HOMER

HOMER
German Scholarship
in Translation

Translated by

G. M. WRIGHT and P. V. JONES

with Introduction by

P. V. JONES

CLARENDON PRESS · OXFORD
1997

Oxford University Press, Great Clarendon Street, Oxford OX2 6DP

Oxford New York

Athens Auckland Bangkok Bogota Bombay
Buenos Aires Calcutta Cape Town Dar es Salaam
Delhi Florence Hong Kong Istanbul Karachi
Kuala Lumpur Madras Madrid Melbourne
Mexico City Nairobi Paris Singapore
Taipei Tokyo Toronto Warsaw

and associated companies in
Berlin Ibadan

Oxford is a trade mark of Oxford University Press

Published in the United States
by Oxford University Press Inc., New York

© P. V. Jones and G. M. Wright 1997

British Library Cataloguing in Publication Data
Data available

Library of Congress Cataloging in Publication Data
Homer: German scholarship in translation / translated by G.M. Wright
and P.V. Jones: with an introduction by P.V. Jones.
Includes bibliographical references.
1. Homer—Criticism and interpretation. 2. Epic poetry,
Greek—History and criticism. 3. Odysseus (Greek mythology)
in literature. 4. Achilles (Greek mythology) in literature.
5. Trojan War—Literature and the war.
I. Wright, G. M. II. Jones, P. V. (Peter V.)
PA4037.A5H59 1997 883'.01—dc21 96–54624
ISBN 0–19–814732–5

1 3 5 7 9 10 8 6 4 2

Typeset by Hope Services (Abingdon) Ltd.
Printed in Great Britain on acid-free paper by
Biddles Ltd., Guildford & King's Lynn

Preface

We translate here ten important and influential articles and extracts from books by German Homeric scholars—three general, three on the *Iliad*, four on the *Odyssey*. The occasional passage has been omitted, but nothing has been added.

The purpose of the Introduction is not to summarize what the papers say, but to review or push forward aspects of their arguments. The discussions are not of uniform weight or length.

The translation aims to be accurate rather than beautiful. It is primarily the work of Dr Wright, though Dr Jones must take final responsibility for the finished product. Dr Jones wrote the Introduction, and the indexes are the work of Barbara Hird.

P.V.J.
G.M.W.

Department of Classics,
University of Newcastle upon Tyne
September 1995

Contents

Introduction

P. V. JONES

Strasburger (pp. 47–70) is interested in the essentially agrarian nature of Homeric society and the way in which the military world of the hero is integrated into it (see further Redfield 1983; Griffin 1986*b*). But as Strasburger was well aware, the sociology of a literary artefact looks like a contradiction in terms: a book is not a society. At the same time, one cannot avoid the question of the extent to which the world of the poems at any moment reflects (a) society or constructs a society or is simply in the business of constructing itself (that formulation is far too neat, but we have to start somewhere) and each discipline will bring its own priorities with it (for a good survey of the archaeological problem and an attempt to correlate archaeological 'layers' with 'layers' of the Homeric epics, see Sherratt 1990). Historians will look for history, sociologists for sociology, folklorists for folklore, mythographers for myth, oralists for orality, and so on.

If we agree, however, that the Homeric poems do not make sense *purely* as history, or myth, or folklore (etc.), the overriding question which brings all these competing interests together is how they *do* make sense. That is to suggest that the ways in which they make sense lie outside the sum total of their aggregate parts.

First, banally, the poet has to structure the story. For the *Iliad*, he chooses the wrath of Achilles—which he ties closely in with a wider exploration of the meaning of heroic ideals (see Hainsworth 1993: 50–3). Then he has to find the means to articulate it—in the *Iliad* again, the battle over gifts (see Donlan 1993 for the sociological importance of this device). Then again, a child of his time, he must convert his story into a heroic 'here and now'. It is doubtful if the poet of the *Odyssey*, for example, knew anything about Ithaca (Heubeck 1989: 13–14), or whether the poet of the *Iliad* had a clear conception of what a heroic palace looked like (Kirk 1990: 193), or the Trojan plain (Thornton 1984: 150–63)—except for his own poetic purposes. But he is also an oral poet, and a constant throughout Homeric epic is the shaping of events into typical oral form: at *Odyssey* 8. 500–20, for example, Demodocus sings of the sack of Troy and it is entirely typically articulated—departure, ambush, council, fate, attack, *aristeia*, divine aid (Hainsworth 1984: 116–17, 131).

But it is not all plain sailing. The poet has inherited a tradition of story-telling, which may contain inherent contradictions or fail to suit the story he wishes to tell. He must solve these problems. He can do this, for example, by ignoring them entirely, or acknowledging them but skating round them, or confronting them head-on.

In his *Histories* 2. 114, for example, Herodotus proves that the Trojan War as described by Homer was impossible. What king in his right mind, he argues, would have allowed his city to be besieged for ten years and destroyed because his son had run off with his enemy's wife? Herodotus is, of course, quite right. Homer deals with this problem by ignoring it.

Again, the Trojan War lasted ten years. It involved the gathering of a massive army of leaders from all over the Greek world, just to bring Menelaus' wife back from the distant land of Troy. What was in it for the heroes? Bar the raiding, not much. At *Iliad* 1. 149–60, Achilles argues that its only purpose was to bring τιμή to Menelaus and Agamemnon, and Agamemnon does not disagree: nor does he offer any better reason. In fact, as a historical or cultural construct, the whole expedition in the form that Homer presents it looks terribly unlikely; and as for a ten-year siege of Troy, the poets obviously had trouble working out what the heroes would actually have been doing for all that length of time, and failing to win as the story required (see Jones 1995). Here, then, is an area where Homer acknowledged the problem, but on the whole swept it under the carpet. None of this is to imply that there was not an actual Trojan War of some sort, nor that gatherings of large expeditions e.g. of the sort needed for the attack on Knossos, and minutely described in the Catalogue of Ships in Book 2, were impossible (J. K. Davies 1984: 87–110; Hainsworth 1984: 111–35, esp. 121–2). All it does imply is that Homer is not a historian.

Invention comes in too. The 'king' of the Greeks (see further below) is Agamemnon. He must have an *aristeia* at some stage. But what if the tradition has not given him one? The poet will make one up. As Hainsworth (1993: 233) shows, the list of victims of Agamemnon's *aristeia* in Book 11 contains not one great hero, and all have Greek names. It is, as Hainsworth suggests, an *ad hoc* invention to fill a need (see Willcock 1977).

A problem that Homer confronts head-on is that of Achilles' great speech to the embassy in *Iliad* 9. The fact is that the conflict *can* be settled there and then. It is, after all, settled in Book 19. But the poet does not want it settled in Book 9: the plot of the *Iliad* (that is, the tragedy of Achilles) hinges on its rejection. The poet is therefore in a position where the embassy must be rejected, and rejected once and for all. As Reeve (1973) makes clear, it cannot keep on coming back with improved offers—a point Achilles makes at the start of his reply to Odysseus at 9. 311. Homer must therefore construct an argument for Achilles to which the embassy cannot possibly make a positive reply. That means, for example, that an apology from Agamemnon (which, if Book 19 is anything to go by, seems essential) cannot be mooted as part of a settlement. Increased compensation cannot be made the issue. Indeed, the problem must be seen to be intractable. This is what Homer achieves. Achilles' long, intense, and powerful reply leaves the embassy with nothing to respond to though, as Edwards (1987*b*: 232–4) shrewdly points out, it is all miraculously in character: exactly the sort of reply one would expect from a man like Achilles. It is left to Diomedes to get it right at 9. 699–703 when he wonders why the Greek leadership bothered to make the offer in the first place, and continues 'Achilles will fight when he decides to' (9. 702–3). Precisely. That is exactly what Homer was aiming at all along—because he had no other target he could aim at—and when Diomedes makes this analysis, no further discussion is needed. The issue is, for the moment anyway, settled.

Since the *Iliad* and *Odyssey* both centre on heroes, in particular on one great hero in each poem, and the issue of that hero's status in relation to those around him is articulated as the key problem, the question of authority and leadership looms large in both poems. It is therefore strange that βασιλεύς, which appears to be a term connoting the highest authority (and so usually translated 'king') should be so notoriously difficult to pin down. In Homer, there is not one βασιλεύς but many βασιλεῖς, and their powers are not those of 'kings' as we understand them. In other words, Agamemnon is not an official, hereditary ruler of the Greeks at Troy disagreement with whom is an act of treason. His official position as leader of the expedition—top βασιλεύς, in other words—arises simply by virtue of the number of troops he has brought with him. Now Homer may be reflecting historical reality here—a world where authority is his who can make it his own, by whatever means (number of troops, size of household, charisma). Certainly in the *Odyssey* no one spells out clearly the source of Odysseus' claim to be ruler of Ithaca, and how either marriage to Penelope or the mastery of Odysseus' household would affect the matter (it is not a matter of heredity, if *Odyssey* 1. 389–402 are anything to go by: see West in Heubeck and others 1988: 59–60). But it suits Homer's purpose in the *Iliad* if Agamemnon's position is ambiguous, because that is the only way in which Achilles' attack on him can become a moral issue rather than simple rebellion (Hainsworth (1993) on 9. 160–1, and for the status of king on 11. 46).

Now as far as Linear B goes, βασιλεύς is a term for a minor official (Janko (1992) on 13. 582–3) or local landowner (Edwards (1991) on 18. 556–7) (for the term, see Ventris and Chadwick 1973: 121, 409). Further, as Hoekstra 1979: 97–9 shows, βασιλεύς in epic is an innovation. (See also Hoekstra 1965: 140 ff. on the problem of formulae and Homeric culture.) Whatever its history, in the hands of epic (or Homer) it has developed a fuzziness well suited to Homer's purposes. Rihll (1992) makes the point particularly well. Agamemnon has no 'throne', no 'blue blood', no 'treasury', no 'officials'. His power exists 'only as it is asserted: say it often enough and loud enough and people will believe it' (Rihll's parallel with Zeus, who clearly has no *unchallenged* right to command, is telling). In other words, a leader led because he could persuade those under him to *be* led, not by any divine right (*pace* Strasburger). If he overstepped the mark of what others would tolerate (as Agamemnon did with Achilles), he was in trouble.

The problem comes with seeing history in all this. Rihll (1992: 50) (cf. Rihll (1986), Halverson (1985)) suggests the poems may reflect 'a particular sort of monarchy in the making' and points out that Thucydides (1. 13. 1) has no 'aristocratic' stage: 'the Homeric *basileis* are followed directly by the development of strong, centralized power: tyranny.' But one could as well argue that Homer (or epic) has created a (fictional) model of leadership precisely to accommodate the demands of poems like the *Iliad* and *Odyssey*. In other words, any conclusions we wish to draw about anything other than narrative strategy must take narrative strategy fully into account before we can be confident of their validity.

If we are to read 'history' into Homer, we have to define 'early' and 'late', and the temptation then is to talk in terms of early 'primitiveness', and later 'complexity' or 'sophistication'. The argument could hardly be more self-defeating. Imagine the consequences, for example, for art history: who comes earlier, the Lascaux cave-painter or Jackson Pollock? We face the same problem when we examine the development of the oral tradition. Ring-composition, for example, has often been thought of as a 'naïve' or 'archaic' device for ordering the narrative, characterized primarily by a tight *structural* balance of the concentric rings. The central importance of **Lohmann's** work (pp. 71–102) on ring-composition in the speeches of the *Iliad* is to show that ring-composition is in fact extremely flexible, and that *thematic* repetition in particular is very common. As a result, much more of the text of Homer becomes susceptible to a ring-composition style of analysis; at the same time, Lohmann makes it more difficult for us to talk of 'early' and 'late' in relation to this device.

Lohmann's work is now receiving something of the recognition it deserves, and is frequently cited in the Cambridge commentaries (Kirk and others, 1985–93). Edwards (1991: 44–8) puts the device in its wider context: it is of a piece with hysteron-proteron, where a series of questions (a b c d) is answered in reverse order (d c b a, e.g. 6. 254–70), but is especially marked by its central core (often a paradigm in speeches, as Lohmann points out) surrounded by concentric rings. Edwards takes up Van Otterlo's point that ring-composition is 'not so much repetition of the beginning of a passage at its end, as anticipation of the end at the beginning', but stresses that both aspects are 'present and significant' (48). Janko (1992) in particular uses Lohmann to show how ring-composition can be used for literary purposes, e.g. 417–18 (on 16. 830–63) and to defend a text against analytical attacks, e.g. 324 (on 16. 64–82) and 326 (on 16. 83–100), though he is not above criticizing him (see e.g. 159 on 14. 83–102).

Lohmann's work builds, of course, on Van Otterlo's original observations, which have themselves given rise to speculation about the extent to which ring-composition may be a device that works on a larger scale than the structuring of speeches, digressions, and so on. Richardson (1993: 4–14) raises this question in relation to Whitman (1958: 249–84), who argued that in fact the whole *Iliad* took the form of one gigantic concentric ring. I am sympathetic to Richardson's approach, but feel there is more to be said on the matter.

Whitman's argument that the *Iliad* itself is concentrically structured, illustrated in diagram form by a ten-section pull-out chart at the back of the book, each section divided into concentric subsections, itself runs the risk of circularity (in more senses than one) unless it is possible to show that other epics have been so composed: otherwise, how can we determine what the criteria for determining concentricity are? Bertman (1966) responded to the challenge and attempted to show that the *Odyssey* too was concentrically structured.

The attempt is not successful. For example, *Odyssey* 3. 1–101 are made to match 3. 329–472 (fig. 5, p. 23). But while the sequence of events in 1–101 is marked 1–9 consecutively, the sequence in 329–472 is marked 1 7 9 7 1 2 5 6 3 4 8. The reason for the problem is perfectly clear: in 1–101, we have the opening sequence of a scene of reception, in 329–472 the closing sequence (see e.g. the chart in Reece 1993: 20–9). Far from going round in a circle, the scene progresses with linear logic from arrival, welcome, entertainment, discussion, libation, and bed, to getting up the next morning, sacrifice, and departure. The strain of forcing this single sequence into a concentric ring structure is shown when, for example, Telemachus emerging from the boat (3. 12–31) is set against him emerging from the bath (3. 466–9).

Bertman is no more successful, it seems to me, on the large scale. His fig. 8 (p. 25) tries to show how the whole *Odyssey* is concentrically organized, and sees a structural comparison between Books 5–12 ('1. Calypso learns that Odysseus must leave her to go on a journey 2. Odysseus goes to bed with Calypso 3. Odysseus recounts his adventures to the Phaeacians') and Book 23 ('1. Penelope learns that Odysseus must leave her to go on a journey 2. Odysseus goes to bed with Penelope 3. Odysseus recounts his adventures to Penelope').

Bertman's tortuous heroics do not convince. But they are still useful because they highlight the problems of this approach. The major problem seems to me how we decide what the units of structuring are. On the broad scale one would think first and foremost in terms of typical scenes, and would include any sort of structured scene from the 'typischen Szenen' of Arend (1933) to the more broadly defined *xenia* sequences of Reece (1993), since these seem to be the building blocks which the poet thinks in terms of. It is clear the Bertman–Whitman analysis does not approach the matter in this way.

Then again, it has always seemed to me intrinsically unlikely that any poet would put himself in a position where, having told the story in the order a b c d e f g h i j k l m n o p in Books 1–12, he would then, at the start of Book 13, have to tell it all over again, only in reverse order, p o n m l k j i h g f e d c b a, and expect by this process to construct a satisfying epic with an intelligible plot-line.

But it is not fair to judge Whitman by Bertman. It has been widely accepted that Book 1 of the *Iliad* sets up a sequence which is 'reversed' in Book 24. Whitman's analysis goes as follows: (Book 1)

1. Plague and funerals
2. Quarrel and seizure (of Briseis)
3. Thetis and Achilles (appeal to Zeus)
   —Journey to Chrysa—
4. Thetis and Zeus (adoption of Achilles' cause)
5. Quarrel on Olympus.

His analysis of Book 24 runs:

5. Quarrel on Olympus
4. Thetis and Zeus (modification of hero's cause)
3. Thetis and Achilles (message from Zeus)
   —Journey of Priam—
2. Reconciliation and restitution (of Hector's body)
1. Funeral of Hector: laments of (*a*) Andromache (*b*) Hecuba (*c*) Helen.

The structuring is impressive: this is indeed the way the story goes, and the sequence does indeed 'reverse'. But the question is— why does it reverse? It seems to me that we have three possible answers: (i) because the poet has a passion for concentricity; or (ii) because this is the inevitable consequence of the logic of the narrative; or (iii) because a concentric structure emerges if the content of Books 1 and 24 is defined in this way.

We can immediately see the reason for the 2-3-4-5 sequence. In both books, Thetis is called upon to mediate between Achilles and Zeus on a matter of honour involving the seizure of a person. In Book 1, it is Achilles who wishes to influence Zeus: in Book 24 it is Zeus who wishes to influence Achilles. The effect is indeed one of pleasing 'reversal', and this is why the poet has chosen to begin and end the *Iliad* in this way.

But is it the desire for 'reversal' that is driving the narrative? Is it not rather a combination of the issue at hand and the nature of the relationship between Achilles and his mother, i.e. the internal logic of the story? The *Iliad* is a tale of wrath and crisis, and the main engine of the plot is Achilles' obstinacy and the closeness of his relationship with his mother. Homer chooses to open and close the *Iliad* with a crisis that brings both of these main features of Achilles' character into play. Is it really his desire for a concentric structure that is driving him?

A fair man will agree, I think, that in this case the poet can have his cake and eat it. The logic of the plot produces an elegant ending which mirrors the opening in a most satisfying way. But that is not the end of the matter. We still have a third possibility—that a concentric structure inevitably emerges if the content of the books is defined in the way Whitman defines it.

Whitman's first point of comparison, for example (Book 1—plagues and funerals, Book 24—Hector's funeral), strains credulity to breaking point. Greeks die and are buried in Book 1 because Agamemnon has refused to return Chryseis, and Apollo has sent a plague. In Book 24, Hector is already dead, and the dispute is whether he will be buried or not. There is no point of connection between the two. But it is in any case possible to define the content of *Iliad* 1 in a quite different way, and arguably one in terms more appropriate to the apparent thought-processes of the oral poet—that is, by thematic analysis. Edwards (1980), for example, produces a full thematic analysis of *Iliad* 1, and his scheme bears little relation to Whitman's. A similar thematic analysis of *Iliad* 24 might look like this:

> 1–2: end of assembly.
> 3–21: scene of sleeping (but Achilles fails to sleep).
> 22–76: assembly of the gods (discussion of the dead Hector's plight).
> 77–119: sending a messenger (Iris to Thetis).
> 120–40: reception scene (Thetis and Achilles).
> 141–87: sending a messenger (Iris to Priam).
> 188–280: preparation for journey (Priam and Hekabe).
> 281–321: libation, prayer to Zeus and omen.

322–31: departure.

331–48: departure of Hermes.

349–469: journey of Priam and meeting with Hermes.

469–676: Achilles and Priam: *xenia.*

677–91: secret departure of Priam (Hermes).

692–783: Priam's arrival at Troy and lamentations for Hector.

784–804: burial of Hector.

A fair man comparing this with Edwards' analysis would again, I think, agree that on these terms there is no structural relationship between Book 24 and Book 1. On the other hand, the fair man would be justified in arguing that themes are irrelevant: they are bearers of meaning, not the meaning itself. And that really is the point. We are talking about how we define the content of oral epic, what we mean by declaring that these features are or are not *comparanda.* To give a crude example: I can declare that an animal possesses eyes, nose, ears, legs, lungs, heart, brain, reproductive organs, and is a Professor of Latin. But on that definition *alone* I could equally well declare it is a dead fieldmouse. In other words, differences are even more important than similarities. What is certain is that if you are looking for similarities, you will find them.

What we are ultimately talking about here is the possibility of literary significance. It is a question that applies across the epic. If we do not wish to argue that there is significant patterning on the very largest (i.e. Whitmanic) scale, what about the smaller scale? Hainsworth (1993: 325, on 12. 61–79), for example, argues that the four admonitory speeches of Poulydamas to Hector have 'a certain sameness', but does not wish to assign that to intimate connection (as Lohmann does; cf. Janko 1992: 137 on 726–47) but rather to the poet's possession of a 'pattern for prudent admonition'.

At least we can advance by trying to ascertain (*a*) that the connections are actually there in the text and not overshadowed by the differences, and (*b*) that there are enough examples of such significant connections to suggest that they are typical of Homeric technique. Nevertheless, I am inclined to believe that there are good reasons why intimate connections (and so comparisons) between passages perhaps widely spread are in any case likely.

In general, the poet's consistent use of digression and delay suggests very strongly indeed that the audience paid close attention to the plot. If the audience at *Iliad* 16. 1 has forgotten what Patroclus was doing at *Iliad* 11. 599–848, or why he was doing it, it may as well go home. I do not deny, of course, that Patroclus' behaviour at the start of Book 16 is fully explained by his reference to the wounding of the Greek leaders at 16. 22–9: but Achilles' string of irrelevant questions at 7–19, for example, seems calculated to throw off the scent any audience who did not know they were irrelevant and thought they might actually lead somewhere. Homer's handling of the scene, in other words, is predicated on his confidence in the audience's capacity to stay with the story-line.

The audience, in other words, is attuned to paying attention over large stretches of epic. Even more important, it is attuned to epic *Kunstsprache*. Now the nature of that language is special to epic, and since one of its most obvious characteristics is its repetitiveness at the level of word, phrase, line, and scene, it would be slightly surprising if any listening audience—particularly one of long experience—was not sensitive to it. In this context, the existence of any pattern (e.g. 'for prudent admonition') or frequent repetition (such as arming) offers a context which almost compels comparisons to be made. When a pattern is repeated as frequently as e.g. the *xenia* scenes in the *Odyssey* (see e.g. Reece 1993) or an unpatterned 'theme' as frequently as the mutilation of corpses in the *Iliad* (see e.g. Segal 1971), the poet is almost inviting the audience to mix and match (cf. also Edwards 1987*a*).

That is why I am sympathetic to Richardson's conclusion (1993: 14) that over the scope of the whole epic we are likely to be dealing with repeated, but linear, themes (or *leitmotifs*, to use the musical analogy he adopts) which inevitably repeat themselves and may give the epic the appearance of concentric structure; and why I think we are permitted, in certain circumstances, to see literary significance in their articulation (cf. e.g. Taplin 1992: 74–82 on four visit-scenes in the *Iliad*).

Ring-composition is a general feature of much classical literature from early Greek lyric (Fowler 1987: 53–85) to Roman poetry (Cairns 1979: 192–213). It is interesting that it was not consistently identified in specific terms by the ancients and did not feature in their rhetorical handbooks (Lohmann 1970: 2; Edwards 1991: 45 n. 58). On the subject in general see also Thalmann (1984: *passim*), who writes without knowledge (evidently) of Lohmann's work.

To **Fränkel's** masterly work on similes (103–23) I have no observations to add. In introducing the reprint of this major work, Ernst Heitschel had this to say in 1976:

'It would be well worth examining afresh the theses and interpretations in my book *The Homeric Similes*, which was written a long time ago.' This suggestion, however, which Hermann Fränkel himself made twenty years ago (*Gnomon* 28 (1956), 569 n. 1), does not seem to have been followed up with the necessary caution by anybody so far. For then[1] certainly as now, there was criticism of detail as well as of principle; yet there has been no new discussion of the problems of the subject as a whole. So it should be desirable and justified that the original observations and interpretations be made accessible again through a reprint, approved by the author.

Having appeared at the time as a Göttingen inaugural dissertation, the book was the first major publication of its author who—as we can today say in retrospect—is one of those scholars who in the twenties asked new questions and opened up new areas of classical scholarship. For the author himself, however, this analysis was the first of the series of his preliminary works which eventually made possible the great comprehensive description of early Greek literature *Dichtung und Philosophie des frühen Griechentums* (first published in 1951, tr. as *Early Greek Poetry and Philosophy* (Blackwell, 1975)). Even today, more than fifty years later, the book provides us with the only comprehensive discussion of its subject matter. What was new was the attempt to disassociate the explanation of the Homeric similes from exclusive reference to the so-called *tertium comparationis*, the 'point of comparison'; instead it is shown how in these 'incidental remarks of the author to his listeners' (*Gnomon* 3 (1927), 570) reality and image as complete entities illuminate each other through the development of every single detail of the whole. In this the author resists the temptation to define through a formulaic abbreviation what 'the' Homeric simile actually is; he is justifiably wary of such abstract creations of scholarship: what is discussed here are concrete texts which are supposed to be understood from their context. In this his joy of discovery has admittedly led him occasionally to adopt an extreme position; in these cases, subsequent discussion has been able to make one or two modifications and of course in the meantime new questions have been asked and new observations made. But the fundamental thesis as it had been developed from the interpretation of the individual similes at the time has stood the test of time; Fränkel himself described it once again later in the following words (*D. u. Phil.*[2] 45):

---

[1] Of the reviews written at the time, the following are known to me: W. Andreae, *Lit. Zentralblatt* 74 (1923), 447; M. M. Assmann, *Museum* 30 (Leiden, 1923), 149; S. E. Bassett, *Cl. Phil.* 20 (1925), 191; K. Meister, *DLZ* 44 (1923), 178–80; J. A. Scott, *Ph. Q.* (1922), 235 f.; J. T. Sheppard, *CR* 36 (1922), 168 f.

[2] *Early Greek Poetry and Philosophy* (Blackwell, 1975), 41 (retranslated).

'Ancient epic knows only linear representation and the simile adds a second, parallel line alongside that of the narrative. The doubling gives the matter greater weight and the listener, who is compelled to reconcile two disparate images, is led to think through the situation thoroughly. The similarity of the two images is not restricted to individual traits; rather the structure of the scene or the course of the action as a whole is similar. The stereoscopic double view provides a new vividness. The more richly a simile is elaborated, the more brightly it illustrates the general situation for all the participants at the same time. Again, in the interaction of the two images, the mood and fundamental attitude of the protagonists come to the fore more powerfully than in plain and reticent narrative alone. Hope, greed, impulse, determination, worry, anxiety, terror, disappointment and resignation: they hardly ever transmit themselves more directly from the characters of the story to the sympathetic listener than in the indirect workings of the "artistic device" of the similes.

The similes merely suggest the parallelism without executing it point by point. What is missing in one of the images is reflected on to it by the complementary counter image. And beyond what is verbally expressed in words on either side, much more emerges from the background of the simile, since most of the similes are typical and the listener is familiar with the types. For in the same way that each part of a narrative expresses more in its context than it would in isolation, so the individual simile gains in content through the fact that the listener remembers the family connections of the image.'

All I would wish to say is that an analysis of similes as brilliant as Fränkel's (though more compressed and taking full advantage of later work), with full reading-list, is to be found in Edwards (1991: 24–41).

At *Iliad* 6. 371 (picked up by ring-composition at 374), Hector, who has announced his plan to leave Paris' house and return home to see his wife (365), 'did not find white-armed Andromache at home, but she, with her child and well-robed nurse, was standing on the tower, wailing and lamenting'. **Schadewaldt** (pp. 124–42) saw high significance in this failure to find, and he was right to do so (cf. Kirk 1990: ad loc.): as he goes on to explain, the key to understanding the scene lies in the interaction (or lack of it) between the different worlds of male and female.[3]

---

[3] We are grateful to M. M. Willcock who drew our attention to this paper and allowed us to see an English version of it which he had produced.

In fact, this failure to find the person for whom one is looking is unique in the *Iliad*. In all such typical scenes of arrival bar this one (Arend 1933), the arriver always finds the person (s)he is looking for first time. Such 'non-finding' is non-existent in the *Odyssey* too.[4]

Homer's purpose in upsetting our expectations at this point is part of the wider narrative strategy he adopts to prepare us for the meeting between Hector and Andromache. At 6. 103 Hector, advised by Helenus to tell the women of Troy to make an offering to Athena in an effort to ward off Diomedes, leaves the battlefield. At 6. 237–311, he transmits the advice (and the women do as he tells them), but he now lets out that he also intends to visit Paris and bring him back into the battle (280). So at 313 Hector sets off for Paris' house. At 340–1, Paris tells Hector to wait while he fetches his armour, or to go and he will catch him up, and Hector (presumably taking advantage of the delay) now announces that he will also visit Andromache (365). It is at this point that he does not find her at home, but (we are told) on the tower *with her child and nurse*. And so Homer prepares us for an encounter not just with Andromache, but with Astyanax too.

This is a magnificent example of a Homeric digression, carefully motivated and well set-up.[5] The 'he did not find' element helps the digression on its way, and signals in a most unexpectedly striking way the clash between the two different worlds, of the male and the female, which Schadewaldt analyses so well.

This raises a general issue about the status of negative utterances in Homer. In the case we have been looking at, there is no problem. In typical scenes of arrival, the arriver usually 'finds' the person he is looking for (cf. Reece 1993). This is a fixed element in arrival scenes, part of the poet's data-bank for such incidents, and if he chooses to modify such an element either by stating that it did not

---

[4] *Odyssey* 24. 222 does not count because Odysseus was not looking for Dolios; neither does 5. 81 because Hermes was not looking for Odysseus. The only modification occurs when visitors meet the wrong people first, e.g. 1. 106, where Athena, sent to consult Telemachus, finds the suitors before Telemachus comes out to greet her. This is not found in the *Iliad*.

[5] Cf. Morrison (1992: 63–71), who argues that Homer is somehow 'misdirecting' his audience here because he wants to pose 'alternatives to the tradition and the *Iliad*'s plot that produce epic suspense'. I feel this makes too many assumptions about the expectations of Homer's audience.

take place or omitting it, we are entitled to ask why and look for a reason. In a famous article Armstrong (1958), for example, examines typical scenes of arming to show how Homer turns to full literary effect Patroclus' failure to take Achilles' spear with him into battle. Expectations have been upset, but there is a reason for it. We could say the same of the *xenia* sequence in the Cyclops episode in *Odyssey* 9, where Polyphemus upsets every standard of expected behaviour in his reception of Odysseus.

Because of their inherent repetitiveness, typical scenes are a rich field for this kind of investigation. For example, at 16. 367, Antinoos describes how the suitors lay in wait for Telemachus. When sun set, he says, 'we did not sleep by night on shore, but awaited divine dawn sailing in our swift ship at sea'. Since we know that 'beaching ships by night to sleep' is a typical Homeric practice (e.g. 9. 150–1), we are right to argue that, though this negative occurs outside the full typical scene of landing, tying-up, and sleeping, Antinoos' words reflect typical practice.

The typical scene of 'coming to land' offers another example. At 9. 136–7, Odysseus is actually coming to land, and relates how easy landfall was on the island opposite the land of the Cyclops: 'there was a harbour with good anchorage, where there was no need for moorings (πεῖσμα), or to cast anchor (εὐνὰς βαλέειν) or make fast with lines (πρυμνήσι' ἀνάψαι)'. But these are exactly what were usually needed—see e.g. *Iliad* 1. 436–7, etc. The poet, in other words, emphasizes the untypicality of the landfall by working through the typical landfall sequence, only in the negative (he does the same at 13. 100, where ships that arrive at the harbour of Phorkys ἄνευ δεσμοῖο μένουσι). That this landfall sequence exerts powerful compositional pressure on the poet becomes even clearer at 9. 178: though Odysseus has gone out of his way to say lines were not needed and the ships simply ran ashore and beached (9. 149), when he leaves with his men for the land of the Cyclops 'I ordered my men to embark and untie the lines' (ἀνά τε πρυμνήσια λῦσαι). Such is the pressure by association that the typical can exert.

So far we have been on safe ground. The existence of undisputed typical structures to which we can appeal has secured the argument: 'This negative usually occurs in typical scenes as a positive: we are therefore dealing with a norm which has been modified: we are entitled to ask why.'

That raises a broad question about the status of negatives. We cannot, of course, conclude that when we have a negative, we therefore have a modified norm. But I assume it is worthwhile trying to establish norms for Homeric poetry, because we are interested in the poet's workshop. If we can argue that a negative utterance cuts across the expectations of the audience, we get a closer look into it.

At 9. 92–3, for example, Odysseus sends his men to meet the Lotus eaters, and 'they did not plan death for our men, but gave them the lotus to taste' (οὐδ᾽ ἄρα Λωτόφαγοι μήδονθ᾽ ἑτάροισιν ὄλεθρον). Do we conclude that, when the poet described strangers arriving on a foreign shore, it was typical for them to meet trouble, and what is surprising about this episode is that they did not? It is possible. At 10. 115, Odysseus' men arrive at the land of the Laestrygonians, and Antiphates 'planned horrible destruction for them' (ὃς δὴ τοῖσιν ἐμήσατο λυγρὸν ὄλεθρον). After all, new arrivals often wonder if the people they have come across are god-fearing or hostile (e.g. *Odyssey* 6. 121, 9. 176, 13. 202).

Homer's territorial descriptions in the *Odyssey* are very rich (see Hainsworth 1969: 1–2). When a ship comes in to land, for example, the harbour is usually described, and typically it is good for anchorage (4. 358, 6. 263, 9. 136, 10. 87, 93, 12. 305, 13. 100), and has a water-supply (4. 359, 9. 140, 12. 306, 13. 109), and a cave (9. 141, 12. 317, 13. 103). Entrances can be high (10. 87, 13. 97) and narrow (6. 264, 10. 90). We are dealing, then, with the typical. The untypical, consequently, carries that much more force. When Odysseus is swimming along the coast of Scherie looking for a landing place, he is unsuccessful—οὐ γὰρ ἔσαν λιμένες νηῶν ὀχοί . . . (5. 404); when he reaches Amnisos, there is a cave there, but he puts in ἐν λιμέσι χαλεποῖσι, μόγις δ᾽ ὑπάλυξεν ἀέλλας.

I am arguing here that, under certain conditions, we may be able to use negatives to talk about audience expectations and typical Homeric practice. Certain epic situations, in other words, call to the poet's mind certain methods of handling them. Typical scenes are an obvious example, and I have worked by analogy with such scenes to other stretches of narrative, where there is evidence that we may be dealing with the same sort of phenomenon. It is a question of how far one can go. Territorial descriptions, for example, are fruitful. Consider the typical descriptions of lands (cf. Hainsworth 1969: 1–2): Telemachus describes the plains of Sparta and their crops (4. 602–4), contrasting them with the *absence* of plains on Ithaca (4. 605, cf. 607), and its animal-rearing capacity (goats and horses, 4. 606). At 9. 21–7, Odysseus describes Ithaca as 'rough but good for rearing young men' (the only territory described as 'rough' in the *Odyssey*). At 13. 195, Odysseus finds Ithaca's 'paths, harbours, cliffs and trees' very different in the mist, but Athena at 13. 242–7 describes it as 'rough, no good for running horses, lacking plains, but not poor'. She lists its copious corn, wine, rain, and dew, and its pasture for goats and cattle, its woods and watering places. Meanwhile, the land of the Cyclops has (9. 110–11) wheat, barley, wine, and rain, and its adjoining island (118–35) woods, goats, water-meadows (good for vines), and good ploughing land. One can compare Syrie (15. 403–6) with its good land, good for sheep and cattle, wine, and grain; Libya (4. 85–9), with its amazing sheep (three lambings a year, constant cheese, meat, and milk); and even Utopia (19. 111–14), with its black land, wheat, barley, trees bristling with produce, sheep, and abundance of fish (a unique element). One is reminded of Phaeacia (7. 114–21) and Calypso's cave (5. 63–73). This all suggests a typicality of description, which may have the effect of turning a stronger light on the negatives: Cyclops' lack of ἀγορά most famously (9. 112, cf. 6. 266, 10. 114), but also lack of cultivation (9. 109, cf. 123, and the miracle lands of Phaeacia and Libya). As I said, it is a matter of deciding how far one can go.

At the end of his famous article on Achilles' decision, **Schadewaldt** (143–69) raises the issue of the interaction between freedom and necessity in Homer, and argues that Achilles exercises freedom in the purest form by willingly submitting to, or perhaps rather aligning himself with, fate.

It seems to me clear that Homer has been wrestling with this as a problem of narrative strategy throughout the *Iliad*, and I summarize here the conclusions I have argued more fully in Jones (1996). It is apparent that Cyclic epic (with which, we can assume, Homer was acquainted) deployed oracles with the utmost frequency (Kullmann counts seventeen in our existing summaries), but the only two of significance in the *Iliad* are that Troy will fall and Achilles will die. Neither will be fulfilled beyond the end of the *Iliad*, and to that extent they could both, in theory, have been omitted. The reason why they are included is obvious enough: without them, the dimension of tragic pathos would be missing.

Introduction

It seems to me that Homer has two problems to solve here if he is to make sense of a world in which free heroes work within the context of ineluctable fate: how is he to handle the gods? And how is he to handle fate?

The world of the gods which he depicts in the *Iliad* is not oppressive, mysterious or dark (see Willcock 1970, in Wright 1978: 61–2 for a good summary of the different sorts of 'meaning' that can be attached to the whole range of the gods' participation in human affairs). The gods themselves are shown to be quite candid about their motives and interests, and to support their favourites openly and ruthlessly (often face-to-face), and humans, even if they are ignorant of what the gods are planning, are never (as far as I can see *in what they actually say*) oppressed by that ignorance. When humans talk about the gods, they do so almost exclusively in terms of the gods' ability to help or hinder them. Mortals rarely express either fear of the gods or even respect for them (which does not mean they feel or express *dis*respect for them). What mortals do is acknowledge the power and right of the gods to act in any way they choose, while they express in prayers the desire that the gods will (this time) help them rather than the other side. For mortals, in other words, gods act as they will for whatever reason, but at least they do not seem to act *wholly* at random, and can be appealed to in terms which have a sporting chance of being granted. That is about all there is to it, *as far as one can tell from the way the characters talk.* The fact that there are so many gods, all with competing desires, gives humans a better chance of finding someone on their side, of course; and the fact that so many mortals have immortal parents also bridges the gap.

Fate, however, is a less tractable literary device. True, it is the 'will of the poet', as Edwards (1987*b*: 136) emphasizes, but if something is fated, that is the end of it. There is nothing anyone, even the gods, can do about it. Consequently, if Homer is to pull the 'fate' card out of the pack, he runs the risk of upsetting the elegant balance of power he maintains between men and gods and of compromising the sense of freedom with which his heroes are invested. With fate pulling the strings, all humans can do is walk—or be dragged—puppet-like to their destiny.

Homer's narrative strategy for dealing with this problem seems to me to have two supports: first, a fate whose terms are either revealed only gradually to the participants (as in Achilles' case) or not at all (as in Patroclus' and Hector's, cf. Taplin (1992: 198) on Patroclus); and second, an insouciance or forgetfulness on the part of the gods to what is fated, so that even they seem unaware that such-and-such a course of action is inevitable. The fact that fate (which means with very few exceptions 'the moment a man dies') is seen not to be in the gift of the gods, but something spun for a man the day he is born quite outside the ambit of divine interference, helps further to distance the gods from it.

In these ways the text of the *Iliad* never quite reveals its hand. Gods are both all- and partly powerful, humans both wholly and partly free. When it suits the poet to play the 'ineluctable fate' card, he can do so; when it suits him to play the 'agonizing tragic choice', he can do so. In this sense, Schadewaldt is quite right to emphasize that Achilles' choice is both free and fated and yet does not strike the reader as paradoxical. Homer has plotted a narrative strategy that enables him to produce precisely that result, without compromising the power and grandeur of the gods (on which see Emlyn-Jones in Emlyn-Jones and others 1992: 90–103). It is also a strategy all of a piece with the independence which seems so characteristic of the Homeric hero. Whatever claims that respect for others or the need for communal activity may make upon a hero (see e.g. Zanker 1994), the individual's need to affirm his own 'competence, potency and power' remains at the heart of Homeric ethics (Rowe 1983: 268–9). As Rihll (1992: 50) puts it, 'Akhilleus is not the deviant hero, nor champion of the people nor defender of the meek. He does not seek to change the world. He seeks his own freedom; freedom of action and freedom to live.'

Reinhardt's paper on the place of the Judgement of Paris in the *Iliad* 'is, or should be, a landmark in Homeric studies' (Griffin 1980: 195 n. 49). The story of the Judgement occurs in full detail in Cyclic epic, in the *Cypria* (*EGF* p. 31. 7–11). But most scholars prior to Reinhardt, agreeing with Aristarchus that Homer did not know the story of the Judgement of Paris ('otherwise he would have mentioned it all over the place'), athetized *Iliad* 24. 25–30, where the story is alluded to. In this paper, however, Reinhardt argues that the reason why the Judgement does not feature strongly in Homer is that the tone of a mighty, Olympian epic is unsuited to what is a somewhat unheroic episode in folklore. The story does, however, surface—discreetly and by implication—in a form suited to the manner of the *Iliad* in a number of passages where Athena and Hera are shown to be in conflict with Aphrodite. In this sense, however much Homer assigns the course of events to the rape of Helen, or fate, or the will of Zeus, the Judgement of Paris does lie behind the *Iliad* and explain the hostility of the two goddesses to Troy.

Unfortunately, as M. Davies (1981) rightly pointed out, Reinhardt did not give any reason why the incident should appear in the one place where it does come unambiguously to the surface (*Iliad* 24. 25–30), nor did he deal adequately with the severe problems that the passage itself poses, which caused Aristarchus to delete it.

Erbse (1977: 518–23) gives the full scholiastic details; M. Davies (1981) and Richardson (1993: 276, on 23–30) offer bibliographies, put the problems in perspective, and suggest solutions, while Stinton (1990: 17–75) is necessary reading both on this issue (esp. 17–22) and the exploitation of the Judgement of Paris by Euripides (the only classical Greek in whose work it frequently recurs).

The main problems are:

(i) Why is Poseidon associated with the goddesses whose hatred of Troy sprang from the Judgement of Paris (26)? Poseidon's reason for hating Troy was nothing to do with Paris, but because Laomedon, Priam's father, had not rewarded him for building its walls (*Iliad* 21. 450–2). But myth is the most notoriously flexible of mediums, adding and discarding motives at will. For example, when Poseidon argues in the passage above that Apollo should be on the Greek side, not the Trojan, since he too did unpaid service as a herdsman for Laomedon, Poseidon is offering a radically alternative account to that which he came up with at *Iliad* 7. 452–3, where he says both he *and Apollo* built the walls (see Richardson (1993) on 21. 441–57). Consistency does not worry Homer: Poseidon is associated with the goddesses of the Judgement of Paris because, as a great protagonist of the Greeks, he must have been interested in any circumstances which could be used as a reason to attack Troy. Observe too that the poet does not involve Poseidon in the Judgement itself. He is forgotten by the time we reach 29 (θεάς is telling).

(ii) 29–30 are most inappropriate: νείκεσσε does not mean 'judge', and μαχλοσύνην means 'madness for sex' (it is a punishment), when what Aphrodite gave Paris was a reward, Helen. De

Jong (1987: 120) explains this all very neatly by citing this passage (and a string of others) as examples of 'implicit embedded focalisation', by which she means that 29–30 are to be read not as 'documentary' evidence but as Athena and Aphrodite's thoughts on the matter. If this is true, it explains both νείκεσσε (Adkins 1969: 20 had explained this passage in the same sort of way) and μαχλοσύνην.

(iii) Finally, if the whole passage is somewhat elliptical, Richardson (1993: 278) is surely right to point out that this is characteristic of epic summaries.

If, then, we accept that the passage should stand, we have to ask (as Reinhardt did not), why here? M. Davies (1981) argues that Homer is continuing a theme begun in Book 1—that of human and divine conflict. In Book 1, the conflict between humans on earth rages on, while that between the gods in heaven is settled; but in Book 24, it is the conflict between the gods that will rage on, to issue in the destruction of Troy, while that between humans is settled. The Judgement of Paris reminds us of the background to this ancient and deadly dispute.

This is surely on the right lines (and is supported by Bremer 1987: 40–1). Book 24, through the death of Hector, actually signals the future destruction of Troy, which has been the purpose of Athena and Hera all along (4. 20–54). At this unique, climactic moment it is an appropriate poetic strategy to replay the whole course of events, and put the present in the perspective of the past (so common a feature of Homeric epic technique—see Austin 1966; Jones 1992).

It is also worth noting that not only do we get the Judgement of Paris, but the marriage of Peleus and Thetis too, where the dispute over the golden apple set events in train (24. 60–3—as we should expect, no golden apple is mentioned). Further, if Reinhardt is right to see an equally ancient folklore motif in the two contrasted brothers—'bad' Paris vs. 'noble' Hector—it becomes even more effective that, at the moment of the noble brother's death, we should be explicitly reminded of the bad brother's role in creating the situation out of which his brother's death was so tragically to arise.

Klingner's paper (192–216) seems at one level very *passé* because we no longer find the debate between analysts and unitarians particularly instructive. Oral theory rules the roost, and it finds no problem with the *Telemachy*. Milman Parry (1971: 454) points out that the *Telemachy* could hardly stand by itself—it has no plot, no denouement, and Telemachus himself is both too young to achieve anything significant in the course of it and in a situation where, under the guidance of Athena, and then with the help of Peisistratus, all he has to do is listen, and possibly learn, from others (cf. Hölscher 1978: 57). Besides, we are awaiting the return of Odysseus, who cannot be upstaged by his son. Doubtless there were epics about someone like Diomedes, and doubtless much of their interest derived from the fact that Tydeus was his father (about whom there must also have been epics), but it is obvious Telemachus is not that sort of hero. In its present form, the *Telemachy* could have been conceived only as the prelude to a much greater epic about Odysseus himself and it is very difficult to imagine circumstances in which it could ever have been anything else.

But if the terms in which Klingner analyses the first two books of the *Odyssey* seem old-fashioned, the judgement he brings to bear upon the text is extremely relevant. Today debate centres not on 'analysis' but on the nature of the relationship between oral poetry and literary criticism. The importance of Klingner's paper is that he gives no evidence of understanding the impact of oral poetry upon the *Odyssey* at all. He treats it, in other words, as a purely literary text. Yet the results he comes up with are not merely acute in themselves; I cannot see that even the hardest Parryist could find grounds *on principle* on which to complain about them. This does not make oral theory irrelevant: far from it. What it does mean is that a sufficiently acute and sensitive mind, working closely from the evidence of the text alone, does not need to be conversant with oral theory to produce striking and important results. This, of course, is not a recommendation: it is simply an observation (cf. Martin 1989: 1–4).

What Klingner does so effectively is to tease out the strands of thought or ideas which run through the opening two books of the *Odyssey* and form the basis of plot and character: Telemachus' despair, the absence of Odysseus, the plague of the suitors, and so on, all designed to show why Odysseus is so urgently needed, and why Athena's intervention takes the form it does, and to lay the groundwork for his return. Klingner shows us, in other words, the poet in his workshop, the thinking which has gone into making the opening of the *Odyssey* what it is. These ideas are, of course, realized in oral form. But the ideas control the form—not the other way round. Further, Klingner goes on to try to explain how those ideas are articulated into an effective sequence. One gets a strong sense of the poet as the technical master of his medium and of a medium that is fully capable of responding to the demands the poet makes of it (see e.g. Foley 1990: 277, where even type-scenes are shown to be capable of extreme variation in context).

This, of course, does not mean that the poet is an unfettered creative genius. But the range of ideas he has at his fingertips is very wide indeed. Some of them are highly formulaic in articulation (i.e. tend to appear in closely related verbal and metrical shape). Others resist close formular analysis. The point is, it would be instructive to know, first, the extent to which the poet's ideas on any topic were limited; and second, the extent to which the poet was able to develop *wholly* different ways of saying the same things (see further e.g. Austin 1975: 11–80, and for a summary of the current state of thinking about formulas, Hainsworth 1993: 1–31).

The argument is one from analogy. First, typical scenes (Arend 1933) consist of fixed patterns of action. Thus in the typical scene of arrival someone 'leaves', 'arrives', 'finds someone' (often 'doing something'), and so on. There is variation and imagination in the elaboration of each detail (e.g. you have to leave somewhere and arrive somewhere, all of which can be briefly or extensively described), but the action-plan remains the same. The listener *usually* knows what is going to happen next at the level of action sequence. The language can be highly repetitive.

Second, formulae demonstrate scope and economy. To take the issue to extremes, in a perfect Parryist oral world, every potential gap in the metrical line would be fillable with a noun + epithet combination (scope); but for each gap, there would be only one combination possible (economy) (see Parry 1971: *passim*). This rigid view of the oral poet's technique is now discredited (see e.g. Shive 1987): but since Homeric epic is still (surely) oral in style, it would be surprising if the poet was able to create verse free from and unfettered by constraints. Thus the listener can often complete a line of epic poetry before (s)he hears it: (s)he knows what is coming next at the level of diction.

Fenik's work on battle scenes brought these two ideas together. While battle scenes were not as tightly structured as typical scenes, yet the number of action-plans permissible seemed to be quite limited. Second, while the action-plans could be realized in a very large number of ways, there was not total freedom of expression (Fenik 1968, and cf. Willcock 1992: 65–6; Thornton 1984: 93–103 is also apposite).

Fenik showed how the models of composition proposed by Arend and Parry could be fruitfully brought together and extended to cover other areas of diction (Parry almost foresaw this in his review of Arend in *CPh* 31 (1936), 357–60; also in Parry 1971: 404–7). It was the level of repetitiveness in battle scenes that made his work possible. We have then a challenge. How far is it possible to identify other areas of Homeric composition with a level of repetitiveness which will make them accessible to a Fenikian style of analysis? If successful, we would gain yet further insights into the poet's workshop, on the level of both composition and possibly diction too. For one large, important, and only partly explored area of Homeric scholarship is that of the synonym.

Paraskevaides (1984) has looked at single-word synonyms. That is a straightforward enough task. But can we go further? The possibility raises itself of comparing the diction of what look like repeated ideas, whose status as an 'idea' is guaranteed because they occur in the context of a repeated scene or sequence.

This is a murky world, and one which must, by definition, resist analysis by concordance. But it dangles another tantalizing possibility before us as well: that of being able to say something about Homeric invention. Hainsworth (1978) comes up with a typically elegant and subtle statement of the relationship between diction and invention: 'it is verbal dexterity, not verbal inventiveness, that is the epic's strong point' (50). But it all depends where you start from. At the level of formula, true: but may it not be possible to identify 'invention' at moments when the poet expresses what seems to be a common idea in a wide variety of ways, in response to the needs of the story? I cannot deny that this would be dexterous, since the poet is manipulating formulae. But I think that, within the context of a formular system, this reasonably counts as 'invention' too. You do not automatically call a builder 'uninventive' because he continues to use bricks.

For example, at *Odyssey* 1. 5 the poet says that Odysseus tried to

save himself and his friends: ἀρνύμενος ἥν τε ψυχὴν καὶ νόστον
ἑταίρων. I can find parallels for this idea only at 9. 421–2 εἴ τιν'
ἑταίροισιν θανάτου λύσιν ἠδ' ἐμοὶ αὐτῷ | εὑροίμην, 11. 105 αἴ κ'
ἐθέλεις σὸν θυμὸν ἐρυκακέειν καὶ ἑταίρων, and 23. 253 νόστον
ἑταίροισιν διζήμενος ἠδ' ἐμοὶ αὐτῷ. This uncomplex idea seems to
me to have attracted a most uneconomical spread of realizations. Is
not this invention at work? If the reply to that is 'the language is
still formulaic' (which it is), we can reply, 'Maybe, but the basic
idea is being most inventively realized.'

Let me advance the argument by taking some speeches and part-
speeches of Penelope. I mark (a), (b), (c), etc. those ideas which
turn out to be repeated.

1. *Odyssey* 1. 337–44

"Φήμιε, πολλὰ γὰρ ἄλλα βροτῶν θελκτήρια οἶδας,
ἔργ' ἀνδρῶν τε θεῶν τε, τά τε κλείουσιν ἀοιδοί·
τῶν ἕν γέ σφιν ἄειδε παρήμενος, οἱ δὲ σιωπῇ
οἶνον πινόντων· ταύτης δ' ἀποπαύε' ἀοιδῆς   340
λυγρῆς, ἥ τέ μοι αἰεὶ ἐνὶ στήθεσσι φίλον κῆρ
τείρει, ἐπεί με μάλιστα καθίκετο πένθος ἄλαστον.
τοίην γὰρ κεφαλὴν ποθέω μεμνημένη αἰεὶ
ἀνδρός, τοῦ κλέος εὐρὺ καθ' Ἑλλάδα καὶ μέσον Ἄργος."

Context: Phemius has been singing of the difficult return of the
Greeks from Troy (326–7) while the suitors listen 'in silence' (325).
Penelope descends and speaks.

339–40: οἱ δὲ σιωπῇ | οἶνον πινόντων (the metrical equivalent of οἱ
δὲ σιωπῇ | ἧατ' ἀκούοντες, 325–6) is typical: Penelope, like
Telemachus, is always talking of and complaining about (1) *the
suitors' consumption of the household*. Here she identifies their wine
consumption. This is because dinner has finished (1. 150—I do not
think we need to believe that the suitors had stopped drinking
because they had 'satisfied their desire' for it).

342: Penelope is (b) *suffering grief*. I note that ἐπεί με μάλιστα
καθίκετο πένθος ἄλαστον is a unique expression in Homer (developed from e.g. 4. 108 ἄχος αἰὲν ἄλαστον, 23. 224 ἵκετο πένθος): a
powerful way for Penelope to express her feelings for the first time
in the *Odyssey*. In particular, her grief has been ἄλαστον for nearly
twenty years now—a key feature of the plot (cf. Hölscher 1978: 58).

343: Penelope (c) *desires/remembers her husband*, (d) *a man of fame
throughout Greece*. This couplet will be repeated. West in Heubeck

and others (1988), *ad loc.* comments that κεφαλή 'is generally associated with the dead' in Homer, a feature of Penelope's dilemma that is, again, crucial to the plot. κλέος too is a central epic motif, already mentioned by Telemachus (1. 240–1) and as important for Penelope as it is for Odysseus (24. 196–8) (Segal 1983 and Katz 1991: 29–9 make somewhat heavy weather of all this).

2. *Odyssey* 18. 201–5

> "ἦ με μάλ᾿ αἰνοπαθῆ μαλακὸν περὶ κῶμ᾿ ἐκάλυψεν.
> αἴθε μοι ὣς μαλακὸν θάνατον πόροι Ἄρτεμις ἁγνὴ
> αὐτίκα νῦν, ἵνα μηκέτ᾿ ὀδυρομένη κατὰ θυμὸν
> αἰῶνα φθινύθω, πόσιος ποθέουσα φίλοιο
> παντοίην ἀρετήν, ἐπεὶ ἔξοχος ἦεν Ἀχαιῶν."   205

Context: Penelope has been sleeping while Athena beautifies her. Now she awakens.

201: (e) *a wonderful sleep.*

202–3: (f) *expression of death-wish.*

203–4: (b) *I am suffering grief.* ὀδυρομένη κατὰ θυμόν signals the grief context clearly enough, and the extension αἰῶνα φθινύθω (developed by association with e.g. 5. 106–1, αἰών | φθινέτω) is a moving addition, triggered perhaps by 18. 180–1: ἀγλαΐην γὰρ ἐμοί γε θεοί, τοὶ Ὄλυμπον ἔχουσιν, | ὤλεσαν, ἐξ οὗ κεῖνος ἔβη κοίλης ἐνὶ νηυσίν.

204–5: (c) *desire for my husband.* Note ποθέουσα and cf. 1. 343.

205: (d) *a man of fame.* ἀρετή and ἔξοχος replace κλέος of 1. 344. Again, this is a unique combination, developed out of e.g. 4. 629 = 21. 187, 22. 244 (the suitors) ἀρετῇ δ᾿ ἔσαν ἔξοχ᾿ ἄριστοι. Penelope is readying herself to marry an inferior (18. 272–3): hence she remembers Odysseus' superiority to all other Greeks. At 4. 725 she calls Odysseus, resoundingly, παντοίης ἀρετῇσι κεκασμένον ἐν Δαναοῖσιν, a dramatic reworking of the idea.

The (b) (c) (d) idea-sequence is a replica of 1. 342–3 above, but the mode of expression is entirely different. This is verbal dexterity: is it not also inventive?

3. *Odyssey* 21. 68–72

> "κέκλυτέ μευ, μνηστῆρες ἀγήνορες, οἳ τόδε δῶμα
> ἐχράετ᾿ ἐσθιέμεν καὶ πινέμεν ἐμμενὲς αἰεὶ
> ἀνδρὸς ἀποιχομένοιο πολὺν χρόνον· οὐδέ τιν᾿ ἄλλην   70

μύθου ποιήσασθαι ἐπισχεσίην ἐδύνασθε,
ἀλλ᾽ ἐμὲ ἱέμενοι γῆμαι θέσθαι τε γυναῖκα."

Context: Penelope has fetched Odysseus' bow from the store-room and is announcing the contest. She begins:
68–9: (a) *suitors' consumption of the household*. The expression is unique, but is close in form to 2. 305 ἀλλά μοι ἐσθιέμεν καὶ πινέμεν, ὡς τὸ πάρος περ. The conjunction of 'eating and drinking' is found again at e.g. 10. 460, 12. 23. It is metrically identical with 23. 8–9 οἵ θ᾽ ἐὸν οἶκον | κήδεσκον καὶ κτήματ᾽ ἔδον βιόωντό τε παῖδα (not that this could be substituted: but the variety is striking).
70: (g) *my long-departed husband*.
71: (h) *the suitors' desire to marry Penelope*.
These three ideas make a crisp summary of the situation of the *Odyssey*: Odysseus is long gone, so the suitors can make merry with the property of the house and force Penelope into marriage. This is wholly appropriate at the moment when Penelope thinks she is about to have a new husband chosen for her.

4. *Odyssey* 23. 15–19

"τίπτε με λωβεύεις πολυπενθέα θυμὸν ἔχουσαν   15
ταῦτα παρὲξ ἐρέουσα καὶ ἐξ ὕπνου μ᾽ ἀνεγείρεις
ἡδέος, ὅς μ᾽ ἐπέδησε φίλα βλέφαρ᾽ ἀμφικαλύψας;
οὐ γάρ πω τοιόνδε κατέδραθον, ἐξ οὗ Ὀδυσσεὺς
ᾤχετ᾽ ἐποψόμενος Κακοΐλιον οὐκ ὀνομαστήν."

Context: Eurycleia has awoken Penelope to tell her of Odysseus' arrival and the slaughter of the suitors.
15: (b) *Penelope's grief*. πολυπενθέα θυμὸν ἔχουσα is a deeply emotional expression at this high point of the epic, πολυπενθέα being used only here of the θυμός, and promptly contradicted by Telemachus at 23. 97, who accuses her of ἀπηνέα θυμὸν ἔχουσα!
16–17: (e) *a wonderful sleep*: The only verbal comparison between this expression and that at 18. 201 is the use of a form of καλύπτω.
18–19: (g) *my departed husband*.

These passages have obviously been carefully selected to reveal a nexus of associated ideas: (b) occurs three times, (a), (c), (d), (e), and (g) occur twice, and (f), (h) once. Their methods of expression also vary rather considerably. In an established context, where one idea sets up another, this range of variety is impressive.
    Let us now look at 18. 250–80:

Τὸν δ' ἠμείβετ' ἔπειτα περίφρων Πηνελόπεια·　　　　250
"Εὐρύμαχ', ἦ τοι ἐμὴν ἀρετὴν εἶδός τε δέμας τε
ὤλεσαν ἀθάνατοι, ὅτε Ἴλιον εἰσανέβαινον
Ἀργεῖοι, μετὰ τοῖσι δ' ἐμὸς πόσις ἦεν Ὀδυσσεύς.
εἰ κεῖνός γ' ἐλθὼν τὸν ἐμὸν βίον ἀμφιπολεύοι,
μεῖζόν κε κλέος εἴη ἐμὸν καὶ κάλλιον οὕτως.　　　255
νῦν δ' ἄχομαι· τόσα γάρ μοι ἐπέσσευεν κακὰ δαίμων.
ἦ μὲν δὴ ὅτε τ' ᾖε λιπὼν κάτα πατρίδα γαῖαν,
δεξιτερὴν ἐπὶ καρπῷ ἑλὼν ἐμὲ χεῖρα προσηύδα·
'ὦ γύναι, οὐ γὰρ ὀΐω ἐϋκνήμιδας Ἀχαιοὺς
ἐκ Τροίης εὖ πάντας ἀπήμονας ἀπονέεσθαι·　　　260
καὶ γὰρ Τρῶάς φασι μαχητὰς ἔμμεναι ἄνδρας,
ἠμὲν ἀκοντιστὰς ἠδὲ ῥυτῆρας ὀϊστῶν
ἵππων τ' ὠκυπόδων ἐπιβήτορας, οἵ κε τάχιστα
ἔκριναν μέγα νεῖκος ὁμοιΐου πολέμοιο.
τῷ οὐκ οἶδ' ἤ κέν μ' ἀνέσει θεός, ἦ κεν ἁλώω　　　265
αὐτοῦ ἐνὶ Τροίῃ· σοὶ δ' ἐνθάδε πάντα μελόντων.
μεμνῆσθαι πατρὸς καὶ μητέρος ἐν μεγάροισιν
ὡς νῦν, ἢ ἔτι μᾶλλον ἐμεῦ ἀπονόσφιν ἐόντος·
αὐτὰρ ἐπὴν δὴ παῖδα γενειήσαντα ἴδηαι,
γήμασθ' ᾧ κ' ἐθέλησθα, τεὸν κατὰ δῶμα λιποῦσα.'　　270
κεῖνος τὼς ἀγόρευε· τὰ δὴ νῦν πάντα τελεῖται.
νὺξ δ' ἔσται ὅτε δὴ στυγερὸς γάμος ἀντιβολήσει
οὐλομένης ἐμέθεν, τῆς τε Ζεὺς ὄλβον ἀπηύρα.
ἀλλὰ τόδ' αἰνὸν ἄχος κραδίην καὶ θυμὸν ἱκάνει·
μνηστήρων οὐχ ἥδε δίκη τὸ πάροιθε τέτυκτο,　　　275
οἵ τ' ἀγαθήν τε γυναῖκα καὶ ἀφνειοῖο θύγατρα
μνηστεύειν ἐθέλωσι καὶ ἀλλήλοις ἐρίσωσιν·
αὐτοὶ τοί γ' ἀπάγουσι βόας καὶ ἴφια μῆλα,
κούρης δαῖτα φίλοισι, καὶ ἀγλαὰ δῶρα διδοῦσιν·
ἀλλ' οὐκ ἀλλότριον βίοτον νήποινον ἔδουσιν."　　　280

Context: Penelope is facing the suitors in the hall and preparing to announce her intention to remarry.
251–2: (i) *my beauty is destroyed.*
253: (g) *my departed husband.* I note this same sequence (i) (g) occurs again at 18. 180–1 in quite different words: ἀγλαΐην γὰρ ἐμοί γε θεοί, τοὶ Ὄλυμπον ἔχουσιν, | ὤλεσαν, ἐξ οὗ κεῖνος ἔβη κοίλης ἐνὶ νηυσίν.
254–5: (k) *my kleos, should he return.*
256: (b) *my grief and god-sent troubles.*
257: (g) *my departed husband.*
(His instructions to Penelope.)

272–3: (h) *my marriage impends.*
274: (b) *my grief.*
(Suitors' irregular marriage-practices.)
280: (a) *suitors' consumption of the household.*

This is worth comparing with 19. 123–36:

> Τὸν δ' ἠμείβετ' ἔπειτα περίφρων Πηνελόπεια·
> "ξεῖν', ἦ τοι μὲν ἐμὴν ἀρετὴν εἶδός τε δέμας τε
> ὤλεσαν ἀθάνατοι, ὅτε Ἴλιον εἰσανέβαινον   125
> Ἀργεῖοι, μετὰ τοῖσι δ' ἐμὸς πόσις ἦεν Ὀδυσσεύς.
> εἰ κεῖνός γ' ἐλθὼν τὸν ἐμὸν βίον ἀμφιπολεύοι,
> μεῖζόν κε κλέος εἴη ἐμὸν καὶ κάλλιον οὕτω.
> νῦν δ' ἄχομαι· τόσα γάρ μοι ἐπέσσευεν κακὰ δαίμων.
> ὅσσοι γὰρ νήσοισιν ἐπικρατέουσιν ἄριστοι,   130
> Δουλιχίῳ τε Σάμῃ τε καὶ ὑλήεντι Ζακύνθῳ,
> οἵ τ' αὐτὴν Ἰθάκην εὐδείελον ἀμφινέμονται,
> οἵ μ' ἀεκαζομένην μνῶνται, τρύχουσι δὲ οἶκον.
> τῷ οὔτε ξείνων ἐμπάζομαι οὔθ' ἱκετάων
> οὔτε τι κηρύκων, οἳ δημιοεργοὶ ἔασιν·   135
> ἀλλ' Ὀδυσῆ ποθέουσα φίλον κατατήκομαι ἦτορ."

Context: Penelope is talking with Odysseus the beggar in the hall
late at night.
124–9: ((i), (g), (k), (b)) = 18. 251–6.
130–3: (h) *marriage to suitors.* (= 1. 245–8)
133: (a) *suitors' consumption of the household.* (= 1. 248)
134–5: (l) *suitors pay no attention to anyone.*
136: (c) *desire for Odysseus*
136: (b) *I suffer grief.* These two ideas are here compressed into a
single line—considerably different from e.g. 1. 343 and 18. 204.
The whole line could have been expressed as Eumaeus does at 14.
144: ἀλλά μ' Ὀδυσσῆος πόθος αἴνυται οἰχομένοιο (cf. 14. 169).

One could go and extend the basic analysis (e.g. the run at 4.
681–95, 722–41, 810–23 is rich in new and old ideas and expressions). One could then look more closely and discuss the aesthetic
reasons for this or that mode of expression, this or that sequence,
this or that emphasis. One may lay the foundations for new
thoughts about formulae and synonyms. For example, the ideas
that I have highlighted are not unique to Penelope: under (a) *suitors' consumption*, there is a great deal more evidence one could take
into account, since characters are constantly talking about it. Try
the following careful selection:

Introduction

1. 160 ἐπεὶ ἀλλότριον βίοτον νήποινον ἔδουσιν
2. 57–8 εἰλαπινάζουσιν πίνουσί τε αἴθοπα οἶνον | μαψιδίως. τὰ δὲ πολλὰ κατάνεται.
2. 203 χρήματα δ' αὖτε κακῶς βεβρώσεται
2. 312–13 ἐκείρετε πολλὰ καὶ ἐσθλὰ | κτήματ' ἐμά
3. 315 μή τοι κατὰ πάντα φάγωσι
4. 318–20 ἐσθίεταί μοι οἶκος ... μῆλ' ἀδινὰ σφάζουσι καὶ εἰλίποδας ἕλικας βοῦς
4. 686–7 βίοτον κατακείρετε πολλόν, | κτῆσιν Τηλεμάχοιο δαίφρονος
11. 116 οἵ τοι βίοτον κατέδουσι

And so on. Dexterity, certainly: invention too?

And all the time, surprises are in store. At 18. 256 above, Penelope tells us her troubles are sent by the gods: τόσα γάρ μοι ἐπέσσευεν κακὰ δαίμων. At 4. 722, she expresses the identical idea in a quite different way: περὶ γάρ μοι 'Ολύμπιος ἄλγε' ἔδωκεν. If one wants the same idea expressed as a whole line, one can toy with the possibilities raised by e.g. κήδε' ἐπεί μοι πολλὰ δόσαν θεοὶ οὐρανίωνες (9. 15), αὐτὰρ ἐμοὶ καὶ πένθος ἀμέτρητον πόρε δαίμων (19. 512), καὶ δέ μοι ἄλλα θεοὶ δόσαν ἄλγεά τε στοναχάς τε (14. 39), (οἷον) ἐπεί νύ μοι ἄλλα θεοὶ κακὰ κήδε' ἔτευξαν (1. 244). These are not mutually substitutable as they stand: but the range of expression is wide and notable.

In a formular system, the poet has no option but to work with his formulae. But this does not deny him the ability to be inventive. He can be inventive in their manipulation and recombination. There is more to this than dexterity. It is the point at which art and craft cross.

To return to Klingner. His analysis of the sequence of ideas the poet feeds into his narrative raises the important question of the different forms these ideas might take and how the sequences themselves are chosen and articulated. There is much work beyond the simply formulaic to be done here.[6]

One of the major issues which **Reinhardt** (217–48) explores here is how the poet converts folk-tale into epic, and he argues that Homer takes the simple actions of folk-tales and creates out of them epic 'situations', in which character can be deepened and the

---

[6] Martin (1989: 146–230) illustrates another level of complexity of diction when he discusses the rhetorical repetitiveness of the language of Achilles.

psychology of human feelings and relationships explored (on the same lines see Hölscher (1988), who emphasizes the anonymous nature of the folk-tale, as opposed to the epic, hero, and cf. Peradotto (1990: 32–58) for a discussion of the differences between the narrative of folk-tale, where desires are fulfilled, and of myth, where they are not; and cf. in general Slatkin (1991)). Of course we do not know precisely what Homer (or his tradition) had to work with. Nevertheless, the argument that the tales of *Odyssey* 9–12 are folk-tale in origin is undisputed; and it is worth speculating what Homer might have done to convert them into the present text. The argument is, of course, circular, unless we have reason to believe that folk-tales follow some ineluctable laws of construction, which do (or do not) apply to Homer. Since I think there are such laws, I proceed.

In *Odyssey* 9–12, on which I shall concentrate, the poet (or 'his tradition') faces three particular problems: (i) he has to see how far the broad structure of each folk-tale fits the *Odyssey* (thus, Odysseus has companions: does the folk-tale? Can they be worked in?); (ii) he has to Hellenize the folk-tale, i.e. make it accessible to a Greek audience; (iii) he has to find some way of stringing the folk-tales together so that, however disparate the tales are in origin, they blend together in the *Odyssey* as a convincing composite, suited both to the needs of the story and to the character of their teller, Odysseus. This, perhaps, is the severest problem of all. I take the problems one by one.

(i) At a Berlin conference in 1908 Axel Olrik (1909) ambitiously defined a number of 'laws' which he felt underlay the composition of most European folk-tales, sagas, legends, and myths (which he lumped together under the term *Sage*). These 'epic laws', as he called them, are above any individual's control: all the folk narrator can do is blindly obey them. Set against the folk-tale's 'over-whelming uniformity . . . national characteristics seem to be only dialect peculiarities' (131). If this sounds unnecessarily mechanis-tic—and after all, once similarities have been defined it is the dif-ferences that are interesting—some of the laws can still be usefully applied to the *Odyssey* tales of Books 9–12. I list them here in roughly the same order as Olrik, combining and adapting laws where that can be usefully done.

(*a*) The law of opening and the law of closing. The *Sage* 'begins by moving from calm to excitement, and after the concluding event, in which a principal character frequently has a catastrophe, the *Sage* ends by moving from excitement to calm.' In other words, tales do not begin or end abruptly: they wind up and wind down again. This is well exemplified in the *Odyssey*, where throughout Books 9–12 Odysseus is constantly landing, investigating, undergoing an adventure, and then extricating himself from it.

(*b*) The law of repetition and the law of three, sometimes four. In *Sage*, things are rarely done once, but usually three (or four) times. Thus Hector runs three times round the walls of Troy; three times Patroclus charges the walls of Troy, but on the fourth Apollo attacks him. Three times Odysseus gives Cyclops a swig of wine, three times he drinks it (9. 361); three times Cyclops milks the flocks (9. 244, 308, 341), three times he seizes companions and eats them (9. 289, 311, 344); three times Odysseus tries to grasp the ghost of his mother Anticleia, three times she eludes him (11. 206–8); three times a day Charybdis swings into action (12. 105–6).

(*c*) The law of two to a scene. The interaction of more than two characters at any one time is very rare in *Sage*. What is interesting about the *Odyssey* in this respect is that Odysseus is a first-person narrator: does he then 'count'? Should we expect plenty of 'I' + x + y? The problem is then compounded by the presence of Odysseus' men: one has ' "I" + men' before one has even started. In fact, the spirit of this law is maintained: there are very few *clearly* integrated three-sided conversations or interactions in Books 9–12 (i.e. narrator + men + y, or narrator + y + z, or no narratorial presence but x + y + z). For possible exceptions, though they could all be characterized as two-sided conversations if one insisted, see e.g. 9. 287–96 ('I' + Cyclops + men)? 9. 446–61 ('I' + Cyclops + ram)? 9. 491–542 ('I' + Cyclops + men)? 10. 233–43 (Polites + men + Eurylochus + Circe)? 10. 428–45 ('I' + men + Eurylochus)? 11. 333–84 ('I' + Arete + Echeneus + Alcinous)?

(*d*) The law of contrast. This is a correlative to the law of two to a scene. The pair in the foreground at any one time, in other words, tend to be strongly contrasted (young and old, large and small, good and evil, etc.). This is meat and drink for Books 9–12: Odysseus and his men are paired in this way throughout, as are Odysseus and/or men vs. 'villain'.

(*e*) The law of initial and final position. 'Whenever a series of persons or things occurs, then the principal one will come first.

Coming last, though, will be the person for whom the particular narrative arouses sympathy.' It is difficult to apply this law to a story told by a first-person narrator whose primary aim is to generate sympathy for himself. One notes, for example, the sympathetic Elpenor at 10. 522 ff., who comes 'last' in the sense that he is the last single companion with whom we have contact before Odysseus goes down into the Underworld: but this law seems inapplicable.

(*f*) The law of patterning. Situations repeat themselves in *Sage* in a way quite unlike real life. But one of the typical ways in which Homer works is to turn folk-tale into life which is as 'real' as possible, especially by suppression of the overtly magical elements (see Page 1973: *passim*). Formulaic repetition is an inevitable feature of oral epic (see (*b*) above, and cf. landing—sending ambassadors ahead—seeing smoke rising from the land, etc.), but this is realistic anyway, and not quite what Olrik meant.

(*g*) The law of tableaux scenes. Every *Sage* has a grand, central moment that etches itself indelibly on the memory. This law, so obviously exemplified by e.g. the blinding of the Cyclops and Odysseus and his men's meeting with Circe, does not particularly help us understand how the poet set about converting folk-tales into the *Odyssey*.

(*h*) The law of the single strand (which links with the law of unity of plot). *Sage* does not go back to fill in missing details. If such background information is necessary, it will emerge in the dialogue. This is broadly true of each tale as an individual unit, but is not quite true of the tales as a whole, since the poet is at pains to forge links between them. Thus in the course of Books 9–12 we look forward and back across the tales in a way that would be meaningless if the poet were recounting one tale and no other. So at 9. 197 we are told of the wine Odysseus was given by Maron during the earlier Ciconian adventure.

(*i*) The law of concentration on single character ('the greatest law of folk tradition'). This law will be inevitably fulfilled if the tales are not third-person narrative but told by the hero-narrator. Homer has a major problem to face here with Odysseus' companions, i.e. giving them a role which makes them more than cyphers but less than Odysseus himself (cf. Telemachus). Indeed, given folk-tales' concentration on the clash between a villain and a single hero, it must have required considerable effort to find a creative role for Odysseus' companions, and they do indeed move in and out of the action rather uneasily at times. Nevertheless, the role the poet finds for them is, in the end, of critical importance: they are further examples, like the suitors, of the way men bring disaster upon themselves (cf. 1. 7, 32–43, 12. 340–419).

(ii) Hellenization of the tales. We are on firmer ground here, and a few examples will suffice of how Homer turns 'neutral' folk-tales into Greek folk-tales. Cyclops' father is a Greek god Poseidon (9. 412); Cyclops knows of Zeus and the Greek custom of *xenia*, though he chooses to ignore it (9. 273–8); the Cyclopes had a sooth-sayer, Telemos (9. 509); Aeolus is most hospitably Greek (10. 14–15); the land of the Laestrygonians has many Greek features (an *astu* (10. 104), an *agora* (10. 114), etc.); and so on.

(iii) Adaptation of the tales to suit the particular needs of the *Odyssey*. At one level, the Hellenization of the tales gives them a form of surface unity. But they are still heterogeneous as a collec-tion, and need blending together to make a convincing whole. At least the problem of location solves itself, since Odysseus is on the move. When one adventure has finished, he moves elsewhere to have another one.

But Homer is also at pains to draw the connections between the tales, to give them a unity they did not originally possess. He describes, for example, the journeys between each location, the storms, landfalls, nights ashore, hunting expeditions for food, and so on. As the ships move on to their next port of call, the men often remember what has just happened to their comrades (e.g. 9. 62–3, 12. 8–15); Odysseus reminds them of what they have been through (e.g. 12. 209–12); and prepares them for what is to come (e.g., fol-lowing Circe's instructions, at 12. 154–64). At 9. 196–205, Odysseus takes wine to the Cyclops given him by Maron during the earlier Ciconian adventure.

Then again, Homer links the tales into the mainstream of the *Odyssey*'s plot. Odysseus' account of his adventures after leaving Troy are bound in with his stay on Scherie at 11. 335–84; when Cyclops prays to Poseidon to ensure that Odysseus will return home late, having lost all his men (9. 528–35), the poet has placed the Cyclops incident at the very heart of the story of Odysseus' return.[7]

---

[7] Hölscher (1978) points out that Radermacher in *Die Erzählungen der Odyssee* (Vienna, 1915) found a reference to an American Indian folk-tale in which the hero

Thematically, too, Homer forges links. The conflict between Odysseus and his men, for example, is built into the tales as a constant issue: e.g. 9. 43–4, 96–9, 224–30, 10. 28–45, 266–73, 12. 270–95, 339–52. This feature certainly cannot have been there in the 'original' stories. Again, the *xenia* sequences are not simply a matter of Hellenization. They are of high thematic importance in a tale where the hero will return home to find all rules of *xenia* in disarray.

In particular, De Jong (1992) has shown how cleverly the poet suits the narration of the story to the character of Odysseus. The story may, once, have been a third-person narrative. But Homer has not turned it blindly into a first-person narrative without further thought. For example, Odysseus' words ring with the vocabulary of judgement usually used only by speakers (Griffin 1986*a*), not by the third-person narrator: the story, in other words, is personalized, made to feel like a first-person, not a third-person, tale.

Burkert's paper (pp. 249–62) raises an issue of great interest to scholars: the relationship between the *Iliad* and *Odyssey*. One has, of course, to assume for the sake of the argument that the *Odyssey* is later than the *Iliad* (not an assumption shared by all) and that in the essentially oral cultural world of Greek speakers of the eighth/seventh century BC it makes sense to talk of one poem 'referring' (in whatever way) to another.

Burkert argues that the story of Ares and Aphrodite in *Odyssey* 8 was composed in the light of the *Iliad*: and that the ethically serious divine world of the *Odyssey* here acknowledges the element of burlesque in the divine world of the *Iliad*. The argument depends on structural and verbal similarities between *Odyssey* 8 and passages in *Iliad* Books 1, 14, and 20.

'Poetic allusions . . . cannot be proved or disproved' (Garner 1990: 1, promptly corrected on p. 2; cf. Goldhill (1991: 207–11) on the similar problems inherent in parody). Garner is being extreme, of course, as he ultimately agrees (how much 'proof' do you need to demonstrate that Virgil alludes to Homer, or Milton to both?), but even if we cannot prove or disprove allusions, we can all recognize

---

is told in the Underworld that when he returns home he will find his brothers courting his wife, and that he will live to a happy old age. This is instructive: one cannot be wholly certain that, as Radermacher indicates, there were no links of this sort already existing in a tradition of adventure + homecoming folk-tales. V. A. Propp's *Morphology of the Folktale* (*IJAL* (III) 24, 1958) points in the same direction.

them. Allusion-spotting is in fact a highly pragmatic business. There is, as far as I know, no useful theory to handle it (as even Goldhill admits in relation to the parallel phenomenon of parody, and he should know: Goldhill 1991: 209, cf. Garner 1990: 183–6). Pucci (1987) seems to have no interest in the historical perspective—whether the *Iliad* or *Odyssey* was composed first seems irrelevant to him—but is sensible enough on the problems of allusion (p. 19). The Greek literary theorists also say virtually nothing about it, though the literature (as they knew) indulged in it endlessly (Garner (1990) illustrates this in relation to Greek tragedians' use of Homer).

Modern discussion must start with Rutherford's fine paper (1991–3). Here, he argues that the *Odyssey* was produced after the *Iliad* and is a response to it. The argument proceeds humanely on two legs: first, the broad structural reasons, second, the more intimate textual reasons, for believing that the *Odyssey* poet has the *Iliad* in mind. Structurally, for example, he argues that the *Odyssey* completes many stories left in the air in the *Iliad*—a remarkable coincidence if the *Odyssey* poet did not know the poem. The length of the *Odyssey* is *Iliadic*—suggestive of imitation, because as Griffin (1977) has shown, the *Iliad* is uniquely long. Like the *Iliad*, it centres around a single hero, exploring a complementary theme (the world of peace), within a narrow time-frame, plunges *in medias res*, and at the end leaves the future uncertain. The use of speeches and similes, the handling of moral dilemmas (from which the poet *qua* narrator distances himself) and treatment of the gods, who in both epics 'define more clearly the achievements and the limitations of mortal men', are also striking.

Again, at the level of episode, Rutherford points, for example, to the similarity of the proems, the 'testing' speeches in *Iliad* and *Odyssey* 2, and the climactic deaths in *Iliad* and *Odyssey* 22. He points out that both epics end with funeral rites, and emphasize the father–son theme. He also discusses the similarities between *Iliad* 24 and *Odyssey* 1 (a favourite topic: see e.g. Richardson 1993: 21–4).

At the level of sentence and paragraph, Rutherford offers, for example, the 'I shall not receive him home' topos at *Iliad* 18. 440–1 (Thetis) and *Odyssey* 19. 257 ff. (Penelope); the 'fatal decision' topos in *Iliad* 9 (Achilles must choose a long or short life) and *Odyssey* 5 (Odysseus must choose whether to stay with Calypso and be immortal or return); the reflections of the Trojan War in Demodocus' songs in *Odyssey* 8, and the way characters in the *Odyssey* recall the Trojan conflict (e.g. Nestor at 3. 103 ff., Menelaus and Helen at 4. 235–89, and so on). There are some almost parodic reflections too: e.g. the lion simile used of a warrior at *Iliad* 12 and a naked Odysseus at *Odyssey* 6, or Hector's famous words at *Iliad* 6. 492–3 and Telemachus' imitations at *Odyssey* 1. 356–8, 21. 350–2. Rutherford also picks up the 'end of day' topos at *Iliad* 18. 239 ff. and *Odyssey* 23. 243 ff.

This is an impressive list. It could be extended and deepened with reference to e.g. Clarke (1989: 86–97), Griffin (1987: 63–70), Rutherford (1992: 1–7), Camps (1980: 2–4), while Usener (1990) deals with the subject in massive detail (but see Griffin's rightly hesitant review in *CR* 41 no. 2 (1991), 288–91). But there are two major problems with it. First, the essence of oral poetry is repetition. The *Iliad* and *Odyssey* cannot help but repeat each other, at the level of word, phrase, scene, and scene sequence (see Hainsworth 1984: 115). Second, the language of oral poetry is drawn from a common pool. If *this* quotation in the *Iliad* looks remarkably close to *that* quotation in the *Odyssey*, the one is not necessarily drawn from the other: there may be a shared source on which both have independently drawn (cf. e.g. Fenik (1968) on the relationship between the *Iliad* and *Aethiopis*).

Rutherford is, of course, well aware of this. He agrees that his argument is 'cumulative and tentative . . . intended to stimulate further discussion' (38). My problem with it, however, is that I do not see that it proves the case he wants to make. Rutherford has certainly shown that there exist rich and suggestive connections between the two poems, but it seems to me that he could have written in exactly the same terms of (say) *Macbeth* and Aeschylus' *Agamemnon*, without claiming that he was thereby proving that Shakespeare was *au fait* with Aeschylus. In other words, Rutherford's article strikes me as an important contribution to a literary, not a historical, debate.

Rutherford would be justified in replying to this, 'Agreed. But the similarities are there. What are we to make of them?' It may be that we must just assume intertextual allusion was a common feature of oral poetry. I have, after all, no problems with allusion over a wide spread of narrative in the same text (above, 9 ff.): why not between texts? I would be happier, however, if we could come up with a cultural context within which such intertextual allusion would make sense. One possibility is that Martin (1989) is right about the competitiveness of oral poets. Usener (1990) certainly takes the view that the *Odyssey*-poet is a rival of the *Iliad*'s, picking up Iliadic themes and challenging its values. Allusion from one poem to the other, then, would show that the poems are by different authors, and the *Odyssey*-poet was attempting to upstage the *Iliad*-poet.

But that itself is open to the objection that there are few, if any, passages where it can be convincingly shown that the *Odyssey*-poet is *taking on* the *Iliad*, as opposed to drawing from a common pool or reflecting the different values of a different poetic *mise-en-scène* (cf. Lloyd-Jones 1983: 30–1). Let us take a major difference between the two poems, that the *Odyssey* is the poem of μῆτις and the *Iliad* of βία. There is in fact plenty of both in each poem (e.g. the βία of Odysseus when he kills the suitors, and the μῆτις of Priam when, metaphorically naked to his enemy, he supplicates Achilles with no less cunning than that with which Odysseus supplicated Nausicaa). Further, it is not exactly surprising if βία is dominant in the *Iliad*, a poem of war, while the folk-take world of much of the *Odyssey* equally lends itself to resolution by μῆτις. Nevertheless, it is commonly agreed that the meeting in the Underworld between Odysseus and Achilles at 11. 467–540 looks like a conscious attempt to set one sort of heroism against another.

But in what terms? Odysseus indicates the trouble he has getting home (481–2), and praises Achilles as once lord of the living and now of the dead (483–6). Achilles replies that he wishes he were still living, even as a θής (488–91), before enquiring after his son and his father, whom he can no longer help (492–503). The only point of difference between them is that Odysseus has survived. Survival is certainly a heroic priority, but the price of an early death is worth paying if κλέος results (see Hainsworth 1993: 44–53), and for Achilles, it surely has. Besides, there are many other dead in Hades with whom Odysseus converses: there is no sense that Achilles' death is somehow uniquely important.

If Homer wished to contrast the heroism of the two, it may seem flat-footed to demand some reference to Patroclus or Hector, or to Odysseus' triumphs and Achilles' failures: Homer, after all, can be as suggestive in silence as he is in utterance (e.g. Ajax at 11. 563–4). But that leaves the example of Clytaimnestra and Penelope to consider. There is no reticence there about Homer's intentions in comparing the loyal and disloyal wife (11. 428–53). I do not understand what advantage there was for Homer in remaining silent about the competing heroism of Achilles and Odysseus if that is what he wanted to highlight. I conclude that in the meeting between Odysseus and Achilles, two sorts of heroism are not being compared. What we have is an especially pathos-filled meeting in the Underworld between heroes from the Trojan War, the central point of which is that the dead Achilles placed such a high value on life.

I do not see on what grounds it is possible to say whether the *Odyssey* was consciously competing with the *Iliad* or complementing it, imitating it or correcting it, or even engaging in a dialogue with it. But what Rutherford has shown is that the one can cast powerful light on the other. This is where Burkert's paper comes in. There is no doubt that the use of the gods in the song of Ares and Aphrodite in *Odyssey* 8 presents severe problems. Burkert's attempt to solve those problems by reference to gods in the *Iliad* seems to me the right way to set about the problems, and to illuminate both the *Iliad* and the *Odyssey* in the process. Whether we are justified in seeing direct textual allusion, however, is not so straightforward a matter. I end by suggesting there may be something to be said for the view of Nagy (1979: 41–3; cf. Nagy 1992: 22 n. 62) that in the *Iliad* and *Odyssey* we are dealing with different traditions of poetry, which have been in existence for a very long time and because of that long history of development cannot help but 'respond' to one another in general terms.[8]

Erbse's paper (263–320) tackles one of the issues at stake in determining whether the ending of the *Odyssey* (which, for the sake of argument, I take to mean 23. 297–24. 548) is authentic, i.e. composed by the same poet who (substantially) composed the rest of the poem.[9] Erbse takes on the linguistic case against authenticity made by Page (1955), and demolishes it. This is not to deny that some of his arguments plead special cases as strongly as Page's did: the argument 'how else could the poet have said it?', for example, is particularly open to objection. But (as Erbse is well aware) the linguistic case alone does not entirely resolve the problem.

[8] I cannot subscribe to all Nagy's views on this matter.
[9] Renate Oswald in *Das Ende der Odyssee* (Graz, 1993) takes the bizarre view that the *Odyssey* ended at 23. 245, though she is sound enough on the other issues.

Introduction

Those who argue that cultural/historical problems loom large at
the end of the *Odyssey* tend to run into the same sort of brick wall
that Erbse constructs in relation to the linguistic problems: the
unique situation at the end of the *Odyssey* requires unique handling, and merely because a phenomenon occurs once in Homer is no
evidence that it is non-Homeric. The geography of the second
nekuia at the start of Book 24, for example, does indeed look very
strange, but if the poet insists on describing the route down to
Hades, it must look strange: he has never done it before in the detail
he is aiming at here (cf. *Odyssey* 10. 507–15, 11. 13–22, *Iliad*
23. 72–3). There is no *prima facie* reason why any of the detail he
selects should not have been available to him (Heubeck in Russo
and others (1992: 360–1) on 24. 11–14). Again, whatever the problems raised e.g. by the Laertes scene, Lord (1960: 177–9) shows
that recognition of a newly returned son by a parent, occurring
after the son has revealed himself to everyone else, is thoroughly
typical of return stories. After the attention Laertes has received in
the earlier part of the poem, it is unthinkable that now, of all times,
he should be left in the air.

That leaves literary/aesthetic grounds. Here, it seems to me, the
end of the *Odyssey* does look like a botch. Unfortunately, standards
of proof in this area are not rigorous, and one man's opinion set
against another's looks like the feeblest kind of subjectivity. One
can only offer a comparative argument, and ask whether in logic of
plot structure and control of narrative the last book of the *Odyssey*
comes up to the general high standards reached elsewhere, e.g. in
Books 1, 5–6, 9, and 21–2. It seems to me it does not. This is not
to deny that parts of it are excellent, and clearly build on what
has gone before (e.g. the Halitherses–Eupeithes assembly at 24.
413–71, the Telemachus–Odysseus interchange which brings such
joy to Laertes at 24. 502–15). But Page's analysis of the overall
effect of the last lines of the *Odyssey* in particular seems to me well
said (Page 1955: 112–14; cf. West 1989: 128–30).

It can be agreed that whoever composed the end of the *Odyssey*—
the main composer or not—did so with the rest of the *Odyssey* in
mind. That he did not do it very well seems to me at least arguable.
Even Homer nods, of course, but it is worth considering in what
circumstances one can imagine the poem being extended from an
original ending at 23. 296.

Two approaches seem especially fruitful. West (1989: 131–4) is perfectly content that the *Odyssey* should have ended at 23. 296, since epic did not see the need to tie up loose ends in what was an almost infinitely extendable sequence. The poet simply chopped out the bit he wanted to deal with, and dealt with it (so the *Iliad* does not tell of Achilles' death, etc.). She then observes sharply that Eugammon of Cyrene's *Telegony* does not start where our *Odyssey* ends—for it begins with the word οἱ μνηστῆρες ὑπὸ τῶν προσηκόντων θάπτονται (Davies, *EGF* p. 72, l. 3). Since Cyclic epic did not usually trespass on Homeric ground but skirted round it, it looks as if Eugammon's *Odyssey* ended before 24. 417 (where the suitors are gathered and buried). So Eugammon buried the suitors, and sent Odysseus off on a long further series of adventures culminating in his death at the hands of Telegonus, his (non-Homeric) son by Calypso.

West argues that by the time of the Panathenaea (sixth century BC), neither the infinite extendability of the story nor an ending at 23. 296 which left the whole issue of blood vengeance and state harmony unresolved would have been acceptable and suggests that it was then that our ending was composed. This strikes me as persuasive, if one can reasonably assume that the late eighth/early seventh century BC would have felt differently. After all, it is not as if revenge for death is a theme unknown to epic.

Seaford (1994: 38–42) builds on West's argument by arguing that it was the development of the city-state mentality that brought about this ending. Seaford in fact argues that much Homeric epic can be shown to be infused with such a mentality, and, rejecting the idea of a single composer, sees the development of the composition of the epics as we have them as a process extending over two or three hundred years, from the eighth century BC well into the Classical period. This makes far too many *a priori* assumptions about what it was and was not possible for an eighth/seventh-century epic poet to do with his inherited material and is clearly overstated. Nevertheless, West's argument fits in neatly with his hypothesis, and Seaford adds convincingly to it: 'the wedding pattern in the *Odyssey* (i.e. the reunion of Odysseus and Penelope culminating at 23. 296) is a private affair, reconstituting the household of Odysseus, but leaving the public issue of vengeance unsettled . . . the disjunction in the narrative . . . implies . . . the growth of a sensibility which could no longer do without settlement of the public issue . . . with this growth, the reaction to private violent

revenge becomes harder to exclude from a satisfactory solution.'
Seaford admits that the settlement in our text of the *Odyssey* (reconciliation imposed by Zeus and Athena with oaths) is not the
same as that which the *Oresteia* will offer (settlement through
human courts of law). But that does not affect the force of his and
West's argument about the cultural-historical circumstances which
could explain why our *Odyssey* ends as it does.

References for Introduction

ADKINS, A. W. H. (1969), 'Threatening, Abusing and Feeling Angry in the Homeric Poems', *JHS* 89, 7–21.

AREND, W. (1933), *Die typischen Szenen bei Homer* (Problemata, 7; Berlin).

ARMSTRONG, J. I. (1958), 'The Arming Motif in the Iliad', *AJPh* 79, 337–54.

AUSTIN, N. (1966), 'The Function of Digressions in the Iliad', *GRBS* 7, 295–312, repr. in Wright (1978), 70–84.

—— (1975), *Archery at the Dark of the Moon* (Berkeley and Los Angeles).

BERTMAN, S. (1966), 'The *Telemachy* and Structural Symmetry', *TAPA* 97, 15–27.

BREMER, J. M. (1987), 'The So-Called "Götterapparat" in *Iliad* XX–XXII', in Bremer and others, 31–46.

—— DE JONG, I. J. F., and KALF, J. (eds.) (1987), *Homer: Beyond Oral Poetry* (Amsterdam).

CAIRNS, F. (1979), *Tibullus: A Hellenistic Poet at Rome* (Cambridge).

CAMPS, W. A. (1980), *An Introduction to Homer* (Oxford).

CLARKE, H. W. (1989), *The Art of the Odyssey* (repr. Bristol).

CONTE, G. B. (1986), *The Rhetoric of Imitation* (Ithaca, NY, and London).

DAVIES, J. K. (1984), 'The Reliability of the Oral Tradition', in Foxhall and Davies, 87–110.

DAVIES, M. (1981), 'The Judgement of Paris and *Iliad* XXIV', *JHS* 101, 56–62.

DE JONG, I. J. F. (1987), *Narrators and Focalizers: The Presentation of the Story in the* Iliad (Amsterdam).

—— (1992), 'The Subjective Style in Odysseus' Wanderings', *CQ* 42 (i), 1–11.

DONLAN, W. (1993), 'Duelling with Gifts in the *Iliad*: As the Audience Saw It', *Colby Quarterly* 29, no. 3 (Sept.), 155–72.

EDWARDS, M. W. (1980), 'Convention and Individuality in *Iliad* 1', *HSCP* 84, 1–28.

—— (1987a), '*Topos* and transformation in Homer', in Bremer and others, 47–60.

—— (1987b), *Homer, Poet of the* Iliad (Baltimore and London).

—— (ed.) (1991), *The Iliad: A Commentary*, v. Books 17–20 (Cambridge).

EGF = M. Davies (ed.), *Epicorum Graecorum Fragmenta* (Göttingen, 1988).

EMLYN-JONES, C., HARDWICK, L., and PURKIS, J. (eds.) (1992), *Homer: Readings and Images* (London).

ERBSE, H. (1977), *Scholia Graeca in Homeri Iliadem*, i–vii (Berlin, 1969–88).

FENIK, B. C. (1968), *Typical Battle Scenes in the Iliad* (Hermes Einzelschriften 21; Wiesbaden).

—— (ed.) (1978), *Homer—Tradition and Invention* (Leiden).

FOLEY, J. M. (1990), *Traditional Oral Epic* (Berkeley and Los Angeles).

FOWLER, R. L. (1987), *The Nature of Early Greek Lyric* (Toronto).

FOXHALL, L., and DAVIES, J. K. (eds.) (1984), *The Trojan War* (Papers of the First Greenbank Colloquium, Liverpool, 1981; Bristol).

GARNER, R. (1990), *From Homer to Tragedy: The Art of Allusion in Greek Poetry* (London).

GOLDHILL, S. (1991), *The Poet's Voice* (Cambridge).

GRIFFIN, J. (1977), 'The Epic Cycle and the Uniqueness of Homer', *JHS* 97, 39–53.

—— (1980), *Homer on Life and Death* (Oxford).

—— (1986a), 'Words and Speakers in Homer', *JHS* 106, 36–57.

—— (1986b), 'Heroic and Unheroic Ideas in Homer', in J. Boardman and C. E. Vaphopoulou-Richards (eds.), *Chios, A Conference at the Homereion in Chios* (Oxford; also in Emlyn-Jones and others (1992)).

—— (1987), *Homer: The Odyssey* (Landmarks in World Literature, Cambridge).

HAINSWORTH, J. B. (1969), *Homer: Greece and Rome* (New Surveys in the Classics no. 3; Oxford).

—— (1978), 'Good and Bad Formulae', in Fenik (ed.) (1978).

—— (1984), 'The Fallibility of an Oral Heroic Tradition', in Foxhall and Davies (eds.), 111–35.

—— (ed.) (1993), *The Iliad: A Commentary*, iii. *Books 9–12* (Cambridge).

HALVERSON, J. (1985), 'Social Order in the *Odyssey*', *Hermes* 120, 129–45.

HEUBECK, A., WEST, S., and HAINSWORTH, J. B. (eds.) (1988), *A Commentary on Homer's Odyssey*, i. *Books i–viii* (Oxford).

—— and HOEKSTRA, A. (eds.) (1989), *A Commentary on Homer's Odyssey*, ii. *Books ix–xvi* (Oxford).

HOEKSTRA, A. (1965), *Homeric Modifications of Formulaic Prototypes* (Amsterdam).

—— (1979), *Epic Verse before Homer* (Amsterdam).

HÖLSCHER, U. (1978), 'The Transformation from Folk-Tale to Epic' in Fenik.

—— (1988), *Die* Odyssee: *Epos zwischen Märchen und Roman* (Munich).

JANKO, R. (ed.) (1992), *The Iliad: A Commentary*, iv. *Books 13–16* (Cambridge).

JONES, P. V. (1992), 'The Past in Homer's *Odyssey*', *JHS* 92, 74–90.

—— (1995), 'Poetic Invention: The Fighting around Troy in the First Nine Years of the Trojan War', in Ø. Andersen and M. W. Dickie

References for Introduction

(eds.), *Homer's World: Fiction, Tradition and Reality* (Papers from the Norwegian Institute at Athens vol. iii, 1995), 101–11.

JONES, P. V. (1996), 'The Independent Heroes of the *Iliad*', *JHS* 96, 108–18.

KATZ, M. A. (1991), *Penelope's Renown* (Princeton).

KIRK, G. S. (ed.) (1985), *The Iliad: A Commentary*, i. *Books 1–4* (Cambridge).

—— (ed.) (1990), *The Iliad: A Commentary*, ii. *Books 5–8* (Cambridge).

KLINGNER, F. W. (1944), *Über die ersten vier Bücher der Odysee*, Sitz.-Ber. Leipzig xcvi. I (Leipzig, also in *Studien zur griech. und. röm. Literatur* (Zurich and Stuttgart, 1964).

LLOYD-JONES, H. (1983), *The Justice of Zeus* (2nd edn., Berkeley, Calif.).

LOHMANN, D. (1970), *Die Komposition der Reden in der Ilias* (Berlin).

LORD, A. B. (1960), *Singer of Tales* (Harvard).

MARTIN, R. P. (1989), *The Language of Heroes* (Ithaca, NY).

MORRISON, J. V., *Homeric Misdirection* (Ann Arbor, Mich.).

NAGY, G. (1979), *The Best of the Achaeans* (Baltimore).

—— (1992), 'Oral Poetry and Ancient Greek Poetry, Broadenings and Narrowings of Terms', in Pinsent and Hurt, 15–37.

OLRIK, A. (1909), 'Epische Gesetze der Volksdichtung', *Zeitschrift für Deutsches Altertum* 51, 1–12, repr. in trans. in A. Dundes (ed.), *The Study of Folklore* (Englewood Cliffs, NJ, 1965), 129–41.

PAGE, D. L. (1955), *The Homeric Odyssey* (Oxford).

—— (1973), *Folktales in Homer's Odyssey* (Harvard).

PARASKEVAIDES, H. A. (1984), *The Use of Synonyms in Homeric Formulaic Diction* (Amsterdam).

PARRY, A. (ed.) (1971), *The Making of Homeric Verse: The Collected Papers of Milman Parry* (Oxford).

PERADOTTO, J. (1990), *Man in the Middle Voice* (Princeton).

PINSENT, J., and HURT, H. V. (eds.) (1992), *Homer 1987* (Papers of the Third Greenbank Colloquium April 1987, *Liverpool Classical Papers* no. 2; Liverpool).

PUCCI, P. (1987), *Odysseus Polytropos: Intertextual Readings in the Odyssey and Iliad* (Cornell).

REDFIELD, J. M. (1983), 'The Economic Man', in Rubino and Shelmerdine, 218–47.

REECE, S. (1993), *The Stranger's Welcome* (Ann Arbor, Mich.).

REEVE, M. D. (1973), 'The Language of Achilles', *CQ* 23 no. 2, 193–5.

REINHARDT, K. (1938), 'Das Parisurteil', in C. Becker (ed.), *Tradition und Geist* (Göttingen, 1960), 16–36.

—— (1948), 'Die Abenteuer der Odyssee', in C. Becker (ed.), *Tradition und Geist* (Göttingen, 1960), 37–125.

—— (1961), *Die Ilias und ihr Dichter* (Göttingen).

References for Introduction

RICHARDSON, N. (ed.) (1993), *The Iliad: A Commentary*, vi. *Books 21–24* (Cambridge).

RIHLL, T. E. (1986), 'Kings and Commoners in Homeric Society', *LCM* 11 (6), 86–91.

—— (1992), 'The Power of the Homeric βασιλεῖς', in Pinsent and Hurt, 39–50.

ROWE, C. J. (1983), 'The Nature of Homeric Morality', in Rubino and Shelmerdine, 248–75.

RUBINO, C. A., and SHELMERDINE, C. W. (eds.) (1983), *Approaches to Homer* (Austin).

RUSSO, J., FERNANDEZ-GALIANO, M., and HEUBECK, A. (eds.) (1992), *A Commentary on Homer's Odyssey*, iii. *Books xvii–xxiv* (Oxford).

RUTHERFORD, R. B. (1991–3), 'From the *Iliad* to the *Odyssey*', *BICS* 38, 37–54.

—— (ed.) (1992), *Homer, Odyssey Books XIX and XX* (Cambridge).

SCHADEWALDT, W. (1965), *Von Homers Welt und Werk* (4th edn., Stuttgart).

SEAFORD, R. (1994), *Reciprocity and Ritual* (Oxford).

SEGAL, C. (1971), *The Theme of the Mutilation of the Corpse in the* Iliad (*Mnemosyne* Suppl. 17; Leiden).

—— (1983), '*Kleos* and its Ironies in the *Odyssey*', *AC* 52, 22–47.

SHERRATT, E. S. (1990), 'Reading the Texts: Archaeology and the Homeric Question', *Antiquity* 64, 807–24 (also in Emlyn-Jones and others (1992), 144–65).

SHIVE, D. M. (1987), *Naming Achilles* (Oxford).

SLATKIN, L. M. (1991), *The Power of Thetis* (Berkeley, Los Angeles, Calif.).

STINTON, T. C. W. (1990), 'Euripides and the Judgement of Paris', in *Collected Papers on Greek Tragedy* (Oxford), 17–75 (orig. *JHS*, Suppl. xi (1965)).

TAPLIN, O. P. (1992), *Homeric Soundings* (Oxford).

THALMANN, W. G. (1984), *Conventions of Form and Thought in Early Greek Epic Poetry* (Baltimore).

THORNTON, A. (1984), *Homer's Iliad: Its Composition and the Motif of Supplication* (*Hypomnemata* 81; Göttingen).

USENER, K. (1990), *Beobachtungen zum Verhältnis der* Odyssee *zur* Ilias (Tübingen).

VENTRIS, M., and CHADWICK, J. (1973), *Documents in Mycenaean Greek* (2nd edn., Cambridge).

WEST, S. (1989), 'Laertes Re-Visited', *PCPhS* 215 NS 35, 113–43.

WHITMAN, C. H. (1958), *Homer and the Heroic Tradition* (Cambridge, Mass.).

WILLCOCK, M. M. (1970), 'Some Aspects of the Gods in the *Iliad*', *BICS* 17, 1–10, repr. in Wright (1978), 58–69.

References for Introduction

WILLCOCK, M. M. (1977), 'Ad Hoc Invention in the *Iliad*', *HSCP* 81, 41–53.

—— (1992), 'Nervous Hesitation in the *Iliad*', in Pinsent and Hurt, 65–73.

WRIGHT, J. (ed.) (1978), *Essays on the Iliad* (Bloomington).

ZANKER, G. (1994), *The Heart of Achilles: Characterization and Personal Ethics in the* Iliad (Ann Arbor, Mich.).

The Sociology of the Homeric Epics

HERMANN STRASBURGER

The age of Homer has been called 'The Greek Middle Ages' by several renowned interpreters of Greek culture and history.[1] Points of comparison with the Germanic and Romance Middle Ages can indeed be found on the small and the large scale. Just consider the parallel which lies in the conquest of a high culture now past its best by the assaults of a fresh and talented immigrant nation, and the ensuing period of pacification and ethnic cleansing, fusion, and settling down. Here, as there, we find the same vigorous, non-literate perspective on life, the prerequisite soil where great heroic epic flourishes. In individual features too, what an affinity there is between the ideals and customs of Homer's heroes and courtly society of the Christian Middle Ages!

Such a comparison is fertile, because it stimulates the imagination into active response but it is precisely here that danger lies too. So from another perspective, people have warned with equal justification against the perpetuation of the notion of 'The Greek Middle Ages', since the differences between the two ages are as great as the correspondences.[2] It is to one of these differences, [492] namely the social structure of the aristocratic society, that I would like to turn my thoughts today. As a set of economic facts, the society was described accurately by various scholars a long time ago—I will just mention Robert v. Pöhlmann, Eduard Meyer, and Johannes

Lecture given on 5 June 1952 during the Conference of German Ancient Philologists and Scholars of Antiquity in Marburg, published in H. Strasburger, *Studien zur alten Geschichte*, i (Hildesheim, 1982), 491–518, reproduced by kind permission of Georg Olms Verlag, Hildesheim.

[1] Thus already Welcker. J. Burckhardt, *Griechische Kulturgeschichte* iv (Stuttgart, 1994), 61; Th. Bergk, *Griechische Literaturgeschichte*, i (Berlin, 1887), 303 (for the period of lyrics: J. 776–500 BC); R. v. Pöhlmann, *Aus Altertum und Gegenwart* (Munich, 1911), 139 ff.; E. Meyer, *Geschichte des Altertums*, iii (2nd edn., Berlin, 1928), 267, 2; U. Wilcken, *Griechische Geschichte* (5th edn., Munich, 1943), 53. Cf. H. E. Stier, *Historia* 1950, 196.

[2] H. Bengtson, *Griechische Geschichte* (Munich, 1950), 51, 3.

Hasebroek.[3] But their insights have not become the common property of scholarship, nor have they been exploited by the scholars themselves to draw the necessary conclusions in the fields of sociology or history of ideas. There are huge tomes about the Homeric age in which its sociology is not touched on at all.[4] So it seems to me worthwhile taking up the question again, even if it only leads to a shift in emphasis . . .

I found few points of contact in my work with the 'analysts'' approach to Homer. From the point of view of social as well as intellectual history nothing, as far as I can see, forbids us from treating the *Iliad* and the *Odyssey* each as a self-contained whole and regarding them as temporally very close.[5] Both epics most probably belong to the eighth century BC. Hesiod's poems should also be located before the end of that century.[6] Although the poets of [493] the *Iliad* and the *Odyssey* also undoubtedly took over individual features from predecessors from older cultural stages—which no longer had any validity in their own century—they still reflect their own time in everything to do with existence (and I am concerned only with this issue)—both in the quasi-reality of the daily life described in the epics, and in the scale of non-material and material values. Conversely, however, we do not want to exclude the possibility that conditions similar to Homer's lifetime had *also* existed in the past. Indeed, 'in view of the great persistence of

[3] R. v. Pöhlmann, 'Aus dem hellenischen Mittelalter', in *Altertum und Gegenwart*, 139 ff.; E. Meyer, 'Die wirtschaftliche Entwicklung des Altertums', in *Kleine Schriften* (Halle, 1910), 99 ff.; id., *Geschichte des Altertums*, iii. 270 ff.; J. Hasebroek, *Griechische Wirtschafts- und Gesellschaftsgeschichte* (Tübingen, 1931), 6 ff. Cf. L. Brentano, *Das Wirtschaftsleben der antiken Welt* (Jena, 1929), 26 ff.; G. Finsler, *Homer*, i (2nd edn., Leipzig, 1914), 98 ff.

[4] A. Lang, *Homer and his Age* (Cambridge, 1906); H. M. Chadwick, *The Heroic Age* (Cambridge, 1912); W. Leaf, *Homer and History* (London, 1915). Also Burckhardt (*Griechische Kulturgeschichte*, iv, 3rd edn. 23 ff.) has missed the essential thing.

[5] Cf. K. Reinhardt, 'Tradition und Geist im homerischen Epos', *Studium Generale*, 4 (1951), 339.

[6] W. Schadewaldt, *Von Homers Welt und Werk* (2nd edn., Stuttgart, 1951), 92 ff.; cf. also H. T. Wade-Gery, 'The Dorian Invasion', *AJA* 52 (1948), 115 f.; id., *The Poet of the Iliad* (Cambridge, 1952). R. Hampe, *Die Gleichnisse Homers und die Bildniskunst seiner Zeit* (Tübingen, 1952), 27 ff. and ills. 7–11 has just published an important new find for the dating of the *Odyssey*: an Attic pot 'from the middle of the 8th century'.

agrarian conditions in times of an economy based purely on natural resources'[7] we have to regard this as generally probable.

When looked at broadly, epic society falls into two classes, which in terms of general contemporary perception seem to be separated by a deep gulf: an upper class of high-ranking or aristocratic families whose power and prestige are very closely connected with the size of their property, and a dependent or servile class respectively. Among these you practically have to count not only slaves and paid labourers but also skilled manual workers (in as far as these had become specialists at all) and the small, and even the medium-sized, farmers. For the farmers too, although free, are completely dependent on the mercy of their noble masters who administer justice to them in accordance with unwritten laws, and at their own discretion grant or withhold *both* protection from being robbed by enemies *and* economic support. They too are oppressed in particular by being compelled to accompany their master on military service. Their subservience is established through the client system typical of a patriarchal society.

On questions of bondage or serfdom, the epics give no definitive information. Helotry probably developed only in the following two centuries. Likewise there are no freedmen either. Through capture in war or seizure by pirates a person suddenly fell into lifelong slavery. Nothing might seem more terrible to us. But the poet of the *Odyssey* describes as the hardest lot on earth that of the paid labourer in the service of a poor [494] farmer (*Od.* 11. 489–91), not that of the slave. Indeed the lot of a slave who served a well-disposed master with the means to keep his slaves well may be tolerable, even enviable. Through his master's favour, the slave can come by a piece of land and property of his own and be married to a slave within the household. In the *Odyssey* such a pair are the old servant Dolius and his wife. They have six sons! (24. 497). One should think of the free small farmers of Boeotia to whom Hesiod recommends the one-child system (*Erga* 376) because the barren land cannot support its population. The *Odyssey* may possibly be idealizing conditions; but the possibility is still real enough, because the slave on a large farm does not run the economic risks of the free farmer. At the same time a large number of children benefits his master. The slave Eumaeus, Odysseus' swineherd, has even

---

[7] R. v. Pöhlmann, *Geschichte der sozialen Frage und des Sozialismus in der antiken Welt*, i (2nd edn., Munich, 1925), 18.

bought a slave for himself from his own means, who serves him during meals (*Od.* 14. 449–52). The relationship between rulers and slaves on Odysseus' estate is informal, even warm. Again, the free and noble origin of slaves to a certain degree makes itself evident here as well. Thus the social position of a slave varies widely, depending on the attitude and wealth of the master, and cannot be rigidly categorized.

The normal occupation of people in Homeric times is agriculture. Several crafts are indeed beginning to break away, e.g. the potter or the carpenter. The blacksmith and leatherworker have an especially important role through the production of weapons. Skills which require a peculiar talent—of doctor, seer, and bard— are equally specialized. But most essential goods are produced as far as possible by the farmer on his own estate. The women spin wool and use the fabric for making clothes. The farmer himself takes to the mountains, fells trees, and builds his own chariot (*Il.* 4. 482 ff., with the references mentioned next). The example of the heavy iron discus which Achilles offers as a prize in the games is especially pretty: with this amount of iron the winner, whether shepherd or ploughman, [495] will have enough smith's material for years and will not have to make his way to town (*Il.* 23. 826–35, cf. Hes. *Erga* 432). So craftsmen are beginning to settle in the centre of town.

But town dwellers in our sense do not otherwise exist. Those who are called ἀστοί are squires or farmers who have their residence in a town. Here we have to be clear what a town actually is in Homeric times. The territory of a community is called πόλις in Homer and Hesiod, and the collective noun for its inhabitants is δῆμος, exactly as it will be among later Greeks. But we must concentrate on the real meaning of the thing, not on these words which are still lacking the most important element of the content which we retrospectively and instinctively attach to them: the specifically political.[8] The community has no power nor does it have an administrative machinery. The assembly of the army in the *Iliad* and the peaceful assembly of the people in the *Odyssey* are mute assemblies, in which the crowd receives announcements and instructions. Expressed in Roman terms: there are only *contiones*, no *comitia*. It

[8] Cf. for the following V. Ehrenberg, *Der griechische Staat* (Gercke-Norden 3; Leipzig, 1932), 8 f.

is true that the community has executive leadership, the king, and his council, the *gerontes*; but it has not elected these authorities; their natural authority is based on hereditary nobility. If we disregard the subordinate body of the so-called heralds, the criers, then the glimmerings of a community order can be seen only in their jurisdiction, exercised by the king himself or the *gerontes* (*Il.* 18. 503), according to uncodified law as we have already said. But the king, that is, the greatest lord of the manor, and the *gerontes* are the leaders of the richest landowning families. Basically the *polis* is still nothing more than the settlement centre (fortified, it is true, in most cases) of a tribal community which makes its living from the land. We must not be surprised that in Homer no villages are mentioned, since with the exception of its possible fortification the *polis* is still a village in character and according to modern scale is also in most cases a village in size as well. The intellectual and economic centre of gravity then seems to lie on the countryside surrounding it; the world of private [496] concerns, life in the family and on the estate, dominates the formation of culture. The *polis* serves more as a meeting place and protective fortress. Protective fortress is probably also the original meaning of the word πόλις (ἀκρόπολις > πόλις). In the action of the Homeric epics, although there is a pronounced individualism which everywhere threatens to destroy the weak bonds of a community held together by a common purpose, which is in fact mainly a military community, there does rule a kind of political order at least in the respect that people show towards the authority of the king and the doctrine of the divine right of the aristocracy. Hesiod on the other hand—certainly less the representative of a new era than of a group which has so far been mute on the literary level—demonstrates an attitude which emphatically rejects anything political. For him, the basic form of human existence is the agriculture of individual landowners (*Erga* 21–39). In his opinion, lawsuits are settled honestly man to man on the spot; a decent person stays away from the *agora* and its quarrels (cf. *Il.* 16. 387; 18. 497 ff.; *Od.* 12. 440). Hesiod's distrust of human justice and especially that of the aristocratic judges, and in general of the effectiveness of morality in the community (*Erga* 202–73), is profound. In Hesiod's rules of life in the appendix of the *Erga* (695 ff.), it is remarkable that the authorities receive no mention. In his opinion, human community can exist only in the most cautious communication with friends and neighbours.

The embryonic idea of the *polis* in its actual sense, the state community, is in Homeric times still fighting a serious battle to assert itself against that reckless stubbornness which fights only for the interests of the clan—though in the following centuries, that idea will win. For the time being, in general, if you lump together all these communities which are internally so loosely organized—not to mention that this net of *poleis* by no means covers the Greek world without any gaps yet, but still seems unevenly spread owing to the unorganized individual settlement within the area occupied by the tribal community—the result is still a picture of severe fragmentation. In terms of developmental history, there is obviously a *decline*, since, under the leadership of Mycenae, Greece had already once formed a cultural [497] unity, indeed possibly even a kind of political community, as soil-finds and the *Iliad* confirm for each other.[9] So an urban bourgeoisie based on trade and industry shows only feeble signs of emerging in Homeric times. Country life and its needs determine the culture of the so-called town. In particular, there still seems to be missing a merchant class which is economically independent of the aristocracy, would be capable of bridging the gap between great and small, and as a free middle class could work towards the strengthening of a political system of law and order. But mercantile shipping, which is beginning to blossom, is already laying the foundations for the formation of a stratum of merchants. This *must* become a privilege of a special new class of society, since the large aristocratic landowner and, even more, the small farmer are tied to the soil. The story of the *Odyssey* is indeed the best illustration of the extent to which the estate economy must suffer because of the lengthy Viking voyages of its masters, the pirate excursions across the sea. For them, wars against neighbours on land and brief invasions are the more suitable means of enrichment. One can be a farmer *and* have a ship, though; especially if, as the inhabitant of an island, one has a part of one's farmland or pastures on the neighbouring mainland—and *vice versa*, of course— like Noemon who lends his only ship to Telemachus (*Od.* 2. 386; 4. 634–7). For rowing, one enlists *thetes* or slaves (4. 644). Hesiod, as it seems, owned two ships, one large, and a small one lying in Aulis. But he never went any further in them than across the straits to

---

[9] S. Fr. Matz, *Griechische Vorgeschichte* (in *Das neue Bild der Antike* (Leipzig, 1942), i), 28 ff.; id., *Handbuch der Archäologie*, ii (1950), 303; J. F. Daniel, 'The Dorian Invasion', *AJA* 52 (1948), 107.

Euboea to put his crop surpluses on the market in Chalcis (*Erga* 618–94).[10] This means that, as a peasant, he also did some modest trading in order to support his estate. But in the *Odyssey* we also meet the real merchant with [498] ship and 'comrades' who sails great distances to barter (1. 182–4; 8. 161–4). Since the boundaries are fluid, the type easily turns into that of the adventurer and pirate (*Od.* 14. 191–359; 15. 403–81), people who at the time of the poet dominate the seas. People like to blame the more experienced Phoenicians for the disreputable aspects of this (*Il.* 23. 744; *Od.* 15. 415 ff; cf. Herodotus 1. 1) but the Greeks certainly participate in this activity themselves. If trade and seafaring are less important in the *Iliad*, we may not infer from this a lower degree of development. Bartering across the sea, which must indeed have been considerable already in Mycenaean times, also occurs in the *Iliad* in several places (7. 467; 9. 71 f.; 21. 41; 23. 747; 24. 751 ff.), and its similes offer quite a few images of sailors on the high seas (*Il.* 7. 6; 15. 381, 624 ff.); in these cases, it is certainly not just warriors at sea that are meant.

Nevertheless, for the Greeks of this period, distant seafaring and trade as an end in itself are something that is thought of as modern.[11] Therefore, in the heroic world of the epic, such activities appear only at the margins, tainted with the flavour of the suspect or even contemptible (*Od.* 8. 159 ff.). Why aristocratic society should despise the merchant will have to be discussed later.

My real purpose is to understand more precisely the special character of the ruling class in Homeric times. Precisely because the special attention of the poet is turned on it, we have to contend with greater difficulties and possibilities of misunderstanding here than when we look at the lower classes of society. The latter are without doubt described fairly true to the life of his own time, stylized of course, but not glorified and archaized.[12] But since the poetic motifs of the main action of both epics concern the aristocracy, especially the kings, we have to expect that these represent early stages of poetry, overlaid by stocks of material, and thus hierarchies of spiritual and social values from a longer series of later [499]

---

[10] Hasebroek, *Griechische Wirtschafts*, 38 f. Differently judged by M. Pohlenz, *Der hellenische Mensch* (Göttingen, 1947), 347.

[11] G. Busolt, *Griechische Staatskunde* (3rd edn., Munich, 1926), 173.

[12] Cf. C. M. Bowra, *Tradition and Design in the Iliad* (2nd edn., Oxford, 1950), 121 and 191.

centuries. But the discrepancies which must result from this are not seriously to be found in the spiritual–sociological sphere but only in that of antiquities (with which I need not concern myself) and institutions. Nothing in the picture of the Homeric order of society is less clear—even if you separate the *Iliad* and *Odyssey* into two different worlds—than the legal position and power of kingship.[13] The only one of the many kings in the *Iliad* who still has something left of the splendour of real kingship is in fact Agamemnon, with whom Menelaus and Nestor are the most likely to bear comparison. Here memories of the real power-structures of Mycenaean times are reflected.[14] Agamemnon can, if he wants to, still give away whole cities as presents together with their inhabitants, and treasures on top of that. With these gifts of atonement which he offers to Achilles (*Il.* 9. 122 ff.), compare Priam's ransom money for the corpse of Troy's best man (*Il.* 24. 229 ff.; cf. *Od.* 21. 274 ff.). These are the gifts of a rich landowner—in other respects too Priam is characterized in such terms. Ultimately in the *Iliad*, the original relationship of rank between Agamemnon and Achilles (around which the legendary motif of their anger was able to crystallize) remains unclear. One would like to think that it must have been the relationship of an absolute ruler to a subject, to a defiant vassal who as a fighter was the better man. But in the general tenor of the *Iliad*, Agamemnon has sunk down to a not overly respected *primus inter pares*. One does not really understand—Thucydides (1. 9) had already thought about this—how he raised a levy of so many who were equal in rank and kept it together for so long for the sake of a private feud. But it was obviously not important enough for the poet of our *Iliad* (and rightly so from the poetic point of view) to clarify the situation. What fascinated him were the thought-processes involved in settling the quarrel of the kings and here [500] everything is as full of light and as precise as is the real world of country life in the similes. That means: the great poet himself uniformly invented the arguments in the main action of the *Iliad*, out of the feeling and the spirit of his own time.[15] For no one will think it possible that the poet of the *Iliad* methodically carried out

[13] Cf. Chadwick, *The Heroic Age*, 387 f.
[14] On Nestor: R. Hampe, 'Die homerische Welt im Lichte der neuen Ausgrabungen', in *Vermächtnis der antiken Kunst*, ed. R. Herbig (Heidelberg, 1950), 11 ff.
[15] Bowra, *Tradition and Design*, 253; Wade-Gery, *AJA* 1948, 116; H. Fränkel, *Die homerischen Gleichnisse* (Göttingen, 1921), 100.

historical research into the intellectual culture of the Mycenaean period. His archaizing is of a far more innocent nature. The social colouring stems without exception from the world of living, current ideas—no differently, incidentally, from the *Odyssey*. As it does not matter what is called a 'town' in Homer but what a *polis* actually is according to its description, so we must not make assumptions about the word 'king', since in Homer it no longer describes a separate class above the aristocracy.[16] Rather, in the multitude of the so-called kings in the *Iliad* as well as in the *Odyssey* (where the same relationship is repeated on a smaller scale—but Penelope's suitors who are also called kings are really no more than small barons) and again in the majority of the kings in Hesiod, we have, historically speaking, the many-headed ruling class which we might call the aristocracy—that means, the highest class of society of the Homeric age. This order provides all the protagonists of human action in the *Iliad* and mostly in the *Odyssey* too and is described far more comprehensively in both epics than any other class in its habits and particular world view; indeed, it is at the same time the class for which the poets write.

It is also quite obviously this class which stamped its own characteristics onto its century. Through the vitality of the two immortal poems, these continue creatively to have their immense influence on the Greeks, on the whole of Antiquity—even on us. There is probably complete agreement—and I do not exclude myself—that the Homeric poems stem from an aristocratic world, an age of courtly ideals.[17]

[501] On the other hand, it does not seem at first to be a contradiction but a statement of purely economic historical significance, if historians who have read the epic against the trend, so to speak, remark—I take over a formulation by J. Hasebroek: 'The Homeric world is an agrarian one, and so the property conditions of Homeric aristocracy too are based first and foremost on agriculture and cattle breeding.'[18] It cannot escape any reader of Homer that Odysseus, according to his economic form of existence, is actually a big estate-owner, and that we also have to imagine the heroes of the *Iliad* as living in such a setting in peacetime. But does this exclude a genuinely aristocratic lifestyle, a fulfilment in courtly

---

[16] Cf. Chadwick, *The Heroic Age*, 364.

[17] See esp. Schadewaldt, *Von Homers Welt und Werk*, 116 and *passim*.

[18] *Griechische Wirtschafts*, 10.

ideals? In principle, not at all. And so Eduard Meyer describes the life of the ruling order of Homeric times in the following way:

It is characteristic of the aristocracy to love conspicuous displays of its prosperity and its power, and to unfold its rich and comfortable luxury for all to see. The aristocrat appears in splendid weapons with a large retinue, keeps magnificent horses, hounds and lap dogs (*Od.* XVII 310). When he is not preoccupied with war or his own business—which in real life played a far larger role than in the epic's idealized picture—he leads, before the eyes of the crowd, a comfortable life of pleasure, together with his comrades of the same class: one banquet follows another, spiced with singing and dancing performed by professional singers and dancers . . . (*Geschichte des Altertums*, iii (2nd edn., Berlin, 1928), 340).

Other scholars colour the picture slightly differently, but taken as a whole, the opinion still predominates that the aristocracy of the Homeric age is 'a kind of feudal aristocracy whose men divide their life between fighting, hunting and feasting while the women supervise the maids in the house'.[19]

But this view is too one-sided, and cannot be justified even from the *conscious* picture painted by the poets (as it were from a reading *with* the trend of the poetry).

[502] First, the alleged unceasing feasting of the Homeric heroes. Who is actually feasting all the time? The Phaeacians: a fairy-tale people. The suitors of Penelope: undisciplined offspring lacking the strong hand of control. Finally: the gods. Their cheerful pleasure is supposed to illustrate precisely their higher bliss, which distinguishes them from the human race: 'But they, they remain | in perpetual feasts | at golden tables' while man is smitten with misfortune and hard work; not only does Hesiod lament like this (*Erga* 174 ff.) but so do the poets of the *Iliad* (24. 525 ff.) and *Odyssey* (1. 348 ff.; 4. 197 f.; 20. 201 ff.). The *Iliad* does not contain any banquets which indicate a permanent state of affairs. Eating and drinking are mentioned with epic relish, but are only a way of describing life with maximum clarity, like the indication of the breaks in the day, the putting on of arms, or the harnessing and unharnessing of horses. If in the *Odyssey* (except for the cases mentioned already) there is feasting together, then it is accounted for explicitly—and this is precisely what is significant: in Pylos (3. 5 ff.) because a great

---

[19] E. Auerbach, *Mimesis* (Bern, 1946), 27. Cf. Burckhardt, *Griechische Kulturgeschichte*, iv, 40. R. Harder, *Eigenart der Griechen* (Freiburg, 1949), 20 ff.

sacrifice in honour of Poseidon is being celebrated, in Sparta because of a double wedding in the royal family (4. 2 ff.). Naturally, the banqueting scenes are executed with relish, because dwelling on ideal existence heightens the festive mood which belongs to the epic. But they are not supposed to be an everyday phenomenon of aristocratic life; as we see, just the opposite.

On the other hand, work is omnipresent in the heroic world, in the *Iliad* no less than in the *Odyssey*. Wherever the *Iliad* allows glimpses of peace and the everyday life of the nobility, there is useful activity in the centre, not recreation, amusement, or sport. Of women, it is generally regarded as natural that their fingers do not rest for a moment. Not only does the king's daughter participate in doing the laundry; the queen herself also takes up her spindle immediately after the meal at a festive meeting. Even goddesses made their clothes themselves. It is not perhaps the roughest dirty work in which the people of high rank participate themselves. But basically [503] everyone can do every kind of work and gets down to it wherever it may be necessary.[20] The reader of the *Iliad* is most certain to find the sons of kings and noblemen out in the fields guarding the cattle. Thus engaged, they can, if nothing else, still dream and, like Anchises and Paris, have a good chance of an undisturbed visit from gracious goddesses. But it is not Arcadian bucolic ideals that introduced this motif into poetry. The pasturing of herds is—and before tribes settled down was even more so—the most pressing, continuous work of the day. This is so typical that, in the legend of the founding of Troy, even the god Apollo has to graze herds of cattle on Mount Ida while Poseidon builds the wall around Troy for King Laomedon (*Il.* 21. 448). Noblemen, in order to save male personnel—which is not exactly abundant—enlist their sons for this work as long as they are good for nothing better; so they too learn how to handle cattle straight away. It is virtually expected, from the outset, that one will meet noble young men out in the fields. After his landing on Ithaca Athena appears to Odysseus as a young shepherd, as the text says: 'of a fine figure, as the children of rulers are' (*Od.* 13. 222).

Paris has a hand in the building of his house (*Il.* 6. 314). His brother Lycaon is keen to make himself a chariot (21. 37 f.). Odysseus himself constructs his bed and bedchamber out of wood

---

[20] Finsler, *Homer*, i. 123; cf. Bowra, *Tradition and Design*, 245.

Hermann Strasburger

(*Od.* 23. 189–204). Laertes, who in his youth was a great warrior (he is several times called *heros*), had also cultivated land for his estate by the sweat of his brow at exactly the same time (*Od.* 23. 206 f. Schol. ad loc.). When Odysseus comes home he finds him doing hard and simple work (226 ff.). It is not emphasized that he is working despite the fact that he is a lord, but that he is doing it at such an advanced age (255). Probably the thought is that he is working in the place of his missing son, whose presence would have enabled him to retire (*Il.* 5. 153 f.; 4. 477 ff. = 17. 301 ff.). And if Odysseus as a boy was given at his request by his father a row of special fruit trees as a present (336–44), this can [504] have happened only with the intention that he himself should tend them. At least the motif (introduced at the very climax of the recognition scene between father and son!) shows the intimate connection between the nobleman and his work on the estate. In the reply of the beggar Odysseus to the suitor Eurymachus (*Od.* 18. 356–80), competence in agriculture on the one hand and in war on the other is praised as the ideal of a stout-hearted man (cf. *Od.* 20. 378 f.). The people's assembly in Book 2 of the *Odyssey* is dissolved with the words (252): ἐπὶ ἔργα ἕκαστος: 'each to his property!' Again, Antinous, the ringleader of the suitors of Penelope, describes a possible departure of the suitors as a return ἐπὶ ἔργα (*Od.* 2. 127 = 18. 288). So even the noble good-for-nothings know where their place is—at work—and that the least they must do is be there.

Work then and personal competence at running an estate belong, at least in the *Odyssey*, to the highest ideals of nobility. I point out in passing how this notion in several important places is interconnected with the notions of genuinely royal quality (*Od.* 18. 356 ff.; 19. 109 ff.; cf. Hes. *Erga* 255 ff.; *Od.* 24. 205 ff., 365 ff.) and how at the end of the *Odyssey* the unification of these qualities makes the three representatives of the legitimate royal household (grandfather, father, and son) logically stand out as winners in distinction to the mere quantity of degenerate usurpers. In saying this, I know that I am provoking an objection from the analysts that in doing so I am taking my material from the 'youngest strata' of the epic and that the conclusions are irrelevant to the time of the *Iliad*. As already indicated, I do not believe that the sociology of the *Iliad*, *Odyssey*, and Hesiod's *Erga* allows us to distinguish three different periods of time. What is important is the sector of the field of vision, which depends on the respective action and on the personality of the poet. What the *Odyssey* says explicitly here is taken for granted in the *Iliad*. How else could it happen that in the *Iliad* even gods and goddesses rarely fail to harness and unharness their horses themselves and scatter their fodder for them (*Il.* 5. 369; 8. 50; 13. 23 and 35 f.)? It is obvious that the people for whom the poets sing—and these are precisely the aristocrats—are closer in their daily lives to the rustic world [505] than to the heroic one. It is true that they are a warrior people in origin: it is true that they see the epitome of manliness in battle and that they warm their hearts on the memory of their own feats of arms and ideals of superhuman heroism in battle. Their military expeditions are so to speak the festival days of their lives. So the improbability of the battle descriptions matters less to such listeners; in fact, as the fulfilment of their wildest dreams, it is unconditionally welcome. How long speeches can be delivered in the thick of battle, how heroes in heavy armour can move around like athletes, how wounds that have just been inflicted can suddenly be healed—they do not ask questions on these topics. The more fairy-tale-like the heroic world, the better! The quasi-realistic images of dying are skilfully deployed individual features. But in the sphere of his everyday reality, Homer's listener demands plausibility. Horses must have their fodder! (*Il.* 6. 187–9; 8. 503 f., 543 f.; 24. 350). With justification have people counted the Homeric gods' and heroes' love of horses among the 'noble passions'.[21] For horses as battle companions are particularly close to man (Hehn);[22] select ones among them can even talk or weep (*Il.* 17. 426–40; 19. 404 ff.). But here one sphere merges inseparably into the other. The bull too appears in the heroic similes. It is one of Zeus' forms of disguise. Pasiphae falls in love with a bull. Later, the conception is familiar to the Greeks and Romans—and why should this not be all the more the case for the early period?—that cattle are working animals and man's companion (references: Hehn, p. 39). At Priam's departure (*Il.* 24. 247–80) the king's sons themselves must harness the chariot. The technical process is precisely described! In doing this they are urged on by their father with words of abuse: 'Liars! Dancers! Sheep thieves! Goat thieves!' This is the way an old farmer grumbles on his farm. Of the horses it is observed that Priam had looked after them and

---

[21] Schadewaldt, *Von Homers Welt und Werk*, 116; Harder, *Eigenart der Griechen*, 21.

[22] V. Hehn, *Kulturpflanzen und Haustiere* (4th edn., Berlin, 1911), 39 ff.

fed them personally (cf. 5. 271). A village situation! We do not like
to imagine the mighty tyrants of Mycenaean times, who made hosts
of servants [506] or war captives pile up the Cyclopean stone blocks
of their palaces,[23] the lords of Mycenae and Tiryns, to have been
people like this. The so-called Palace of Priam (6. 242)[24] is imagined only very vaguely. The poet imagines an unpaved inner court-
yard, since otherwise, when he is mourning for Hector, the king
would not be able to grovel in the dirt the way he does (24. 161 ff.).
The real royal fortresses (legend's reflexes of a submerged reality)
do not occur before the *Odyssey*: high-roomed palaces shining with
splendour (4. 43–136; 7. 84 ff.; cf. 3. 386 ff.).[25] But when, in front
of this colossal background, Alcinous suggests that they all jointly
contribute to the guest presents for Odysseus, because it would
necessarily be difficult for him alone (13. 15); or when Menelaus
invites 'neighbours and close friends' to the wedding, and the question can be raised whether one can take on the entertainment of two
strangers in the king of Sparta's palace or whether they should be
sent away to a different host (4. 15–36); then all this does not illustrate a living idea of the poet of Mycenaean royal splendour and
'royal' conditions, but an imagination which feeds on the simple
rustic world of a poorer period. The scales of value too which are
shown in the *Iliad* as well as the *Odyssey* in the lists of presents and
competitive prizes lead on the whole to absolutely the same conclusion. The stylized 'king' in the description of Achilles' shield is a
lord of an estate who is supervising the harvest (*Il.* 18. 550 ff.). The
shield of Achilles, by the way, which is in fact a kind of image of
human life, gives us (so to speak) a statistical handle. The images of
life and work on the land in it completely outnumber the few scenes
which already breathe something like an urban air. Again, the war
it depicts centres round the values of agricultural possession, especially herds of cattle, which in reality seem to have been the most
important target for booty.[26] [507] This reference is important for
the reason that the description of Achilles' shield does indeed stylize life but does not glorify it, like the similes which are woven into
the battle scenes. Nevertheless, an analysis of the similes leads to

[23] On this Pöhlmann, *Aus Altertum und Gegenwart*, 160 ff.

[24] Finsler, *Homer*, i. 117; H. L. Lorimer, *Homer and the Monuments* (Cambridge, 1950), 431.

[25] On this Lorimer, *Homer and the Monuments*, 406 ff.

[26] *Il.* 1. 154; 11. 671 ff.; *Od.* 20. 49 ff.; 23. 357 and *passim*. Hesiod, fr. 96, 1. 10 f. Rz.

exactly the same result. After what has been said, I will probably not have to labour the point that the similes which have been taken from rural life—in the *Iliad* they are by far the most numerous—are not supposed to reflect the heroic events of battle in a reality perceived as inferior but in the reality in which the nobleman himself lives and moves. It is *for this reason* that it causes no ripples at all in the heroic world if the advancing battle line is compared to mowing reapers (*Il.* 11. 67) or a dogged pair of fighters with two farmers who quarrel at the border of the field about every inch of soil, measure in hand (12. 421), or the Trojan army lusting for battle with a herd of sheep bleating wildly and waiting in confusion to be milked (4. 433)—just to take only a few of the numerous even more extreme examples.

Heroic epic is saturated with images and concepts from the rustic imagination. Kings and noblemen have as their name of honour ποιμὴν λαῶν (shepherd of peoples). Towns are called εὔπωλος (rich in foals: *Il.* 5. 551) or ἱππόβοτος (feeding horses: 4. 202) or πίειρα (fat: 18. 342). The rich man is called πολύμηλος, πολύρρηνος, πολυβούτης, πολυλήϊος (14. 490; 9. 154; 5. 613: rich in sheep, cattle or wheat), the poor man ἀλήϊος (9. 125). A frequent epithet of important heroes, as of whole tribes of people (Hesiod fr. 16 Rzach[2]), is ἱππόδαμος (tamer of horses). But the heroes do not ride in battle, nor do they drive the chariot themselves either. So the image stems from the training of wild horses.[27] The marking of the time of day is also described with rustic images. Noon is called 'the time when the woodcutter prepares his meal' (*Il.* 11. 86–9; cf. *Od.* 13. 31–4), evening 'the time of unharnessing bulls' (*Il.* 16. 779 = *Od.* 9. 58). We are led into the *polis*, the rural town, by the description: [508] 'the time when the judge leaves the market for his dinner' (*Od.* 12. 439 f.). In order to sing the praise of young girls, the *Iliad* has an expression which encompasses a whole piece of cultural history in itself; the maidens dancing in a round are not called 'the charming ones' but 'the ones who bring in cattle' ἀλφεσίβοιαι (18. 593, referring to the suitors' gifts which they will win for their fathers through their marriage). In order to suggest the charm of virginity, the *Odyssey* compliments Nausicaa by calling her a παρθένος ἀδμής ('the untamed one': 6. 109 and 228; of the taming of young horses and mules). Both epithets also occur in the

---

[27] Cf. also the simile 15. 679–84 with Finsler, *Homer*, i. 101 f.

Hymn to Aphrodite (82, 119, 133). In this context we shall think of those proper names which carry a whiff of the stable: women's names: Ἀλφεσίβοια, Μελίβοια, Φερέβοια (Hesiod fr. 57 Rz. Athen. 13. 557 a–b); these first three not in Homer but all the following ones are: Ἐρίβοια (*Il.* 5. 389), Περίβοια (21. 142), Πολυμήλη (16. 180), Ἱπποδάμεια; men's names: Βουκολίων (6. 22), Βουκόλος (15. 338), Πολύμηλος (16. 417), Θρασύμηλος (16. 463), Εὔμηλος (2. 764), Ἐχέπωλος (4. 458; 23. 296), Ἱππόδαμος (11. 335); all from a heroic, i.e. good, family. But the major heroes in Homer do not have such names; more will have to be said about this.

Enough references for now. They should have shown that in Homeric times the nobleman is closely associated with agricultural work, at least in his *outward* life. He is both knight and great farmer combined, and his arrogance towards the small farmer does not stem from different lifestyle but from the size of his property. This distinguishes him sharply from the knight of the German or French Middle Ages, who does not work and despises the class of farmers, and who really lives only for the noble passions and ideologically cuts himself off from the world of work.[28] But as the knight of the Christian Middle Ages [509] consciously and on principle rejects the ways of the life of work, the peasant, and the merchant class as something inferior, and expels them from the world of his ideals, so now the more important question arises as the real crux: did rustic utilitarian thinking as a fundamental attitude work its way in Homeric times too into the world of courtly ideas, did it do so as culturally structure-forming, or is the contact of the two spheres of life restricted to the outward form of existence and activity?

The answer is foregone. Already in the examples given, the outer world can often no longer be separated from the inner. It can hardly any longer be regarded as a merely external consequence of the structure of the economy if, among the heroes of the *Iliad*, the value of a woman, calculated above all in relation to her efficiency at

---

[28] A revision of this view for the 'simple basic strata of the medieval knightly nobility' is suggested by H. G. Wackernagel who starts from the observation that in Switzerland in many places knights' fortresses were firmly connected with estate farms which were mainly engaged in cattle and dairy farming: Wackernagel, 'Burgen, Ritter und Hirten', in *Schweizerisches Archiv für Volkskunde* 47 (1951), 215 ff. (I owe the reference to R. Merkelbach.) Parallels can also be found in the Nordic culture area. But it will hardly be possible to find that which gives Homeric time its special character: the farming class included in the *ideals* of a *highest* knightly class of society and in a refinement of forms of expression which seems courtly.

work, is with the most precise matter-of-factness assessed against that of cattle or cooking pots (23. 262 ff.; 702 ff.). An agricultural sense of economy is deeply and inextricably embedded in cultural attitudes, and is crossed in a most peculiar way with a sense of heroic nobility, and a delicate sense of honour. These features frequently appear on a large and small scale in both epics. I must be satisfied with a few examples which can be easily isolated.

Achilles, who represents the extreme standpoint of honour, still declares, just like a farmer, that basically he has no business being at Troy; he says 'for the Trojans have not wronged me, since they have not driven away my cattle or horses nor destroyed the fruit of my fields' (*Il.* 1. 154 ff.).

In Book 5 of the *Iliad* we listen to a conversation between the archer Pandarus, leader of the Lycian auxiliary troops, and Aeneas. Pandarus is annoyed that his marksmanship is denied success and now almost regrets that he did not set out with horse and chariot as his father had actually advised him to do. Now he describes how in his farmstead at home (the house of a king!) he has eleven chariots, neatly spread with blankets, [510] and next to them in the stable his horses, which feed on white barley and grains of spelt. When, against his father's advice, he did not set out in a chariot, he did this out of consideration for his horses, which were used to plentiful fodder and ought not to suffer from hunger in the besieged city (*Il.* 5. 180 ff.). How movingly the farmer comes out here!

Iphidamas, a Thracian, who set out to fight for Troy immediately before his own wedding, falls at the hands of Agamemnon (11. 241 ff.). 'Thus he fell to the ground and sank into the iron sleep of death—(the undeniably high heroic pathos of the scene should be noted)—unlucky man! For he fell when he was fighting for his country, far from the wife he had just married but had no joy of, though he had given so much to win her. He had paid a hundred head of cattle at the time, with the promise of a thousand animals to follow, mixed sheep and goats . . .'.

When Glaucus and Diomedes exchange their armour as a sign of guest friendship the poet remarks: 'But Zeus the Son of Cronus must have robbed Glaucus of his wits, for he exchanged with Diomedes golden armour for bronze, a hundred oxen's worth for the value of nine' (6. 234 ff.).

Achilles believes that he has to justify to the dead Patroclus the fact that he is returning Hector's corpse, but he does not justify himself in terms of the will of the gods or the imperatives of human feeling, but in terms of the splendid ransom gifts, of which he will also give to him, Patroclus, his fair share (24. 592–5).

Athena's comfort and encouragement to Odysseus on the night before the suitors are killed (*Od.* 20. 49 ff.) are quite strange: 'You and I could be surrounded by fifty companies of men-at-arms, all thirsting for our blood, but you would still drive away their cattle and sheep.'

In the story of the contest of the suitors for Helen's hand in Hesiod (fr. 94–6) it is taken for granted from the start that the richest suitor will win the bride. So clever Odysseus sends no bridal gifts himself. As he foresaw, Menelaus wins because he gives most.

[511] Such a rustic world is the natural breeding ground for the most sober self-interest, which always has its starting point in the interest of one's own family. Thus in her lament for the dead Hector Andromache prophesies the following fate for her orphaned son (22. 487 ff.):

'Even if he escapes the horrors of the Achaean war, nothing lies ahead of him but hardship and trouble, with strangers eating into his estate. An orphaned child is cut off from his playmates. He goes about with downcast looks and tear-stained cheeks. In his necessity he looks in at some gathering of his father's friends and plucks a cloak here and a tunic there, till someone out of charity holds up a wine-cup to his mouth, but only for a moment, just enough to wet his lips and leave his palate dry. Then comes another boy, with both his parents living, who beats him with his fists and drives him from the feast and jeers at him. "Out you go!" he shouts. "You have no father dining here."'

This passage vividly records how in this aristocratic society harsh rustic self-interest obscures the aristocratic *esprit de corps*, or rather, how the latter is just a disguise for the former. The class structure of this society is entirely based on the principle 'might is right'; honour is enjoyed in it only by the person who knows how to defend his property with the sword against predatory neighbours, if need be (this is also a basic motif of the *Telemachy*).

For the *Odyssey*, the importance of material ideals has been better recognized in scholarship. I refer especially to the essay by Felix Jacoby: 'Die geistige Physiognomie der Odyssee' (*Antike* (1933), 159 ff.). Jacoby writes (pp. 178 f.):

The cultural attitude of the *Odyssey* poet in contrast to the Homeric one (scil. of the '*Iliad*') is everywhere markedly bourgeois in the true sense of the word. One single but dominating motif of each of the two epics is enough to make this clear: let us sum them up in terms of honour ($\tau\iota\mu\dot{\eta}$) and property ($\chi\rho\dot{\eta}\mu\alpha\tau\alpha$) in doing which we can feel free to think of the modern contrast between a 'trader's' and a 'hero's' spirit. Both are closely connected in so far as in every society, perhaps especially in an aristocratic one, social rank is connected with property; property is a precondition of a man's prestige. But it is not the fact which matters here, but the scale of values. And there is no doubt that the *Iliad* emphasizes honour, the *Odyssey* poet (who in this is contiguous with Hesiod but not congruent) property.

After the robust expressions of a rustically mercantile spirit [512] of the age which I have just quoted from the *Iliad*, I cannot consider this evaluation as correct. On the contrary: if you allow for the differences in material, the fact that for the *Iliad* the basic heroic colouring is given through its setting and action, while in the *Odyssey* the rustic background, like the main theme which is full of questions of civil and private law, invites us to indulge in materialistic ideas—in view of this I find the basic utilitarian attitude in the *Odyssey* moderate and refined compared with the less refined unaffectedness of the *Iliad*. It certainly makes a difference whether one wants to measure the 'cultural physiognomy' of the two epics in terms of the poetic action, i.e. the illusion which the poets intend to produce, or in terms of the historico-cultural reality from which they involuntarily speak. But I do not see either in what way Odysseus is supposed to be more bourgeois and less heroically minded than Achilles. There is a considerable parallelism between them in the issue of their conflicts. Both Achilles and Odysseus are affronted in the matter of a possession, which to them is at the same time an object of personal affection. Both are filled with wrath and an irreconcilable thirst for revenge. Neither forgives his offender (Achilles/Agamemnon, Odysseus/the suitors), both refuse the gifts of atonement offered to them since the 'heart-wounding humiliation' cannot be wiped out by material atonement. But Achilles finally ends the feud (even though he does not forgive), and returns to the normal decencies of human contact, although the insult done to him was unnecessary, malicious, and intentionally hurtful. Odysseus, however, does not forgive, and takes a terrible revenge, although the suitors had not intentionally hurt him at all, and material atonement could very well have solved the problems. For the suitors had wooed his wife only on the firm assumption that he would never return, and consumed his property—according to the custom of all bride wooing—only till such time as the bride would make her decision; if they were impudent in their feasting, that was only to put Penelope under pressure. The poet has to work very hard to make credible, to a down-to-earth evaluation, the wickedness and violence of the suitors, which allegedly reach up to the sky (17. 565). Nevertheless Odysseus insists on revenge, which, in [513] his situation, is neither necessary nor wise, because for him as for Achilles the question of honour is the really important one. So in the *Odyssey* too the main motif has been intentionally elevated into the heroic sphere. The feature that Odysseus comes home and has to kill the suitors was probably, in the original story, quite simple and, so to speak, necessary by nature, but when located in the context of the ideas of a problematically sensitive time, it takes on a more extravagant character, which drives man beyond his natural limit.

But enough of this. As a last touchstone for the question how far the class of farmers and of knights were a unity in the nobility of Homeric times I would like to consider whether our poets are not after all conscious of some conflict here, and whether they perhaps do make a value distinction between a specifically rustic and a specifically courtly lifestyle and way of thinking.

On this question, I believe that I may from a broad overview of both epics deduce some rough findings which allow me to answer it in the affirmative. It strikes me that the 'rustic' element—if I may categorize by key words—whether in a trait of character, or in a comparison, or in the colouring of a setting, is seen far less in the main action and its protagonists than in the minor figures and minor action. The further we go from the foreground of the stage to the background, to the scenery which has been merely painted on, away from heroic excess to normal human scale, the stronger the rustic element in the basic courtly tone becomes. It is true that Achilles (or Hector too) feels the strong stirrings of rustic utilitarianism which is literally 'in the blood' of all heroes, great as well as minor; it is true that Odysseus is pleased to see how Penelope, as a housewife worthy of him, tricks the presents out of the suitors; but such features attach to the main characters only in secondary contexts; in primary situations, the great heroes listen only to the mighty call of their fate, which obliges them to activate without restriction the consciousness of their own worth, their honour. The purpose of this trait of character is at the same time to help illustrate how much larger than life they are. It is already a step down the heroic scale of values, when in the embassy to Achilles Ajax reminds the obstinately wrathful hero [514] of the custom which, as a good and sensible norm, as an advance in civilization, so to speak, is supposed to have become established among men: that affronts so hurtful that they cannot really be compensated for, should be allowed to be obliterated through material atonement (*Il.* 9. 632 ff.). It gives us an insight into the treatment of such conflicts in the real world of those times. But apparently this is no longer heroic enough for the imagination of those aristocrats: Achilles is the hero of the *Iliad*. Aristocratic ideals begin to become extravagant. The caste-like separation of worlds which had not happened before, and which for Hesiod from his perspective from below is already a bitterly felt reality, also emerges as a tendency in the treatment of the central motifs of heroic epic.

This differentiation can be shown more precisely in the similes, especially the more numerous ones of the *Iliad*. It is known that they stem predominantly from observations of rural life and nature. If the violence of heroic warfare is illustrated by comparison with the violent forces of nature or violent beasts of prey, then modern people too find this appropriate for the heroic world. But we are puzzled when we find Agamemnon compared with a leading bull (*Il.* 8. 480), Ajax with a stubborn donkey (11. 558), Menelaus with a tiresome stable-fly or even with a cow which is lowing pitifully (17. 4, 570, 742). On the other hand, it is certain that comparison with an animal is not supposed to caricature the hero and his behaviour in battle. If a dying warrior is compared with a bull struggling in a sling (13. 571) or with a writhing earthworm (13. 654), the horrible seriousness of the situation excludes all minor comic intention. Men of Homeric times are so completely involved in the animal world that they regard animals as too good to be used for purposes of disparagement. If the poet wants to light up a hero with a fleeting ray of the comic by an amusing comparison, which is very rare, he does not compare him with animals but with humans (16. 7; 20. 252). But if it is not meant to caricature, the comparison with an animal is still supposed indirectly to characterize the hero. There it becomes obvious that the poet (with his listeners) feels a definite difference of rank between lesser and nobler animals. Achilles or Hector are never compared with bulls [515] or donkeys. Ajax, Menelaus, Agamemnon, etc. are, it is true, also

compared with lions, boars, eagles or forces of nature, but Hector
and Achilles not the other way round also with ordinary animals.
The gods too are excluded from comparison with the latter, except
when, for example, they are drastically abusing each other (as 21.
394 and 421: 'dog fly'). Achilles in turn rises a step higher than
Hector by not just being compared, like him, with noble animals
(the lion, the eagle, the noble hound, or the race horse) but with a
higher symbolism of might, for which the animal is no longer sufficient. His person shines out, widely visible like signs of smoke and
fire from a besieged island town (18. 207 ff.), like a conflagration in
the mountains, a *daimon* (20. 490 ff.), a star (22. 26). In his last fight
Hector through comparison with timid animals sinks again into a
lower category; while Achilles rises through the ultimate conceivable heightening and is not compared any more at all. Only his
spear shines like the evening star (22. 318). With this, he is located
in the sphere of the gods (Apollo walked 'like night').

So there is a kind of precision here; a clearly graded scale of
emotions. From checking through all the similes, we find that the
rustic element forms an indivisible and amicable unity of feeling
with the courtly element in the reality of Homeric times, but that
the ideal is about to abandon its rustic home in search of a more
abstract kind of nobility.

The question about the chronological priority of these worlds is
a difficult one as such. The more common view, I think, is that the
Iliad, the *Odyssey*, and Hesiod reflect to us a historico-cultural
sequence of steps in which we are gradually led from a heroic
courtly world (reflecting Mycenaean royal splendour) into a new
age (in the *Odyssey* still hidden, clear in Hesiod) typified by a commitment to rustic and bourgeois work, ideals of utilitarianism, and
awakening social feeling.

A reverse development seems more probable to me. We know
nothing about the sociology of Mycenaean times and, apart from
the outline of the legend, which reflects the society's earlier power-
structures, it hardly has any important [516] effect on the *Iliad*.[29]
The storms of the periods of migration obliterated the cultural
traces of the old. What follows is sociologically a new beginning, an
era of nomadic farmer warriors who are gradually settling down.
Their purpose in life is agriculture and fighting with their neigh-

[29] Cf. F. Matz, *Handbuch der Archäologie*, ii (1950), 302 f.

bours for food and living space. These wars involve series of plun-
derings and raids, in which ambush plays a larger part than open
heroic conflict and one annihilates the enemy's male population
and abducts their women and children as workers. The typical
object of dispute in these fights is herds of cattle, which people try
to steal from each other. When epic looks back into a quasi-histor-
ical past, heroic life and conflict always centre precisely on these
activities. The tales of Nestor exemplify this point, where the illusion of a simpler past is produced by the artistic device of an earth-
ier colouring, as Schadewaldt has explained for the great tale in
Book 11 (*Iliasstudien* (Leipzig, 1938), 85 f.). As people correctly
realized a long time ago, these images are an approximate representation of reality still valid for Homeric times. The *Iliad*, and
partly also the *Odyssey*, tend to transcend this heroism, which is too
ordinary, in the superhuman world of the imagination—a world
which certainly does not feed on genuine historical memories of a
still greater past, but on brilliant imagination which in fiction satis-
fies the ideals of an aristocratic world thirsting for life and deeds.
This universal transcending of dimensions concentrates in both
epics on the main action and is in both epics probably the work of
the last great poets, who from older and simpler sources designed
the great unified plots. Expressed in terms of cultural history: in
the class of lords, the tendency of the time is to depart from old-
fashioned rusticism towards courtly ideals; it is true that it does not
try to eliminate the rustic element from itself entirely because it is
its basic form of existence, but it tries to suppress it socially, in the
exclusiveness which we may without exaggeration call courtly. For,
as has been said before, while the coarse, [517] rustic element is
restricted in the main action of both epics, the courtly element is
attached to the main characters—without therefore being missing
in the minor action—with a comprehensiveness which is both
emphatic and eloquent. Nearly all the arguments of the heroes are
courtly in the restraint and self-discipline of external as well as
internal manners; courtly decency is the norm for which people aim
again after all their mistakes. I would like to refer only to the formal reconciliation between Achilles and Agamemnon in Book 19,
as one classic example among many. Here the rustic element, at
least the way we understand it as a criterion, has been eliminated
without trace. But then, of course, in battle (as has already been
said by others) brutality is the old norm, chivalry the new.

It should be noted here that social decency, that healthy style of patriarchal benevolence in the relationship of the great landowner to the small farmer and to the estate personnel, is expressly included in this ideal of courtly culture. This manifests itself in greater detail in the *Odyssey*, but the *Iliad* also indicates it sufficiently. Thersites is an impudent fellow, most probably himself a nobleman of minor rank[30] who suffers the rebuke he deserves. Otherwise the great lords use ugly terms of abuse only amongst each other. The client and the faithful slave—at least in the ideal world which the poets show us with complete consistency—are treated politely and kindly. The 'antisocial' behaviour of the suitors who abuse the honest shepherds of Odysseus as 'stupid peasants' (21. 85) and recklessly set a weak maid the same workload as her stronger companions (20. 105 ff.) is supposed to show up the degenerate squires and to put them beyond the pale. Agricultural work, as the basic form of human and noble existence, retains its high prestige and is still included in lordly activity (18. 366 ff.). But if on the other hand the aristocrat looks down on the growing breed of merchant with contemptuous mistrust, he does not do this because the merchant is chasing material profit—the aristocrat does this no less—nor because he is working, but probably for the very reason that the merchant works *less* than he does himself.

[518] In the *Odyssey*, whose sparsely used similes, inserted at high points of emotion, fulfil associative functions which have been especially deeply thought through, the daily work of the farmer receives a special place of honour through a comparison with the heroic life of Odysseus after he has finished narrating his adventures to the Phaeacians:

But Odysseus kept turning his face to the blazing Sun, impatient for it to set, as he was longing to be on his way. He was like a ploughman who yearns for his supper after his two brown oxen have pulled the ploughshare up and down the field all day; the sunset is welcome to him, and his legs are weary as he plods homeward. Like him Odysseus welcomed the setting of the Sun that day.

[30] Proclus re. Aithiopis. Gebhard, Pauly Wissowa *RE* 2nd ser. v. 2459.

The 'Inner Composition' of the Speeches in the *Iliad*

D. LOHMANN

I. THE MORPHOLOGY OF RING COMPOSITION

The morphological investigation of Homeric ring composition should begin with two speeches whose concentric structure was noticed elsewhere a long time ago,[1] although the analyses put forward in those works differ in details. We will first look at Diomedes' speech **6. 123–43**.

	123–6	Introduction: question about the identity of the opponent.
a	127	Threat: Unhappy the parents whose children face me in battle.
b	128	But if you are one of the immortals . . .
c	129	. . . I would not fight with the heavenly gods.
d	130/1	For Lycurgus did not live long either when he quarrelled with the heavenly gods . . .
e	132–9a	Elaboration of the paradigm.
d'	139b–40	He did not live long because he was hateful to the immortal gods.
c'	141	But I would not want to fight with the blessed gods.
b'	142	But if you are one of the mortals . . .
a'	143	Threat: Come closer so that you will reach your destination of death more quickly!

Except for b–b' the analysis corresponds with the scheme which Van Otterlo (*De ringkompositie*, 11) gives. After the short introduction the speech develops almost verse by verse from the threat con-

From: D. Lohmann, *Die Komposition der Reden in der Ilias* (Berlin, 1970), 12–40, reproduced by kind permission of Walter de Gruyter & Co., Berlin.

[1] R. Oehler, *Mythologische Exempla in der älteren griechischen Dichtung* (Diss. Basle, 1915), 9; W. A. A. van Otterlo, *Die ringkompositie als opbouwprincipe in de epische gedichten van Homerus* (Amsterdam, 1948), 11 ff.; W. Nestle, *Hermes* (1942), 66, 3.

ditioned by the situation to the expansively executed narrative of the paradigm and via the same four stages back to the threat formula. Through its formal, almost schematic, character, this structure corresponds very much to the concept of the naïve, archaic character of ring composition: the inner ring components b–d correspond with each other almost exactly (though note the antithesis in b and b'); but the outer ring a–a' does already point to one characteristic feature of Homeric ring composition: the ring components are not identical—the speaker varies the form of the threat. The warning at the beginning is generalized and expressed with provisos; the threatening invitation at the [13] end of the speech with which it corresponds is levelled directly at the opponent (note the intensification).[2]

Achilles' speech at **24. 599–620** is of very similar structure:

a   599–601a   Your son has been released and is lying on the bier. Tomorrow you will see him when you take him home.

b   601b   Now let us remember the meal.

c   602   Niobe also remembered food.

d   603–12   Elaboration of the paradigm.[3]

c'   613   But she remembered food.
[614–17 to be deleted, see below, n. 4]

b'   618–19a   Come then, we also should remember food.

a'   619b–20   After that you shall weep over your child while you take him back to Ilium. He will cost you many tears.[4]

As in Diomedes' speech the paradigm is concentrically enclosed. The components of the inner rings b, c almost exactly correspond

---

[2] In Idomeneus' battle speech 13. 446–54—also structured in ring form apart from the two retrospective introductory verses (at the centre a short genealogy!)—strikingly similar types of threat are used in the outer ring, but in a different order: 1st ring component 448/9, 'Come and face me so that . . .!' 2nd ring component 453/4, 'Now the ships have brought disaster to you, your father and all the Trojans!'

[3] The Niobe narrative itself is thematically divided into three with the earlier history of the gods' punishment (607/8) enclosed by the murder of the children, again in ring form.

[4] That verses 24. 614–17 are interpolated was already seen by the Alexandrians. Today this deletion is largely accepted. (Differently judged by P. von der Mühll, *Kritisches Hypomnema zur Ilias*, Schweizer Beiträge zur Altertumswissenschaft, 4 (Basle, 1952), 384.) Kakridis's arguments are convincing, *Rh. Mus.* 79 (1930), 113 ff. The formal analysis confirms the deletion.

with each other while the outer ring a–a' eludes the usual definition. Significantly it is referred to neither by Oehler (*Mythologische Exempla*, 7) nor by Van Otterlo (*De ringkompositie*, 12).[5] The relation of the final verses to the beginning is clear: actual situation as opposed to the centre, same constellation: Achilles–Priam–the dead man, same theme. In contrast with this, one striking divergence emerges immediately in a certain tension between the corresponding parts of the ring, and this shows how they work: (a) Your son is lying on the bier, tomorrow you will see him when you go home— (a') you will weep for him when you go to Ilium, he will cost you many tears. The relationship is clear: seeing is followed by weeping, there is a chronological connection in 'is lying', 'tomorrow', and an overall continuation of the thought. If the speeches already mentioned have been dominated by purely formal elements, the following example will illustrate a completely different form of this type [14] which is far more characteristic of the way Homeric ring composition works. Significantly here, as also in the following examples, the concentric structure—as far as I can see—has not been noticed up till now (Van Otterlo merely mentions the outer ring 5. 800 : 812, *Die ringkompositie*, 57).

5. 800–13: Athena has come down from Olympus with Hera and approaches Diomedes who idly stays away from battle. The goddess's speech is a typical exhortatory rebuke. The paraphrase:

a	800	Truly, Tydeus begat a child who resembles him little.
b	801	Tydeus was indeed small but he was a warrior.
c	802	Even when I forbade him to fight . . .
d	803–8	Elaboration of the paradigm.
c'	809–10	But I stand by you and call you to fight.
b'	811–12a	But exhaustion has weakened you or you are full of fear.
a'	812b–13	Then you are not Tydeus' son.

Again a paradigm is enclosed by three concentric rings. Strictly speaking the paradigm begins already with the second verse but the actual elaboration, the description, stands in the centre. So the whole is structured like a triptych: (a) before the exemplum, person of Tydeus, (b) exemplum (c) after the exemplum, the counterpart,

---

[5] On the other hand Walter Nestle has drawn attention to the relations between the beginning and end of the speech (*Hermes* (1942), 66, 3).

Diomedes.[6] The relationships between the individual ring components become clear in the paraphrase. But here it is striking that we can still talk about a material correspondence only in relation to the components of the *outer* ring, and even there the milder reproach (a) 'Tydeus begat a child dissimilar to himself' is set against the harsh hyperbole (a') 'You are not Tydeus' son' (intensification). The function of the two remaining rings lies precisely in the contrast, not in their identity: (b) *Tydeus*, admittedly small of figure, was a warrior, but (b') *you* are a weakling and a coward. (c) I forbade *him* to fight (and yet he did!), but (c') *you* I order to fight (and you don't).[7] Grammatically the parts correspond to each other exactly: Tydeus is the subject in a and b, Diomedes in a' and b'; in c and c' both are the object, while the agent is Athena. The contrast has been elaborated right down to the details.

[15] We note that again there is a definite functional relation between the ring components, but this time a different one from that in the outer ring of the Niobe paradigm: There it was chronological succession, here it is intensification and contrast.

The next speech with strictly executed ring composition is probably the most extensive example of this kind in the *Iliad*: 23. 306–48. Achilles has opened the funeral games in honour of the dead Patroclus and the charioteers line up for the race, among them Antilochus, Nestor's son. Then the old father steps up to Antilochus and makes a speech comprising no fewer than 43 verses in which he gives his son detailed tactical advice for the contest.[8] Outside this self-contained passage, however, are the three introductory verses 306–8 in which Nestor praises his son for his knowledge of chariot racing. So, he says, it would actually be unnecessary to instruct him.[9] Nevertheless Nestor does not miss the opportunity to demonstrate his didactic prowess.

[6] The structure: Person A—paradigm—Person B (as counterpart to A) can e.g. also be shown in Horace, *Carm.* 1. 33 where the same triptych-like structure determines the construction. Cf. Kiessling-Heinze *ad loc.* Cf. also *Epode* 10 and E. Fraenkel's note on composition (*Horace* (Oxford, 1957), 24, esp. n. 2).

[7] H. Erbse emphasizes the conscious contrast in this passage, *Rh. Mus.* (1961), 159: 'Tydeus knew how to confirm his courage even when Athena forbade him to fight, but the son, in a situation which demands a warrior's achievements, is tired and cowardly.'

[8] On the figure of Nestor cf. H. Vester, *Nestor, Funktion und Gestalt in der Ilias* (Diss. Tübingen, 1956), esp. 18–23, the interpretation of the speech analysed here.

[9] This passage is for us the earliest example of an introductory topos within the *genus praeceptivum* which was used frequently later. Cf. Horace, *Epist.* 1. 17. 1 ff.:

23. 306–48: The paraphrase:

	306–8	Introduction.
a	309–12	Pessimism.

For you know well how to steer around the turning-post but your horses are the slowest. So I am pessimistic about the result. But though the others' horses are swifter, they themselves are not as intelligent as you.

b	313–18	Act with intelligence!

Come on, my dear son, bring your cunning intelligence (= *metis*) to bear so that the prizes will not elude you. Through *metis* the woodcutter achieves more than through strength. Through *metis* the helmsman steers the ship. Through *metis* one charioteer surpasses another.

c	319–25	General characterization of the charioteer.
1.	319–21	Negative:

He who simply trusts his horses and chariot will weave from side to side without purpose, the horses will drift off course, he will not be able to control them. [16]

2.	322–5	Positive:

But he who has worse horses but knows the 'tricks' will watch the turning-post and turn round it tightly and will not forget to hold a steady course but will steer unswervingly and watch the chariot ahead.

d	326–33	Elaborate description of the turning-post.
c′	334–43a	Practical instructions.
1.	334–40a	Positive:

Drive the team close to the turning-post and lean to the left of the car. Spur on the right-hand horse, give him full rein. The left-hand horse must graze the turning-post so that the wheel hub seems to touch the side.

2.	340b–3a	Negative:

But avoid touching it so that you do not injure your

'Quamvis, Scaeva, satis per te tibi consulis et scis, | quo tandem pacto deceat maioribus uti, | disce . . .'. Q. Cicero begins his instructions for his brother's application for the consulship similarly. Cf. Kiessling-Heinze on the Horace reference.

horses and break your chariot to the joy of the others, and your own disgrace.

b′ 343b But, my dear son, act with foresight!
a′ 344–8 Optimism.
Once you have passed the turning point, no one will catch you up, even if he were driving the godlike Arion, Adrastus' horse which had divine origins, or Laomedon's horses.

The paraphrase clearly demonstrates a completely self-contained structure of a triple-ring composition, indeed even a quadruple one since the two parts of the ring c–c′ again correspond to each other chiastically. It is worth dwelling on this example, because it clarifies particularly well the nature of Homeric ring composition and how it works.

It is striking that this time there is no paradigm in the centre, but a detailed description of the turning-post: striking, first because the examples quoted so far have almost given the impression that a paradigm is a regular feature of a multiple ring system, and second, because this is the only extended speech of Nestor's in the *Iliad* which, in spite of its extremely didactic tone, does without the paradigm so typical of this speaker. [We will return to this.] Let us first look at the individual rings, moving from the inner to the outer. The inner ring c–c′ deals with the technique of turning. Here the special relation in which the ring components stand to each other strikes us at once. The first ring (319–25) pays no attention to the actual situation, but, abstracted in time and place, deals with the way in which first a bad and then a good charioteer will steer his horses round the turning-post. In the second ring component (334–43a), the speaker applies the criteria just developed to the concrete case, instructing Antilochus first how to steer the horses, second, how not to. So we observe in [17] Homer for the first time a conscious differentiation between abstract, general discussion on the one hand, and concrete application to a situation on the other or—to use the conceptions of school rhetoric coined for this—the distinction between the general and the particular.[10]

In the ring b and b′, the encouragement of his son to use his intelligence is executed in detail in b, but summarized in b′ in a

[10] Cf. H. Lausberg, *Elemente der literarischen Rhetorik* (2nd edn., Munich, 1963), 40 para. 82, 1 and 2.

single half line (343b),[11] though it clearly alludes to b (the form of direct address!).

There is a striking feature to the outer ring a–a'. We have seen from the Athena speech in Book 5 discussed above (pp. 73–4) that ring components can stand in contrast to each other; but there, though we had a juxtaposition of different persons, both ring components complemented each other in terms of content. Here the second ring component *contradicts* the first one in terms of content: 'I am pessimistic about the result, since your opponents' horses are faster. When you have passed the turning-post no one will catch you up . . .'. Pessimism—optimism!

Here a new aspect of ring composition comes to light and in the 'archaic' poet it is a surprising one. Nestor's speech does not, like a didactic lecture, simply *describe* the process of a chariot race at the critical phase when one drives round the turning-post but in the way it is composed *it becomes* a chariot race:

a: The situation before the turn. Its pessimism is psychologically sound: I am pessimistic, the horses of the others are faster.

b c d c' b': The process of turning, visually clearly composed, and, in the centre, that around which everything 'turns', the turning-post.

a':   The situation after the turn: nothing can now go wrong, even if the others had Arion!

The subject-matter determines the form: the composition becomes a programme. Ring composition in the image of the chariot race: driving there—turn—driving back. We see a bridging of a period of time and through it the connection of time of action and time of narrative. This ingenious structure has certainly nothing to do with previous conceptions about the archaic character of ring composition.

[18] As for the form of multiple ring composition, we must correct the assumption that it was not developed before Pindar—in whom it feels far more 'archaic' (thus L. Illig, *Zur Form der pindarischen Erzählung* (Diss. Kiel, 1932), 59). Indeed, this is probably not even true for Homer, since the play with form we have

---

[11] The correspondences in a ring system are not dependent on the length of the ring components. Sometimes a concisely formulated theme is elaborated broadly in the second ring component or vice versa—as in this case—a whole group of verses is resumed again by few words. What is important is the thematic connection.

observed here is not characteristic of the beginning of a compositional development but points rather to a stage of maturity.[12]

2. 23–34: At first sight the Dream's messenger speech in Book 2 of the *Iliad* does not seem structured in the slightest by the laws of ring composition according to the traditional definition. But if we look at it in its thematic structure then again a concentric structuring does emerge, yielding hard information about the morphology of ring composition. The paraphrase:

a	23–5	You are asleep? A man who gives wise counsel, carrying such great responsibility, should not sleep all night!
b	26a	Exhortation: Now listen to me! (1)
c	26b–7	Authorization:[13] I am the messenger of Zeus who is concerned about you.
d	28–32	Messenger's order: (= 2. 11–15) You are to arm the Achaeans, since now you can capture Troy. Hera has brought all the gods round. Sufferings have been inflicted on the Trojans . . .
c′	33a	Authorization: . . . by Zeus (ἐκ Διός)
b′	33b–4a	Exhortation: But you, remember it! (2) and do not forget it! (3)
a′	34b	. . . when sweet sleep releases you.

The two verses (33–4) which conclude the composition after the actual messenger's order in the centre may be condensed and brief, but they still keep the exact order of themes. That the surface length of the ring components which correspond with each other does not need to tally has already been emphasized,[14] but this example also shows that, in spite of clear thematic demarcation, the

---

[12] The Nestor speech has always been a stumbling block for critics. The 'strangely contorted course . . . of its thought development', the 'clumsy and not always clear description' led to the verdict: 'failed beginning of didactic poetry', 'late addition!' (Ameis–Hentze App. VIII, 51). Modern analysis makes the clumsy poet 'B' responsible for it (Von der Mühll, *Kritisches Hypomnema zur Ilias*, 238). It is superfluous to enter into the different accusations; the clear composition speaks for itself.

[13] For the typical phenomena of a messenger's speech cf. A. Fingerle, *Die Typik der Homerischen Reden* (Diss. Munich, 1939), 252 and 266.

[14] See n. 13! That the addition 'from Zeus' (33a), which does not belong to the verses repeated from Zeus' speech 2. 8–15, is supposed to point back to the authorization was already seen by Fingerle, *Die Typik*, 268: 'The addition ἐκ Διός in the report speech B 33 serves the rounding off (frame technique!) . . .'.

individual parts now and then merge into each other both syntactically and metrically over the verse. We will keep an eye on the phenomenon [19] of the poet syntactically breaking up or obscuring
the thematic structure. The compositional technique already
observed above, i.e. that the second ring component continues the
first, shows itself neatly in the second ring (b–b′) in the three
imperatives which belong together: Listen! (b)—Remember it!
(b′)—Do not forget it! (b′).[15]

The centre of the speech this time is the report of Zeus' order
which is repeated literally here (= 2. 11–15),[16] though framed by
the speaker's additions.[17]

5. 815–24: The literal report of an order, this time placed in the
mouth of the man who received it, lies also at the centre of
Diomedes' reply to Athena's rebuke in Book 5 which was discussed
above (5. 815–24). The report of Athena's order (819–21 = 5.
130–2) is framed on each side by two apologetic verses, in which
Diomedes rejects the reproach of cowardice (817–18) and excuses
his order to retreat (822–3). Also the outer parts of the speech
(815–16 and 824) clearly refer to each other through the 'I recognize' formula (each time a god is the object). This has been placed
emphatically at the beginning of the verse and results in a double
ring composition.

14. 42–51: As Diomedes remembers Athena's order, so
Agamemnon here remembers Hector's threat. Here too the report
of the threat is placed in the centre of a multiple ring composition:

a	42–3	Nestor! Why are you leaving the battle and coming here?
b	44	I fear that Hector will now fulfil his word.
c	45	. . . as he once threatened when he was talking among the Trojans,
d	46–7	Hector's threat: That he would not return home before he had burned the ships and killed the men (47 = 8. 182).

[15] This phenomenon of the interrupted group of three will also show itself as
characteristic of ring composition.
[16] Only the pronouns have been changed correspondingly.
[17] This procedure can straight away be observed again in the speech to the elders
following Dream's announcement in 2. 56 ff. where now Dream's speech (this time
as direct speech and slightly shortened at the end) is framed by Agamemnon's additions. Cf. also 8. 413–24.

c'	48a	Thus he spoke.
b'	48b	Everything is now being fulfilled.
a'	49–51	Really! Now the other Achaeans too like Achilles are angry with me and do not want to fight.

[20] Here the report of Hector's threat is framed by the fear that it might be fulfilled.[18] The outer ring is functionally striking. A reproachful question to Nestor ('why are you leaving the battle?') corresponds with a generalizing self-referential answer (characteristic of Agamemnon's delusion): Now no one wants to fight any more because the Achaeans are angry with me.

15. 502–13: A representation of Hector's threat also occurs in Ajax's speech 15. 502–13, again in the centre of a double ring composition. But here it is not so much that the threat is reported as that it is vividly and pictorially described. The appeal, a counterpart to the preceding speech by Hector intentionally placed here,[19] is a fine example of a strictly structured general's speech:

a	502–3	Appeal: Disgrace! Now our destiny is either death or salvation and the defence of our ships from disaster!
b	504–5	Do you believe that after the ships have been captured everyone could return home on foot?
c	506–8	(Hector's threat:) Do you not hear how Hector is driving on his people, urging them to burn the ships? He is not inviting them to a dance but to battle.
b'	509–10	For us there is no better tactic than to fight it out at close quarters.
a'	511–13	Appeal: Better to choose death or life once for all than to languish by the ships for a long time, defeated by inferior men!

The beginning and end ring respectively (a–a') feature an appeal with the alternative 'life or death'. The second ring (b–b') features

---

[18] The same structure is found in Achilles' speech 18. 6–14 where Thetis' prophecy (9–11) is framed by the anxious foreboding of its fulfilment: 8 the generally expressed apprehension, 12/13 the direct statement: Patroclus is dead. The components of the outer ring 6/7:13/14 are referred to each other through the counterpart of the disorderly flight towards the ships and the ordered withdrawal to the ships. So, a double ring composition.

[19] Well noticed by Fingerle, *Die Typik*, 86.

the prospects of the Greeks, in which b brings the—ironically over-stated—false expectation and b' brings the correction.[20]

[21] **16. 200–9:** Inserted direct speeches, like the indirectly reported speeches remembered by the speaker, usually stand in the centre of a ring composition. Here we mention only Achilles' appeal to the Myrmidons (16. 200–9). The outer ring (200 : 209) features an appeal like that by Ajax just analysed (a prohibition—a' order, the rhyme of the two imperatives at the end of the verses underlining the reference). The second ring (b 201–2 and b' 207–8) recalls the time when the Myrmidons were hungry for battle in vain and made accusations against Achilles: these accusations, inserted in direct speech, form the centre of the composition.

24. 253–64: Priam's invective against his sons is also characteristic of the morphology of Homeric ring composition.

a	253a	Appeal: Hurry!
b	253b–4	Curses: Wicked children! Disgraceful sons! If only you had all died instead of Hector!
c	255–9	Lament: How unfortunate I am! I fathered the noblest sons, but none of them is left—neither Mestor, nor Troilus, nor Hector . . . (epithets, detailed description)
b'	260–2	Curses: Ares killed them all, and only the despicable ones remain—the liars, jugglers, and dancers, the stealers of rams and goats!
a'	263–4	Appeal: Will you not prepare the cart at once and put everything in so that we can complete the journey?[21]

The general and concise appeal at the beginning (a) corresponds to the detailed elaboration at the end (a'). The invective in the second component (b'), is likewise expanded and excessively heightened, while in the reflective centre (c) Priam reminisces and grieves for his dead sons with a detailed lament. In contrast to the rings this section has the distinct flavour of a monologue.

---

[20] Also in other instances the poet expresses this contrast between (false) hope and reality through ring components which refer to each other. Cf. 16. 830 ff.: 836b and 22. 331 f.: 335 f. (These two passages are referred to each other through comprehensive composition; 18. 324/7: 329/32; 21. 583 f.: 588b f.; similarly the contrast 8. 497/501 : 526 ff. (Today's hope was false—hope for tomorrow.).)

[21] Otterlo, *Die ringkompositie*, 60 notes the outer ring.

22. 378–94: In the following example too, Achilles reflects in monologue form at the centre of a double ring composition:

a   378–80   Friends! Since the gods have allowed us to overcome this man who has done more damage than all the others together . . .

b   381–4   Appeal: Come! Let us make an attack on the city to see if the Trojans will abandon it or stay! [21]

c   385–90   Reflection: But what was my heart considering there? Patroclus lies unburied. I will not forget him as long as I live. But even if one forgets the dead when one is in Hades, I will still think of him, even there.

b'   391–2   Appeal: Come! Singing the song of victory let us return to the ships with the dead man!

a'   393–4   ('Song of Victory') We have gained great glory. We have killed divine Hector to whom the Trojans used to pray as to a god.

Without doubt this speech constitutes a special case within the *Iliad*. For the speaker to revise an original intention so radically is otherwise usual only in the 'monologues',[22] and significantly the poet uses here the formulaic verse typical of monologue reflection (385). The analysts' critical approach to Homer produces a more or less foregone conclusion: 'that the original ("Since we have killed Hector, come then, back with him in triumph!") has been interrupted by an improper thought (381–90) which has been tossed in . . .' (Von der Mühll, *Kritisches Hypomnema z. Ilias*, 342).[23] According to Von der Mühll the author of the insertion is the poet 'B'—whose addition, with all its 'clumsiness', would still have created a speech structurally typical of Homer.[24] That a speech 'develops', i.e. that the point of view of the speaker can somehow change in its course in other contexts than monologues, can be shown precisely in the morphology of ring composition. (Cf. the 'development' from pessimism to optimism in Nestor's speech 23. 306 ff. p. 77).[25] [23]

[22] Cf. 11. 404 ff.; 17. 91 ff.; 21. 553 ff.; 22. 99 ff.

[23] Cf. also Ameis–Hentze, App. p. 16; Schwartz, *Entstehung der Ilias*, Schriften der wissenschatlichen Gesellschaft in Strassburg, Heft 34 (1918), 27 ff.

[24] Even after the proposed deletion a simple ring composition would remain in whose centre (untypically!) would stand the appeal formula.

[25] In more recent times the speech 22. 378 ff. has played a part in the discussion about the priority of the '*Memnonid*'. W. Schadewaldt sees in Achilles' self-interruption (385) the seam between the material taken over from the *Memnonid* and

23. 570–85: The following example shows a different kind of development. In the course of the chariot race Antilochus has used unfair tactics against Menelaus. Menelaus takes him to task in front of the assembled audience:

a 570–2 Antilochus! You have shamed me and impeded my horses by cutting in front of them with your slower team.

b 573–4 But come, Argives, arbitrate impartially.

c 575–8 Let no one say: 'By lying, Menelaus defeated Antilochus and won the prize of the horse for himself' (NB direct speech).

b' 579–80 Come, let me arbitrate and no one will find fault with me.

a' 581–5 Come, Antilochus, stand in front of the team, take the whip with which you drove your horses, touch the horses, and swear by Poseidon that you did not deceitfully impede my team on purpose.

The outer ring (a–a'), whose second component clearly continues the first, is plainly separated from the central part through the change of address. We will see that change of address nearly always means a caesura in the structural scheme. So here the speech

independent continuation: 'Homer leaves at this place the path of the *Memnonid* which he had pursued up to that point' (*Von Homers Welt und Werk*[4] (Stuttgart, 1965), 169). Kullmann (*Die Quellen der Ilias*, Hermes-Einzelschriften, 14 (1960), 39 f.) defends Schadewaldt's thesis against the objections of Hölscher (in *Gnomon* 27 (1955), 394). A. Lesky even regards it as the decisive argument in the discussion about the priority of the *Aethiopis*. (*RE* Suppl. XI (1967), 75 f.). In spite of everything the thesis does not seem sound to me. The clearly structured construction of the speech can of course not be the only argument against it (for the construction method involving whole blocks of verse does not exclude the possibility that one of these blocks of themes could have been taken over from another place). However, the speech is well motivated in this form and at this place—which Kullmann denies—for two reasons: (1) After Hector's death and the confusion of the Trojans which necessarily follows, from the point of view of military expediency an immediate attack on the city would indeed be the only logical consequence. Instead of this, the army withdraws for funeral ceremonies by which Troy gains time to overcome its panic. As regards his audience, the poet can overcome this logical discrepancy most easily by bringing up the conflict openly in Achilles' behaviour; at the same time he underlines with this the depth of his piety towards his dead friend. (2) Here the poet, with the 'affective reaction of Achilles which can only be interpreted in psychological terms' (Kullmann, *Die Quellen der Ilias*, 39), has made use of an artifice which is also used in the remaining speeches by Achilles consistently, even if not always as clearly, to characterize the hero. We will have to deal with this phenomenon in a different place.

develops from the 'dialogue type' to the '*agora* type' and back
again. Also the inner ring b–b′ shows a development which is not
dissimilar to the one proposed just now for Achilles' speech at 22.
378 ff.: the speaker revises his general request to the listeners for an
impartial arbitration and now declares *himself* ready to make it.
(The invitation formula 'come' at the beginning is used without
any difference for his own decision too, when he invites himself to
arbitrate.) The imaginary direct speech is placed in the centre.

17. 19–32: The change of address shapes the structure of Menelaus'
threat speech against Euphorbus in an even clearer form. Here the
change of addressee has been shifted into the outer ring:

a   19–23   To Zeus: Father Zeus! It is not good to boast excessively (NB *gnome*). Neither the panther's, the lion's
nor the boar's courage (*menos*) is as great as that of
Panthus' sons. [24]

b   24–5a   Hyperenor did not enjoy his youth either . . .

c   25b–7a   (Elaboration of the paradigm) When he insulted
and resisted me and said I was the most cowardly of
the Danaans . . .

b′   27b–8   He did not, I say, come home on his own two feet
to the joy of his wife and parents.

a′   29–32   To Euphorbus: So I will break your resolve to
fight, too. But it would be better if you retreated
and did not resist before you come to grief! Even a
fool sees what has happened (NB *gnome*).

The centre (c) with the inner ring (b–b′) attached to it—the killing
of Hyperenor (14. 516 ff.) recalled by Menelaus—functions as an
apotreptic paradigm.[26] The parts of the outer frame (a–a′) are only
loosely related to each other: (a) Prayer-like lament over
Hyperenor's '*menos*'—(a′) turning to Euphorbus himself, threat to
break the '*menos*', connected with warning advice.[27] The pointed
position of the two *gnomes* at the beginning and at the end of the

---

[26] It is in accordance with Homer's compositional technique that in the following
answering speech 17. 34–42 the same 'paradigm' as the central part—significantly
with a changed function: the warning precedent becomes the reason for revenge!—
is framed in ring form by two threats 34/5 : 41/2.

[27] A similar change between general speech and prayer is found in Ajax' speech
17. 629–47. There the address to Zeus is at the end (645–7), and is clearly referred
to the lament at the beginning (629–33) where Zeus is mentioned in the third person. Cf. also 8. 228–44; 13. 620–39; 19. 270–5.

speech respectively is striking. The compositional significance of such *gnomes*, which can be observed frequently, will occupy us again in a different place. As parts of a ring they are generally related to each other formally or in terms of content. Here they are contrasted (a) 'It is not good to boast excessively—(a′) but even a fool sees what has happened'. Here, too, through this contrast the popular antithesis between empty words and hard facts becomes obvious.[28]

From the speeches analysed so far[29] we can draw some safe conclusions about the nature of Homeric ring composition.

1. The Outer Rings: Their function clearly goes beyond the purely formal *structural* task, e.g. bringing a digression to a conclusion, resuming a thought, and so on. The relationship of a–b–c [25] to a′–b′–c′ is only rarely exhausted by a more or less literal repetition of the same expression, but a′–b′–c′ normally constitute the *complement*, the *completion* of the argument, the thematically necessary rounding-off or *intensification* of the thought. This complementary function of the ring components can take different forms: variation, intensification, correction (p. 82), change of address (p. 83), chronological continuation or bridging, thesis/antithesis, general/particular formulation, detailed elaboration/general summary, prohibition/order (p. 80–1), question/self answer (p. 80), illusion/reality (p. 80–1 with n. 20).[30]

---

[28] Cf. 2. 337 f. : 342 f. (ring!); 20. 200 ff. This relation may be the reason for the rephrasing of the proverb παθὼν δέ τε νήπιος ἔγνω (Hes. *Opp.* 218) which Plato *Symp.* 222b attests as the correct phrasing (see E. Ahrens, *Gnomen in griechischer Dichtung* (Diss. Halle, 1937), 29 f.). Then the reference in Book 17 would be primary to 20. 198 (the latter reference seems to be interpolated).

[29] The examples discussed comprise only a part of the speeches in the *Iliad* with a purely concentric structure. Above all, the merely simple ring compositions, which naturally exceed the multiple ones in number, have not been considered since speeches with several rings are more informative for a morphological analysis. Individual cases will have to be referred to in a different context.

[30] In this characterization, which of course in the first place starts from considerations of content and logic, one important functional aspect has not been considered, the differentiation into 'inclusory' and 'anaphoric' ring function as elaborated by van Otterlo (see esp. his introduction). The observation that the second ring component either concludes a thought or continues it is of great importance for the ordering function in the course of the speech. Also, the different thematic 'rank' of the individual rings would have to be differentiated more precisely. (So in most cases the innermost ring, especially in decidedly descriptive passages, exempla etc., has hardly any thematic value of its own but belongs (inclusively) as introduction and conclusion firmly to the centre.) These (formal) differentiations would have to be observed but cannot be executed in detail here. They also result immediately from the text.

2. Rings–Centre: A further characteristic of ring composition becomes apparent in the relationship between the outer rings and the centre. Three centres of speeches from our series of examples contained mythological *exempla*, the fourth example contained the detailed description of a turning-post; and further examples contained direct or indirectly reported speeches, descriptions, personal reminiscences or reflections. In other words, all central parts usually contain some sort of *narrative* element, whereas conversely the outer rings (mostly ring a, sometimes also ring b) regularly refer immediately to the actual situation in hand, particularly through threats, invective, censure, exhortations, prohibitions-orders, appeals, and personal initiatives.

These observations are of the greatest importance for our further morphological investigations. For in speeches as in epic generally there is a continuous interchange between *progressive* and *descriptive* passages, i.e. on the one hand continuation of action, argument, activity—on the other hand descriptions, digressions, and pauses. As further investigation will confirm, the descriptive passages are normally in the centre of a closed composition of ring shape.

This observation also clears up the question raised above (p. 76) why Nestor in his didactic speech about chariot racing [26] unexpectedly omits a paradigm. There is no room for two descriptive passages in one closed ring composition. The elaborated image of the turning-post compositionally replaces the paradigm.

Naturally this more contemplative, reflective, central part of the ring composition refers mainly to events of the past. As a result, in most cases a 'chronological gradient' develops between the rings and the centre; i.e. concentrically structured speeches or parts of speeches very often develop from the present to the past and back again to the present.[31] In general the following rule can be established: the rings are topical and refer to the immediate situation, while the centre illustrates and describes.[32]

[31] So the technique of chronological 'backrun' emphasized above all by Schadewaldt (*Iliasstudien*, 83 f.) can be explained from the morphology of ring composition. (Ed. Fraenkel, Aeschylus *Agamemnon* (Oxford, 1950), ii. 119 with n. refers to a remarkable example of this chronological graduation in Aeschylus, *Ag.* 184–205.)

[32] That these structural laws are valid for the majority of speeches or parts of speeches composed in ring shape will emerge more and more clearly in the further course of the investigation. Nevertheless there are also cases where rings and centre are morphologically exchangeable. Very rarely is the morphological relationship really the other way round. In Eurypylus' tripartite pleading speech to Patroclus

3. 'Building-Brick' Pattern: Furthermore, a structural law can be derived from the speeches we have discussed which does not relate only to ring composition but will turn out to be a basic principle of Homeric compositional technique in general. It has had to be emphasized several times that it is not the word-for-word correspondences which specifically characterize Homeric ring composition so much as the *thematic* connections. This means that it is the thematic substance of the ring components and the centre that is relevant to the overall structure. The literal correspondences help bind the structure together but only rarely actually constitute the ring itself. This can be observed most clearly in Nestor's speech (23. 306–48) discussed above at pp. 74–7 ff. The individual parts of the speech, ring components as well as centre, are lined up as clearly distinguished thematic entities: 'The team is at a disadvantage—appeal to intelligence—behaviour of the bad and the good charioteer—turning-post—[27] how Antilochus should, how he should not steer—appeal to intelligence—After the turning-post his team has the advantage.' Thematically self-contained, the elements are placed side by side without any sliding transitions, like building bricks, in such a way that a clear concentric structure emerges.[33] The image of the 'building bricks' will prove itself methodically fertile throughout the course of our investigation, both as a heuristic principle of structural analysis, and as a starting point for our question about the poet's compositional technique.

Now the image of the 'building bricks' in turn fits the observation that the *individual* thematic units again frequently demonstrate an interior structure built up on the same principles as the larger structure (as also the other way round, the larger structure as a thematic unit can be a building brick of a larger compositional unit). With this we now touch the principle of the combined speeches and beyond this that of the Outer and Comprehensive Composition. For clarification, only a few speeches should be

11. 823–36 the exhortation, the plea for medical help (828–32), is enclosed in ring form by the description of the unfortunate plight of the Achaean army: a (823–7) 'No help anymore for the Greeks, the best lie wounded'—a' (833–6) 'Of the doctors one is wounded, the other one in battle.' But this exception precisely proves the rule developed above through the fact that the exhortation part in the centre is elaborated descriptively through the reference to Achilles and his teacher in the art of healing, Chiron.

[33] That this thematic delimitation is sometimes concealed through verse technique or syntactically had to be mentioned before (cf. above, pp. 78 f.!).

quoted here which, with their concentric overall structure in their individual parts, again show interior structuring:

7. 124–60: Nestor's speech of exhortation begins and ends with the reproach of Greek cowardice[34] in the face of Hector: A. 124/34 corresponds to A'. 159/60. (Note the variation between the indirect invective at the beginning and the direct reproof at the end!) The paradigm itself (B), conventionally framed (132/3a : 157 f.),[35] is again in itself structured like a triptych through the arms digression in the middle part: (a)133b/7—(b)138/49—(a) 150/6 (note the chronological step back).[36] So there is a concentric structure to the whole speech. The invective at the beginning, however (i.e. A, the first ring component of the outer ring), is itself structured in ring form through the reminiscence of the encounter with Peleus. So the ring has the following broad pattern:

A. Invective

a   124/6   Alas, great suffering affects the Achaean country, and Peleus the noble would lament loudly . . .

b   127/8   . . . who once in his house joyfully asked me about the race of all the Argives (note the chronological step back in the reminiscence). [28]

a'   129/31   If he now heard how *all cringe away from Hector* he would raise his hands and beg the gods to die.

B. 132–58   Paradigm (double ring composition, cf. above).

A'. Invective:

   159/60   But of you, the best of the Achaeans, *no one dares to stand up to Hector*.

23. 69–92: This phenomenon becomes even clearer in the speech of Patroclus when he appears to Achilles in his dream (23. 69–92). Apart from the two introductory verses 69/70, the speech shows a simple ring composition corresponding to the morphological laws of structure already observed: The exhortations to burial, expressed generally and justified through the wandering of the soul in the first ring component (71–4), are in the second ring compo-

---

[34] The reproach of cowardice as a ring around a positive counter-example is also in 4. 370–400; 5. 633–46.

[35] Cf. 11. 670 : 762a; 23. 629 : 643a.

[36] Van Otterlo, *Die ringkompositie*, 16–18, further differentiates between 136 : 150b and 137 : 150a but presumably it is correct to refer the whole complex 150–6 as a chronological continuation to 133b–7 with literal reminiscence in 137 and 150.

nent (82–92) elaborated in detail, and frame a contemplative centre piece, the lament about the separation caused by death, connected with the prophecy to Achilles (75–81). But again, both ring components also show a ring-shaped interior structure, the first very formal (71 gates of Hades: 74 the wide-gated house of Hades), but the second with a clear digression, in the memory of their shared youth (82–92),[37] as follows:

a	82–4a	Exhortation: Do not bury my bones apart from yours but together,
b	84b	as we grew up in your house together.
c	85–8	Reminiscence: When Menoetius brought me to you because of the unfortunate killing on the day when I involuntarily killed Amphidamas' son.
b′	89–90	Then Peleus received me into his house and raised me as your henchman.
a′	91–2	Exhortation: So, too, shall one common urn contain our bones (92 disputed, see Ameis–Hentze ad loc.).

23. 272–86: Like the rings, the centre too can often be divided into parts. Achilles' speech to open the chariot race 23. 272–86 begins and ends with an invitation to compete at the games for the prizes on offer. This outer ring A/A′ frames a detailed explanation B by the speaker why he and his horses are not participating in the contest:

A	272–3	Atreides and you other Achaeans! Here are the prizes in the arena that wait for the charioteers! [29]
B	274–84	His own refusal to compete:
1.	274–9a	No participation by Achilles.
a	274–5	If we were fighting to honour someone else I would carry off first prize.
b	276–8	For you know the quality of my horses . . . (descriptive elaboration of the team).
a′	279a	But I stay back . . . (note the syntactic connection with the next part).
2.	279b–84	No participation by the horses.
a	279b	And so do my horses (sc. stay back).

---

[37] Van Otterlo recognizes both rings, *Die ringkompositie*, 23.

b   280–2   For they lost their glorious charioteer who often used to pour oil over their manes and wash them . . . (Description, reminiscence).

a′   283–4   They both mourn for him, their manes hang down and they stand full of grief.

A′   285–6   You there, prepare yourselves, those of the Achaeans who trust in their horses and chariots! (Chronological continuation of A.)

The passivity of Achilles and his horses is explained, one after the other, in the centre of the speech and in both cases a descriptive, explanatory part (b) is inserted so that two parallel ring systems, which belong closely together thematically, form the centre of the whole speech.

The following example, which is to conclude our morphological analysis of ring composition, also shows the influence of 'Parallel Composition'.

23. 457–72: The chariot race in Book 23 is entering its last stage. The teams approach the ring of spectators again. Idomeneus recognizes them first from a look-out and reports (in the mode of a '*teichoscopy*'):

a   457–60a

1.   457–8   Friends! Can *I* alone see the horses or can *you*, too?

2.   459–60a   It seems to me that different horses are in the lead, with another charioteer showing himself.

b.   460b–1   The horses of Eumelus probably suffered some mishap in the plain, those which led up to that point.

c   462–4   For I saw them swing round the turning-post first but now I cannot see them anywhere, although my eyes are looking over the Trojan plain everywhere.

b′   465–8   (Detailed conjectures about the damage): Perhaps the reins slipped from the charioteer's hands and he could not turn . . ., and he probably fell out, the chariot broke, and the horses escaped.

a′   469–72

1.   469–70a   But you also, rise and look! I cannot make it out clearly.

2.   470b–2   It seems to me that a man of Aetolian race is in the lead, a ruler among the Argives, Tydeus' son, Diomedes!

This speech is an excellent example of Homeric ring composition. The 'report' in the rings refers to the situation (note [30] the intensification of tension which would do credit to a modern reporter: the person of the winner only gradually emerges at the end,[38] with the name Diomedes coming last), reflection and theoretical considerations[39] make up the centre (b, c, b').

Both components of the outer ring again show a clear division in two, but their parts this time do not stand in chiastic, but in parallel, relationship to each other, i.e.: a (1) Can I alone see the horses or can you, too?—a' (1) But you also, rise and look! a (2) It seems to me that different horses are in the lead, with another charioteer.—a' (2) It seems to me . . . to be Diomedes.

The speeches discussed last belong strictly speaking to the combined structures since the pure concentric form has already been broken, in the two last examples even through the principle of 'Parallel Composition', the morphology and function of which will have to be investigated by several examples in the next section.

2. THE MORPHOLOGY OF PARALLEL COMPOSITION

Compared with ring composition parallelism stands out less clearly as a compositional principle in the speeches of the *Iliad*. Speeches structured purely in parallel are rare. The actual importance of Parallel Composition shows itself in the combination of the different principles. The clear morphological and functional difference from ring composition with its preponderantly narrative tendency is to be explained by several examples which are particularly suitable for illuminating the nature and the rhetorical function of Parallel Composition.

18. 254–83: Patroclus has fallen. Achilles through his mere appearance has frightened the enemy back and is waiting for Hephaestus' weapons. In this breathing-space before the decisive battle the Trojans take counsel. Poulydamas the warner urgently advises retreat into the city (18. 254–83). The speech belongs to the 'combined' forms. It clearly consists of two parts, the first of which is

---

[38] For this reason, against Aristarchus and many modern scholars, I keep verse 471.

[39] A necessary bridging of the time during which the team comes closer and becomes recognizable. This too is amazingly reminiscent of the practices of modern sports reporters.

enclosed in ring shape (254–66a, cf. Otterlo, 65). The paraphrase of part I: [31]

I.   254–66a   Strategic suggestion for the situation.

a   254–6   Now consider well, friends! For I advise you now to march to the city, not to await morning by the ships. We are lying far away from the wall.

b   257–65   Description of the situation:

1.   257–60   So far: As long as Achilles was angry with Agamemnon the war against the Achaeans was easier. I used to enjoy sleeping by the ships hoping to conquer them soon.

2.   261–5   Future: But now I very much fear Peleus' son, he will not want to tarry in the plain . . ., but he will fight for the city and the women.

a'   266a   Exhortation: But let us march to the city! Obey me!

(Note the antithetical bisection of the centre with the exact correspondences: I used to enjoy—I fear, prospect of conquering the ships—fight for city and women).[40]

To this strategic advice a passage now connects itself with the introductory words ὧδε γὰρ ἔσται (266b) in which the speaker analyses and weighs up against each other the two contrary possibilities which result from the situation: staying or retreat. Here we are concerned with this part of the speech.

II. 266b–83   Analysis of the two alternatives.
     266b   Transition.

1.   267–72   1st alternative: We stay.

a   267–8a   Now *admittedly night* has held Achilles back.

b   268–70a   But if he finds us *here tomorrow*, storming *in arms*, many a man will get to know him well!

c   270b–72   Fate of the Trojans: Gladly will they then arrive *in Ilium* who just manage to escape. But *dogs and vultures will eat* many . . .

     273   Transition: But if we obey me . . .

2.   274–83   2nd alternative: We retreat.

a'   274–6   *At night admittedly* we will keep our strength in the market place. Towers, gates and doors will protect the city.

---

[40] Strikingly similar in content and structure is the centre of Ajax' speech 13. 813–16 which is enclosed in ring shape by the threat 810/12 and 817/20.

b' 277–9   But *tomorrow* we will stand *on the towers in arms*. All
              the worse then for Achilles if he attacks us!

c' 280–3   Achilles' fate: He will retreat *to the ships* . . . He will
              not penetrate into the city, before that *the dogs will
              eat him*!

The two antithetical parts of the alternative have a completely parallel structure which maintains the chronology: (a) At night—(b)
The next morning—(c) Fate of the Trojans/fate of Achilles.

The congruence of composition is veiled through the non-con-
gruent syntax and (in (2)) through the verse structure. The conscious contrasting goes right down to the details: [32]

a: Night (only) is holding Achilles back—towers and fortifica-
     tions protect the city.
b: Morning: Achilles storming along in his arms will find us here.
     Many a man will then get to know him well!—We will stand on
     the wall in arms, all the worse for Achilles if he wants to attack!
     (Even the veiled tenor of the threat corresponds both times,
     the unveiled threat follows under (c).)
c: The Trojans in flight to the city, many are eaten by dogs and
     vultures!—Achilles retreats back to the ships, otherwise the
     dogs will eat him!

This second part of the speech is in its structure a classic example
of strategic analysis. Clearly set out, considering each case precisely, it is the rational report of a 'military theorist'. Take only one
verse out of the speech and the whole well-constructed building
collapses.[41]

How consciously the poet chose the structure of the speech is
shown by the observation that he recalls it in later speeches twice,
with clear reference to Poulydamas' speech. In Hector's answering
speech 18. 285–309, which in all details is a mirror-image of the

---

[41] Compared with this the verdict of Homeric analysis seems incomprehensible:
'Here as there . . . (this concerns the relationship between the Trojans' council and
events which happened before) the same inclination to exaggeration, the same lack
of unity in the characterization, the same breadth of description . . . The piece suffering most from these flaws is the speech of Poulydamas in which, particularly after
the deep despondency which is expressed in the first part, the confident, the even
boastfully challenging tone at the end displeases greatly.' (Ameis–Hentze, App. VI,
120 f.) Düntzer deleted 266–83, Ameis–Hentze suggest 257–66. Today one does not
delete any individual parts but gives the whole 'bad' speech to the 'editor' (Von der
Mühll, *Kritisches Hypomnema zur Ilias*, 276).

D. Lohmann

warning speech discussed just now,[42] the 'analysing' second part follows the same chronological scheme as in Poulydamas' speech. Against the two alternatives of the warner, Hector sets up his own strategic analysis:

a 297–302 *Now* have your meal and put up guards! (300/2 a sarcastic remark aimed at P. follows).[43]

b 303–6a *But tomorrow* (cf. 277) we will attack the ships *in arms; but if Achilles* really rises, *all the worse for him!* (cf. 278).

c 306b–9 I will not flee from him but resist him, whether he wins or I (fate of both of them!).

But the poet develops the motif still further at 19. 56–73: Achilles reconciles himself with Agamemnon (part I, 56–66)[44] and now is keen to fight: part II, 67–73:

a 67–8a *Now* I end my anger, I must not be angry ceaselessly (cf. 18. 267).

b 68b–71a But drive the Achaeans to war *soon* so that I can still test the Trojans, *whether they want to sleep by the ships!* (cf. 18. 278, 306, esp. 259!).

c 71b–3 But I believe that he will *gladly* bend his knees *who escapes* my spear (cf. 18. 270 f.).[45]

Again the same chronological structure, at the same time the unmistakable literal reminiscences. The repetitions, together with structural connections, thus take on a different complexion concerning the overall composition of the epic (a complexion which has not been noted enough so far). The example shows that with our poet we must expect connections of this kind which link longer passages. More about this in the later chapter about 'Comprehensive Composition'.

[42] This belongs to the sphere of 'External Composition'.

[43] The three verses disturb the connection. They, like the concluding *gnome* 309, do not seem to be original.

[44] This passage is a remarkable ring composition: (a) 56–8 Was the quarrel about a girl of advantage to us? (b) 59–62 (reflecting) If only she had died then! (a') 63–4 To Hector and the Trojans it was of advantage. But the Achaeans will probably think about our quarrel often. (Question and self answer, cf. above p. 80.) (The two superfluous verses 65/6 (= 18. 112 f.) have rightly been deleted here. See Ameis–Hentze App. VIII.)

[45] The arch closes itself in 21. 606 ff.: After the two prophecies from the mouth of a friend and of an enemy the fulfilment of what has been prophesied follows (see G. Scheibner, *Der Aufbau des XX. und XXI. Buches der Ilias* (Borna, 1939), 56).

94

But let us return once more to Poulydamas' speech! The governing principle of composition here is parallelism. It is clear that the topic determines the structure: to the rational, unemotional, analytical investigation before us in the second part of the speech in particularly pure form, the poet also applies the rational form of parallel structure. This does not mean that speeches show more ring composition the more strongly the temperament of the speaker emerges;[46] the actual reason for the differentiation observed lies in the fact that a rational, analytical speech as a rule is less inclined to descriptive expansions. Poulydamas' speech in the second passage is of the same uniform 'rhetorical density'. There is no tension between progressive and descriptive passages, nowhere does the speaker allow himself to be led astray into lengthier descriptions.

14. 83–102: Let us consider a further example. Agamemnon (for the third time within the *Iliad*, after his *'peira'* in Book 2 and the corresponding suggestion in Book 9 which is meant seriously) calls for departure home whilst already developing a detailed plan for retreat (14. 75–9). Odysseus contradicts him in a speech which is not only remarkable compositionally but also illuminates the art of Homeric character depiction: 14. 83–102. [34] As most speeches, this one is also structured into three sections: I. 83–7, II. 88–94, III. 95–102, which step by step develop from the emotional at the beginning to the emphatically rational at the end and whose thematic progression in each case (again tripartite!) is the same. At first the thematic analysis of the first passage, which is characterized by the emotion of indignation, is not easy. But the three themes (which are differentiated more clearly in the following parts) are recognizable: a: Reference to *Agamemnon's plan* developed in the preceding speech (83), b: *Criticism* and rejection (which lies in the indignant question, the strong address: ill-fated man! and in the following unreal wish, 84 f.), c: *Obligation of the general* (84b–7). This last motif, which is dealt with in detail, constitutes in the form of an unreal wish a norm of heroic ethics: Only the brave man is justified in commanding the brave.[47]

---

[46] It will become obvious later that in passages of strong emotion, as a rule, 'free sequencing' is used.

[47] This dialectic system of relationships between ruler and subject puts both sides under obligation elsewhere in the *Iliad* too, cf. the reversal of this relationship in 1. 231 and 293.

These three themes (plan—criticism—ruler's obligation) determine (now with clearer differentiation!) the structure of the second
and third passage:

II. 88–94

a'   88–9   *Ag.'s plan*: So thus you want to give up the city of
                 the Trojans for the sake of which we suffered much
                 misfortune.

b'   90–1a   *Criticism (of the others!)*: Be quiet! So that no other
                 Achaean will hear this word . . .

c'   91b–4   *Ruler's obligation*: . . . which a man should not use
                 who knows how to say sensible things and is a car-
                 rier of a sceptre and whom as many peoples obey as
                 you command.

III. 96–102[48]

a''   96–7a   *Ag.'s plan*: You who call us to draw the ships into
                 the sea during battle.

b''   97b–102a *Criticism (of the speaker!)*: So that even more will
                 happen according to the Trojans' wish . . . for the
                 Achaeans will not stand their ground but they are
                 looking away and desist from fighting. Then your
                 plan will be frustrated.

c''   102b   *Ruler's obligation*: . . . Shepherd of peoples!

The relationship of the first components (a) is of conventional style.
These show that the morphological law of complementary function
deduced from ring composition (cf. above p. 85) is also valid here:
After the general retrospective hint 'What kind of a word did you
use there!' (a) follow the two special parts of the strategic plan
which complement each other by polarization: To give up the city
[35] (a')—To pull the ships into the sea (a'').[49] More revealing is
the relationship of the other parts to each other: criticism (b) and
ruler norm (c). Whereas the first part restricts itself to a general
invective, in the second one the speaker quotes the criticism 'of the
others' to be expected, and only in the third part do his own and
actual objections appear. But more important than the contrast
between anonymous and personal criticism is the practical difference. Odysseus passes over the ethical arguments of the heroic
moral code with astonishing ease (Be quiet! The others might hear

---

[48] The caesura verse 95 is probably to be deleted (after the Alexandrians).

[49] Cf. for instance the same polarization 2. 140/1.

this word which a king just does not use . . .) in order to reveal the inner logical contradiction of the strategic plan with cool rationality. This form of *praeteritio* is a well-calculated means of heightening the sharpness of the criticism. (I do not need the ethical arguments of the others—the plan is simply stupid!).[50]

Logically the reference to the obligation arising from Agamemnon's position as ruler—broadly elaborated as an ethical norm in parts I and II (84b–7 and 91b–4)—is reduced at the end to two heavily exposed words which as it were make up for the honouring address formula left out at the beginning: Shepherd of peoples! This after Odysseus has disqualified Agamemnon with mocking superiority in two respects (first as king who offends against the ethics of rank, second as strategist who offends against common sense).[51] The unspeakable sarcasm of this pointed address [36] at the end becomes very clear through the structural analysis of the speech.[52]

The similarity to the ethos of the Poulydamas speech of Book 18 discussed above is obvious: it is mainly centred on rational argumentation; there the designing, here the refutation, of a strategic plan, admittedly directed at a military superior but delivered from the clear security of intellectual superiority.

[50] In the distancing from the emotional and the turning to rational argument, the characterization of the 'man of many counsels' becomes visible, which has been executed by the poet quite consciously and consistently. It is the same Odysseus who, before the assembly of the army in Book 2 of the *Iliad*, after referring to disgrace, breaking one's word and cowardice (284–90), weighs up without passion and argues rationally, and calls for understanding of the behaviour of the Greeks (291 ff.); who quite unheroically, against the will of Achilles (who is urging people into battle), makes sure that breakfast is taken before the battle (19. 155–72), who, as the objective diplomat of Book 9, does not appeal to human bonds like Phoenix or to the ethic of friendship like Ajax. He is also the hero of Book 13 of the *Odyssey*, who trusts only in his own cleverness and is reserved even towards his divine helper Athena. All this does not mean that Odysseus rebels on principle against the demands of heroic ethics. Significantly he 'decides' explicitly to follow the precept of heroic honour in his monologue 11. 404–10, but again he does this in an extraordinarily unemotional and 'calculating' manner.

[51] As a general, Agamemnon mostly cuts a sorry figure in the *Iliad*. Cf. for this S. E. Bassett, 'The Ἁμαρτία of Achilleus', *TAPhA* 65 (1934), 48–58; E. Valgiglio, *Achille eroe implacabile* (Turin, 1956), 12; Vester, *Nestor*, 26 f.; and esp. E. Kalinka, *Agamemnon in der Ilias* (Vienna, 1943), *passim*. We will come back to the role of the king, which is drawn with striking contempt.

[52] Kalinka, *Agamemnon*, 61 f.: 'A vocative whose mockery as the end of the whole speech consciously heightens its bitterness.' For the sarcastic end position of an 'honouring' expression cf. e.g. Horace, *Sat.* 1. 6. 110 '. . . praeclare senator!'. Generally, the place at the end suits this kind of biting mockery: cf. the exposed position of the sarcastic remark 'pudicissimam uxorem' in Petronius 112. 3.

8. 5–27: The speech by Zeus in which he forbids the gods to participate in battle 8. 5–27 is likewise delivered from a superior position, characterized by mockery and threatening sarcasm. Apart
from the two introductory verses[53] the speech consists of two
approximately equal parts (I. 7–17, II. 18–27) which each have the
same three-stage thematic structure:

I.	7–17	Specifically on the situation:
a	7–9	*Peira* of the gods: No *female* or *male* god is to *try* to frustrate my word, but you must all agree so that I will complete this quickly.
b	10–16	Threat: Whoever is disobedient will return to Olympus disgracefully beaten, or I will hurl him into Tartarus . . .
c	17	Zeus' power: Then you will realize *by how much* I am *the strongest of all gods*.
II.	18–27	General (Play of the imagination):
a'	18–20	*Peira* of the gods: Well then, *try* it so that you will know it! Suspend a chain from heaven and suspend yourselves from it, all *the gods and all the goddesses!*
b'	21–6	Threat: With all your effort you would not be able to pull down Zeus but if I wanted to I would pull you up, earth and all; then I would fasten the chain round the rock of Olympus and everything would be suspended high in the air.
c'	27	Power of Zeus: *By this much I surpass gods* and men.

The second part repeats the first one right down to the details
and in this the individual passages (which vary strongly from
each other) almost correspond with each other even in terms of
extent.[54]

Morphologically the example does [37] not quite fit in with the
speeches discussed just now: the clearly descriptive expansion of
the threat in second place recalls phenomena of ring composition.
However, the particularly rational character of the speech (in con-

---

[53] Verse 6 is missing in several manuscripts and should probably be deleted.

[54] The numerous factual stumbling blocks which have offended people since the
Alexandrian epoch in individual verses cannot be solved through structural analysis.
They concern above all parts I and IIb. A deletion of 25/6 with Zenodotus would
doubtlessly tighten up IIb (ring 21 : 24). I also think that the Hesiod reminiscences
15/16 seem suspect. For the latter see Von der Mühll, *Kritisches Hypomnema zur
Ilias*, 144–6.

trast for instance to other (pathos laden!) threat-speeches of the *Iliad*, cf. 1. 225 ff.; 293 ff.) shows itself in the fact that part I, which refers to the concrete situation, is repeated in exact structural correspondence as an abstract construction of thought (part II). This threat does not spring from the immoderate wrath of an Achilles or the hatred-filled pathos of Homeric battle speeches, but from the cold sarcasm of a tyrant, conscious of his power, who with obvious relish and with playful imagination thinks up grotesque ways of proving this power of his (cf. esp. 21 ff.!).[55]

This rational playing out of dreamed-up possibilities which are detached from the situation (if a happens then b will follow) often determines the parallel structure pattern (so also in the speech by Poulydamas analysed above, see above, pp. 91 ff.). So the soliloquies have a preponderantly parallel structure.[56] They are mostly structured in a stereotype fashion into protasis and apodosis, with the individual passages showing great differences of size.

22. 99–130: Hector's monologue 22. 99–130 thematically consists of the weighing-up of three possibilities: (1) to flee into the city; (2) to implore Achilles for mercy; (3) (as 'least evil') to dare a decisive battle. The first two possibilities are rejected, the third one remains as the best solution. In the execution a parallel structure is clearly aimed for:

I.   99–110:

a   99   1st possibility: (εἰ μέν κε . . .) If I go into the city . . .

b   100–8a   objection: then Poulydamas who warned me before will abuse me . . . but I did not obey. Now that I have destroyed the people, I fear the Trojans lest one of them abuse me . . . (This passage is structured in ring shape in itself through the reflection

[38]   101/4 and the abuse of Poulydamas and the Trojans 100 : 105/8a.)

---

[55] Zeus' threat 15. 222–8 (itself centre of a ring composition 221 : 229 f.) also shows a similar structure within the smallest space. It likewise shows a parallel structure in twofold alternation 'Action of Poseidon—Threat of Zeus' (222/4a–224b/5–226/8a–228b). Also here the calculation of the tyrant: 'Let us suppose that Poseidon had disobeyed . . .'.

[56] On the four monologues see esp. Schadewaldt, *Iliasstudien*, 61–3, for further literature, likewise *Von Homers Welt und Werk*, 300–3.

c   108b–10   It would be far *better* for me to return home after killing Achilles or to be killed by him in glory (3rd possibility).

II.   111–30:

a′   111–21   2nd possibility: (εἰ δέ κεν . . .) But if I submitted to him . . . (Hopeful, detailed visualization of this thought in one single anacoluthic period of 11 verses!)

b′   122–8   Objection: (introduced by the formulaic verse 122 typical of monologue) But what was my heart considering there! He will not have pity on me, he will kill me even if I am unarmed like a woman. Now one cannot chat like maiden and youth . . .

c′   129–30   *Better* again to start the fight as quickly as possible. We want to see to whom the Olympian will grant glory! (= 3rd possibility).

Through the distribution of the third possibility (decisive battle) into both parts, the formal result is a parallel structure consisting of three passages which, however, through the variable expansion of the individual parts, breaks up the usual frame. Rational weighing-up and emotional excitement penetrate each other—an excellent study of the psychological situation in which Hector finds himself.

21. 553–70: Corresponding phenomena can be observed in Agenor's speech 21. 553–70, which shows a similarly shaped structure. Again there are three possibilities whose working out gives the speech its structure (note the remarkable variation compared with the Hector monologue!): (1) to flee into the city; (2) to flee into the plain; (3) to resist. The structure:

I.   553–5   1st possibility:
a   553–4   Into the city.
b   555   Objection.
II.   556–66   2nd possibility:
a′   556–61   Into the plain.
b′   562–66   Objection.
III.   567–70   3rd possibility:
a″   567   Resisting.
b″   568–70   Hopeful prospect.

Apart from the fact that the third possibility, which in Hector's speech through its distribution into parts I and II appears significantly merely as 'lesser evil', here stands with equal rights after the two rejected solutions, the correspondences to Hector's monologue are clearly recognizable. The same introduction of the *protaseis*, the detailed hopeful visualization of part IIa ('. . . In the evening I would then be able to wipe off the sweat and return home').[57] Furthermore, the monologue formula appears at 562 (= 22. 122) which here has its place at the same spot within [39] the composition, namely between the two parts of the second alternative.[58]

11. 404–10: Odysseus' monologue in Book 11, which also has a parallel structure but according to a law of construction different from the two monologues in Books 21 and 22, sounds scanty and unemotional. There, in a game of premise and conclusion, different possibilities with their prospects of success were strung together. Here, the same alternatives are weighed up against each other respectively in two phases, between which a clear break in the speaker's perspective reveals itself: the same facts are considered once from the point of view of personal safety, and on the other hand from the viewpoint of the normative, the heroic moral law.

404a		Exclamation.

I. Personal

a	404b–5a	1st alternative: Fleeing is a great evil!
b	405b–6	2nd alternative: Resisting and being captured is more horrible!

II. Normative

a′	408	1st alternative: Cowards flee!
b′	409–10	2nd alternative: Brave men must resist!

The well-known formulaic verse 407 separates both phases. The discrepancy lies in the second alternative in each case. The 'decision' itself remains unexpressed.[59]

---

[57] This is certainly not the conclusion to the 'if-clause', but is still part of the protasis. Correctly Ameis–Hentze to verse 556.

[58] In both cases the formula verse for Von der Mühll (*Kritisches Hypomnema zur Ilias*) comes 'amazingly too early' (p. 327) since 'in the normally used pattern' it 'has to stand before the "decision" ' (p. 334). A bold setting up of a norm for two out of four monologues! In the monologue-like speech 22. 378 ff. too the same verse does not stand before the 'decision' (391 ff.) but likewise before the reflective part 386 ff., cf. above p. 82 f. What is 'amazing' is how, from a phenomenon which can be proved to be typical, an offence against a 'norm' can be adduced which then leads to analytical conclusions.

[59] Cf. for this B. Snell, *Philol.* (1930), 144 f., Schadewaldt, *Iliasstudien*, 62. Menelaus' monologue 17. 91–105 is similarly structured. However, the order of the

D. Lohmann

[40] From the examples analysed, the peculiarity of Parallel Composition has emerged quite clearly. All the speeches had a preponderantly rational tendency: strategic propositions and planning,[60] examining and weighing up.[61] The influence of the emotional became conspicuous where longer expansions broke through the structure (for instance in Hector's monologue!). It was characteristic of almost all the speeches that they were concerned with abstract conceptions, analyses, the working out of theoretical possibilities.

alternatives in the second phase is reversed, so that the following 'mirror image' structure results: (a) 91/3 1st alternative: If I leave Patroclus any of the Achaeans who sees it will be angry with me! (b) 94/6 2nd alternative: But if I fight against Hector on my own many will encircle me! (Parallelism through protasis and apodosis) 97 Formulaic verse. (b') 98/9 2nd alternative: If someone defying the *daemon* wants to fight against a man whom a god honours, then disaster will come over him. (a') 100/1 1st alternative: Therefore none of the Achaeans who sees that I yield to Hector will be angry.

Now a third compromise solution joins itself to this (not quite harmoniously!).

[60] Cf. for this also 21. 531–6 (twice (a) instruction: keep gate open—shut it; (b) Reason: fear); in combined speeches: 7. 77–86; 8. 502–22 (twice individual instruction—purpose); 12. 67–74; 12. 322–8; 17. 156–63.

[61] Cf. on this: 5. 180–91; 9. 412–16; 17. 220–32 (triple variation of the theme 'service and service in return'); 24. 488–502 as well as referring compositionally to it through AeK 534–48.

Essence and Nature of the Homeric Similes

H. FRÄNKEL

A. 'THE PURPOSE' OF THE SIMILES

1. 'He spun like a top'; 'he fought like a lion'; 'you are like a flower'—it would not be easy to define 'the' purpose common to all of these three very simple comparisons. So it is unlikely that we will be able to demonstrate a uniform purpose for the Homeric simile, which was refined to the limits and developed in many very different ways. Attempts to do so have been too narrowly or too broadly conceived to say anything definite. The opinion which is probably put forward most frequently is that the function of the simile is illustration, i.e. to make the unknown clear through juxtaposition with the known, or the invisible clear through the visible. Many a scholar has succumbed to the temptation to make the degree of vividness the yardstick of the simile. We probably do not need to refute this opinion in detail; the three modest examples we have just given do it conclusively enough.

Much more profound and apt is Plüss's definition that the simile should give an 'idea or picture' of the main event which is 'strong in emotion'. The definition is very apt for the second and third of the similes mentioned above but not for the first. The reason for this is that Plüss virtually excludes the issue of the vividness of the similes because for him, strangely, there are only two alternatives: either the simile illustrates, or it provokes emotion. So he accepts only the ideas of emotion which a simile arouses and completely dismisses the image behind them as a mere means towards an end. The simile as such is violated in this process; for in this definition of purpose there is nothing which refers particularly to a comparison. Achilles' speech in *Iliad* 9, for example, also give us an 'idea strong in emotion' of the nature of the hero.

From H. Fränkel, *Die homerischen Gleichnisse* (Göttingen, 1921), 98–114, reproduced by kind permission of Vandenhoeck & Ruprecht, Göttingen.

2. But so far we gladly agree with Plüss: it is only the emotion ('atmospheric content') which gives the most beautiful similes their actual life; it is in most cases more important and effective than illustrative clarity. If similes merely aided the imagination which envisaged things concretely they would generally fall back on the very well known. But numerous images, set in the wild forest or the barren mountains, far beyond what was actually needed in the circumstances, do not transfer the listener into surroundings most familiar to him, but lead him to places he rarely goes to, which surround him with romantic excitement—the places where dangers lurk, where great, exciting adventures beckon and where all is remote isolation. A lion hunt was certainly not an ordinary event, however often it is recounted in a simile; but for the person who had once joined in one, it was a high point of his life and the memory triggered off in him a vivid sensation of furious combat and a deadly earnest struggle. So he was also deeply moved by the descriptions of the wild sea, the raging storm or gathering thunderstorm, a mood which made him receptive to the grandeur of the heroic poem. Thus we could explain admittedly not 'the' sole purpose of 'the' similes but still 'one' effect of 'some' Homeric similes—the one which stimulates or arouses feelings. This effect is reinforced by the refreshing leap into a totally different world, and by the way in which the obscure nature of the comparison [99] spurs the imagination into activity. Let us have a further look for other kinds of effect.

3. Related to the one mentioned just now is the reinforcing effect. Through a simile, the bard can dwell on a subject for longer and so to speak double the narrative's impact, when otherwise it would simply hurry him along. Furthermore the simile can make something which is difficult to imagine, e.g. miracles, more comprehensible and clearer.

In particular, it can express moods, feelings and ethos and couch the abstract in sensory pictures.

It can spatially unify confused elements and firmly make the many into one. It turns a host of soldiers into a cloud, or a fleeing army into a hounded animal which tries to get away from its pursuer.

It can draw together confused elements into a single time sequence and by looking back, by pointing to the future or a combination of both, it can embrace a large stretch of the action in one single vivid image. So e.g. on the night of Odysseus' return, his twenty years of troubles and sufferings seem like the burden of a single long, hard day of work which is now coming to an end. So in these cases the special effect is achieved by compression.

In other cases the similes gain their effect through the very opposite, i.e. exaggeration: 'as fast as a horse, as an eagle'. Furthermore one could talk about dramatic similes (comparison with a lion) and about characterizing ones (comparison with a donkey, with an octopus).

Finally one should not forget that quite a few similes are there simply as an embellishment of the performance, without any special effect being aimed at in the particular case.

Nothing would be gained by trying to enlarge and complete such analyses. There is an infinite number of types of effect. Hardly any simile would fit exclusively into one of the types which have been or would have to be established, or would not serve several or many 'purposes' at the same time—if one dares to apply the notion of 'purpose', even if it be poetical purpose, to artistic creation at all. More simply and more correctly we can say: for the epic bard the simile is there and given, a feature of his style and he uses it in any way he likes.[1]

B. THE WORLD OF THE SIMILES

1. It is in the nature of similes that all of a sudden they draw the listener into a quite different world from that of the narrative. The secret of their tremendous effect lies in the bridged contrast, in the juxtaposition of sameness and difference.

But what *is* the world of the Homeric similes? Winter (Gercke-Norden *Einleitung in die Altertumswissenschaft*[3] (Leipzig-Berlin, 1927), ii. 162) thought that it was that of the Aegean (Minoan–Mycenaean) age; that this was the period when similes were created and that post-Mycenaean times had produced only [100] watered-down repetitions and imitations of those old similes which had been so freshly and vividly painted. Indeed he believes that he can distinguish the post-Mycenaean similes from the Mycenaean ones according to their degree of vividness. Against this, Platt concluded

---

[1] Cf. the valuable remarks by W. Moog, *Zeitschrift für Ästhetik* vii. 353 ff.

specifically from the Homeric similes in a short but significant essay (*Journ. Phil.* 24, 28; 1896) that 'the civilization of the Homeric poets is not Achaean but Ionian in every particular'.[2] Who is right?

Platt's work, apart from some slight exaggerations, is convincing. The proof that within the epic, which is in all other respects archaizing, the world of the similes stands out as sharply modern and probably Ionian is a complete success. But: only those similes are listed which lead precisely to that conclusion, and these in fact come predominantly from the *Odyssey* and the later parts of the *Iliad*. So all that has been proved—and Platt did not set out to show anything else—is that some of the similes escaped from the archaizing narrative of epic to reflect the Ionian life the bards experienced.

We will not go into detail about Winter's analyses, which are sensitive and full of ideas; we shall discuss only the question of the relationship to Aegean culture, i.e. to Aegean art.

2. The world of the similes is certainly not identical with that of Mycenaean paintings. Very many deviations can be found.[3] Nevertheless none of the older styles of art comes as close to the similes—especially to the 'unmodern' ones which Platt does not consider—in terms of content, attitude, and representation as the Aegean. Images so rich in figures, full of movement, observation, and sensitivity from nature and from human life do not reappear until Hellenistic times.[4] Art had later to relearn such an ability to see events as a whole: it took several centuries for it to grow beyond the lining up and putting together of single figures regarded as independent or at most groups of pairs. This unconditional subordination of all individual traits to an action accomplished with passion and devotion; this organic versatility, free but never styleless; this mixture of subtle observation of nature with bold invention about nature: all this links Aegean art very closely with the epic similes. And the same is true of their content and attitudes. The

---

[2] In the same way F. Poulsen (*Der Orient und die frühgriechische Kunst* (Leipzig, 1912), 168 ff.) establishes, admittedly exaggeratedly, the close relations between the Homeric poems and the monuments of the 10th–8th cents. with the help of an amazing amount of mainly antiquarian individual material.

[3] They are especially emphasized by U. von Wilamowitz, *Kultur der Gegenwart* (Berlin/Leipzig, 1910) i. 8, p. 12.

[4] Cf. M. Heinemann, *Landschaftliche Elemente in der bildenden Kunst bis Polygnot* (Bonn, 1910), 7 ff.

correspondences with art on the continent seem especially close.[5] Here, complete, detailed scenes in similes are depicted for us in paintings; e.g. the lion hunt, with warriors armed with spears on a Mycenaean dagger, and the boar hunt with dogs which drive the animal into the spears of the hunters on Tirynthian frescoes. The roaring bull which has had its foot tied up by a man and the fights between bull and man on the Vafio beakers—the frequently depicted bull games—remind us of those similes in which a struggling bull is being dragged along in fetters or a [101] roaring bull is being mastered by strong youths to the joy of the god watching the fight. The massive silver bull's head of Mycenae, the one in stucco relief from Cnossos, and so many other images of bulls lying down in a herd or fighting with a lion also correspond in their attitude to the dramatic bull similes in Homer. The Aegean axe cult finds its correspondence in the extensive admiration which the similes show for the woodcutter and the carpenter, and in the unique comparison of the hero's soul with a sharp, flashing axe. We find some favourite animals of Aegean art (dolphin, octopus, and fish) in the simile, though not often; we are at once reminded of the flying fish of Phylacopi from the fact that fish are often depicted as leaping in Homer. So in terms of content, Aegean art is fairly close to the similes,[6] and in terms of attitude and representation it is almost identical with the world of the similes. But before we begin to evaluate and interpret this fact, we have to define more closely the relationship of the poets of the similes to nature and their environment.

3. We have been anticipating for some time one weighty objection to our whole way of looking at this; namely, that the sensitivity which generally characterizes our interpretations is quite unhomeric, even though in every single case the attempt was constantly made to understand the similes in the spirit of Homer.

We could reply to this that one can argue about the Homeric spirit; that Wilamowitz, and others, have taught us to recognize, through what is in fact only a thin veil of conventional language and description technique, the rich, versatile, and fluid abundance of subtle and very subtle images of mood and character. Such a reply would be fully justified and in making it we would have defended

---

[5] Cf. G. Rodenwaldt, *Tiryns* (Mainz-Rhein, 1912), ii. 203.

[6] If e.g. the butterfly occurs from time to time in Aegean art but never in the epic there need be no further reason for this than that the artist selected animals with a decorative effect for his plates of jewellery.

part of our interpretation, accurately, as it seems to us, against this criticism.

But only part. The essential part would still remain unfinished. In a certain respect, the assertion that the spirit of the similes is not that of the *Iliad* (we want to restrict ourselves to this work to begin with) is quite true. And indeed this can be proved without going back to our interpretations—or to any interpretations at all. For what is described in the similes—whatever it may *mean*—must have come from a quite different way of thinking from that of the epic.

4. In the simile, bulls or oxen are often slaughtered; they resist the people who are pulling them, they struggle, they roar, they collapse prone. In the narrative, cattle are slaughtered often enough, they do nothing. They are simply objects. We hear nothing about the resistance they put up, about their lowing,[7] their dying;[8] without a sound, without a soul, without a life of their own, they fall. Not that the poet did not have time for such [102] details. He has plenty of time for the most precise description of all the *human* tasks involved in slaughtering, however unimportant they may be.

In the simile, a horse breaks its halter and thunders after the herd, mane flying, conscious of its beauty. In the narrative, many a team gallops along; the whip is applied and then 'it flies not unwillingly'. It seems to be as subject to the hackneyed phrase as it is to the whip. Once in the narrative, horses are allowed to stumble (*Il.* 6. 38), once to stand still, neighing (*Il.* 12. 51), once one is even allowed to be seriously wounded (*Il.* 8. 81). But of course only to embarrass the hero. Occasionally, too, a few other things are said or hinted at about horses—their speed, value, colour, and markings. But these are simply qualities which are important to the owner of the animal. The horses of the *Iliad* have no life of their own.[9] If, in an exceptional case, they are to be given a soul, a miraculous intervention is needed: then they are immortal animals, weeping with human tears and talking with human voice.

In the *Iliad* there are no seasons, and there is hardly any weather. Zeus intervenes with supernatural miracles like bloody dew (11. 53),

---

[7] Exception perhaps *Il.* 23. 30 f.

[8] Different is the slaughtering of the lambs *Il.* 3. 292 ff.; but here there are special reasons which only a detailed interpretation of the whole passage could reveal.

[9] A slight exception is 8. 188 f. and perhaps also 23. 281 f.

lightning or thunder (8. 75, 133, 170, 405; 17. 593; 20. 56),[10] night during the day (16. 567, 17. 268). But he causes storms, rain, and snow almost exclusively in the simile.[11] No cloud ever gathers in the sky.[12] It is true that the sea rises when the gods rush across it;[13] but apart from this, it contents itself with its epithet 'loudly roaring' and comes to life only in the simile.[14]

In the *Iliad*'s narrative, the whole of nature serves its masters, humans and gods. It is always present when it is needed. If the warrior wants to throw a stone he needs only to reach for it: it will lie there at hand, exactly the right size. But nature will never obtrude. It stays in the background, and would never dare to intervene in human action in any positive or decisive way, not even to lead a modest life of its own beside it. Even in order to contribute any atmospheric shading, it has to clothe itself in the garment of the simile and so stand *beside*, rather than step *into*, the narrative.[15]

[103] 5. So to Platt's sentence: 'It can be seen from the similes how much the poets are archaizing', we can add a second point: it can also be seen from the similes how much they stylize their own perceptions. With the simile the poet not only leaps from the heroic world into a different one, but also from an artificially restricted, one-sided view of the world into an unaffected, natural one.

[10] A thunderstorm seems to be counted among miracles rather than natural weather. In fact it appears only rarely in the simile. In the same way the gates of clouds of 5. 751, 8. 395 and miraculous clouds like the ones of 23. 188 do not belong to 'weather'. Of course it is difficult to distinguish between the two but this is necessary here.

[11] Exception: *Il.* 12. 253 where Zeus harms the Achaeans through wind and dust. *Il.* 16. 374 perhaps means 'the wind was blowing above below the clouds'.

[12] 17. 372 f. at least the clear sky is mentioned expressly; but really just to establish the contrast with the cloud of dust in which the area of the violent fight is wrapped.

[13] 13. 29, 18. 66, 24. 96; the winds 23. 214, 230; Iris jumps in at 24. 79.

[14] Exceptions: 18. 402 and 8. 392 where Poseidon's interference in the fight is the cause (390). A surf simile follows (394) so that here for once the same natural event and the simile about nature, which both create a mood, come up together into and next to the narrative.

[15] On Homer's feeling for nature in general cf. Moog, *Zeitschrift für allgemeine Psychologie* xii. 151 ff. According to his collections it seems that trees and plants are most easily accepted into the narrative. Unhesitating as the Homeric bards were concerning the placing of the props necessary for the action, they would not have had difficulty in discovering that they could command the weather as freely as Zeus could. And their artistic maturity as we otherwise know it must have told them that even without 'as . . . so' two images presented next to each other could blend in mood. So it was not a lack of ability but of volition, if they did not incorporate their representations of nature immediately into the narrative.

Perhaps this leap is an escape; perhaps the decrease of the similes in the *Odyssey* can be traced back to the fact that this epic admitted the powers of nature and animals in a less affected way. In the *Odyssey* there is winter with cold, rainy nights and cool mornings; there are land and sea beasts of which one is afraid; a sea which determines men's fate; a dog described as a pathetic figure; there are beggars and poor, dependent people; cold, nocturnal winds which can be fatal for an exhausted person; physical hunger which does not need to be excused through a detailed speech as an all-too-human failing (cf. *Il.* 19. 221–32). In the *Odyssey* there was also a bitingly cold, snowy night at Troy (*Od.* 14. 475 f.), and a thunderstorm which prematurely ended a battle (24. 42) . . . It is very strange that the same *Iliad* poets were able in the narrative to celebrate the self-importance of mankind and overlook nature, but that in the similes they put animal, storm, and rock next to their heroes as contrasting images of equal value. But it does not seem impossible.

6. We now have to try to appreciate afresh the correspondences between the art of Aegean culture and the similes, and to determine which must be traced back to a blood relationship, and which to a matter of choice. And indeed many of them come into the latter category. A fresh feeling for nature, which wants to describe the sublime in image or song,[16] will constantly of its own accord go back to large, strong animals like lions and bulls. If, furthermore, [104] the

[16] The pictorial decoration on Homeric weapons corresponds to the symbolism of the similes; the snake, the emblem of the fury of battle, is also represented on Agamemnon's armour (*Il.* 11. 26). His sword-belt too was decorated with a three-headed snake (11. 39) while on that of Heracles there were represented 'bears, boars, furious lions, battles, fights, murder, and killing of men' (*Od.* 11. 611). Indeed also in the simile boars and lions are again and again the images of heroism; only the bear is new here. The helmet with the boars' tusks which Odysseus puts on in *Il.* 10. 261 was surely supposed to give his wearer something of the strength and courage of the boar. With its strange shape and arrangement of decoration it has been proved as Aegean by W. Reichel (*Homerische Waffen* (Vienna, 1901), 101); in the same way Homeric image symbolism too can be recognized on Aegean (lion hunt, predators hunting ducks, lion choking a bull together on the one dagger) and post-Aegean weapons (snakes, lions and eagle on the shield from the Idaean cave, Poulsen, *Der Orient*, ill. 78). For obviously such representations are not mere decoration; they have an inner relationship with the use of the object. So in fact the lions run on to the point of the dagger and help to generate a heavy thrust. All these relations become clearest on [Hesiod's] shield of Heracles; for here images of men's battles and images of animals' battles (in the sense of the similes but with oversharpened symbolism), and emblems of events of battle which have become physical (Eris etc.), stand next to each other as equal; all this is conveyed by words but meant as a visual work of art.

pictures of scenes are quite often similar, then a good deal of this similarity is a result of the representational abilities of Aegean pictorial art, which, as far as time is concerned, need not have corresponded to the representational abilities of epic poetic art. In summing up we can say: Aegean paintings show a truly poetic shaping of scenes; they share their sensitive view of nature and several peculiarities of selection of material with the Homeric similes. So the world of the similes probably preserves, as does the epic generally, memories of that culture which in the East seems to have had a long afterlife. Alongside these similes which are eternally young but inherited from olden days there are, as we have seen, modern ones. So 'the' world of the similes does not actually exist; any kind of material (including the mythical) is equally welcome. Only the world of epic narrative, which of course is supposed to be left behind in the simile, is generally avoided.

C. THE RELATIONSHIP OF THE SIMILE TO THE NARRATIVE

1. When the bard inserted a simile into the epic narrative, his imagination hung in a state of suspense between two different but similar images. But the narrative's rhythm did not cease; indeed, it was meant to and had to penetrate the simile which was meant to serve the narrative and constitute a part of it. On the other hand, the image contained in the simile, once it had appeared, would fight uncompromisingly to take on a life of its own. The result of the conflict cannot be dogmatically predicted, but can at best only be described afresh for every single case.

The peculiarity of Homeric language and of the Homeric view of the world makes this investigation all the more difficult. Order and logic have not yet remotely gained the kind of influence they have on our thought and language. With the same ease with which the eyes wander from right to left, so frequently the description shifts from one person to another, from one event to another, sometimes to return straight away, sometimes to dwell there. Instead of cohering into images which at least remain static until they have been fully described, the action flows on constantly, just as one experiences it in real life. Again, as they are experienced in real life, aural images and visual impressions are also represented impressionistically, not explained: cause, effect, accompanying consequences, which analysis later differentiates, remain undifferentiated, equal and autonomous parts of the same event. And all these images of events involving people, animals, and things are not observed with detached curiosity, but are felt with vivid and dramatic sympathy in many places and at the same time.[17] Of course, language cannot remotely cope with all this abundance. But then it is talking to Homer's listeners. From the [105] few hints given by the bard, such people are able to create the most vivid and animated image of the whole event, however many details are involved, with maximum speed, clarity, and sensitivity. In the same way, we are able instantly to convert scanty hints, hastily thrown out, into an unbroken logical sequence of conclusions. So if we want to read Homer, we must learn to see, *behind* the words, which are only of little importance, the image with its affective content, which alone is important. For example, we have to learn that when the bard says: 'his armour rang with the weapons of the Trojans'—we are supposed to hear in this drumming and rattling the bravery of the Achaean hero who threw himself into the middle of the enemy, attracting their spears as he did so.

It is precisely that which makes up the unique poetic magic of Homeric poetry,[18] which gives that radiant freshness to the Homeric similes, which also creates the greatest difficulty for scholarship. Even if those images could be completely recaptured, just as the bard intended them, they will never receive fixed contours, never allow themselves to be reduced to such simple patterns that one could precisely measure the degree of similarity, let alone think about counting up the 'points of comparison'. Therefore we have to content ourselves with general impressions and with a description of some typical features.

The general impression is that the size of the simile roughly corresponds to the content of comparison. The more detailed a simile is the more comparison value it normally also contains, whether in its execution the image is expanded to make it broader or intensi-

[17] On the other hand many things are completely pushed away by what follows, are forgotten and no longer valid (but can also be brought out again as desired). But since in most cases we do not know what in each case was removed from consciousness in this way and what on the other hand still continued to have an effect, this factor too makes interpretation much more difficult rather than simplifying it.

[18] Certainly everything which has been explained here is valid for all poetry, not just for the Homeric kind. But for the latter it is most valid because it was allowed to build itself up on a way of speaking and thinking which had been minimally influenced by logical and causal standardization.

fied, giving the colours stronger radiance (e.g. *Il.* 13. 178), or finally clarified, to outline the object or event meant as clearly as possible. This proposition is of course only very generally valid. Strong variations can be shown. But it is not true that the similes should, on principle, constitute an elaboration of a motif once given which is completely free and independent of the narrative. This view is also refuted by some facts which demonstrate a strong inter-relation between simile and story, and vice versa. Thus:

(*a*) simile and narrative often complement each other, so that the one would be incomplete without the other; for instance, in the way that the main action runs on in the simile;

(*b*) sometimes the beginning and the end of the event described in the simile is deliberately chosen to coincide exactly with the beginning and end of the comparison;

(*c*) in order to heighten the similarity with the narrative, in quite a few cases the image in the simile is poetically shaped by the free imagination of the bards in such a way as to violate nature.

On the other hand the image of comparison often contains features which disrupt the [106] comparison. It is very easy for the event described in the simile to be developed beyond the point in time at which it ceased to run parallel to the narrative. So in *Il.* 11. 481 we see the lion swallowing its prey; but Ajax does not really want to 'eat up' Odysseus but on the contrary to save him. Again, in *Il.* 17. 678 the eagle kills the hare whereas Menelaus only wants to give Antilochus some friendly advice. In other cases, however, we do not feel any element of disruption, although the development of the simile still seems to overshoot the mark. This happens when the mood or ethos is so important that it is allowed to have its full effect in the simile, whereas this is forbidden to it in the narrative—or at any rate forbidden for the time being. Thus Achilles in *Il.* 18. 318 groans over Patroclus' corpse like a lion which has been robbed of his cub and furiously pursues the hunter; or at *Il.* 4. 275 the shepherd at the approach of a storm drives his sheep into the cave, whereas the Trojans will in fact have to hold their ground against the approaching enemy in the open field. In cases like this the simile gains a virtually contrastive force. The simile shows us how our feelings would advise us; in the narrative, however, we are shown what resolute bravery must accomplish contrary to our natural instincts. This contrast is probably nowhere more impressive than in *Il.* 11. 86.

3. But we do not want to enter into specific instances again. We shall simply identify one example in which the conflict between the serving position of the simile and its striving for independence becomes very obvious. In *Il.* 16. 161 the bard had compared the Myrmidons hurrying to the danger zone with wolves trotting down to the stream. Having vividly described them there, he should have stopped and reverted to the narrative. But he simply could not resist reporting as well how the animals 'lap the dark water from the surface of a deep spring with their slender tongues, belching gore'; and since this act of drinking had no point of comparison, he put it in the future to indicate intent. However, he painted the scene so colourfully that we do not see it as indicative of future intent but as fully and brilliantly here and now.

It is in this tension between the two images, which appear neither completely the same nor completely different, that the special charm of the comparison lies. It is not our task to give the reason for this. But everybody will feel that a simile which was correct in every respect would be just as dull and boring as the one which fits in with the narrative in only one point is disturbing and absurd in effect (from Homer we can only give one example of this: *Od.* 4. 791).

[107] D. TYPES AND VARIATIONS

1. There are some similes which give the impression of striving to be original (e.g. the black-pudding simile); but they are the exception and seem to be of younger origin. Most of them are typical, i.e. in their content and wording they have much in common with other similes. Indeed one complete, long simile is used verbatim twice. So it appears that the bard had a number of readily available images at his disposal. This conjecture is confirmed when we see how, in one instance, the bard is tempted by the ambiguity of a word to insert a simile which had been devised for a completely different context. Again, in a battle scene which deviates from everything which is normal, a series of four comparisons occurs, whose individual traits contradict the narrative in question—whereas they would fit excellently into a normal battle. So they had originally been created for a normal battle, but been taken over without adaptation (or without complete transformation).[19] So for typical battle

[19] The bard was able to do it without damage, for the simile can tolerate even far stronger deviations from the narrative. So this observation is not supposed to imply any criticism.

scenes there existed equally typical similes. Again, if the events were varied, the simile could be adapted with them. Now in one instance, through the mistake of a rhapsode, two variations of the same simile have been preserved alongside each other; we were able to find a third in a different place. So the variations too could become as typical as the complete similes.

2. If one now looks more closely at the variations produced over the whole range of the similes, one finds that basically nothing is fixed. Everything can change. Individual components of images are exchanged—so the lion and the boar. Some of the words can stay and yet the sense can be altered,[20] or the same sense can be put into new words. The content of what we are looking at can remain, and yet the mood can change completely: so the gleam of the hero's armour is sometimes compared with an evil and sometimes with a beneficent fire; sometimes with a beautiful star, sometimes with an evil one which brings disease. A comparison which was valid for both the outward appearance and for the mood can become a pure image of mood, a mere painting of the soul. The mood and with it the image of the simile can remain, and yet the base of what we are looking at can change completely: a particularly strange but understandable phenomenon. Finally the event can change but the sphere in which it takes place can remain: whether the narrative is about the fish which has been caught, or the diving oystercatcher, the victim or the conqueror. Images of fishing [108] always have something wretched about them.

So everything seems changeable. But almost without exception what is valid for nature is also valid for the epic poet: *Non facit saltus*. Without a leap the one flows into the other. It was precisely this that made the images comprehensible to the original listener and interpretable by us. The new and different joins itself to the old and familiar. Every time the old is most lovingly absorbed, newly and freshly felt, shaped and transformed, the new which joins it is not alien. The unique and the familiar blend most beautifully into the stylish. Everywhere there is diversity in unity, there is fullness of teeming life in the calm order of the cosmos.

---

[20] Even one of the similes repeated verbatim has a different meaning in both places.

3. If a comparison could adopt different forms in order to adapt itself for different use, so the bard also had more than one image at his disposal for numerous typical processes; he had the choice, he could change. But he could also place several comparisons next to each other, could visibly expand the abundance over which he ruled. So in one place (*Il.* 14. 394) the three images of attack come one after the other; each of the three fills a couplet and the fourth couplet rounds them off; 'But neither the thunder of breakers on the beach, driven in from the deep by a northerly gale; nor the roar of the flames when fire attacks the forest in a mountain ravine; nor the wind's moan in the high foliage of the oaks when it rises to a scream in its wrath, is so loud as the terrible war-cry that the Trojans and Achaeans raised as they fell upon each other.' It sounds quite similar to the triple image of *Il.* 17. 20: 'We know the courage of the panther and the lion, and the fierce wild-boar, the most high-spirited and self-reliant beast of all; but that, it seems, is nothing to the prowess of these sons of Panthous with their famous ashen spears!' (cf. also *Il.* 22. 262 ff.).[21] Sometimes also the same narrative subject is represented twice in one single simile.[22] So the hostile forces which Hector disperses are on one occasion seen simultaneously in terms of the two images typical of a mass of warriors—cloud and the surge of the sea—whereas the attacker, as often, appears as a gale: 'he fell on the rabble, like a full gale when it strikes from the West and scatters the white clouds that the South Wind has marshalled; when the great billows start their march and the foam flies high on the wings of the travelling wind' (*Il.* 11. 305). This double image of the hosts of Achaeans in the simile would be felt as embarrassing if individual details of the relationship between the simile and the narrative did not recede into the semi-conscious in the face of the overwhelming overall impression.[23]

4. But far more often, two or more symbols are presented as a choice ('*x* or *y*'). So of the three symbols of an attack which we

---

[21] *Od.* 13. 81 ff. the two images of the horse and the bird usual for the ship are joined together in a peculiar way.

[22] Apart from the example mentioned in the text cf. also *Il.* 5. 87, where ἕρκος (πολέμοιο) and γέφυραι (πολέμοιο), both metaphors for the same chain of warriors, appear next to each other, and *Il.* 12. 146.

[23] A not very fortunate attempt to unite several similes for the same object to one overall image was also ventured, *Il.* 2. 478.

found run together in *Il.* 14. 394, two appear again run together in a short comparison [109] in 13. 39: 'Like a high wind *or* a conflagration the massed Trojans were sweeping on in the wake of Hector son of Priam with indomitable fury.' The attacking heroes are compared to lions greedy for flesh *or* boars of formidable strength as in *Il.* 5. 782 (= 7. 256). The bard actually goes rather further when in 11. 292 he makes Hector incite his men against the Achaeans in the way a hunter incites hounds against a wild boar *or* a lion. So here the image as a whole remains fixed, whereas part can be chosen at will. But the individual traits which are thus left in suspense through the 'or' formulation are not always, as here and often in other places, incidental. It can happen that one of the main carriers of the image of the simile remains in suspense like this. A fully executed image of pursuit (*Il.* 8. 338) leaves it open whether we want to imagine the person pursued either as a lion or as a boar. Such indeterminacy gives a certain pallor or unreality to the process of the simile so that we do not forget that this is just an interlude of smaller importance which is interrupting the main process.[24]

5. Two or more detailed similes can also be put next to each other, without explicit connection. If every individual simile already means a doubling of a part of the narrative, it is only one step further down the same road if the similes are multiplied. So we find in *Il.* 2. 144: 'The Assembly was stirred like the waters of the sea in a storm' (detail) . . . 'or when the west wind falls on a cornfield (detail), thus the Assembly was stirred.' Again, whole series of similes appear of which one sometimes seems to add virtually nothing new to the preceding one, but sometimes the following simile adds something new and different to the description of the narrative. For 'new features are not always added; the earlier ones return, develop the picture . . . Every image of Homer's is a musical painting; the given note vibrates in our ear for a while longer; when it wants to die down, then the same string sounds again and the earlier note returns intensified; all the voices unite into full harmony.' Besides, in the course of these similes a certain progress of the action is

---

[24] The bard is then also prevented from furnishing the image with characteristic individual traits which would fit only one of the simile carriers given as a choice. I wonder whether Ameis-Hentze-Cauer for *Il.* 15. 273 are right in relating the 'rock' to the goat and the 'wood' to the stag?

unmistakable, besides the many notes which simply repeat and
intensify themselves: while the similes march past us one after the
other, the army is gathering and arranging itself. Where an
immense crowd of people and the gradual ordering and shaping of
the masses are supposed to be described, there the description too
must be allowed calmly to spread the rich abundance of its images,
one after the other.[25]

[110] E. THE HISTORY OF THE HOMERIC SIMILE

1. For primitive man the whole world is full of similarities with the
events of his own life. He interprets events of nature after the pattern of human ones, and so by a process of unconscious transfer-
ence sees similarity in all things (cf. *Il.* 3. 3). And these similarities
which confront him everywhere—sometimes genuine, sometimes
apparent—are not for him a mere game of chance: he is always
inclined to refer them back to intrinsic relationships. Divine will
sends omens of what is to come to humans; whatever happened in
the heavens and in the air, whatever striking happened at significant moments, will soon correspondingly happen in human life too
(*Il.* 2. 326 and in other cases). Man himself can also cement such
relationships in solemn speech, through the oath ('just as this holy
staff will never grow green again, thus I will not . . .' *Il.* 1. 234), or
the curse ('just as this sacrificial wine is running down to earth, thus
may the brain of the one who breaks a contract splash out' *Il.* 3.
300), or magic (no Homeric example; ἐπαοιδή is mentioned *Od.* 19.
457). Again, we may see in the old epic similes a little more than an
artistic device; in many cases the poets certainly believed that their
comparisons revealed a mysterious connection which really
existed. So the assertion 'he has the heart of a stag' has its direct origin in the comparison 'he is cowardly like a stag'. So too it is said of
Agamemnon that he is made 'of dog', of canine essence because he
is so impudent. And if a hero's soul is like a shining and consuming
fire, this fire burns in the man's eyes; indeed it can physically blaze
out of his body and his arms. The bright gleam which plays on the

[25] One can assume the most different reasons for the fact that sometimes frequently changing images follow each other in tremendously quick succession. It is
probably most correct to link this with the mobility of the Homeric imagination
which willingly glides over from one object to another and is able to forget equally
well as retain images which have just been unfolded.

leader's bronze armour does not resemble fire accidentally or mechanically, but it is a visible aura of the heroism which glows inside him, a glittering, threatening sign and forewarning of his fiery, deadly rage and fury.

2. Such features in particular point to the antiquity of some comparisons and their origin in experience, independent of the actual poem. And in the same way alongside the studied and symbolizing comparisons there surely existed from the beginning others which were intended for immediate understanding and precise characterization, and finally those which were thrown up instinctively and randomly, in a spirit of pure play. Epic poetry took up images of this kind—particularly to start with those of the first kind, if need be also of the second—and shaped them into a highly developed stylistic device long before the epics which have come down to us. For in their oldest parts the simile is already there ready in artistic shape, though not as something rigid and dead but still full of movement, in continuous transformation and capable of recreation. It is 'coined form which develops as it lives'.

We found various forces operative in this development of the similes.[26] The image of the simile attracted illuminating detail. And the more one became absorbed in a comparison, the more new points of comparison one found [111] in addition to the first one(s). Sometimes, the freshly discovered point of comparison became even more important to the bard than the original one; then the focus of the simile shifted. Special cases again and again compelled him to give the comparison a particular twist. He continued to develop the images of comparison, often giving free rein to his imagination and without regard for scientific accuracy; he creatively deepened, extended, and enriched them in the same way as the epic heroic legend. Indeed, occasionally, the simile seems to move towards the animal fable. New comparisons originated through the connection of independent individual images, through the crossing of different types of similes. Sometimes an image was initially invented for a process which was at the same time physical and psychic: an excited mass of people, seething, roaring, surging on, is similar to the surging sea; but then it becomes a mere picture of the soul: his heart was surging like the excited sea. In the later

---

[26] What has been explained elsewhere in connection with the material shall not be repeated here. It is just called to mind very briefly.

strata of the epic we find more technical similes and similes from daily life, in the older ones more dramatic images of landscape, hunting, and herds.[27] The later similes strive for originality and often deviate from the conventional. Many of them are more tender and sensitive than the older ones.

3. All these developing forces will not have come into play only at the moment when the similes we have to hand received their final shape. They will have operated for a long time before. And since nearly all of them tended towards extension and enrichment, the earlier stages of our similes must have been shorter and simpler. At the very beginning there was a very simple basic form at least for one group. We saw there that all[28] Homeric horse similes, however different from each other they were, still had one feature in common—'as quick as a horse'. The simile always related to speeding ships or fast-running men. Only one simile bucked this trend, where other features (the proud, noble gait, the splendid beauty of appearance) definitely dominated the foreground. But precisely this simile was still connected with the narrative by the turn of phrase: 'so quickly his knees carried him'. This revealed that this comparison too originated from the simple 'as quick as a horse' and that the more dominant features were nevertheless later and had been included subsequently.

When it comes to other types of material, the similes arrange themselves quite spontaneously into family trees, at the top of which there is the short comparison such as 'he fought like a lion' or 'he overcame him as a lion does the ox' or 'the army approached black as a stormcloud'. From such simple structures, which still appear quite frequently in our Homer, the similes developed. In order to connect them with the narrative the bard often retained the old coupling 'as black as', 'as fast as' etc. without making allowances in expression as well for the fact that the content had been extended and changed.[29] The bard hoped to be understood even like this; Homeric language was awkward in dealing with the abstract. The [112] task of expressing the core of the comparison briefly, but strikingly and without pedantry, would be desperately

[27] Cf. H. Immisch, *Die innere Entwicklung des griechischen Epos* (Leipzig, 1904), 21 f.

[28] We disregard the strange *Il.* 15. 679.

[29] In *Il.* 6. 513, however, in the apodosis before the 'so quickly' something was added about the shining appearance.

difficult even if the most perfect language was available. This peculiarity has always misled interpreters[30] from the beginning.

4. As has a second one. If the comparison grew into a simile
through gradual extension, the most natural form was that the further extension should append itself to the original concise version.
In *Il.* 23. 133 it is said 'the cloud of infantry followed'. In *Il.* 4. 274
we read the same; but joined to this is a long simile: 'as when a
goatherd saw a cloud coming up from the rock' etc. Or: in *Il.* 17.
132 Ajax places himself in front of Patroclus' body to protect it ὥς
τίς τε λέων περὶ οἷσι τέκεσσιν. The comparison could end here for
the essential point has already been made; but it continues with a
relative clause ᾧ ῥά τε νήπι' ἄγοντι etc. The short comparison often
ends the line, as here, and the extension begins the next one.[31] All
this is easily understood if the development really took place in the
way we assume. But similes structured like this can easily give the
impression that the bard initially wanted simply to give the short
comparison; that it was only subsequently that, carried away by the
image which has risen before him, he indulges in further elabora-
tions. But appearances are deceptive; in reality such a structure
shows only the biogenetic prehistory of the genus. Giving this
structure to similes had long ago become a fixed, traditional form
for the bards of our *Iliad*. Instead of unfolding the individual features of the elaborated image one after the other before an unpre-
pared listener, the poet first shows it in a clear ground-plan in order
then to extend it richly and splendidly in front of his eyes. This
extension happens so quickly, so easily and unaffectedly that it is as
if the only driving force were the artist's sheer pleasure in the structure he is creating. And yet he hardly ever forgets that this construction, as a whole and in its parts, should not be a free and
independent ornament, but a clearly determined part of a large
whole. From the free and unaffected way in which some similes
seem even subsequently to develop themselves from an anticipated
main point of comparison, from the way they seem to slide without
a will of their own from one idea to the next, Cauer wrongly

---

[30] It can of course not be taken for granted that the coupling gives the oldest origin of the simile in every case. But through such cases as the ones described the bard
became accustomed to regarding the coupling as an unimportant and subordinate
part of the whole which he could choose at will.

[31] For this reason very many similes can be deleted without difficulty, and without leaving a gap, by people who find them uncomfortable.

concluded that the similes were nothing but a reckless and unrestrained play of the imagination, stimulated by the short comparison, the point of comparison.[32] This error pays the highest tribute to the Homeric style. For 'a beautiful end-product may, even must, follow rules; but it must appear to be free from rules'.[33]

5. The history of the similes would be incomplete without a consideration of which were the oldest materials for similes. Our results so far offer a good basis to determine this. We may regard as old such motifs as [113] have a long prehistory, are present in rich and widely ramified variety, and are deeply rooted in epic language. On the other hand, those materials are young which make use of the form of the simile (already completely developed) without ever having themselves gone through the earlier stage of the short comparison. These, naturally, then have no family tree of their own.

Thus all the seafaring similes show themselves as late.[34] The motif of seafaring did not itself become one which formed series but it subsequently entered into other series of similes. Twice, the poet makes the wave—a frequent description of an attacker—smash into the ship instead of surging against the shore. Once, the leaders who otherwise urge their people forward to the attack as the gale does the wages, are compared with a favourable wind which drives the ship forward and relieves the labouring sailors of the effort of rowing, just as the intervention of the leaders relieves the men of the heaviest burden of battle. Yet another seafaring simile belongs to the frequent passages in which the gleam of armour is compared to a fire which (according to the mood) is evil or beneficent: the armour of Achilles returning to battle shines like a fire which signals rescue to shipwrecked sailors. In the other similes, the features which refer to seafaring are quite insignificant and unimportant and could be substituted at will by others. And in the same way as the seafaring comparisons are unconnected with each other, so they also lack any connection with epic language. None of the turns of phrase so familiar from Attic tragedy of the 'helmsman' of the state

---

[32] P. Cauer, *Grundfragen der Homerkritik*[2] (Leipzig, 1923), 411; however, in the following explanations he abandons this point of view again.

[33] Schiller to Körner, 15 Nov. 1793.

[34] Just as in plastic arts the ship appeared only in the geometric style. To the Aegean epoch seafaring must have seemed prosaic and purely functional. It is also missing on Achilles' shield.

or the army[35] or of the 'haven' as the emblem of security etc. has a counterpart in Homer.

On the other hand, alongside the innumerable and closely connected similes from pastoral life, there is the phrase ποιμὴν λαῶν. The hunting images and the animal comparisons are inseparably connected with these. The comparisons from agriculture seem to be less richly developed and less unified in their inner connections. But the powerful images of the roaring sea and the unshaken rock, of the raging gale and the stormcloud, of the falling tree of the primeval forest, of the evil snow, of the wild torrent which in its rage pulls everything away with itself, of the star and the fire: they and their relatives all belong to the core of the stock of similes.[36] Did those generations which created the style of the similes really spend their lives in the wilderness, in free untamed nature? Did they see the content and highest goal of their existence in the battle with beasts of prey, in the care of their herds, in hunting and war? Or had they already become cool, sedate [114] and orderly town-dwellers who, if they wanted to describe the great and sublime, turned their thoughts away from the daily life which surrounded them?

[35] The ancient interpretation of Zeus' epithet ὑψίζυγος as the rower or helmsman of the world is therefore wrong. Linguistically too it is more than forced. It can hardly be ascertained what kind of image underlies it; most likely, probably that of the scales.

[36] Isolated very old elements may also be found elsewhere. But here we are concerned with the unified groups of material with and on which the style of the epic simile developed.

Hector and Andromache

W. SCHADEWALDT

I

On the advice of the seer Helenus, Hector has gone from the battlefield to the city (6. 237). His mother Hecuba and the women of
Troy are to make a supplication to Athena, to ask the goddess to
restrain the onslaught of Diomedes, who is causing havoc among
the Trojans outside the city.

Hector has gone from his mother to Paris, to fetch that dilatory
warrior back to battle. He finds him busy with his weapons, and
Helen among her women (6. 321). He speaks seriously to him: the
men are dying outside, around the wall and the city, and yet it was
for his sake that the war had flared up. Paris is ready; he will soon
catch him up within the city. Helen curses herself and her life with
this dishonourable husband, but still (she says) her brother-in-law
should sit down; he has so many troubles because of her and Paris;
to both of them Zeus has given such an evil fate, of which men will
still speak in the future. Hector declines; he must go back to the
Trojans, who have great need for him out there. But he asks her to
get her husband moving, and let him hurry himself up, to catch him
up still within the city. 'I myself will in the meantime go to my
house, to see my servants and my dear wife and my little son. For I
do not know whether I shall come back to them again, or whether
the gods will overcome me this time at the hands of the Danaans'
(6. 360–8).

> So speaking Hektor of the shining helm departed
> and in speed made his way to his own well-established dwelling,   370
> but failed to find in the house Andromache of the white arms;
> for she, with the child, and followed by one fair-robed attendant,
> had taken her place on the tower in lamentation, and tearful.
> When he saw no sign of his perfect wife within the house, Hektor

From W. Schadewaldt, *Von Homers Welt und Werk*[3] (Stuttgart, 1959), 207–29.
Reproduced by kind permission of K. F. Koehler Verlag GmbH.

stopped in his way on the threshold and spoke among the
    handmaidens: 375
'Come then, tell me truthfully as you may, handmaidens:
where has Andromache of the white arms gone? Is she
with any of the sisters of her lord or the wives of his brothers?
Or has she gone to the house of Athene, where all the other
lovely-haired women of Troy propitiate the grim goddess?' 380
    Then in turn the hard-working housekeeper gave him an answer:
'Hektor, since you have urged me to tell you the truth, she is not
with any of the sisters of her lord or the wives of his brothers,
nor has she gone to the house of Athene, where all the other
lovely-haired women of Troy propitiate the grim goddess, 385
but she has gone to the great bastion of Ilion, because she heard that
the Trojans were losing, and great grew the strength of the Achaians.
Therefore she has gone in speed to the wall, like a woman
gone mad, and a nurse attending her carries the baby.'
    So the housekeeper spoke, and Hektor hastened from his home 390
backward by the way he had come through the well-laid streets. So
as he had come to the gates on his way through the great city,
the Skaian gates, whereby he would issue into the plain, there
at last his own generous wife came running to meet him,
Andromache, the daughter of high-hearted Eëtion; 395
Eëtion, who had dwelt underneath wooded Plakos,
in Thebe below Plakos, lord over the Kilikian people.
It was his daughter who was given to Hektor of the bronze helm.
She came to him there, and beside her went an attendant carrying
the boy in the fold of her bosom, a little child, only a baby, 400
Hektor's son, the admired, beautiful as a star shining,
whom Hektor called Skamandrios, but all of the others
Astyanax—lord of the city; since Hektor alone saved Ilion.
Hektor smiled in silence as he looked on his son, but she,
Andromache, stood close beside him, letting her tears fall, 405
and clung to his hand and called him by name and spoke to
    him: 'Dearest,
your own great strength will be your death, and you have no pity
on your little son, nor on me, ill-starred, who soon must be your widow;
for presently the Achaians, gathering together,
will set upon you and kill you; and for me it would be far better 410
to sink into the earth when I have lost you, for there is no other
consolation for me after you have gone to your destiny—
only grief; since I have no father, no honoured mother.
It was brilliant Achilleus who slew my father, Eëtion,
when he stormed the strong-founded citadel of the Kilikians, 415

Thebe of the towering gates. He killed Eëtion
but did not strip his armour, for his heart respected the dead man,
but burned the body in all its elaborate war-gear
and piled a grave mound over it, and the nymphs of the
    mountains,   420
daughters of Zeus of the aegis, planted elm trees about it.
And they who were my seven brothers in the great house all went
upon a single day down into the house of the death god,
for swift-footed brilliant Achilleus slaughtered all of them
as they were tending their white sheep and their lumbering oxen;
and when he had led my mother, who was queen under wooded
    Plakos,   425
here, along with all his other possessions, Achilleus
released her again, accepting ransom beyond count, but Artemis
of the showering arrows struck her down in the halls of her father.
Hektor, thus you are father to me, and my honoured mother,
you are my brother, and you it is who are my young husband.   430
Please take pity upon me then, stay here on the rampart,
that you may not leave your child an orphan, your wife a widow,
but draw your people up by the fig tree, there where the city
is openest to attack, and where the wall may be mounted.
Three times their bravest came that way, and fought there to
    storm it   435
about the two Aiantes and renowned Idomeneus,
about the two Atreidai and the fighting son of Tydeus.
Either some man well skilled in prophetic arts had spoken,
or the very spirit within themselves had stirred them to the
    onslaught.'

    Then tall Hektor of the shining helm answered her: 'All these   440
things are in my mind also, lady; yet I would feel deep shame
before the Trojans, and the Trojan women with trailing garments,
if like a coward I were to shrink aside from the fighting;
and the spirit will not let me, since I have learned to be valiant
and to fight always among the foremost ranks of the Trojans,   445
winning for my own self great glory, and for my father.
For I know this thing well in my heart, and my mind knows it:
there will come a day when sacred Ilion shall perish,
and Priam, and the people of Priam of the strong ash spear.
But it is not so much the pain to come of the Trojans   450
that troubles me, not even of Priam the king nor Hekabe,
not the thought of my brothers who in their numbers and valour
shall drop in the dust under the hands of men who hate them,
as troubles me the thought of you, when some bronze-armoured

Achaian leads you off, taking away your day of liberty,   455
in tears; and in Argos you must work at the loom of another,
and carry water from the spring Messeis or Hypereia,
all unwilling, but strong will be the necessity upon you;
and some day seeing you shedding tears a man will say of you:
"This is the wife of Hektor, who was ever the bravest fighter   460
of the Trojans, breakers of horses, in the days when they fought
   about Ilion."
So will one speak of you; and for you it will be yet a fresh grief,
to be widowed of such a man who could fight off the day of
   your slavery.
But may I be dead and the piled earth hide me under before I
hear you crying and know by this that they drag you captive.'   465
   So speaking glorious Hektor held out his arms to his baby,
who shrank back to his fair-girdled nurse's bosom
screaming, and frightened at the aspect of his own father,
terrified as he saw the bronze and the crest with its horse-hair,
nodding dreadfully, as he thought, from the peak of the helmet.   470
Then his beloved father laughed out, and his honoured mother,
and at once glorious Hektor lifted from his head the helmet
and laid it in all its shining upon the ground. Then taking
up his dear son he tossed him about in his arms, and kissed him,
and lifted his voice in prayer to Zeus and the other immortals: 475
'Zeus, and you other immortals, grant that this boy, who is my
   son,
may be as I am, pre-eminent among the Trojans,
great in strength, as am I, and rule strongly over Ilion;
and some day let them say of him: "He is better by far than his
   father",   480
as he comes in from the fighting; and let him kill his enemy
and bring home the blooded spoils, and delight the heart of his
   mother.'
   So speaking he set his child again in the arms of his beloved
wife, who took him back again to her fragrant bosom
smiling in her tears; and her husband saw, and took pity upon her,
and stroked her with his hand, and called her by name and spoke
   to her: 485
'Poor Andromache! Why does your heart sorrow so much for me?
No man is going to hurl me to Hades, unless it is fated,
but as for fate, I think that no man yet has escaped it
once it has taken its first form, neither brave man nor coward.
Go therefore back to our house, and take up your own work,   490
the looms and the distaff, and see to it that your handmaidens

ply their work also; but the men must see to the fighting,
all men who are the people of Ilion, but I beyond others.'
　So glorious Hektor spoke and again took up the helmet
with its crest of horse-hair, while his beloved wife went home-
　　ward,   495
turning to look back on the way, letting the live tears fall.
And as she came in speed into the well-settled household
of Hektor the slayer of men, she found numbers of handmaidens
within, and her coming stirred all of them into lamentation.
So they mourned in his house over Hektor while he was living   500
still, for they thought he would never again come back from the
　fighting
alive, escaping the Achaian hands and their violence.

                              (*Il.* 6. 369–502: trans. R. Lattimore, Chicago, 1951)

2

[212] We look first at the outside frame, and are immediately conscious of the hand of a poet who plans, organizes, constructs.

The 'act' of 'Hector in Troy' is an insertion into the battle action
of the *Iliad*, and the conversation between Hector and Andromache
is the third and longest of the three scenes which make it up—
Hector with his mother Hecuba (6. 242–85), Hector with Paris and
Helen (312–68), and Hector and Andromache (369–502). Before
this group of three scenes stands a short introduction (237–41), and
at the end is an epilogue (503–29). In the middle, after the Hecuba
scene, is inserted the narrative of the supplication to Athena, which
the goddess refuses (286–311). The whole is constructed precisely,
but without obvious design, as if nothing more than a slice of life.

The 'Introduction' shows Hector at the Scaean Gate surrounded
immediately by women and girls, who ask him about sons, brothers,
husbands. It is a 'crowd scene', aimed, as often in the *Iliad*, at out-
lining the general picture of the situation at the beginning, out of
which the important 'individual scenes' then arise clearly. Greek
tragedy later imitated Homer in the shaping of such 'expositions'.
Here the introduction strikes the keynote which runs through the
whole act: danger outside for [213] the army, anxiety and apprehension within the city. The emotional mood of the Andromache
scene is foreshadowed.

The final scene of all (503 ff.) advances the action on an external
level and back to the fighting. Hector has left Andromache, Paris

overtakes him, and the two brothers, reconciled, leave the city. One should appreciate the atmosphere here too. Paris is brimming with courage and strength like a horse which has broken free from its halter and merrily makes for the open country to bathe. And Hector's words at the very end (526) are optimistic: '. . . that we may set up the mixing bowl to the immortal gods in freedom in the palace, having driven the well-greaved Achaeans from Troy.' The poet needs this optimism after so much sadness, to give the act a tangible conclusion, and to link it with the heroic actions of Hector which have been provisionally granted to him.

From this outer framework grow Hector's three meetings. Throughout, the emotion increases and deepens, up to the meeting with his wife, which is evidently the purpose of it all.

The meeting with Hecuba takes place because Hector is supposed to bring about the supplication to Athena which is the reason for his return to the city. But there is more to the scene than that. A new mood, heavy with anxiety, is heard in the concern of a mother (254): 'My son, why have you left the fighting and come here? Surely because the Achaeans are exhausting our people, and you wished to raise your hands to Zeus from the highest part of the city. I will bring you wine, to make a libation to the god, and to give you strength.' And further: the first meeting shows Hector as a son, the second a brother and brother-in-law, the third a husband and father—three degrees of kinship, three levels of emotional bonds. And in all three relationships, Hector is the same; the man who cannot delay, since he must get back to the battle. For this manly attitude of Hector, the poet has created a wonderfully simple image: Hector [214] refuses the wine his mother offers him, 'for fear that it may curb his will and he may forget his prowess'; so in the next meeting he will refuse to sit down when kindly urged to do so by Helen; and this refusal of female comfort offered to him will finally show in greater depth in the scene with Andromache.

Still more directly does the second stage, Hector's visit to Paris and Helen, prepare for his meeting with Andromache. Immediately before the main scene the poet constructs a contrasting scene, to make the main scene's effect that much stronger. Before the pair Hector–Andromache comes the other pair Paris–Helen, in a diametrically opposed relationship. The weakwilled (523), inconstant (352) husband with his strong-minded wife, aware of honour and weary of her unworthy existence, contrasts with the hero and his simply loving wife, the mother of his son. Counterpoint is one of the most constant stylistic devices in the creative invention of the *Iliad* poet. It forces the reader's gaze along a particular line, and avoids any need for authorial comment. And the poet controls this device with such unobtrusive certainty that one does not notice the artistic intention to which one is nevertheless subject.

3

The same melancholy anxiety which has been evident from the beginning of the act hangs over the meeting of Hector with Andromache herself. It is concentrated now in the thought of Hector's approaching death.

At the beginning there are Hector's own words to Helen, that he does not know if he will see his family again. At the end of the scene there are the lamentations of the women in Hector's house, as if he were already dead. So much more tangible has the thought of death become in the course of the scene. In the scene itself, it is this that motivates both actions and words. Thinking of his possible death, Hector looks for his wife. Her anxiety for him, [215] when she heard of the defeat outside, drove her up to the wall. Anxiety about death initiates Andromache's speech, and it is with that thought that Hector's speech ends; his very last words (487 ff.) are about death in battle. In short, the whole meeting is conditioned by and imbued with this premonition. Hector is as good as dead already. We shall later consider what function the meeting of Hector and Andromache thus fulfils in the context of the *Iliad* as a whole.

The events themselves of the scene stream past us as if in full flood, but nothing becomes blurred. The individual parts are shaped and structured there too as clear as crystal. One can give them headings: *Searching and finding* (369–406), *Speeches* (407–440–465), *Coming together* (466–93), *Parting* (494–502). Everything is directed towards the goal of *Coming together*. The construction and nature of these stages of the action may be illustrated by a few suggestions, so that many other easily observed details automatically emerge for every reader when he looks at the passage himself.

Searching and Finding

What is special and meaningful in this prelude lies in the way the poet moves his two figures before he brings them together. He scorns the most obvious solution. For he could have arranged that Hector found Andromache where he looked for her, at home, weaving, or, like Helen, among her maids. But he does it differently. Andromache has left the house when Hector gets there. She has run to the tower at the Scaean Gate, almost out of her mind with anxiety. Hector, when he hears this, also hurries to the Scaean Gate. We do not hear that he himself has any intention of looking for his wife there, and the next phrase (393), 'whereby he would issue into the plain', gives us rather the impression that he intended to go straight back to the fighting if he did not meet her. But Hector does meet her. For she too [216] is already on her way back to the house. Why do the characters go back and forth like this? Why this delay in their meeting?

Delay creates suspense, and with the suspense grows the significance of what we have been waiting for. Hector ought not to come to his house in the casual way that any husband pops in to see his wife at home during a break from work. The meeting of Hector and Andromache is the single, and last visible, meeting of the two in the whole story of the *Iliad*. It had to be raised out of the common and everyday to the height of something lasting and essential. The poet achieves this through the simple movement of his characters. Before they find each other, they must first fail to find. And how brilliantly is this mutual failure achieved! While the husband looks for his wife in *her* sphere, the house, she has already been driven by her anxiety for him to approach *his* sphere, the tower, to look out for him on the battlefield. The same longing sends them across and past each other and apart, and when Chance—one can also say Providence—finally brings them together after all, this meeting, which was first endangered, but still in the end achieved, has the effect of something heartfelt and necessary, without a word being expressly said about it.

Much more could be said about the shaping of the details of this prelude. An inner drive controls the movements of both characters. But the husband remains composed and acts with self-control, as if fulfilling a duty, while the wife is 'like somebody out of her mind, like a mad woman', in the manner of women who suffer, hysterical, giving themselves to the pain. And how impetuous she is, in hurrying, urging, running. This again is a contrast with the broad calm of the housekeeper answering Hector's question. Again, this 'mad' anxiety of Andromache is not an everyday thing, but an advance indication of the catastrophe which is approaching. Or consider how the poet, at the very moment when Andromache finally comes near, stops the movement and gives an explanation of [217] her background, her father and her home, the two names of her child, of which the second reminds us in passing of Hector's vocation as defender of Troy.

After all this, we recognize Homer the dramatist, and see that it is not the case that his epic resembles a continuous stream, without beginning or end. Only very superficially may that seem so. The actual body of Homeric epic is as carefully constructed, as full of tension, as consciously articulated, as it could be. In particular, Homer creates movement, action; he *directs* his characters, and directs them in such a way that the hearer understands from mere observation what their position is, and in what relationship they stand. The poet saves words, particularly in circumstances where words could easily be obtrusive. Instead of them he uses restrained gestures. It is so right at the end. The father's silent smile at the sight of his son, the weeping wife coming close to him, the touch of a hand. This art of suggestion—hardly 'art'—derives from a great restraint in observing human affairs.

The speeches now arise out of this 'psychological' preparation. And as they speak, the two characters, who have just come together, move apart.

The Speeches

The two speeches present an archetypal 'dispute'. The wife, taking the lead, and pleading with strong emotion, tries to bring the husband over to her side, so that he may preserve himself for her sake and that of the child. The husband resists her, firmly persevering in his mission, but with understanding.

The parties to the dispute are not characters whose so-called personal individuality is reflected in their language, or who pride themselves on the uniqueness of their thoughts and feelings. Nor is it a question of philosophical doctrines embodied in ideal figures, with wavy scrolls coming out of their mouths [218]. Nor again is this a kind of debate about who is right, as so often in the *agons* of late tragedy. Here the loving wife and the fighting husband stand opposite each other, and two worlds assert themselves in them, two basic realms of life, which although they fit together like two hemi-spheres become increasingly aware of their incompatibility.

Andromache speaks from an archetypal calling as a wife, nur-turer, and preserver of life. Her realm is the house, the family, with father, mother, brothers, child, and husband. She wishes to keep safe and preserve. And her demand is for natural happiness, saying to her husband, 'Be here!'.

In Hector, male heroism speaks. He alone is Troy's protection; his realm is the battlefield outside. His 'happiness' is action. Simple existence and life are expendable. All his efforts are directed towards duty and glory, in which his value as a man is realized and will live on into the future.

So both wife and husband speak from the full, total necessity of their existence, which was sketched out for them in the law accord-ing to which they grew up, was shaped and hardened through the discipline of their rank and through their fate, and confirmed by the role which they now aim to fulfil. It is the fact that they each speak from the totality of their own personal position that makes their speeches so important and 'human'.

Andromache's speech is overwhelmingly subjective. She senses in Hector something that she does not understand, which separates him from her—that 'stubbornness', 'strength of will' (*menos*), that heroic impetuosity in him which drives him into danger and indeed to death. (The poet represents this self-destructive force of heroic impetuosity twice in lion similes: 12. 41 ff., especially 46; 16. 751 ff., especially 753. Andromache speaks of it again at 22. 457 ff.) It is this which in her first words sparks off the outburst arising from her love for him, in which she too is so impulsive. The suppressed emotion shows in the 'jerkiness' of the first sentences, which run on with enjambement line after line (407–12). For her, his heroic impulse is heartlessness, lack of pity. And her whole speech turns into one [219] single, widely extending plea for pity, that he should preserve himself for her and the child. (A so-called 'ring-composition': 407–31, 411 ff.–29.)

Her father and brothers were killed; her mother died of grief. She has only Hector now; and even more, combined in him, she has all that the others had been to her. She speaks very naturally and feelingly of the warm comfort that he gives her (412). As the value of her husband grows for her in the enumeration of the bereavements she has suffered, she dwells for a long time on the past. And in dwelling on what fate has brought up to this point, she raises an ominous presentiment about the future. For in the background the menacing (and yet again gentle) figure becomes visible of the man who will soon kill her husband as well, Achilles.

The circle of her speech is completed by the request that Hector stay on the city wall. But her anxiety makes her go further. With the claim of her love, the wife ventures into his male sphere, when she presumes to dictate to him a strategy for defence. Anyone who cuts out this end of the speech (433-9), as Aristarchus first did, expects the wife of Hector to ask her husband to act dishonourably. Her appeal that he should stay by the wall becomes acceptable and reasonable only through the details of the plan that she gives and the reminder of earlier attacks there. In her loving lack of understanding, this reasoned argument is in itself affecting. Her useless attempt to follow obstinately the dictates of her love and control her husband in war as well, which is 'men's business', is the final logical step of her anxious heart.

Andromache is not a hero's wife like many in German saga and many Spartan wives and mothers. She does not achieve the inner strength of Helen, who urges her husband into battle. The poet could not place that sort of wife next to Hector. Nor does she have the greatness of the divine mother Thetis, who admittedly [220] warns her son of his coming death with quiet words (18. 95), but calmly approves of his resolution (18. 128), and even acts to help him. On the other hand, one should not make the mistake of unconsciously letting the picture of the Homeric Andromache blend with the sentimental female figures of the bourgeois, idyllic minor epics of the eighteenth century. Andromache's love has a quality that is absolute and elemental; it is not for nothing that the poet describes her in her anxiety as 'like a woman gone mad'.

Hector's speech in reply reflects the self-assertion of a man and his world against the constricting pressure of the woman. Against her agitation there comes from her husband a massive calm; against the lack of understanding which arose from her love there comes from him an understanding which adds a great gentleness to the firmness of his speech.

Hector appeals to obligations which are both external and internal. He is concerned about the talk of the citizens, which in that society was the inflexible source of honour or dishonour; and through it, perceptible in a sense of 'shame', there comes to the hero 'from outside himself' what we would call 'duty'. But this duty—always to be the best, to fight in the front of the battle, not to dishonour the reputation of his father and to protect his own reputation—is precisely what he as a man of princely blood has 'learned'. What was once a matter of instruction and example has long since become second nature to him through his breeding. No part of his being opposes it.

That is Hector's reply to his wife—not a matter of refutation, because there are two worlds in conflict here, but the clarification and vindication of his natural and moral need to show his 'defiance', a trait which to her mind is only self-destructive and without pity.

But this perseverance of Hector in what his origin and nature prescribe for him is actually strengthened by his foresight of the future. Before Hector too stands the destiny of his death. But because he is the defender of Troy, for him, unlike for his wife, this fate expands immediately into the common fate of his people, in fact into the coming destruction of holy Ilium. The words [221] which bring about the famous line, 'For I know this thing well in my heart . . .' (447), make an abrupt change in Hector's speech; but the theory that they are 'borrowed' from elsewhere (4. 164–5) is not a sufficient explanation. Behind this knowledge of the future destruction lies an unspoken 'But all the same!' To fight, Hector does not even need hope.

Unnoticed, his thoughts go further. His vision of the future is narrowed, and everything else is pushed into the background behind the single destiny of his wife. Just as Andromache looked back to the deaths of her father, mother, and brothers, to replace all of whom she now has Hector alone, so Hector looks forward to the approaching miseries of his parents and brothers, and the pain of all of them troubles him still less than the pain of his wife when some man drags her away, and she must be a slave in Argos, Sparta, or Thessaly, and the inquisitive local people point at her and recognize in this humbled figure the wife of Hector. One must feel how the husband's sympathy wells up in the description of these accumulated details in one single unbroken sentence,[1] and how the

---

[1] Not noticed by most editors and translators who punctuate heavily at the end of line 461. Even after 463 it is better to put a colon than a full stop, since 464–5 gathers up everything which came before.

agonizing thought of his own name dishonoured in the humbling of his wife blends in with this, until his feelings finally force themselves out in the wish, 'better dead before that!'

One can see without further explanation how the two speeches, in their thought and their shape, in their parallels and contrasts, show detailed correspondences with each other. Each of the two characters is painfully anxious about the fate of the other. But, although bound together by their pain and love, they are still in essence deeply separate from each other, for personal happiness and greatness do not naturally or automatically come together.

Coming Together

At this point the action takes a sudden and unexpected turn. A third person takes a decisive part in [222] events, and effectively brings their separation to an end. This third party is the child, the boy Astyanax.

Once again it is necessary to observe the language of gesture, in the acts of reaching out, taking, and passing on, and to interpret it accurately. This kind of interpretation might be suspected of daring to attribute to Homer's descriptions the possibility of ambiguity, or symbolism. This would not be the first time this happened to the poet. No! This is not 'symbolism'. But what we do have is the brilliant exactness of an intuitive wisdom, which simply perceives what is alive (where lesser ages would beat their brains out) and cannot perceive it any differently than by perceiving in it the simple meaning of life.

The father stretches out for the child. The nurse is still carrying it. The child is terrified and cries out; he struggles against his father in the shining helmet and waving crest. The parents laugh; the helmet must be taken off. Now the child comes to his father. He kisses him and prays. After his prayer, he now hands the child to its mother. And she, who previously cried, and now has to laugh after all, thus laughs amid her tears. And Hector caresses her. It is the only physical tenderness from the husband in the whole scene.

The movement of the child to the father, and from the father to the mother, forces the figures visibly together. At the end, the three of them form (one would like to say) a closed group as if in sculpture . . . The development of the wife's moods is equally clear in thematic terms. Her laughter, drawn forth by the child, does not overcome her tears, but combines with them, both equally valid.

And what, from inside, created this coming together? A happy incident, and a solemn look, one close after the other.

The simplicity of a child's nature, which Homer knows well [223] (cf. 15. 262, 16. 7), forces them, in spite of everything, to the relief and release of laughter. But that is not all. The hero finds in his child an unexpected opponent. And when this small champion of the wife in his own way protests against his father's military appearance, this time his complete simplicity is stronger than all the passionate intensity in the world. What the wife failed to achieve on the large scale, either by passionate exhortation or by rational advice, the child manages for a moment on the small scale. The bronze helmet with its horse-hair plume is put on the ground. And with the child in his arms, the father has now entered the world of those who are closest to him.

Then he prays.

Now he sees in the child his son. Once again the future opens before his sight, but now with all that is painful removed. The hope which he did not entertain for himself transfigures his spiritual legacy to his son. He prays that in this preserver of his blood and race his own self may be preserved and enhanced, as protector of Troy, defender of his fatherland; and that the manliness of his son may bring joy to the mother.

In hopes, longings, wishes, man experiences in the most simple and basic way his impulse towards the ideal; and a particular case lies in what parents hope for in their children. Also, Hector's wishes for the future of his son have this power of rising above the distress and conflicts of the present; and as they look up to the still dormant picture of the future son, in whom the enhanced personality of the father will be the mother's joy, the two parents are as one.

The coming together of Hector and Andromache has now reached its goal. As Hector sees his wife, uncertain between laughter and tears, his heart opens up. She had begged for 'pity', and now he does 'pity' her. Now for the first time he actually answers her speech, by consoling her.

[224] 'Unhappy woman', 'Impetuous one', 'Driven by an incomprehensible force, a demon'—with the same untranslatable word (*daimonios*) she had begun her argument against him. In her

unrestrained indulgence in the passion of her suffering, he now senses the same mysterious force of an uncontrollable, unpredictable impulse, as she saw in his fighting. And he speaks further, and for the first time openly, of what has been on her mind, the possibility of his death. No man's weapon can wound him unless it is fated. That is his consolation for her, and it is certainly a consolation which inspires confidence, or at least strength to endure. Hector's heroic mission is not diminished by it, but rather justified in a new way. Wherever his sense of honour may drive the noble hero, wherever glory may lure him, he cannot escape his fate, the portion allotted to him. The thought has broadened into the religious sphere, as Homer understands religion—as an affirmation of what cannot be altered.

Parting

Moments of inner exaltation strengthen human beings for their life, but in life they also pass, and reality makes its prosaic demands. One can hardly express in how matter-of-fact a way and how austerely Homer separates again the togetherness of the husband and wife, unconcerned for the more tender desires of many of his later readers. The two spheres, home and war, which our interpretation attempted to recognize and distinguish from the beginning, are now harshly juxtaposed. And Hector warns that they must return each to his and her own sphere. It is one of the places in early epic where we hear an advance echo of Plato. What awaits them is the dull everyday principle: that each of them—the wife with her spinning, the husband in the field—should 'attend to their own task' (Plato, *Republic* 433a, b).

A few touches bring the scene to an end. Hector takes up his helmet, his wife finds it hard to leave him, and her tears [225] flow again. And as in his house the women, overcome by weeping, mourn for Hector, although he is still alive, as if he were dead, so from that time on, whatever feats of arms Hector will still accomplish, he remains for the audience of the *Iliad* a man forfeit to death.

The deeply convincing realism—the complete naturalness and instinctive truth in the meeting of Hector and Andromache—rests on the fact that in this particular husband and wife Homer truly made husband and wife meet, and thus placed the meeting on one of the great basic polarities which sustain human life. Such composition by polar contrasts is one of the main strengths of Homer, to whom everywhere in his poem the reality of the world discloses itself in the opposition of the great polarities.

4

The end of the scene directs our view beyond its boundaries. How does the meeting of Hector and Andromache fit into the whole of the *Iliad*? We will limit ourselves to facts.

This recommends itself for this reason alone that some scholars have really believed that the act 'Hector in Troy' once existed as an independent 'single lay' (with a now-lost opening showing Hector in the presence of Priam and the Trojan counsellors: see Wilamowitz, *Die Ilias und Homer*[2] (Berlin, 1916), 310–11; G. Jachmann, 'Homerische Einzellieder', *Symbola Colonensia* (1949), 1 ff.). But the number of possibilities in the evolution of a great work of literature cannot be so restricted by the making of a few stylistic judgements and the discovery of a few 'inconsistencies', together with the inferences drawn from them, that only the one or the other explanation remains valid. A poet who e.g. works 'scene by scene' may easily rouse the suspicion of having not only composed from previously existing sources, imitating and inventing, but also taken over pre-existing 'single lays' word for word. Such a poet, moreover, particularly if he composes for oral performance over a period of several days, will also have to create transitions, back-references, foreshadowings, in which it is not always possible [226] to be certain to what level of exactness everything has to be 'motivated'.

The 'act' *Hector in Troy* is an episode when viewed from the standpoint of the battle narrative of the *Iliad*. But this 'episode' is of decisive importance for the great opposition between Achilles and Hector, which comes more and more strongly into the foreground from the beginning of the third and longest day of fighting (Book 11), and, after the killing of Patroclus by Hector (Books 16 and 17), becomes virtually the single theme of the poem. The great opponent of Achilles could not remain a mere outline. He had to be developed into a character, close to the hearer and familiar both as a hero and as a man, with his own personality and destiny. This is the achievement of the act *Hector in Troy*, with its three meetings of Hector with Hecuba, Paris/Helen, and Andromache. We cannot conceive the *Iliad* without it. It belongs to the group of acts in the

first third of the epic (Books 1–7) which make us familiar with characters, things, and relationships, together with the 'view from the
wall', 'Agamemnon's review of the army' lined up in battle formation, and the 'quarrel of Achilles and Agamemnon' in the first book.
One can observe how the most important heroes of the great drama,
Achilles, Agamemnon, Odysseus, Paris, Menelaus, Diomedes, and
so on, are here introduced. The poet has, not without reason, saved
the development of the figure of Hector to the end of this first part
of the *Iliad*. Hector's stay in Troy shows him as the defender of the
city to which he belongs, just as his following duel with Ajax (Book
7) shows him as a great fighter. His meeting with Andromache constitutes the 'internal' climax of this whole two-sided presentation of
Hector. Here his argument with her, who is nearest and dearest to
him, reveals most clearly his true character.

Over Hector's meeting with Andromache lies the gravity of the
danger to which the army is exposed outside on the plain. Without
Hector's mood, one weighed down with concern, the poet could
not have developed his character so deeply. For the sake of this
invention, [227] he had to put up with a Hector who removed himself from his army in a situation of great danger. In my opinion, jus-
tifying this 'improbability' by means of a religious errand for
Hector was not a bad device. The danger to the Trojans came about
with an easy and smooth transition from the advance of Diomedes;
and Diomedes is emphatically named in Andromache's last words
(437) (Wilamowitz, *Die Ilias und Homer* (Berlin, 1916), 307). That
connects our act *Hector in Troy* in the sixth book closely with the
aristeia of Diomedes in the fifth. A bond back to the third book is
made in the meeting with Paris and Helen. Helen speaks of her husband with the same sad contempt (6. 344) as she did on his inglori-
ous return from his duel with Menelaus (3. 399, 428) (cf. also 3. 139
ff.). That Hector at first supposes an anger in Paris that keeps him
from the battle (326) is no reason at all for assuming an older and
different stage of the poem. Anger was the noble weakness of these
lords, whose lives were dominated by strong instincts; it was a common theme of early Greek epic, as also of the epics of related
peoples, and thus was sufficiently likely to be taken up in passing.

The Hector–Andromache scene, like the whole act of *Hector in
Troy*, is closely tied in with its context, the first third of the *Iliad*,
which broadly and diversely develops the situation and lays the
foundation for what happens later.

Through the meeting of Hector and Andromache runs the thought of Hector's later death, and by the end this thought becomes a certainty for the listener. In that respect the sixth book looks forward, long before Hector begins his *aristeia* in Books 11 to 18, to his death in the duel with Achilles in Book 22. The meeting with Andromache is the 'last' time the two of them are together. An observant reader can work it out that Hector returns once more to Troy (7. 310), and must presumably also have seen Andromache again. But that is of no consequence to the poet, [228] because he does not *show* the husband and wife together again. But he *does* show us Andromache again at the end of Book 22 (after Hector's death) in such a way that we cannot fail to think back to the Andromache of Book 6.

The connections of Book 6 with the end of the *Iliad* go still further. Clearly recognizable echoes connect the speeches of Briseis and Achilles in Book 19 (19. 287–300, 321–37) and that of Priam in Book 24 (24. 486–506) with Andromache's in Book 6. But at the end of the last book, three women really do raise the cry of mourning for the laid-out corpse: Andromache, Hecuba, Helen—the same three whom Hector encountered in Book 6. In Andromache's speech here some thoughts from the earlier encounter are heard once more.

Finally, the connections with Achilles. Achilles was present in the background at Hector's meeting with Andromache. Andromache spoke of the killer of her father and brothers, and without knowing it thus named the future destroyer of her husband. That Andromache also knows of the reverent respect, the gentleness of Achilles, agrees with his portrait in the rest of the *Iliad*.

The poet had an eye on the figure of Achilles in another way too when he portrayed Hector in Book 6. We saw that Hector's imminent death becomes a certainty for the hearer particularly at the end of the scene. But the poet avoided giving Hector himself the certain knowledge of approaching death, which Achilles has had since his first meeting with his mother (Book 1). Hector thinks of death, he expects it. He believes that Troy will be destroyed at some future time. But all the same he hopes for his son. He will make good his quarrel with Paris when they celebrate the feast of freedom and have driven the Achaeans from their country (6. 526). It appears that the poet knew what he was doing when he placed Hector, in the Andromache scene, in the shadow of coming [229] death, but withheld from him the clarity and freedom of action which comes from the certainty of death, which belonged only to the greatest hero of the *Iliad*, and to no other. This can only become fully clear later, from Achilles himself.

Achilles' Decision

W. SCHADEWALDT

I. SUMMARY AND TRANSLATION

Patroclus has been killed.

Wearing Achilles' armour he had gone out at the moment of greatest danger, extinguished the fire which had already fallen on one Achaean ship, and driven the Trojans back again onto the plain. Sarpedon and many others have succumbed to him. But he forgot Achilles' warning to return after he had thrown back the enemy, that Apollo was the Trojans' friend. Struck on the back by Apollo, so that his armour fell from his body, he was wounded by Euphorbus, slain by Hector, and fell under Troy's walls.[1]

Now the battle is over his corpse. Menelaus has quickly taken revenge on Euphorbus for Patroclus' death, but Achilles' weapons are now Hector's spoil. While they continue fighting painfully under the blanket of mist, back in the camp Achilles as yet suspects nothing of his friend's death. He has heard only an obscure prophecy from his mother: that he will conquer Troy not without him and not with him. Then Zeus grants victory to the Trojans, and Ajax sends Menelaus to tell Antilochus to take news to Achilles. Tears spring to Antilochus' eyes and he leaves without a word. Now they pick up the dead man to carry him back. The Trojans follow like a pack of hounds after an injured boar, constantly giving way when he turns on them. The battle rages like a fire roared on by a gale; and the Achaeans carry the dead man away like mules, sweating and straining to drag a tree-trunk down to the valley by a steep path; and as a wooded ridge on the edge of the mountains [235] blocks the water streaming towards the plain, so the two Ajaxes set themselves against the mass of Trojans. But on the other side, Aeneas and Hector attack from behind and the Achaeans flee screaming, like a swarm of crows from a hawk.

From: W. Schadewaldt, *Von Homers Welt und Werk* (Stuttgart, 1959), 234–67, reproduced by kind permission of the Schadewaldt family.   [1] *Il.* 16. 786 ff.

Abandoned pieces of armour litter the edges of the ditch, and there is no check to the fighting.[2]

Book 18, verses 1 ff.

So they fought on like burning fire, and Antilochos came quick-footed with the news for Achilleus. He found him in front of the horned ships. His mind was foreboding what had indeed come to pass, and (5) in dismay he spoke to his own great heart: 'Oh, why are the long-haired Achaians once more being driven in terror across the plain back to the ships? May it not be that the gods have brought that hateful sorrow on my heart that my mother once revealed to me, saying that (10) while I still lived the best of the Myrmidons would leave the light of the sun under the hands of the Trojans. It must surely be that the brave son of Menoitios is now dead—obstinate man! I told him to come back to the ships once he had driven away the enemy fire, and not face Hektor in full fight.'

(15) While he was pondering this in his mind and his heart, the son of proud Nestor came up close to him with his warm tears falling, and gave his painful message: 'Oh, son of warrior Peleus, there is terrible news for you to hear, which I wish had never happened. (20) Patroklos lies dead, and they are fighting over his body. It is naked now—Hektor of the glinting helmet has his armour.'

So he spoke, and the black cloud of sorrow enveloped Achilleus. He took up the sooty dust in both his hands and poured it down over his head, soiling his handsome face: (25) and the black ashes settled all over his sweet-smelling tunic. And he lay there with his whole body sprawling in the dust, huge and hugely fallen, tearing at his hair and defiling it with his own hands. And the serving-women that Achilleus and Patroklos had won in war shrieked loud in their hearts' grief, and ran out (30) to flock round the warrior Achilleus: all of them beat their breasts with their hands, and the strength collapsed from their bodies. And to one side Antilochos mourned with his tears falling, and he held the hands of Achilleus as his glorious heart groaned: he was afraid that Achilleus might take a knife and cut his own throat. (35) Achilleus gave out a terrible cry, and his honoured mother heard him, where she sat by the side of her old father in the depths of the sea, and she wailed loud in response. And the goddesses gathered round her, all the daughters of Nereus who were there in the deep of the sea. There were Glauke and Thaleia and Kymodoke, (40) Nesaia, Speio, Thoë, and ox-eyed Halië, Kymothoë and Aktaia and Limnoreia, Melite, Iaira, Amphithoë, and Agaue, Doto and Proto and Pherousa and Dynamene, Dexamene and Amphinome and Kallianeira, (45) Doris and Panope and famous Galateia, Nemertes and Apseudes and Kallianassa: and Klymene was there and Ianeira and Ianassa, Maira and Oreithyia and lovely-haired

---

[2] 17. 722 ff.

Amatheia, and all the other daughters of Nereus who were there in the deep of the sea. (50) The silvery cave filled with them; and they all beat their breasts together, while Thetis led the lamentation: 'Listen, Nereids, my sisters, so you can all hear and know the sorrows in my heart. Oh, my misery! Oh, the pain of being mother to the best of men! (55) I bore a son who was to be noble and strong, the greatest of heroes, and he shot up like a young sapling. I tended him like a plant in the crown of a garden, and sent him out with the beaked ships to Ilios, to fight the Trojans. But now I shall never welcome him back (60) to Peleus's house—there will be no home-coming. And yet all the time I have him alive and looking on the light of the sun, he is suffering, and I can give no help when I go to him. But even so I shall go, to see my dear child and hear what it is that has come to grieve him now he is withdrawn from the fighting.'

(65) So speaking she left the cave, and the others went with her full of tears, and the swell of the sea parted round them. When they reached the fertile land of Troy, one after another they came up on to the shore, where the Myrmidons' ships were beached close-crowded around swift Achilleus. (70) His honoured mother came and stood by him as he groaned heavily, and with a high wail she took her son's head in her arms, and spoke winged words in sadness for him: 'Child, why are you crying? What pain has touched your heart? Tell me, do not hide it. Look, all that you asked has been brought about (75) by Zeus, when you held out your hands and prayed that all the sons of the Achaians should be penned back by the sterns of their ships through want of you, and be put to terrible suffering.'

With a heavy groan swift-footed Achilleus said to her: 'Mother, yes, the Olympian has done all this for me. (80) But what pleasure can I take in it, when my dear friend is killed, Patroklos, a man I honoured above all my companions, as much as my own life. I have lost him, and Hektor who killed him has stripped the huge armour from him, that lovely armour, wonderful to see, which the gods gave as a splendid gift to Peleus (85) on the day when they brought you to a mortal man's bed. If only you had stayed in your home with the immortal goddesses of the sea, and Peleus had married a mortal wife! But as it is there must now be countless sorrow for your heart too, for the death of a son you will never welcome (90) back to his home—since my heart has no wish for me to live or continue among men, unless first Hektor is struck down by my spear and loses his life, and pays me the price for taking Patroklos son of Menoitios.'

Then Thetis said to him with her tears falling: (95) 'Then, child, I must lose you to an early death, for what you are saying: since directly after Hektor dies your own doom is certain.'

Swift-footed Achilleus answered her in great passion: 'Then let me die directly, since I was not to help my friend at his killing—he has died far away from his native land, (100) and did not have me there to protect him from destruction. So now, since I shall not return to my dear native land, since I have not been a saving light to Patroklos or my many other companions who have been brought down by godlike Hektor, but sit here by the ships, a useless burden on the earth—(105) I, a man without equal among the bronze-clad Achaians in war, though there are others better skilled at speaking—oh, that quarrels should vanish from gods and men, and resentment, which drives even a man of good sense to anger! It is far sweeter to men than trickling honey, (110) and swells to fill their hearts like smoke—such is the anger that Agamemnon, lord of men, has caused me now. But all this is past and we should let it be, for all our pain, forcing down the passion in our hearts. And now I shall go, to find the destroyer of that dear life, (115) Hektor—and I shall take my own death at whatever time Zeus and the other immortal gods wish to bring it on me. Even the mighty Herakles could not escape death, and he was the dearest of men to lord Zeus, son of Kronos; but fate conquered him, and the cruel enmity of Hera. (120) So I too, if the same fate is there for me, will lie finished when I die. But now my wish is to win great glory, to make some of the deep-breasted Trojan and Dardanian women wipe the tears with both hands from their soft cheeks and set them wailing loud, and (125) have them learn that I have stayed too long now out of the fighting. And do not try to keep me from battle, though you love me—you will not persuade me.'

Then the silver-footed goddess Thetis answered him: 'Yes, child, this is true—it is a good thing to save your stricken companions from stark destruction. (130) But think, your fine armour of gleaming bronze is in the Trojans' possession: and Hektor of the glinting helmet is glorying to wear it on his own shoulders—but I do not think that he will have his pride in it for long, as his own death is close on him. No, you must not enter the fray of war (135) until you see me returned to you here—in the morning, at the sun's rising, I shall come bringing you beautiful armour from lord Hephaistos.'

So speaking she turned away from her son, and facing her sisters of the sea she said to them: (140) 'You now go back into the broad lap of the ocean, to visit our father's house and the old man of the sea, and tell him everything. I shall go to high Olympos, to Hephaistos the famous craftsman, to see if he will give a glorious set of gleaming armour for my son.'

(145) So she spoke, and her sisters quickly slipped down through the swell of the sea. And then Thetis, the silver-footed goddess, went on to Olympos, to bring back glorious armour for her son.

(trans. M. Hammond, Harmondsworth, 1987)

[240] 2

The whole of the *Iliad* is divided into three great acts.

1. The net of widely spreading preliminaries and other earlier events (Books 1–9).
2. The day of the great fight, which sways this way and that, which, with the advance of the Trojans up to the ships towards evening, fulfils the promise which Zeus made to Hector in the morning (Books 11–18).
3. Achilles' heroic battle: from his reconciliation with Agamemnon, his arming and setting out, up to Hector's death and the reconciliation brought about by the great double settlement— the funeral of Patroclus, and the ransoming of Hector's corpse (Books 19–23/4).

The story of the wrath of Achilles emerges only gradually from these varied events, but increasingly in a more concentrated way, like a stream which, in its long upper reaches, is hardly distinguishable from the many tributaries which feed it, but which then establishes its direction and, despite a number of backward loops, does not deviate from it and ends in dominant flow. But where the middle reaches flow down to the lower ones, a sudden fall interrupts it. It is here that the reader of our scene is standing. What he experiences is collapse, and a new turn.

How much that has been promised is now fulfilled! The Achaeans are defeated, as Zeus promised to Achilles through Thetis; Hector and the Trojans are victorious by the ships. But the fulfilment is implicated with disastrous loss. At the moment when Achilles' unbending wrath yields, duty now demands that he take revenge. Vistas of greatness open up for him, but greatness which can be achieved only by death.

At this turning point of events, dominating the *Iliad's* whole field of vision, stands our scene, the decision of Achilles.

[241]   3

Its narrower field of vision is the *Patrocleia*, the 'act' which extends from Patroclus' departure to the rescue of his corpse.[3] It comprises two clearly distinguished actions: Patroclus' *aristeia* (Book 16) and the fight over his body (Book 17). The *'aristeia'* and the 'fight over a body' are traditional, basic themes which the poet modifies and

---

[3] Schadewaldt indicates a footnote for p. 241 in the text but does not actually give it later.

147

develops in many ways in his *Iliad*. Here in Patroclus' *aristeia* he created the most beautiful of all his *aristeiai* (after Achilles' great one, that is), and out of an otherwise narrowly limited theme of the 'fight over a body' there developed a long song, filling a whole book.

After a 'prelude', which with the sending out of Patroclus by Achilles makes for the inner (16. 1–100) and outer (130–256) preparation, the *aristeia* rises in a three-stage structure: (i) expulsion of the enemy from the ships (257–418); (ii) fight with Sarpedon and the latter's death (419–683); (iii) Patroclus' death (684–863). Quite a few older prototypes can still be sensed under the surface, but not distinguished; and it should be mentioned here without elaborating in what masterly fashion the individual parts are structured throughout.

A 'fight over the body' by nature does not permit movement in one direction only. As in a painting a pair of fighters stands fixed over the man killed in battle, so here too the dead man becomes the centre of a fluctuating conflict which lasts for a long time. After two brief solo feats on either side—Menelaus' revenge on Euphorbus and the stealing of the armour by Hector (17. 1 to 139)—the battle starts afresh with mutual speeches of encouragement from the leaders, Hector's rearming, and exhortations to the two armies (140, 184, 212, 237). Then the narrative develops via a long chain of smaller individual scenes until it comes to rest on the fate of Achilles' horses (426–542). In between, individual parts are juxtaposed in doublets: Antilochus suspects nothing and neither does Achilles (377, 401); twice there is an agitated speech from Zeus (201, 443). [242] The final stage of the act stands out clearly. On either side, Athena and Apollo call the men afresh to battle (453, 582). Finally, since Zeus gives predominance to the Trojans (593), Antilochus is sent to Achilles (640–701), and the body is rescued (708–61). The image of this withdrawal, five similes packed together, makes evident not only the development of the course of events, but also its many different facets—the yielding and turning, the heat of battle, the dragging off of the body, the resistance, the flight.[4] This results in a finale, carried by the polyphony of exterior and interior conception, which is sometimes shaped out and sometimes not, as only the Homeric simile can create it.

Our scene has been in preparation for a long time throughout the

---

[4] Differently U. v. Wilamowitz, *Die Ilias und Homer* (Berlin, 1916), 152 ff.

course of this act. Already at Patroclus' departure, our eye looks forward to what is to come, to Achilles. He, the absent one, is present in the narrative several times, and especially in the 'fight over the body' we feel his growing proximity.

Already in the prelude, some apparent concern communicates itself to us as Achilles warns his friend about the attack on Troy, and about Apollo (16. 89). And this intensifies when at their farewell he prays: 'May Zeus grant his follower strength and victory and bring him back safe.' The poet adds (16. 249 f.) that Zeus granted the one but refused the other. Again, at the beginning of the last part, when Patroclus rushes towards his death (16. 686 f.), the poet says: 'If Patroclus had obeyed Achilles' words he would have escaped.' Later, after Patroclus' fall, the words with which Hector mocks the dying man (16. 837) concern Achilles. 'And Achilles, great as he was, did not help you! And yet he certainly drove you on repeatedly while he stayed behind, and you went out with orders not to return until you had split Hector's bloody cuirass.' Achilles had done exactly the opposite, and his great grief later in our scene (18. 100) is that he did not help, as Hector says mockingly here.

[243] Menelaus wants to save the corpse for Achilles (17. 104, 121), and his doubt how Achilles would be able to save it without any weapons (17. 711) exactly prepares us for the later salvation of the dead man by Achilles (18. 202). Here one of those instant vistas opens itself up by which Homer usually makes simultaneous events in different scenes visible. We see Achilles still unsuspecting, soon afraid, soon to know, back in the camp (17. 401); and as in our scene a prophecy of his mother's will suddenly become clear to him in his foreboding, so here another enigmatic saying, which he quickly seizes on, remains obscure to the unsuspecting Achilles.

Towards the end, the internal impetus of the plot towards Achilles becomes so powerful that a straight side path is made to branch off the main event with the sending of Antilochus to him (17. 640). The way the thought occurs to Ajax, the way he relays it to Menelaus, and Menelaus takes it up, crosses the battlefield to Antilochus, passes on the order, and Antilochus rushes off—this is not idle expansion: by this means, we are guided for a time along that path which then, in the background, leads on to Achilles. And so we approach the passage in which our scene is embedded, at that exact moment when, in the field, steps are being taken to rescue the body, but at the end of which the rescue itself is again endangered. It is that 'fertile' moment, shortly before the climax of the danger. Later, when Thetis has departed, the retreat with the body continues. Now comes the greatest emergency: Hector grabs the dead man by the foot. Then, summoned by the gods' messenger Iris, Achilles arises and terrifies the Trojans by the fiery gleam of his appearance, the trumpet sound of his cry. Then, speechless, he takes his place by his friend's bier and the sun sets (18. 241).

This embedding of the decision scene into the last stage of the fight for the body had its consequences. Achilles was now able to rescue his fallen friend himself [244] and act for him already here, just as he will avenge him later. And if the rising flood of the Trojan attack, which neither Ajax nor Menelaus could repel, is halted by his mere appearance, without arms, we can already feel here something of the superhuman power to which Achilles increasingly rises after he takes the field.

Besides, the whole ordering of events has two other advantages, one generally technical, one particular.

As the train of action ending here (the *Patrocleia*) and the one starting newly here (the great *aristeia* of Achilles) clamp and interlock, so also the beginning of the *Patrocleia* and the preceding battle for the ships had been clamped together with an overlapping connecting passage (16. 101–24). And this confirms what is valid elsewhere too for Homer's great epic: this epic avoids letting individual 'acts' meet in dead areas. There is supposed to be uninterrupted continuity in the epic, as in life, where endings and beginnings are also intertwined. So the epic contains only few actual incisions or pauses, e.g. before the beginning of the great day of battle (Book 11), roughly in the middle of the *Iliad*.

The effect of this ordering in our particular case is more important. If this same meeting of mother and son had been placed after the *Patrocleia* had finished completely and the dead man had been rescued, it would not, as now, be an island beset by storms of worry and the crisis of battle, and the deep inner decision in it would not be experienced from the tension of pressing events. That precisely was its purpose.

It was great, sure-footed art that succeeded in thus embedding the psychological drama of Achilles' decision in the active drama of great heroes wrestling.

4

The events of the scene itself proceed in three images: (i) Achilles before the ships (18. 1–35); (ii) Thetis and the Nereids at the bottom of the sea (35–65); (iii) Thetis and the Nereids with Achilles (65–147). But this trinity of images is not a mere paratactic sequence of events. From one image to the next, outward activity fades more and more into the background and the spoken word more and more comes to the fore.

First, much activity and many single three-dimensional objects: here the ships, there the log cabin, in the background the battle; and in addition to these, gestures, running, beating of breasts, falls. In the second image, only the glimmering cave is visible and the Nereids rushing there, but Thetis' lament grows beyond this. In the last image, there are only outlines of location and outward action, only the arrival and departure at the beginning and the end, and Thetis taking Achilles' head in her hands. Apart from this, activity and single events have retreated, and the conversation now develops before us as the dominant element. The whole scene is a progression from the visible to the invisible, which can be perceived only by the inner eye.

What the poet allows to develop in this way here is Achilles' decision, which is born from his great grief. Admittedly, he does not describe the real course of events. The apparently most important element, *how* Achilles reaches his decision to take revenge, is passed over.[5] However, the poet is not interested in the actual process, which is perhaps interesting psychologically. He *is* involved with the great realities which condition the decision. And he lets these develop without any gap through the three images which complement each other continuously: the grief which is fate and conditions fate, fate here and now which embraces what has happened and is to come, the figure of the hero who experiences fate in grief and, from the enlightening presence of that all-embracing fate, knows what he has to do.

---

[5] People have been wondering: 'Where is Antilochus then, where are the maids, how is Achilles so changed now!' But it is good Homeric handicraft, to bring to the fore again at a later stage an action in front of which another has momentarily pushed itself. How effusively would one have to praise the skill of an imitative poet who in the first image found the end of an older 'Patrocly' ready (up to 34), then patched a 'connection' (35 ff.) and achieved this!

[246] We will now follow the course of the scene, and observe how Achilles' decision develops in it image by image.

The Grief of Achilles

At the beginning, the motif of 'bad news', which is rich in possibilities, underlies everything. Homer does not concern himself with any psychology of the bringer of the bad news, or explore the 'tragedy' of the bringer of bad news, as Greek tragedy sometimes does later. He does not even make use of his usual 'epic repetition'. Above all, the narrative does not simply run its course paratactically: Achilles already has a foreboding of what is coming. The dreadfulness of events is anticipated in Achilles' presentiment.

This 'anticipation' through presentiment, supposition, knowing beforehand, achieves a great deal in Homer's narrative art. We observe it in small details, e.g. at the beginning of the *Patrocleia* when Achilles already knows what Patroclus wants (16. 17 ff.), and extensive areas of events are affected by it. It contributes considerably to Homer's conciseness (*syntomia*) which the ancients praised many a time. How it gathers in and tightens up the narrative here!

We are drawn into Achilles' mood immediately. We hear Antilochus' message as if with *his* ears. What else would it have to explain, to develop! The event makes itself known through the message and Achilles collapses speechless with grief.

Here the poet has grasped the essence of presentiment in a profound way: metaphysically, not psychologically, as an inspiration in the atmosphere of approaching disaster. Again, the way in which, in such prophetic presentiment, his mother's old unexplained saying about the death of the 'best of the Myrmidons' suddenly springs to his mind and explains itself is not just artistic truth. And precisely in this way the saying has a profound effect: predetermined through the prophecy, Patroclus' fall does not affect Achilles simply as a loss and mere misfortune, but as his *own* fate. [247] The poet shows Achilles' grief through description, seventeen verses of pure description. One is almost frightened by the precision with which the scene unfolds move by move. How the 'modern' poet would ground the image of such grief in the colours of vivid sympathy. But Homer's matter-of-factness is not unfeeling. When the seriousness of an event shows its terrible countenance, such as here, it is as if the poet's eye were silently growing larger, and in the austerity of his gaze, in the concentration of the look which follows the action and fixes it, we feel the most passionate sympathy.

The three-stage structure of the description develops from this. From the sublime silence of the hero's actions as he performs the traditional mourning rituals (23–7) rises the agitated picture of the serving-girls, who having come in lamenting beat their breasts rhythmically according to custom until one after the other they sink down (28–31). Then the 'group of two' separates itself from this throng—here is Antilochus holding down Achilles' hands, for Achilles might kill himself, and then, with Achilles' cry, the whole scene reaches its climax and abruptly ends.

A number of detailed features could be highlighted: for instance, how at the beginning the eye first observes the action, and then its effect, and how it concentrates for a little longer on the sight which has arisen: 'and around the clean tunic the black ash was scattered'. Or: how the same word in the same place links the verse endings which report the disfigurement of his face and hair (24, 27). Or: how the name of Patroclus, where it is mentioned in passing next to Achilles, stands last, full of emphasis (spondaic). However, these details which should show how close an observation Homer's art tolerates and demands should only be touched on here. But, at the end, the comparison should teach us just how far this description of the grief of the *Iliad*'s greatest hero is elevated above anything comparable in the poem.

Priam too is cast down by grief after Hector's death [248] (22. 408 ff.); and when Andromache sees Achilles' horses dragging off her dead husband, she collapses unconscious (22. 466 ff.). On both occasions, the poet also resorts to description, but does not develop it into a very extensive structure. He dwells on individual characteristics, which speak to us symbolically. Priam behaves as if the whole of Troy were already up in flames, and he wants to run out through the gates; when she collapses, Andromache loses the cap which Aphrodite had once given her as a present when Hector was leading her home in marriage. But, above all, the description of grief both times only makes a transition to an immediately ensuing speech, and the speech is the important thing.

On the other hand, Achilles' grief speaks through his gestures, and when the gestures work themselves up into that cry, no speech develops out of it, but the scene changes. Later, when the scene changes back and speech is possible, Achilles' grief has been mastered by the decision he has taken. And later still, when Achilles finally weeps for the dead man, he does so in a controlled lamentation (18. 324 ff., 19. 315 ff.).

It is the wordlessness that is the important element in Achilles' grief. This grief is not an expression, it is an event. First breaking grandly out with all the power of the elemental, later reflectively, aware of fate, clear about the future, determined—it was out of the question to convey this through intermediate stages. The description of grief did not tolerate any 'beyond', it could only break off, disappear from our view behind the picture now pushing itself forward: Thetis and the Nereids.

The Lament of Thetis

Thetis has heard her son's cry in the deep. She sobs, the Nereids run together round her, and Thetis raises her lament among them. The action develops in outline in a series of speedy strokes but its fleeting course is stopped to dwell on a long list of the Nereids' names: a 'catalogue'. Because of its [249] 'Hesiodic style', is it unworthy of the *Iliad* poet, as already the ancient Greek interpreters of Homer thought? But in Homeric epic there are 'catalogues' too. The 'catalogue' as such was no invention of Hesiod, as if it had not existed before; it is very ancient, and for that time not in the least 'unpoetic'. But if you look at it patiently, this Homeric catalogue of Nereids reveals a symmetry and loveliness of formation which elevates it far above the similar catalogues in Hesiod[6] and other ossifying epic.

This list of names is structured into two *Stollens* (39–42, 43–6) and one *Abgesang* (47–8). The *Abgesang* is clearly marked off through the resumption of the initial formula 'there was . . .'. The conjunctions allow us to recognize the structure of the two *Stollens*. At the beginning of each *Stollen* the names hurry past lightly in quick succession (linked by τε), then they move along more heavily (τε . . . καί and καί). In the second *Stollen* the heavier movement begins earlier than in the first. So they grow increasingly heavier, and also the colour and inner fullness of the names seem to grow increasingly in the second *Stollen*.

---

[6] *Theog.* 240 ff., 349 ff.

The poetic gain is not inconsiderable. Only now does the multitude of sea maidens gathering together speak to our senses, indeed in a solemn and magnificent way. This elevates the sea scene, the counterpart to the activity above of the serving-girls round Achilles, above the events on earth. Moreover, at this period names are not mere denotations; and the Nereids are living divinities. In these euphonious names, which are significant names throughout, we sense an aura of the friendly-many-sided sea, of that great, divine element perceptible by the senses, and thus the cruel impression of the first image[7] fades and dies away. So we are already more distanced when we hear Thetis' lament.

It is spoken in the full certainty of the heavy grief which has now broken in upon her. As soon as his mother heard Achilles' cry, she cried; it cried out of her. Even now, there is no enquiry about what has happened, what was coming over him. 'Listen so that you [250] will know!', she begins, as if she were prophesying and revealing something in the course of testifying. She prophesies her fate as a mother, and with it, at the same time, Achilles' fate.

Again, when Achilles called her to him at the beginning of the poem, she had lamented (1. 414 ff.): 'If only it had been granted to you to stay carefree and at ease beside the ships, since Fate has given you so short a life, so little time. But now it seems that you are not only doomed to an early death but besides you suffer more than anyone else.' But at that stage, when everything was beginning, she was dwelling more on the daily toil of his existence. But if, at that stage, she was the one 'who had borne him for disaster' (*aina tekousa* 414, 418), this idea has now been reconstructed to produce a quite unique word formation: 'Woe to me, disaster-hero-bearer (*dysaristotokeia* 18. 54).' She then expands on what this one word comprises and dwells on her son's life, past and future: how he grew up in all the glory of his youth, how she used to cherish him with the care of the gardener,[8] how she sent him away and will never receive him back again. All this has already been decided, as far as she is concerned, and she is conscious of how irrevocable it is.

As a more recent Greek scholar saw so well,[9] Thetis and her

---

[7] 'Pleasant sounding like the splashing of the calm sea it calms down our excitement . . ., makes us receptive for the quietness of the conversation between mother and son', says Wilamowitz, *Ilias und Homer*, 165.

[8] The image of a tree growing up is elaborated more closely in the beautiful simile, *Il.* 17. 53 ff.

[9] I. Th. Kakridis, *Athena* 42 (1930), 66 ff.

women lament after the form and ritual of those who lament for the dead, as if they were already lamenting a dead man in Achilles. Homer had before him Thetis' and the Muses' lament for the actually dead Achilles, a lament which introduced the final episode of his model, the *Aithiopis*, which we now know to be pre-Homeric. What was there intended for the dead Achilles, Homer transferred in the *Iliad* to the still-living Achilles and he achieved a great deal by this transfer. Something like an atmosphere of death now overshadows this scene in which Achilles commits himself to revenge and his own destruction, which means (since Homer is of course not concerned with mere 'atmosphere') that already here the presence of death dominates. (In Hector and Andromache's encounter too, the women were already lamenting for the living Hector as if for the dead (6. 500)).

[251] Finally, through 'anticipation', the scene at the bottom of the sea clearly prepares for the conversation between son and mother which then ensues. Thetis gives vent to her grief for her son in front of her trusty sea sisters. In the conversation with Achilles, her grief for Achilles, like his for Patroclus, will indeed still be audible, yet restrained and perceptible only in the margins.

The Conversation

A narrow, self-contained frame of action encloses the conversation (65/9–138/47).

The simple arrival and departure offered the poet the motive for this. He did not give it in the most concise form, in the quick way that his gods probably move in other instances, as Thetis too did in her first arrival (1. 359) when she rose from the grey sea 'fleeting like a mist'. Here the women move through the sea weeping, and in a long row, as women on geometric vessels often do, they climb up to the shore where Achilles is lying, groaning in his grief, near the ships which have been hauled up together.

Could one ask why the Nereids actually come along, merely to be sent away again at the end without really participating? This arrival and departure join the beginning and the end of the conversation in an incomparably simple way. But other elements, too, have a part to play. It exalts the hero and his grief that friendly deities sympathize with him like this. Aeschylus developed this idea afresh with the Oceanids in his *Prometheus*. Here are a mild glimmer of the fantastic from the depth of the sea, a silver cave, a wandering through the parting waters,[10] all of which plays around the margins of the seriousness of the internal action. In other instances too, the figure of Achilles projects into the world of the elemental–divine quite unlike that of his adversary [252] Agamemnon and his opponent Hector.

What connects mother and son from the first in the conversation is, again, not words, but the silent gesture which in its silence is all the more telling, uniting the two figures as in a 'group' of sculpture: Thetis with her son's head in her hands like that of a dead man. It is a position we know from geometric pictures.[11] But the conversation is not a purely human, intimate expression of togetherness between a mother and her suffering son. Nor is it a clash of two worlds either.

We saw Achilles first through Thetis' anxiety, then through her grief, then we heard in her lament the outline of his fate. Now his own speech reveals the great necessities, inner commitments and comprehensive forces in which he stands and from all this, as decisively as never before, Achilles' fate—we can say just as well: Achilles' true character rises.

Thetis begins in a motherly way: 'Speak your mind!' She had also started in this way when she had first come to him (1. 362 f.). Now she introduces a mild admonition into her consolation: 'For your wish has now been fulfilled.' Already here the beginning and end of the whole action which has been covered come together.

Achilles speaks out. Zeus has fulfilled everything down to the last detail. Empty fulfilment!—His friend has perished, who had been like his own life to him, and his arms are lost to Hector. His speech dwells on the lost arms, a fact which already occupied the ancient commentators. We think what a marvel the pieces of noble, 'divine' handicraft were for those people, and how the warrior is attached to his weapon and loves it as a living being. But the weapon is above all the manifest symbol of a warrior's honour: it is like a piece of the hero himself. Something of Achilles' victorious [253] magic had gone out in Patroclus' arms: and Hector had triumphed over Achilles himself when, earlier on, in the fight 'he put on the imperishable armour of Peleus' son Achilles, which the gods of Heaven had given to Peleus, his father. Peleus, when he grew old, had

---

[10] Cf. also *Il.* 13. 29.

[11] Dresden pot in W. Müller, *Nacktheit und Entblößung* (Leipzig, 1906), tab. V 5. Cf. *Il.* 23. 136; 24. 724.

passed it on to his son. But the son was not destined to grow old in his father's armour' (17. 194). Achilles, too, now comes to dwell on the divine origin of his weapons, and then on the day when the gods presented them to Peleus at his wedding.

Greek artists represented Peleus' wedding as a great solemn feast.[12] Poets like Pindar[13] praised it for its exaltation of mortals by the gods, and Homer must have known it in this form already,[14] since he knows about its presentation of arms to Peleus. Now, entirely corresponding to the old form of the legend in which the sea maiden is forced into marriage with the mortal,[15] it has for his Achilles become the day of disaster, which dragged the divine women who became his mother down into the miseries of mortal existence. With this speech, Achilles has returned to the origin of his own fate, and if his grief for her corresponds with the pain which she suffers for him, this generates a tender harmony between her lament at the bottom of the sea, and his speech here.

But in tracing back the path of her fate, he has also imperceptibly been gliding over into his own future. The fact that he will not return to his homeland is to him a simple 'So it is'. With these words, Achilles' decision is made: we did not see when, or how. Achilles *stands* in the necessity of the fate given to him. We shall return to this.

For Thetis it is only a confirmation of what she had foreseen anyway. She repeats it to him once more, quietly, as if from a melancholy deprived of all hope. And the old, vague prophecy of his early death now turns into a clear prediction: 'immediately after Hector . . .'.

And so begins his great speech, a creation without parallel. [254] The word moves its wings in a truly passionate beat, and magnificently free it forces its way beyond what has passed and what is to come. Now Achilles bursts out from the grip of his 'merciless' harshness. He pulls himself up as if leaping, then bends down once again under the weight of his painful memories, then tightens himself and takes aim. His will is pure as fire. It does not struggle, for it reflects necessity, and sounds in advance the deed to come.

He begins ready to die in the certain knowledge of death, and for this reason doubly ready for revenge; and from here, with a triple 'Now' (101, 114, 121), the great central movement pushes forward.

[12] Cypselus case, Sophilus vessel, François vase.
[13] *Nem.* 4, *Nem.* 5, *Isthm.* 8.   [14] *Il.* 24. 62 f.   [15] Cf. *Il.* 18. 432 f.

Already, with his first word, he is impetuously beyond death.
Immediately after Hector—no, immediately and directly now . . .
Patroclus has died and he has not helped him: so he must *now*
avenge the dead man, he wants to say; but with the argument 'he
won't return home again anyway (γε)' he is again beyond death.
The future which awaits him is precisely *not* only the consequence
of his own decision, but the given reality of fate, determining *him*
no less than the past which has conditioned him. And it draws him
deeply and more deeply back into the past. As his thoughts drive
along and things come up one after the other, and arrange themselves in two series of chains, one after the other (101/6, 107/11),
the poet increasingly makes us feel the torment Achilles is suffering: he did not help Patroclus (he says it for the third time), he did
not help his comrades either who died *en masse*, and he himself was
sitting idly by the ships, a man who does not have an equal in battle—in counsel others are probably better: (here he is thinking of
that first assembly which, it is now indeed clear, did not find him
well advised), and from his pent-up torment breaks out his curse
about strife and wrath, the demon against which not even [255]
reason protects him, so sweetly does it instil itself into man—just as
at the time when the lord of peoples had angered him: Agamemnon. Like a sign of the origin of all evil, his adversary's name thus
comes last of all, and Achilles lets the past be past, under compulsion masters himself and turns to the future. *Now* he will take
revenge and accept death according to the will of the gods. It is the
fate of heroes, the fate of those whom Zeus loves. He recognizes in
Heracles' image the necessity of his death even more profoundly.
Later, through the image of Patroclus 'who also died and was far
better than you' (21. 106), Achilles himself will make the necessity
of Lycaon's death clear to him. But *now* he still wants to gain glory
for himself, and from reflection his speech now rises to a menacing
savagery.

That impetuous, elemental streak, which slumbers 'like a lion'
(24. 572) in these people, now bursts out and his thirst for revenge
dwells cruelly on the image of the coming terrors—doubly cruel,
through the scorn transparent in his indirect way of speaking of the
many tears of women, not the numerous deaths of men.

Looking back one realizes: the forces of the soul, pent up in the
description of grief contained in the first image, are here set free in
Achilles' great speech. The double emphasis of the scene rests on

the description of grief at its beginning and Achilles' speech at its end. A total structure of very finely balanced proportions rises above the three 'images', since Thetis' lament at the bottom of the sea and Achilles' first words in their encounter also leant towards each other. But the weight of this counterbalance has been shifted towards the rear. Symmetry in living poetry is never schematic.

Achilles' great speech is an event no less than his silent grief. The past is being squared, the future is already being shaped. Passion gives internal impulse to the soul. But this passion does not create confusion. It is an expression of the highest prophetic certainty. It [256] covers displeasure, torment, reflection, and thirst for revenge, and in doing so leads to the great dominating realities and reasons out of which Achilles' heroic work is constructed. At the end, the figure of Achilles stands firm above all fluctuation, obsessed with action, ominous, the aura of divine menace surrounds him and will not leave him until Hector has finally fallen.

Thetis says nothing against her son's decision, nor does she lament either—she will tell her troubles once more to Hephaestus (18. 429 ff.). She can only agree, and help her son prepare the ground for his final task. For, however much this mother is attached to her child's life, it has been given to her that she *understands* her son out of her knowledge of the inevitable. In this understanding of her son, in Thetis the *divine* mother has been raised far above the merely loving foolishness of human wives and mothers: Andromache, Hecuba, Penelope.

The end of the scene is shaped with brilliant simplicity: the characters separate. '*You* will dive into the depth of the sea . . . *I* will go to Olympus . . . And the Nereids dived under the waves of the sea . . . She went to Olympus . . .'. There is at the end a consonance between Thetis' order to the Nereids and its execution, and this results in a fading away, as at the close of many a piece of music. And again the spacious halls in the background open up: the depths of ocean where the sympathetic old man of the sea waits, and— Olympus, with Hephaestus, source of the new weapons.

The last word of Thetis' speech to the Nereids paints the radiant splendour of the new armour (*pamphanoonta*). He who from a hundred examples knows the strength and purpose of notions of light in Homer must feel how in this description of his arms' splendour something rather like a prophecy for Achilles rises up here at the end of the scene.

One fact which we have not yet mentioned is of great consequence for the significance of the scene in the whole of the *Iliad*. In the closest proximity to Achilles' decision in Book 18 there is a decision by Hector, and this has obviously been placed there as a counterpart to our scene.[16]

Patroclus' corpse has been rescued and night has closed in. The Trojans now hold council in the field, and Polydamas proposes to return to the city: if Achilles were to meet them outside the next day, anyone who escaped unhurt to Ilium could count himself lucky. Hector contradicts him, arrogantly, imperiously. He refers to Zeus' promise of victory (which was, however, limited only until sunset).[17] 'But if Achilles has really arisen near the ships, so much the worse for him! I will not yield to him . . .'. The Trojans cheer him. 'Fools,' the poet says, 'Pallas Athena had destroyed their judgement.' Achilles' words, that he would overtake the killer of Patroclus, still ring in our ears;[18] Thetis had then confirmed that Hector's death was near.[19] And next day, when disaster overtakes Hector, who will himself face death,[20] the poet will make Hector think back to the voice of the warner Polydamas, and make him become aware of his delusion.

The approaching death of Achilles as well as that of Hector is—as far as they themselves are concerned—decided at the same stage in the plot of the poem. But these decisions are as different in kind as the two opponents, bound by fate, are different in nature.

Achilles *knows* about his death, which he goes to meet in pursuit of his revenge. Hector, in his delusion of victory, in his error-strewn blindness, entangles himself in it.

This difference highlights the greatness of Achilles' decision [258] even more. But it has been prepared in the *Iliad* for a long time.

Hector is already standing in death, but without knowing it himself for certain, in his encounter with Andromache, where his *persona* is outlined for the first time;[21] and at the end of the second day of battle, his *persona* passes into a sinister twilight when, in overbearing delusion of victory, he predicts ruin for the Achaeans on the next day, although the listener has just heard from the mouth of

---

[16] 18. 243–314.   [17] 11. 193.   [18] 18. 114.   [19] 18. 133.
[20] 22. 100.   [21] Above pp. 141 f.

the father of the gods that Hector will be victorious only until the son of Peleus arises (8. 473).

In order to honour Achilles, Zeus through Iris promises Hector victory 'until he should reach the ships'.[22] After heavy fighting, Hector reaches the ships and then stands there, buoyed up with great confidence based on Zeus' promise. 'Bring fire here! And let us all together raise our battle cry! Today Zeus has given us the day which makes up for all the ones past: we are taking the ships which, having landed here against the will of the gods, created so many sufferings for us through the cowardice of the old men who impeded me and the people, every time I wanted to carry the battle to the ships. But if Zeus took our judgement away from us until now, now he drives us on himself and orders it!'[23]

But this confidence is groundlessly maintained, even when Hector, with Zeus' promise fulfilled, has exceeded the height of his deeds. With Patroclus' fall, the poet again moves him visibly into the ambit of approaching death. When, with Apollo's blow, Achilles' helmet falls off Patroclus' head, Homer says: 'never before had dust been allowed to defile this helmet . . ., but now Zeus gave it to Hector to wear: death was near to him.'[24] And from here on, exaltation and delusion continue to remain linked together in the figure of Hector. The poet himself watches him with strangely mixed feelings of admiration, displeasure, and sympathy.

[259] In the middle of the battle he adorns himself with Achilles' weapons—as if he himself had plundered them from Achilles. Then Zeus looks down upon him, and is struck by the monstrosity of the deed which the man, destined to die, dares to commit, but at the same time pities him, and shakes his head: 'Unhappy man! Little knowing how close you are to death, you are putting on the imperishable armour of a mighty man of war, before whom all others quail. And it was you that killed his comrade, the brave and lovable Patroclus, and with irreverent hands stripped the armour from his head and shoulders. Well, for the moment great power shall be yours. But you must pay for it. There will be no homecoming for you from the battle, and Andromache will never take the glorious armour of Achilles from your hands.'[25]

But the god concedes to him as a last favour only a part of the glory which Hector has 'unlawfully' usurped, not all of it. He sees

---

[22] 11. 191 ff.   [23] 15. 718.   [24] 16. 796.   [25] 17. 201.

Achilles' divine horses mourning Patroclus: they are standing fixed like tombstones over the graves of a man or a woman, their heads lowered, weeping, their manes hanging down in the dust.—There he is seized by the same feeling as Achilles in the conversation with his mother: that the divine, in its participation with humans, must also participate in human suffering, and again he shakes his head: 'Poor beasts! Why did we give you, who are ageless and immortal, to King Peleus, who was doomed to die? Did we mean you to share the sorrows of unhappy men? For of all creatures that breathe and creep about on Mother Earth, there is none so miserable as man. One thing I will not have: Hector, Priam's son, shall not drive you and your splendid chariot. Are the arms and the brief exultation they have brought him not enough?'[26]

For Achilles' arms to fall into Hector's hands, Achilles had to lend them to Patroclus when he left to fight. Homeric scholarship long ago recognized this lending of the arms as the poet's own invention. But the particulars are rather meagre. In this way, the poet wanted to make possible the 'inclusion' [260] of the description of the shield—of an existing older 'poem' of which he was ever so fond—or the insertion of the break in the battle.[27] A cleverly invented motif brings its creator ten- and twentyfold fruit. Here, long before the two opponents come to blows, Achilles from a distance has an effect on Hector's fate through his divine arms, which are like a piece of himself. But the god's interpretation guides the listener's view forwards towards the end. In this way, events which span a long period undergo a shift in a definite direction.

Hector is the man unknowingly doomed to die, to whom even the warner speaks in vain, and so he remains in all his greatness. Near death, such a person must weaken, on account of his ignorance. Indeed, before the duel with Achilles, he will remember the warnings to which he had turned a deaf ear, will think of ways in which he could preserve his life at all costs[28] and, unable to withstand the sight of his opponent charging at him, will flee until the goddess dreadfully deceives him and he succumbs to Achilles.

Achilles too, right from the beginning, stands in the shadow of death. But he himself has always been aware of his early death. This consciousness is at first only shadowy. Only in the progress of events does it assume definite features. We distinguish three main stages.

[26] 17.441.   [27] Book 18/19.   [28] 22.111 ff.

In the first book, where the poet lays out Achilles' nature and fate for the whole of the *Iliad*, Thetis and Achilles just talk about Achilles' 'short existence'.[29] In the negotiations with Agamemnon's embassy, he knows through his mother that fate offers him two choices: if he stays at Troy, he will lose his homecoming but win undying glory; if he returns, he will lose his glory but will live long.[30] At the end of the book, Achilles is willing to stay.[31]—In the decision scene, finally, his mother's new prophecy connects his death with his revenge, and fixes [261] it temporally 'just after Hector'. From now on, Achilles is always accompanied by this certain knowledge of his death.

When his thoughts turn to the past and his dead friend, he quietly becomes aware that it had been fated that both of them should redden the same Trojan earth;[32] the same urn will contain the ashes of them both.[33] Or he thinks of his aged father and also knows that the old man lives worried by constant fear of the sad news of his death,[34] and he will not be able to nurse him in his old age.[35] Thoughts of death in the last book generally form the background to Thetis' mourning for her son,[36] as also to the speeches which Achilles and Priam exchange. In the course of the actual revenge itself, our eye again and again glances forward to Achilles' death.

He leaps onto his chariot to drive out, and his horse Xanthus prophesies his death.[37] He says: 'Xanthus, why do you prophesy my death? I know it myself . . .! Nevertheless! I will not desist!' Lycaon entreats him for mercy, but he pushes him away and says: 'Friend, you too must die. Why make such a song about it? Even Patroclus died . . . And look at me. Am I not big and beautiful, the son of a great man, with a goddess for my mother? Yet Death and sovran Destiny are waiting for me too. A morning is coming, or maybe an evening or a noon, when somebody is going to kill me too in battle with a cast of his spear or an arrow from his bow.'[38] The river god presses him hard and, fearing a miserable, watery death, he hastily prays to Zeus: '. . . my own mother, whose false predictions fooled me. She said I should fall to Apollo and his flying darts under the walls of the cuirass-wearing Trojans.'[39] And the dying Hector prophesies that he will die at the Scaean Gate at the hands

[29] 1. 352, 416. [30] 9. 410. [31] 9. 650 ff. [32] 18. 329.
[33] 23. 244. [34] 19. 335. [35] 24. 540.
[36] 24. 85 f., 93 f., 104 f., 131 f. [37] 19. 400 ff.
[38] 21. 106. [39] 21. 273.

of Paris and Apollo. Then he says that he will accept death at whatever hour Zeus and the immortals want to accomplish it.[40] They are, not by accident, the same words with which in our scene too he professes his readiness to die.[41] [262] The poet has set up well in advance a clear counterpart to Hector's death at Achilles' hands in the description of Patroclus' death at Hector's hands. There the dying Patroclus had prophesied Hector's death to him. But Hector did not see his death—did not want to see it: 'Patroclus, why do you prophesy death to me? Who knows whether Thetis' son Achilles might not lose his life before by my spear!'[42]

The lines of fate of the two opponents run through the whole *Iliad*. First, they run with interruptions, so that they lose each other in the mass of battles and events. Then, they converge, faster and faster. In the duel between Achilles and Hector they meet.

But the beginning of our Book 18 is the place where the two lines run closely parallel for a time. In the two scenes of decision they take the same final turn, however different in type and direction.

In all of this we recognize the designing hand of the poet. Through long-term 'anticipation' he oriented the figures of his two main heroes towards their coming death. In this way, he attracted the listener's sympathy especially for these two. In this way, he endowed them, above all others, with their own destiny.

But again, he also distinguished these great heroes from one another. He made the one go to meet his death knowingly and readily. The other drifted towards his destruction, swept away by an 'impulse' which is wholly noble, and under a delusion to which the deity itself initially gave rise and which a not ignoble error makes fatal.

On the whole we find that throughout the *Iliad* both heroes, the one doomed to die without knowing it and the one ready for death in full knowledge, are referred to each other and matched with each other in such various ways that it would have to be a miracle [263] if all that had not originated from the thoughts of *one* man, *one* poet.[43]

---

[40] 22. 355.   [41] 18. 115 f.   [42] 16. 859.

[43] On Hector and Achilles cf. Schadewaldt, *Iliasstudien* (3rd edn., Darmstadt, 1966), 108 f. The interconnection of character and fate of Homeric heroes has recently been worked out by H. Gundert in the characters of Agamemnon, Hector, and Achilles, *Neue Jahrbücher für Antike und deutsche Bildung* (1940), 225 ff.

Two facts which have emerged on the way should be emphasized.

First, from the point of view last adopted, certain parts of the *Iliad* moved closer together. These parts, roughly characterized, were: the prelude to the whole poem (Book 1); the introduction of Hector in the encounter with his wife (Book 6); Achilles' negotiation with Agamemnon's messengers (Book 9); the special prelude to the great decisive battle (Book 11) whose first part[44] sets Hector on his fated course through Zeus' promise of victory, while Nestor's advice to Patroclus in the second part of the book[45] initiates the *Patrocleia*; then the block of the *Patrocleia* with the decision scenes and the reconciliation (Books 16–19); and finally Hector's death (Book 22). Of these parts, the first half of Book 11[46] has up till now been regarded as particularly old, without justification as has been shown elsewhere.[47]

These parts form the structural skeleton of the whole poem. They are the supporting pillars of Homer's original '*Achilleid*'. Homeric scholarship up till now has regarded most of these parts as 'recent' or 'recently revised'. This is justifiable, since in comparison with the mass of sources for which he dug a new bed in his poem, the poet who created the *Iliad* in the eighth century is 'recent'—and he must look 'recent' where he is at his most original and creative.

Second, from the decision scene onwards, the lines of the plot had been interlaced particularly purposefully. Especially through prophecies, which spoke out more and more clearly, the outline image of Achilles' death was continually enriched and completed. The following series resulted: 'immediately after Hector'—Thetis to Achilles;[48] 'through a god and a man'—the horse Xanthus;[49] 'through the shot of a spear or an arrow'—Achilles to [264] Lycaon;[50] 'below Troy's walls through Apollo's arrows'—Achilles in the battle with the river;[51] 'Paris, Apollo, the Scaean Gate'—dying Hector to Achilles.[52] Besides this Apollo, too, seems more and more to assume the characteristics of the future avenger.[53] He threatens Achilles when they meet before Troy, he threatens openly in the gods' council in the last book.[54]

---

[44] 11. 1–596. [45] 11. 597–848.
[46] A 1, Wilamowitz, *Ilias und Homer*, 182. [47] *Iliasstudien*, 1 ff.
[48] 18. 96. [49] 19. 416. [50] 21. 113. [51] 21. 277.
[52] 22. 358. [53] 21. 228; 22. 7. [54] 24. 53.

Are these ever-sharper prophecies a sign that Achilles' death used once to constitute the end of the *Iliad* (Wilamowitz)? I think that we need to distinguish between the 'references in advance' to things which are supposed still to come and the 'anticipation'; as a result of the latter, a future event unfolds its strength in the present—and spends its strength.

Homer had something greater in mind than making the mere fact of Achilles' death the final point of his poem. So he transferred the co-operation of Apollo and Paris, a god and a man, which in the *Memnonid* had been linked with Achilles' death, to Patroclus' death through Apollo and Euphorbus–Hector, and so raised Patroclus' death above that of all the other heroes of the poem. To Achilles' death on the other hand he gave a higher kind of presence than the presence of the merely factual. He left the outer event outside but treated it as a future one in such a way that it was able to unfold its significance fully into the poetic present.

6

From the perspective of a few counter-images, which show the same basic occurrence but shaped differently, we finally look back on Achilles' decision.

In the second part of his *Aeneid* Virgil has given his hero a new 'Patroclus' by his side in Evander's young son Pallas. When in battle the news of Pallas' death reaches Aeneas [265] it affects him deeply. And the hospitable table which Evander had offered to the stranger and the obligation he took on come before his eyes.[55] Later, at the youth's bier, he thinks that he has broken his word and neglected his duty.[56] 'Haec mea magna fides? . . .'

Achilles lacks such a feeling of oppressive responsibility, of his very own guilt. No scruple of the soul torments him. What he has failed to do grieves him, as for example when he says that he let his friend perish,[57] that he did not help him when he died, that he is uselessly burdening the earth;[58] but the torment of repentance does not depress him. He may lament that it was vain when he promised Menoetius the father that he would bring his son home full of glory after Troy's fall;[59] Virgil had this passage in front of him. But,

---

[55] *Aeneid* 10. 515. [56] *Aeneid* 11. 45. [57] 18. 82:
[58] 18. 100 ff. [59] *Il.* 18. 324.

Achilles continues there, Zeus just does not grant fulfilment to all designs of men.

In one of his most beautiful trilogies Aeschylus created a tragic *Achilleid* after Homer's *Iliad*. There, after Patroclus' death, Achilles sees himself in the image of a mortally wounded eagle which by the shaft of the deadly arrow in his body recognizes his own feathers which 'lent wings to' the shot:[60]

> So it is nothing external then, it is our own wing
> of which we die . . .

The course of action of the *Iliad* too is disposed in such a way that Achilles himself becomes the reason for his friend's death. 'He *it is true* had sent him into battle with his chariot and horses', Homer says restrainedly and yet full of significance when Achilles finally stands weeping at his friend's bier.[61] But the Homeric Achilles himself does not say anything about the fact that something which had originated from himself ricocheted back and hit him and swept him away to disaster. He lacks the inclination to become conscious himself of his entanglement with his fate.

Clear, strong, straight feelings stir his heart. But there is no mirror of his soul which deflects and refracts these straight [266] feelings. And complete ignorance of the dangers of that consciousness of Hamlet: 'Thus conscience doth make cowards of us all . . .'. This strength of soul is the special form of *innocence* of Homeric man.

In this 'innocence' is the reason why no conflict, no inner discord affects Achilles, why the poet shows him as the person who *has made* his decision without the development of the decision becoming visible—not in the form in which people in tragedy and in later poetry decide 'consciously',[62] in fact not even in the way in which Homer himself indeed knows decision: as weighing-up, comparing different possibilities of action.

The poet puts such a weighing-up in Hector's mouth when his death is approaching[63]—not in Achilles'. The poet knows very well that strength and volition in man do not always keep step with each other. 'You *are* brave but you let yourself go and do not *want* to'

---

[60] Aesch. *Myrmidons* Fr. 139. Cf. my essay on 'Aeschylus' Achilleid', *Hermes* (1937), 52 ff.
[61] *Il.* 18. 237:
[62] Br. Snell, *Aischylos und das Handeln im Drama* (Leipzig, 1928).
[63] 22. 99 ff.

Hector once says to Paris.[64] In Achilles, strength and volition, being and volition do not diverge.

From all this, which the Homeric Achilles is *not*, comes anew the poet's unique shaping of the hero.

He gave him knowledge of his fate and with that the elevated existence in the presence of the future, a presence out of which his words in our scene express something so essential. In this knowledge of the future his Achilles personifies the complete harmony of a man with the necessity from which he affirms what has been allotted to him and goes to meet his fate.

Does this not also mean: Homer here created the first image of human freedom?

He who looks for freedom only where a will is engaged in struggle will deny it. But what man praises as his freedom is only a kind of different, higher restriction, and beside the struggling will, there is that spontaneous [267] decisiveness which is there where the great character, kindled and penetrated by that which must be, *cannot do otherwise*. One can then say: he wants to, one can also say: he has to; for, whether he wants to or has to, it arises out of his whole being in a state of exaltation which does not know any 'before' and 'after' but only the light, pure presence of what has been and what is to come. In the decision of Achilles, this kind of freedom has for the first time been made word in the west.

[64] *Il.* 6. 522, cf. 13. 234.

The Judgement of Paris

K. REINHARDT

A unique phenomenon in Greek mythology—though it is not clear enough what kind of phenomenon it is—is the story of the judgement of Paris. Consider: the three goddesses come to the shepherd Paris on Mount Ida, and each one promises him something: Hera, dominion over lands and kingdoms, Athena, heroism and victory, and Aphrodite, Helen. Since Aphrodite at least promises something, the story cannot be imagined without the promises of the other two. Which one is the most beautiful? This means: what are the highest fulfilments of the highest wishes of a mortal which the gods can grant him? Paris the shepherd prince is faced with the decision: greatest king? Or greatest hero? Or happiest lover—abductor and possessor of the most beautiful woman of all? Like Christ in the desert,[1] or like Hercules at the crossroads, he is faced with a temptation—except that he, unlike them, makes a choice which brings disaster on himself, his house, and his whole city. This is what happens to a ruler's house, however strongly it be constructed and however rich in sons it may be, once a young prince begins to prefer the goddess of love to Hera or Athena.[2]

From: K. Reinhardt, *Tradition und Geist* (Göttingen, 1960), 16–36, reproduced by kind permission of Vandenhoeck & Ruprecht, Göttingen.

[1] For the Indian parallels to Matt. 4 cf. Joh. Weiss, *Die Schriften des NT* (1907), i. 250; F. Dornseiff, *Zeitschrift für die neutestamentliche Wissenschaft und die Kunde der älteren Kirche* 35 (1936), 134. However, the judgement of Paris is as little related in its meaning to this as it is to the fairy-tale of Cinderella (H. Usener, *Kleine Schriften* (Leipzig, 1912), iv. 73).

[2] For the female beauty contests, Kallisteia, in the cult of Hera on Lesbos and of Demeter in the Arcadian Basilis cf. the references in Martin P. Nilsson, *Griechische Feste* (Leipzig, 1906), 57 and 336; in addition the literature on Alcman's *Partheniae*. Cultic usage is certainly one of a number of preconditions of the story about the judgement of Paris, but the judgement of Paris certainly cannot be traced back to just some *aition* of cult, any more than the story can have been invented to explain how the apple became sacred to Aphrodite, although these things also enter into it. On the other hand, everyone is free to rethink the story as they like into an ancient 'myth' and to imagine that Paris had once been a demon from Asia Minor, and therefore one of the abductors of the pre-Greek goddess Helen etc.

The story appears too didactic to be heroic. Homer does not mention it, with one exception—about which scholars quarrel. Tragedy likes referring to it, but avoids actually staging it. Euripides' *Alexandros*, which put the rest of the story of Paris' youth on stage, left out the [17] judgement of Paris. On the other hand, it *was* represented in one of Sophocles' satyr plays under the title of 'Krisis'. There Aphrodite appeared as Sensual Pleasure, Hedone, putting on perfume and inspecting herself in a hand mirror; Athena as 'Discipline', 'Reason', and 'Virtue' (Phronesis, Nous, and Arete) played games and anointed herself with gymnastic oil. The model for Prodicus' allegory—or parable, whatever you want to call it—of Hercules at the crossroads is unmistakable. But even if the goddesses have here been turned into comic-edifying travesties, located in Attic surroundings, and have almost become personifications of 'abstract conceptions', it still could not be said that Sophocles had treated them in this play totally contrarily to the original spirit of the story. Nowhere else in ancient legend do the gods come so close to allegorical meanings, nowhere else does ancient myth look so similar to parable. The later Stoics, and after them Baroque and Renaissance artists, were not so wrong in this instance to continue freely adapting the story as they felt fit: 'The shepherd on Ida who has to choose between the three goddesses shows how man, if left to himself, becomes by nature the slave of the life of mere sensual pleasure instead of the active and contemplative life (= Juno and Minerva).' So e.g. the 'Interpretation of the Fables' by Natale Conti, 1561.[3]

The story was known to Antiquity from the epic '*Cypria*' called after the Cyprian goddess, a prehistory to Homer's *Iliad* composed in post-Homeric times. Since people with justification regarded this whole cycle of epics complementing the *Iliad* and the *Odyssey*—which they called the 'epic cycle'—as a latecomer's work, finished hardly before the middle of the sixth century, such a story in such surroundings did not seem remarkable.[4] This sort of thing seemed to accommodate itself to the introduction of active personifications with a moralizing tendency, like the consultation of

[3] Quoted after Karl Borinski, *Die Antike in Poetik und Kunsttheorie* (*Erbe der Alten*, 10; 1924), ii. 30. The ancient stories and interpretations can be found compiled by Türk in Roscher's Lexicon of Greek and Roman Mythology under 'Paris'.

[4] The fragments of the epic cycle have been collected and commented on by Erich Bethe, *Homer, Dichtung und Sage*, ii (2nd edn., Leipzig, 1929). On the judgement of Paris ibid. 231.

Themis with Zeus to lighten the earth's burden through the Trojan War, Eris' apple, or Helen's birth from Nemesis, the goddess of 'Retribution': so related spirit [sc. in the story of Paris and Helen and the *Cypria*] reveals itself in related forms.

One discovery overthrew this scholarly chronology. An unquestionable judgement of Paris, the three goddesses one behind the other, [18] Aphrodite as the last, and smallest, and Paris with an overlong arm holding out the apple to her past the other, nobler two, was found, a significant decoration on an ivory comb from the first half of the seventh century (?), excavated by the English in the sanctuary of Artemis Orthia near Sparta.[5] What was the result? Some people updated the *Cypria* by a century or more, and Homer even more; others had the story circulating before the *Cypria* in Antiquity; in this way, they say, the allusion to it could be explained in the last book of the *Iliad* which, by the way, is also late in terms of content.

[5] R. M. Dawkins, *The Sanctuary of Artemis Orthia at Sparta* (London, 1929), 223 and table 127. The combs of this kind were found together with ware of the Protocorinthian and 'first Laconian' style. Protocorinthian ware first appears at the same time as geometric. As the presumed date of our comb, according to Dawkins, we have a span between 700 and 660 (p. 222) or roughly 700 (pp. 209 and 221). We still have to take into account that dating these objects, which were more precious and used for longer, according to pottery of the same time can only with certainty give a *terminus ante quem* (Dawkins, p. 221). If e.g. the comb pictured on table 130 (dying Ajax) was found together with Laconian ware of the third style and is accordingly dated to the first half of the 6th cent. (Dawkins p. 222), we must admit that this dating is practically the only one possible, but this alone does not prove it definitively. For the dating of the ivory in general see Dawkins, p. 231; for the dating of the pottery p. 112.

A. Rumpf, *Festschrift für Poland* (Philologische Wochenschrift, 1932, Nr. 35/38, col. 282) takes over Dawkins' 7th-cent. dating while E. Kunze, *Gnomon* 9 (1933), 14 does not want to regard the comb as older than 600 because of the helmeted Athena and the style.

For the evaluation of the find in terms of literary history and the history of legend cf. Wilamowitz, *Hermes* 65 (1930), 241 ff. and E. Bethe, *Hermes* 66 (1931), 239. Wilamowitz claimed to recognize Zeus in the seated man, and regarded the *Cypria* as the carver's model. Cogent reasons against this are in Bethe. Bethe believes that the judgement of Paris could have been known in Sparta at that time from a 'small epic'. Wilamowitz declares that the bird on the hand of the first goddess, of Hera, is a cuckoo. Athena can be recognized by her helmet. For the older representations of the judgement of Paris in general and the 'bearded Paris' type, cf. Roland Hampe, *Corolla Ludwig Curtius* (Stuttgart, 1937), 145. In view of the original, Hampe regards it as impossible that Paris was holding the apple, as Dawkins's redrawing shows it. If this were the case, the vivid gesture of the left arm past the two other goddesses towards Aphrodite would express the same as what is found in the last book of the *Iliad*: 'he praised her.'

But the most important issue was not tackled, i.e. not whether a story might be older or younger but where, when, and in what relationship to Homer was this sort of story-telling? At what stage of the myth? i.e. one needs to look for the spirit to which the story testifies. But the spirit of the story is diametrically opposed to pretty well everything which one used to imagine as archaic. For—to disregard the individual differences of the scholarly hypotheses— what would be the oldest, deepest-lying stratum of the *Iliad*? However one thinks this enigmatic whole came into being, the more heroic, the greater, the more tragic, the tougher, the bloodier, the more inexorable, so one concluded, the older. According to [19] Jebb, the oldest material would be in Books 1, 11, 16–22.[6] According to Wilamowitz, one of the oldest pieces would be the old Patrocly (and he thought he could restore it, purified from later revisions).[7] According to Bethe, Greek heroic poetry would consist 'in its core of duels between never-changing heroes';[8] so the poem of the wrath of Achilles and whatever else of this kind would have to rank with the oldest in the *Iliad*. But, at the time of those hypotheses, one would not yet have reckoned at all with the possibility that already at the turn of the eighth to the seventh century, the judgement of Paris could have been on everybody's lips. So what should from now on be considered archaic? Do we not have to examine our preconceptions? There would have been enough reason to do this, even without the new find.

In the *Iliad* as well as the *Odyssey*, there are stories mentioned incidentally or retold in conversations which (in terms of their type) do not belong to the form of the great epic. They are allowed to appear only as if at its margin. Even if he had wanted to, the poet 'Homer' could not have put them in the sequence of epic action. Not for the simple reason alone that their events run their course beyond the law of time according to which in Homer's epic the sun rises and sets, and the events between sunrise and sunset reach full and ordered completion in the scope of one epic day. In the *Odyssey* the story about Penelope's piece of weaving belongs to these stories.[9] It is told three times, twice repeated in the same wording, so it

---

[6] R. C. Jebb, *An Introduction to the Iliad and the Odyssey* (Cambridge, 1887).

[7] U. v. Wilamowitz, *Die Ilias und Homer* (Berlin, 1916).

[8] E. Bethe, *Homer*, iii, *Die Sage vom troischen Kriege* (Leipzig, 1927), 8.

[9] Modern interpretations: L. Radermacher, *Sitzungsberichte der Wiener Akademie* (1915), 32 f.

does not appear more than once. Nevertheless, the *Odyssey* can hardly be imagined without it. From where else would Penelope have earned the continuous, inherited epithet 'the prudent', 'the cunning', if she had not outwitted the suitors in the way this story tells? For if the disloyal maid had not betrayed her, her ruse would have succeeded. In the same way, the disloyalty of the maids, which in the epic creates or intensifies epic situations, found itself there as part of the story. But for the following reason, too, that story itself is not allowed to gain admission into the here-and-now of the epic action; for the same reason, too, it must remain among the earlier stories because though the suitors in the *Odyssey* are fools, deceived and blind, even they are not such fools as to allow themselves to be talked into believing for three years that a [20] garment could not be woven in a shorter time. In the *Odyssey*, their foolishness is deafness to the warning voices, blindness to their approaching fate, *hybris*—their foolishness is ennobled, and near-farce is given moral force. But in the same way Penelope, too, is 'the prudent' and 'sensible' one now in a totally different, higher, nobler sense; she no longer tells the suitors such tales as wanting quickly to finish weaving the burial garment for old Laertes . . . But by transforming the stories which precede the *Odyssey* in time, by raising and refining them, the great epic creates epic situations appropriate to itself, which in its own style and tenor make the old motifs sound afresh. It happens, for example, in the *Odyssey* in Book 18, where suddenly Penelope—one can hardly believe one's ears—in sentimental lament makes the delighted suitors believe that when Odysseus parted from her, he had entrusted her—to remarry! She says that now the night so hateful to her is no longer far off: so, according to good old custom, could they please bring presents, rather than just constantly consuming other people's property? The disguised beggar sitting close by hears it, sees through it and is secretly delighted. Penelope shows herself as the cunning one here too. But where the storyteller needs the loom, nightwork, and betrayal, the epic poet of Homeric style needs the intimacy and contrast of souls, and the concealing ambiguity of the spoken and received word.

One sees that it is not always necessary to dissect poetry in order to discover something older behind it. There can be cases in which on the contrary one will reach one's goal sooner by leaving it as whole as possible. Since every radical change of composition, according to Heusler's enquiries into the

Nibelungenlied,[10] always means a change of inner structure too, and since a change of the inner structure always affects not just individual parts but the whole, then the attempts to get to the older and the younger material in one and the same work of poetry solely through the analysis of its composition are likely ultimately to become an exercise in circularity.

The story of the judgement of Paris in the *Iliad* is in no different position from that of Penelope's ruse in the *Odyssey*. The Paris story too is mentioned only once; it, too, is prehistory in a double sense: not only because its events precede the 'wrath of Achilles' but also because it testifies to a spirit which contradicted the epic style—not that, maybe, of the later collectors of material (the 'cyclici'), but all the more that of the *Iliad*. [21] And as the story of the weaving Penelope has an after-effect in the 'great epic' of the *Odyssey* by having its meaning transformed into epic situations, so does the story of Paris in the *Iliad*. As Paris' judgement brings gods and men to interact with each other, so it has its after-effect in the *Iliad* partly in Olympian, partly in human scenes.

The partisanship of the gods in the *Iliad* for and against the Trojans and Achaeans has been explained by scholars after Wilamowitz[11] in terms of influential historical events, of the political circumstances of the time of the Greek migrations; they claim that in such partisanship the situation of the Achaeans is reflected who, pushed out of their Greek motherland, colonized the coasts of Asia Minor, in conflict with native tribes. So, Apollo is on the Trojans' side because, to the Greeks, he had formerly been an alien god from Asia Minor. Aphrodite, too, the goddess of Cyprus, was Asian, and had therefore seemed to them a hostile being, and Ares, a Thracian, all the more so. On the other hand Hera, Athena, and Poseidon sided with the Greeks; Hera and Athena as the national goddesses of citadels and victory, Poseidon as the old mother country's 'Lord of the Earth'; and Zeus, as the highest lord of heaven, stood neutral above everything. The distribution is obvious and seems not just conceived but also realized consistently—but, unfortunately, it changes its face as soon as one begins to ask god after god for his reasons. Should one be allowed to do this? Surely

---

[10] Andreas Heusler, *Nibelungensage und Nibelungenlied* (3rd edn., Dortmund, 1929).

[11] Wilamowitz, *Die Ilias und Homer*, 285 ff.; id., *Der Glaube der Hellenen* (Berlin, 1931), i. 321 ff.

one will have to *decide* to do this: and Homer himself invites us to do so.

Then it turns out that it is true that Apollo for instance is hostile to the Achaeans—but by no means at all costs. First, he sends them the plague, but only because of the injustice which they committed against his priest; then he lets himself be appeased, and as far as he is concerned, everything should now be fine again. Certainly, looking down from Troy's fortress, he encourages its defenders while Athena spurs on the attackers (4. 507); Troy is the city which is his concern (21. 516), here he has his temple (5. 446), the fortress is his residence (5. 460); as he helps Chryses his priest when injustice is done to him, so he protects his city (21. 576). Guarding it from the wall, he wards off Patroclus (16. 701). He does not hate the Achaeans, but he protects the Trojans. Yet his protection too has its limits. In the battle of the gods, humans suddenly seem to him, the noble one who works from afar, too unimportant, too transitory for the gods to fight each other about—a perception different from that of the other gods. Poseidon is even less unconditionally partisan. In Book [22] 7 he complains to Zeus about the defensive wall of the Achaeans (7. 442), which is typical of him. He is easily worried about his divine prestige, but then—no less typical of him—he lets himself all the sooner be calmed down by Zeus, who hands him dominion over the Achaeans' camp for the future. His complaint is a more harmless, Poseidon-like counterpart to the terrible pact over Troy's destruction which Zeus and Hera enter into with each other in Book 4. Another time (20. 293), in the council of the gods, he even intercedes for Aeneas, whom Achilles is threatening. Hera replies to him, not without some sharpness, that what he does is up to him; but that they themselves, Athena and Hera, had sworn enough oaths in front of all the gods that they would not rest until Troy had been burnt—burnt by the sons of the Achaeans. But why would anyone swear so many oaths, and before so many witnesses (in accordance with ancient practice, for which many examples could be cited), if not to commit oneself to revenge, whatever the cost? But what kind of revenge would that be? For what offence suffered? So much is certain: it could not be made more transparent that the help which Poseidon gives to the Achaeans cannot be confounded with the common hatred of the two goddesses for Troy. The only unconditional haters are Hera and Athena; they do not want only to help their own people, they want to destroy others too.

However, with Book 8 the Olympian constellation shifts. It is with this shift in particular that the 'Realpolitik' interpretation of Homer's gods won confirmation for itself. With Book 8, Hera and Athena suddenly become the ones who are anxious and concerned about the Achaeans. But by Book 8 the whole of Olympus is in a different state: for Zeus now lets the Achaeans succumb to Hector solely for the sake of Thetis and Achilles. This arbitrariness of the father of the gods generates the fear that the gods will rebel, a rebellion which can be contained only by the most violent threats. For it is now no longer a matter of the gods simply deciding whether they are for or against Troy or the Achaeans, but of the question: should the whole army of the Achaeans suffer so terribly for the sake of one man, Achilles, and his offended 'honour'? But even here, in this shifted situation, the actual goal of the two goddesses never disappears from view. It is true that the goddesses *speak* before Zeus as if they just felt pity for the poor Achaeans (8. 465), but what they are actually *thinking* as they do this, sitting close to each other, nursing their secret grudge, is revealed in verse 458: destruction to the Trojans! However, Zeus' arbitrariness infuriates virtually 'all the other gods' against him too (11. 78): 'they all' reproach him— but he does not take any notice of it . . . In particular, [23] only now is Poseidon drawn into the pact between Hera and Athena—for Poseidon is a god who in any case is easily inclined to suspect that his rank is not appreciated (the usual fate of the second-born). The triangle Hera–Athena–Poseidon is the answer to the combination Zeus–Thetis. It is true that Poseidon rejects participation in the open revolt which has been suggested to him—in vain Hera reminds him of his old sympathies and of the lovely offerings which the Achaeans in Helice and Aegae gave to him (8. 200 ff.); but as things develop, the two of them in fact play into each other's hands; what open revolt did not succeed in, cunning does achieve[12]—sleep

---

[12] Who would want to doubt that both refer to each other? But according to Wilamowitz, *Die Ilias und Homer*, the poet of Book 8—on him Wilamowitz pp. 42, 57—is a 'late one', at any rate different from the poet of Book 14 (Deception of Zeus). On him Wilamowitz pp. 209 and 232. The poet of Book 14 is also the poet of Book 1; he is, on the whole, the poet of our *Iliad*; see p. 317. But Book 8 is an 'inferior piece of padding', far below the art of even Books 18 and 19, and its poet is younger than Hesiod, a contemporary, probably even a younger contemporary, of Archilochus and Terpander (Wilamowitz p. 58). One must not ask how it happened that this 'inferior piece of padding' could prepare for the excellent Book 14, Zeus sleeping with Hera.

and Aphrodite's girdle. Zeus' love-making only has a purpose for Hera if she can count on her Poseidon despite his refusal. In this way she can harm the Trojans, help the Achaeans, and yet again, when Zeus wakes up, swear to him with the clearest of consciences that she has not been plotting with Poseidon. Which again contributes astonishingly to the improvement of her difficult situation . . .

Through the scenes of the Homeric gods too an older, coarser genre can be perceived, which was also ennobled through the epic: farces about the gods. In the Homeric laughter of the Olympians (1. 599), in Zeus' holy unholy sleep in Hera's arms, we should not forget that stories of cunning, of fettering, of rioting, of secrets the gods have from each other (which occasionally appear in dark hints) point to an existing pre-Homeric 'genre'.[13] Here, too, stories again became [24] situations; through the sublimity of Homer and his time, they were raised to the height of that game which is light and yet terrible through its 'lightness', a game which offended later times so much.

There cannot have been any lack of serious songs about the battles of the gods either. As late as c.500 Xenophanes of Colophon mentions battles of Gigantes and Titans among the traditional rhapsodic subjects at banquets or, to express it in Nordic terms, in the men's hall. The later symposia—the settings of and impulses for so many genres of poetry—are of course nothing else but the

---

[13] Recognizable remains are e.g. 15. 18 (Hera in the hanging torture; by this means Zeus may have forced her to yield in some respect, or it came to a pact, or something similar; cf. with this also 1. 590); 5. 385 (Ares imprisoned in a bronze storage vessel and, through the intervention of a beautiful 'stepmother' of the giant pair of brothers who had put him in prison, freed again with Hermes' help; an apparently amorous adventure of the god of war, similar to his conquest in Hephaestus' house); 18. 394 (Hephaestus, after his birth as a cripple, hurled into the sea by Hera and secretly rescued by the mermaids). An example of the same genre, elaborated with the extravagance of all epic art, is the binding of Aphrodite and Ares in *Odyssey* 8. 266. The Homeric hymn to Hermes is also farce-like, and especially the hymn to Hephaestus as Wilamowitz reconstructed it (*Nachrichten der Gesellschaft von der Wissenschaften*, Göttingen, 1895); the same motifs are also found here: fettering, deceit, disagreement, and reconciliation. I stress that I do not talk here about the age of the individual stories, but about the age of the genre. If, for example, one recognizes something generic in the story of Ares and Aphrodite, it becomes impossible to derive this from the divine scenes of the *Iliad* which, as said earlier, are no longer stories but Olympian 'situations' which interrupt development on earth. Divine farce also existed in Old Nordic mythology: an example is the Thrymsong of the *Edda*. See H. Schneider, *Sitzungsberichte der Bayrischen Akademie der Wissenschaft* (1936), no. 7.

more distant descendants of the heroic social life of the 'kings' with their men enjoying the 'bards' ' songs of heroes and of gods and vagrant jugglers' tricks. At Alcinous' court, the goings-on are admittedly considerably more artistic and more serene, but otherwise hardly different from the ones in the hall of the Norse king Harald Schönhaar in the midst of the scalds, berserker, and vagrant conjurers (Genzmer, *Edda* 2, 191). So there were songs about the gods, among the Greek as among the Germanic peoples, not just for their cult but also for entertainment. But the battles between the gods in the *Iliad*, when compared with similar phenomena, are something so peculiar in the extent to which they go beyond these that from this feature alone a certain poet could be recognized. In the *Iliad*, the Olympians have and do everything that the humans also have and do, as for instance dwarves or elves in fairy-tales have and do everything that the humans do, too—only in a different way. By having and doing everything in the Olympian manner, the Olympians become a genus, a 'phylon'. But even if this is far from being a matter of course (for instance, it is already something alien to the poet of the *Odyssey*), Homer's Olympian world could up to this point still be something more general, something traditional. But the point is that Homer's gods do not just have and do everything in a wonderful and divine way: at the same time without prejudice to their magnificence they also have and do everything in a peculiar way—i.e. *unseriously*. They threaten each other as if it were a matter of life and death, scream, as if they were dying, deceive each other as if they could [25] overthrow each other—but whenever on earth it is a matter of life or death, the gods' struggle dissolves into an 'as if', through which it becomes a game: not because the gods themselves were consciously playing, but because they lack the stake through which alone every action becomes serious—death, destruction, suffering which lays men low, and any diminution of existence. The battle of the gods in the *Iliad* reflects human heroic battles, but without their precondition: danger. This distinguishes these quarrels fundamentally from all gigantomachies and titanomachies, and from Hesiod's *Theogony* too. There the gods are indeed threatened—not to mention the quite different threat they face in Nordic mythology. Let us ask—which is the older? Without doubt, of course, the real threat. Only blind dogmatism could try to eliminate from the older poetic work the mentioning of the Titans and all the things which point to archaic battles between the gods as something supposedly younger. Only in Homer does a seeming threat take the place of a real threat; and through this the existence of the gods takes on something unreal—that is, when looked at from the perspective of a human, faced with real threats. So too the human, in his human transitoriness, like the play of leaves in the wind, when looked at from a divine perspective, represents something transitory, vain, diminished in terms of true being, but in a reversed sense (6. 146; 21. 464). The 'as if' of human existence is permanence, the 'as if' of divine existence is annihilation (the origin incidentally of Parmenides' thought). Both do not just reflect, they also condition each other. As the eternity and magnificence of the gods preserves itself at the cost of the transitoriness and tragic frailty of humans, so the latter in turn preserves itself as the means of human greatness, at the cost of a certain divine failure (according to human standards) which can appear in manifold forms, as a riddle, as a mystery, as fate, as 'beyond good and evil' . . . and beyond this solely in the *Iliad* as sublime unseriousness. Achilles hurls himself into death to avenge his fallen friend; but the father of the gods in all his magnificence can only weep bloody tears over his darling who is doomed to die, his son Sarpedon: Hera does not leave Zeus any doubt: if he wanted to be like one of the mortal heroes, the order of Olympus would be ruined (16. 440 ff.). In order to make this clear, the gods are again and again led by Homer to that brink where their 'game' would *almost* become 'serious'. If Zeus tried in all seriousness to save Troy, his beloved city, he would offend against the pact of [26] the gods, he would break the rules of the game through which alone Olympus preserves itself (4. 25 ff.). No sooner does the pact on earth promise to become the salvation of the troubled peoples, when the pact of the gods immediately nullifies it again. So the humans have to pay with their lives while the Olympians, as the wonderful word goes, simply 'irritate' each other . . . The result is: the scenes of gods in Homer's conception are possible only in a poetic work about human transitoriness, greatness, and tragedy. No other genre, not farce or hymn or theogony or battle of the gods or anything else, indeed not even the epic (apart from the *Iliad* alone) would ever be capable of representing this reciprocal nature of seeming and being, of reflecting and complementing. The *Odyssey* already shows that this conception has been left behind again; its poet sees in the gods hardly anything more than the helpers or adversaries of its heroes, and so stands in this respect, if not as an ethicist, then at least as an epicist on the same stage as the Cyclic poets, i.e. on that stage which, as emerges in so many cases, had also already been the pre-Homeric one. As a stage in style the pre-, like the post-Homeric, is that epic norm which the *Iliad* poet, while seeming to stay within the convention, in fact breaks out of; it is the background, so to speak, against which his profile stands out, the genre without which he would not appear as that which he is.

However—to get back to the topic of the discord between the gods—the shifted situation on Olympus is not the original situation. The original situation is that of Books 1–7 and 20–4. Through the convocation of the gods' assembly and announcement of the gods' battle in Book 20, the old relationship is most solemnly restored by Zeus. By deriving divine friendships and hostilities from the political conditions of a historical epoch, one does not only confuse the poetic situations, but in a bold leap disregards all the hints, all the references in Homer's text. The ones who drive on the action and cause unrest on Olympus, whose passion only makes the Olympian scenes take their dramatic courses, are the two who have conspired together on oath, Hera and Athena. Uninhibited by all other considerations, they alone pursue the one goal: Troy's destruction. In this, Athena at Hera's side in the role of an intriguer against Zeus, is all the greater an enigma since Homeric theology knows the actual character of both of them only as intimately linked with each other. The result of this is again another series of contradictory, and therefore charming, and so again misunderstood, situations which revel in this contradiction. Similarly charming is the contradiction when Hera borrows the [27] magic girdle from her rival (14. 190 ff.), 'smiling' that she has succeeded . . .

After this survey, who would separate the gods into two camps? Olympus knows no reason to hide itself. Book 5 shows the following grouping (418): Aphrodite, wounded in the hand by Diomedes, has fled to Olympus into the lap of her mother Dione, who comforts her and, healing her, wipes the divine blood from her hand. Hera and Athena form a mockers' corner with the intention of 'irritating' Zeus. While elsewhere Hera likes to speak on behalf of Athena, here Athena speaks: 'Cypris must have lured one of the Achaean women into the arms of the Trojans whom she now (!) loves so immeasurably! One of these beautiful ladies evidently wears a golden brooch, and Aphrodite scratched her dainty hand on it when she was fondling her!' 'Now', i.e. since she procured the Achaean girl Helen for the Trojan Paris. But how has Paris, or the Trojans, earned her love? Does she love the Trojans because she is Asian? Whereas the two mockers would be guardian-patronesses of the Achaeans? To reach this conclusion would be to state, according to the old Goethe–Düntzer pattern: 'Homer is mistaken here!' What we have is nothing other than the situation of the judgement of Paris, translated into an Olympian scene, in Homeric style. The scene is now no longer Ida but Homeric Olympus and the circle of the gods . . . but, as on Ida, the two great goddesses, heroic Athena and royal Hera, stand once more against the procuress Aphrodite. What Aphrodite had once promised to Paris on Ida is now generalized by the goddess's mockery; she probably scratched herself a little during business of that sort? What was formerly a story returns as a situation.

The same grouping repeats itself in the battle of the gods (21.423). At Hera's bidding Athena chases after Aphrodite (who is helping up the fallen Ares) and punches her in the breast so hard that she falls down with Ares—'that dogfly', as Hera scolds, who 'yet again' has crossed their path. 'Yet again' points to Book 5. 'May this happen', Athena wishes, 'to everyone who helps the Trojans! Then we would soon be finished with the war and Ilium would be destroyed.' And Hera smiled. Yet Aphrodite did not participate in the battle between the gods at all. If she were Asian, would she not have to fight for the Trojans? In fact, she does not participate in the fighting because she is the goddess of love. The two of them do not fear her as much as they hate her. And they hate her because of her nature. But why? Why only her? Why not the others as well? The only key which unlocks all these enigmas is, again, the judgement of Paris. [28] The dignity of the opposition between Poseidon and Apollo stands out in manly contrast to the divine bickering of the rival goddesses. But rival goddesses—whence? Since when?

After everything else, now too in the last book—which belongs to the poetic design of the *Iliad* as necessarily as anything else anywhere—the hatred of Hera and Athena for Troy (Poseidon is guiltily mentioned in a parenthesis)—is explained even beyond Hector's death, with references to the 'delusion' of Alexandros, who 'censured' the goddesses when they came to his farmstead and 'praised' that one who, to his ruin, granted him fulfilment of his 'lust'. This is in complete harmony with the whole *Iliad*. It is in vain that, even here, people have refused to countenance the judgement of Paris.[14]

But the beginning of Book 4 seems contradictory to all this and needs explanation. Unlike the later scenes, it is not the two female conspirators here but Zeus who [29] begins to 'irritate' the two of them as they sit together. Observe (he says): two female helpers of Menelaus, sitting aside and finding pleasure in looking on! But Aphrodite herself (he says) walks at the side of Paris, protecting him . . . And since 'in order to irritate Hera', Zeus also proposes to put a quick end to the war by giving up Helen, Hera flies into a rage (Athena beside her remains the silent, grudging daughter): how dare he frustrate their sweat and labours (she says)—all their striving for the one end, the ruin of Priam and his sons? The situation here is the same: Hera and Athena against Aphrodite. But the scene is too powerful to make possible here an explanatory reference to

---

[14] *Il.* 24. 29–30. People have partly deleted the verses, partly interpreted them differently. The deletion is impossible because it would mean that this 'hint', which of course is supposed to explain matters, would become all the more enigmatic. Wilamowitz, *Hermes* 65 (1930), 242 first declares Book 24 as 'younger than the *Iliad*', according to his well-known thesis which is probably not shared by anyone today; second, he denies the reference to the judgement of Paris: 'The verses are not sufficient to enable us to recognize the action which the poet presupposes as known, but it was not that of the *Cypria*. It looks as if Paris had disdainfully turned away two of the three women whom he did not recognize as goddesses and received the third. That could very well be a fairy-tale motif which the poet took over. The *Cypria* transformed it effectively.' So here, then, we would have a form of a fairy-tale of the 'feeding of unknown gods'. Paris then would not have insulted the two enraged goddesses as goddesses at all. He regarded them as simply mortals who—one racks one's brains about what the two wanted from him on his farmstead on Ida. I refuse to conjecture what Aphrodite, transformed into a mortal being, should have wanted from him. In short, poor Paris would have become the victim of a deception by the goddesses. The ways and means by which the rejected goddesses would have chosen to show him his error—for presumably they had to do this if their wrath against Troy was to be traced back to this event?—might lead to further complications. There are no limits set to our imagination. The unmistakable words: 'which his evil lust procured for him' are understood in a way I cannot guess. At any rate they are not understood as a 'guarantee' and are not referred to Helen, as if no *Iliad* had ever told us anything about Helen and Paris, as if this did not refer back to that. (Obviously, the first requirement for the tried and tested *Iliad* reader is the blinker.) 'Scolded' and 'praised' is understood as 'reject' and 'accept', which it does not mean at all (see *Il.* 10. 249), and the thought that 'praise' or 'blame' could be appropriate for the judge of a beauty contest is—any explanation seems to be superfluous—simply forbidden to us. Even to think that 'granting' could be connected with 'praising' as origin would immediately plunge us into the bottomless pit: we would be handed over to the judgement of Paris. Onward, then, into the free realm of hypotheses!

the judgement of Paris as happened in the last book. Hera's hatred is enigmatic, uncanny, monstrous. 'Unbelievable goddess!' (says Zeus). 'What have Priam and his sons done to you that was so serious?' he asks. The powerful hatred of the powerful goddess blazes out, lives and justifies itself in its own terms. The judgement of Paris as an explanation would only weaken, but not causally explain, the effect here. Such is the terrible, enigmatic character of the deity—and not just Hera; Zeus himself, once he has decided to destroy a city, will not be different! Hence their pact: if you leave me this, I will leave you that! That the judgement of Paris is not mentioned here is not because the poet did not yet know about it, but because the greatness of events on Olympus had outgrown the spirit of this ancient story. The old motif becomes insubstantial, the epic situation originating from it becomes a vessel for new content.

The judgement of Paris as a story makes sense and has reference only as an introduction to the story of Troy's ruin. This is how the story began: 'Once upon a time there was a king who had a son . . .' But Troy's ruin told in the style of the judgement of Paris—one can imagine this in whatever detail one pleases (as, in late Antiquity, Nonnus' pupil Colluthus and before him the Alexandrians and Romans did; in doing this they also invented the pastoral idyll and the stripping of the goddesses): in any case the story must have been told in a completely different style from Homer's *Iliad*. Quite different in tone from Homer, more fable-like, more novella-like, more parable-like, less heroic and more didactic, not to say more *ainos*-like . . . But the good son in contrast to the bad one, the motif of two dissimilar brothers, starting with the sons of Eve, Cain and Abel, is spread far too widely across the world for there not to have been right from the beginning in this story too the good son, brave Hector, standing next to 'ruinous Paris', Dysparis, as Hector himself rebukes him. In the old [30] *Thebaid*, a hostile pair of brothers destroyed each other and a great army; in the pre-Homeric '*Ur-Iliad*', one good-for-nothing brother destroyed the peerless brother, together with the whole city.

Interpreters of Homer have always seen in Hector only the opponent of Achilles; but in his role as Paris' brother he must be at least as old. Even the death of Achilles is drawn into the play of contrast between the two brothers. As the death of Hector through Achilles (22. 330 ff.)—according to an epic law of composition which would have to be discussed in a wider context—is a reversing variation of the death of Patroclus through Hector (16. 830 ff.), as dying Hector prophesies death to Achilles, as before dying Patroclus does to Hector: thus Achilles' death, after Hector's prophecy, will be the twice-reversed variation of Hector's death, and thus the variant repetition of Patroclus' death. In the same way as Patroclus dies, first hit by Apollo, then by human hand, so will Achilles die, first hit by Apollo, then by Paris' hand (for the reverse order would be unthinkable). Paris triumphs where Hector succumbs. This too must be counted as part of the whole tragedy of Hector.

The story of the unequal pair of brothers continues to have an effect in the *Iliad* and continues in human situations such as the quarrel of the goddesses before Paris in the scenes on Olympus. Take the Trojan episode in the middle of Book 3. Paris, having been snatched away from the duel with Menelaus, the legitimate husband, is transported into his bedchamber and Helen, resisting, is brought to him again. All this happens through the power of Aphrodite, the 'sinister' one, who 'now' loves the couple as dotingly as she would hate them if they did not comply with her wishes any more. This is nothing but the story about the 'abduction of Helen' translated into Homeric form, into the style of an epic episode. In the same way in Book 6 too an episode of the same style, the surprising encounter of both brothers in the fortress of Troy, is nothing else but a transformation, the changing into an epic situation, of the story of the unequal brothers. Here the brave brother, dripping with sweat from fighting, brings out the coward (6. 280 ff.), curses him, meets him (this 'disaster for the Trojans and Priam') checking his arms in his room, but only checking them, the 'wrathful' one, the dubious counterpart of Achilles, and with him Helen, who curses herself for such a husband and laments Hector for her sake and the sake of this 'deluded' one. This shows the people concerned united in an interlocking entanglement [31] pointing at something: the tellable story has transformed itself into a revealing situation, which refers to the past as it does to the future. The abundance of relationships is complemented by Hector's farewell. Hector's farewell to Andromache is juxtaposed with Paris' dubious dignity as the husband of deceived Helen, not just to juxtapose marriage with marriage but also to juxtapose the victim of the ruin with its originator. Hector's curse: 'That I should see him (Paris) coming into Hades!' (6. 285) is the preparatory complement to his foreboding: 'The day will come on which holy Ilium will sink under . . .' (6. 448). Hector, Paris, Helen—united— stand pointing to the beginning and the end. What was historic progression crowds itself into the one episode which builds itself up from its revealing contrasts: before the walls the battle raging, and in the fortress the inner disaster, and Hector, helping and fending off, hurrying from one to the other . . . In addition to the concern about the incapable brother there is the concern about the un- reconciled gods. The order comes to his mother to assemble the matrons, to lay a garment on the knees of Athena Polias and to beg her: may she break the lance of Diomedes—who with Athena's help has now taken Achilles' place as the invincible hero (6. 98)—may she overthrow him herself . . . But Athena refuses to grant this . . . The total situation is one into which an abundance of simultaneous events are crammed—actions whose external purpose (if we inquired) would appear almost incidental, even questionable—a hasty toing and froing, missing and meeting each other. But in this moment of the simultaneous, in this changing encounter of three generations, the total situation comprehends the events as a whole, the past as the future, and binds (pointing at things as through an *Ecce*) one to the other. Diomedes, the one who *now* rages victori- ous—he is not *yet* Achilles; Hector's farewell which seems to be the *last* one—it is *not* the last one *yet*. Threatening clouds are accumu- lating, but one more time day breaks again. But the shadow, which has fallen on the hero and the city, invisibly adheres to both. Such an episode both anticipates and retells in one: the Homeric shape of the pre-Homeric stories of the two brothers, of the abduction of Helen, of Troy's end. *Earlier* events, by being retold, are made a subject for repentance; *later* events, by being anticipated, for worry; through both, the events are pushed into one, internalized, their setting is transplanted into the distressed, foreboding human soul.[15]

[32] The purely negative is not tolerated in the *Iliad*, with the exception only of Thersites, who represents the negation of the world of the *Iliad* (in this the *Odyssey* is different, with its univer- sal juxtapositions of good and bad). So, no Paris can be tolerated in it any longer who, in spite of everything, could not, in his own way, be a hero after all. Just as the periodic form of epic progressions,

---

[15] On the episode of Book 6 see W. Schadewaldt, *Antike* 11 (1935), 149 ff.

comparable to a law of events, again and again approaches an 'almost' in the *Iliad*—a 'nearly' which threatens all order, all measure, all foresight, all nature of things—so also in Paris the doubtful, the unheroic, the common, is nearly touched, but only just nearly touched in order then again to give room to the high-spirited, chivalrous—although it may be felt a tiny bit too much. When they go into battle together, Hector himself must confess: 'Incredible one! No mean-thinking man could despise you' (6. 521). . . . Again, by entering into the *Iliad* Paris is ennobled, elevated, like the suitors in the *Odyssey* who, in spite of their folly and meanness, are again not just scoundrels or fools, and reflect an admittedly degenerate state of society, but one which according to its models is still a heroic one.

Without the judgement of Paris, no *Iliad*. It does not just lie at the basis of individual details, but at the basis of its whole divine–human entanglement. And yet is the *Iliad*, according to its beginning, middle, and end, not an Achilleid? The poem about the wrath of Achilles, his quarrel with Agamemnon and his reconciliation, Patroclus' death and avenging, is, as far as composition is concerned, the main, as well as the framing, action. This progression draws everything else into itself, as if one whirl were causing more and more masses to move. But what does 'frame' and 'filling' mean here? Is not again the wider 'frame' around the *Iliad* Troy's destruction? And so also Helen's abduction? And so also the judgement of Paris? But in the *Iliad* the frame becomes the framed, Troy's destruction turns into an anticipating episode, and the origin of the destruction, the 'disaster-Paris', turns into a minor figure who, in order to fill up the period of wrath in which Achilles indulges for so long, is put among the preludes to the actual tragic events. If this became the main matter, the other had to become an episode. 'How is Achilles and his tragedy concerned with Helen and Paris?', people have been asking for a long time, and not without reason.[16] But only when people [33] concluded from this that the Paris adventures were of later origin, younger vegetation around the old core of the legend, did they overshoot the mark. For in the *Iliad*, two turned into one. The question is not whether old or young, but of what origin, of what spirit.

---

[16] Cf. Bethe, *Homer*, iii. 54 f. But on all these questions see also C. M. Bowra, *Tradition and Design in the Iliad* (Oxford, 1930), 22 f.

The whole of the *Iliad* is something which grew together, let us say, to express it roughly, from two roots. As certainly as one of its roots is that kind of heroic song of which Achilles, singing the 'glory of the heroes' in his tent, is himself an example (9. 189); and as certainly as the majority of its heroes, like Achilles, Aeneas, the two Ajaxes, and so on, are heroes of old tribes or families; and as certainly as the 'wrath of Achilles' is a reproach which can be imagined only as 'sung', as in a poem; and as certainly as the beginning: 'Sing to me, goddess, the wrath . . .' gives the basic chord and tone of the whole symphony of the *Iliad*: so impossible would it seem to imagine the beginning of a work of poetry of this style as: 'Sing to me, goddess, the delusion of Paris . . .'.

Already Herodotus recounted the abduction of Helen, although in the style of the fifth century, as a novella.[17] But it is already a novella if one arranges it as a story in accordance with the statements in the *Iliad*. And novella it remains, from Homer to Ovid, up until the Renaissance . . . But the judgement of Paris belongs to the abduction of Helen as the origin does to the consequence. If Paris were not the darling of Aphrodite, not the hero of the judgement of Paris, then he would not cheat his host out of his wife, as soon as he had visited him. Gods usually visit only that person who already has that in him which the encounter expresses. If one leaves the goddess out of the abduction of Helen, one degrades it into a marriage story, a thing which may seem as important to our time as it would have appeared unimportant to Antiquity.

People have realized with growing certainty[18] that the material of the *Odyssey* is the material of a novella, that one of the old 'home-comer' stories repeats itself in it, of the sort that are spread over the

---

[17] When I talk about novella here, I must ask to be allowed to use the term rather loosely. There are enough definitions which differ from each other, mostly in contrast to legend or to fairy-tale. Literature in J. Bolte and G. Polivka, *Anmerkungen zu den Kinder- und Hausmärchen der Brüder Grimm*, v (1931), 261 f., and articles 'Märchen' and 'Novelle' in Pauly-Wissowa (Aly). So I mean by novella not fairy-tale without its magic nor legend without its gods; rather novella to me is where, instead of the miraculous and fantastic of the fairy-tale, the reflective prevails—be it now something worldly-wise or edifying or revealing man or informed by experience. Novella interprets itself in the telling; fairy-tale does not interpret itself.

[18] L. Radermacher, *Die Erzählungen der Odyssee, Sitzungsberichte der Wiener Akademie* 178: 1 (1915); W. Büchner, *Hermes* 72 (1937), 121; F. Dornseiff, *Hermes* 72 (1937), 352. Wilamowitz, *Sitzungsberichte Berl.* (1925), 59: 'For a long time we did not realize that to a large extent such elements appear as a heroic legend which have no historical content at all, but are to be grasped as fairy-tale or novella.' By historical content here is meant pragmatic history in a heroic disguise.

world and familiar to us through Enoch Arden. [34] The material of the *Iliad* is admittedly less transparent, but that an element of the novella is also present in it can hardly be in doubt any longer. If I might dare to express myself symbolically, I would classify the Achilleid, in its relationship to the story about Paris and Helen, as an element of the 'north' which would have joined itself with a 'southern' kind of material, just as northern and southern elements join in the groundplans of the fortresses of Mycenae and Tiryns. Achilles is the one who knows his fate, who determines his own death out of his own power and inborn tragedy. Death to him is inner certainty, just as it is external fate, yet it comes through no council of the gods, but as through the saying of a *Norne* [Nordic goddess of fate], and with it, what the Achilleid brings with it: military kingship, loyalty, friendship in arms, offence against honour, commitment between princes and comrades beyond death, and retaliation down to the desecration of a corpse, down to the slaughter of the captives in the funeral celebration[19] . . . all this drives like a gale from the north over a southern, lighter, more contemplative world in which one wins through to clarity by resignation rather than by tragically consuming oneself. The contrast between the two worlds does exist, even if we disregard the eye which understands the world while the world reflects itself in it—the eye of the poet. At the time when the *Iliad*, with everything which precedes it in terms of legends, was about to originate, in the epoch of the Mycenaean and geometric styles, between 1200 and 700, the city of Troy lay in ruins, destroyed and burnt, or only just colonized again (though neither by Achaeans nor [35] Argives, but by Thracian tribes which pushed one after the other through migration to Asia Minor).[20] The Hellenic colonization of the area does not start until

[19] Erwin Rohde's much-admired *Psyche* (Freiburg, Leipzig, 1894), 14 ff., explained the horrible funeral ceremonial as a remnant of an older attitude which was almost dead in Homer's time, as a 'rudiment of a more lively cult of the soul of a past time'. He says that the poet here does not seem to feel himself in his element, that with a 'certain timidity' and a 'brevity not at all corresponding to the usual Homeric manner' he passes over the most horrible details; 'it is as if a very ancient, long-tamed savagery were breaking out for the last time'. First, the 'timidity' of the poet is based on the interpreter's purely subjective feeling; second, it is overlooked that this unusual horribleness is already preparing for the reconciliation in the last book; third, one differentiates between 'old' and 'young' as if they were perspectiveless absolutes or as if there could be no other categories.

[20] Cf. Bethe, *Homer*, iii. 14 ff. This has been corrected by the results of more recent excavation (Cincinnati Excavations) in Caskey, *AJArch* (1948), 121 f.: 'The

the end of the eighth century. Let us be clear about this: at the time when that ivory carver in Sparta carved the judgement of Paris onto his comb, the Greeks had only just begun to found Troy as a Greek city. How much older must the judgement of Paris be! Troy's fallen glory loomed like a warning sign into the consciousness of a time which had seen the old glories falling everywhere. People began to reflect, to explain how that came to be, and to tell the story: about the prince who became a womanizer, the goddesses who came to him on Ida, Aphrodite's favour, the revenge of the two offended goddesses and the ruin of Priam and his sons . . .[21]

However, what the abducted woman felt like (presumably in conflict) and how Priam felt when he saw her (probably also in conflict),[22] and how Hector and the others [36] felt about her, the old story will not have asked, or not have asked much. With this question, we step into the realm of great poetry or, if again here we prefer the historical perspective to the aesthetic, into the realm of the great epic and its presumed heroic background and predecessors. The question what a person's inner being looks like was presumably directed originally, and above all, at the hero, and the answer,

latest excavations have not proved Settlement VIIa was destroyed by Achaeans, but they have produced no evidence to the contrary.'

[21] To explain Troy's destruction there was another story which is mentioned incidentally in Homer, *Il.* 21.442. Zeus sent Apollo and Poseidon unrecognized into the service of Laomedon. Poseidon walled the fortress, while Apollo looked after the rich herds. But the hard-hearted king denied them the wage stipulated for them after their time had expired, and threatened to sell them into slavery and to cut off their ears. Full of anger, the gods returned home, whereupon (this is not elaborated any more) Zeus will have decided to destroy Laomedon's family. The story is a more pious counterpart to the judgement of Paris and testifies to the view that Troy fell according to the will of Zeus, because during its foundation its first king had already made himself guilty of a breach of contract and a violation of human and divine law. Thus, next to the novella-like version, runs the legendary one which belongs to that genre to which *Odyssey* 17.485 refers. So even in this all-too-smooth calculation which adds up like this: first the gods were immoral (see the *Iliad*), then they became moralistic (see the *Odyssey*), inconsistencies are not lacking. Unrecognized visits to kings by gods to test them appear e.g. also in the introduction of the Grimnir song in the *Edda* (2.79 Genzmer) etc.

[22] i.e. insofar as by conflict we understand the dynamic principle of psychological transformation and change. In the epic we meet as progression what becomes simultaneous in tragedy. Shape and condition of the simultaneous is reflection. [The last two sentences are open to more than one interpretation and have therefore been translated literally rather than paraphrased.] But when e.g. Priam says to Helen (3.164): 'You are not guilty in my eyes, the gods are guilty' then this means that feelings of a different kind have not remained alien to him, the same feelings with which other old men look at her and against which he defends her.

whether through hints or through alternating speeches, was given in heroic song or in epic of smaller scope. The person who first took the step from the passionately absolute to psychic conflict (which after all is not something to be taken for granted, and so much so that it is alien for instance to the *Odyssey*), i.e. the step from the heroic-superhuman to the problematical-human as we understand it, without in any way diminishing the heroic, but on the contrary in order to elevate it to its greatest height even in the absolute, was no other, as it seems, than the one who also transformed the Paris stories into epic situations . . . the poet of the *Iliad*, the awakener of the Western spirit.[23]

---

[23] On the total world view of the *Iliad* and its not only extensive but especially also intensive totality see Kurt Riezler, *Parmenides* (Frankfurt am Main, 1934), 18 f. I am happy that I am just able to refer to Rudolf Alexander Schröder's 'Gedanken zur Homerfrage' in the *Europäische Revue* (1937) which appeared during printing. Literature published more recently: W. Schadewaldt, *Iliasstudien* (Abhandlungen der Sächsischen Akademie der Wissenschaften 43; Leipzig, 1938); *Homer und sein Jahrhundert*, in *Das Neue Bild der Antike* (1942), i. 51; also his collected Homer essays, *Von Homers Welt und Werk* (1944) [Stuttgart, 1959³]; R. A. Schröder, *Die Aufsätze und Reden* (Berlin, 1939), i. 9 ff. [*Gesammelte Werke*, ii (Frankfurt, 1952), 12 ff.]; Rhys Carpenter, *Folk Tale, Fiction and Saga in the Homeric Epics* (Sather Classical Lectures 20; Berkeley and Los Angeles, 1956).

The Fight for Justice and Departure of Telemachus

FRIEDRICH KLINGNER

In the first four books of the *Odyssey* two stories probably make a special impression on the casual reader's mind. The first is Telemachus' fight for justice with the suitors. In front of the assembled people and gods, he complains about the wicked behaviour of these parasites and demands a solution, but in the duel of words with their leaders, he is deserted by the criminally spineless people of Ithaca, and ignominiously gets the worst of it, although divine signs refer to the imminent return home of Odysseus and a warning voice also speaks up. Yet this only provokes the deluded suitors to commit horribly presumptuous sin. In the second story, Telemachus goes by ship to Pylos and Sparta, is the guest of Nestor and Menelaus, asks about his father, hears stories of the homecomings of Nestor, Agamemnon, Menelaus, and other heroes of the Trojan War, and proves himself in the big wide world into which, hardly grown up, he has stepped from his poor, remote homeland and the stifling misery of his destitute house. Ask the reader how the two stories are connected and he will perhaps be confused at first. For the two stories hardly take each other into account. So too, in the gods' discussions in the first book, Athena announces her plan, and the stories are introduced as two separate topics which are independent of each other (88 ff.):

> ὄφρα οἱ υἱὸν
> μᾶλλον ἐποτρύνω καὶ οἱ μένος ἐν φρεσὶ θείω,
> εἰς ἀγορὴν καλέσαντα κάρη κομόωντας Ἀχαιοὺς
> πᾶσι μνηστήρεσσιν ἀπειπέμεν . . .
> πέμψω δ' ἐς Σπάρτην τε καὶ ἐς Πύλον ἠμαθόεντα
> νόστον πευσόμενον πατρὸς φίλου, ἤν που ἀκούσῃ,
> ἠδ' ἵνα μιν κλέος ἐσθλὸν ἐν ἀνθρώποισιν ἔχῃσιν.

From: Friedrich Klingner, *Über die vier ersten Bücher der Odyssee* (Leipzig, 1944), 15–41, reproduced by kind permission of S. Hirzel Verlag, Stuttgart.

So it may well be that the reader has no answer to the question posed. If he asks Homeric experts, he is perhaps referred to the passage where in the people's assembly, after Eurymachus has refused to comply with obvious justice, the divine sign, and the warning prophet, Telemachus abandons further negotiations over the injustice in his house and asks for a ship: he wants to enquire about Odysseus (he says). [16] He will determine his future course of action in this controversial matter by what he discovers. If he hears that his father is still alive and can return home, he will hold out for another year. But if Odysseus is dead, he will erect a tomb for him and marry-off his mother (2. 209–23). From here, so it may seem, the second theme, Telemachus' departure, logically originates: i.e. from the failure of Telemachus' first enterprise, his attempt to get justice from the suitors before the people. And starting from here, Kirchhoff and his successors have really passed judgement on the whole action of the first two books.[1]

Here in the assembly in Book 2, as Kirchhoff argues, everything proceeds as it should. Telemachus hits on the proposal to depart for Pylos and Sparta only when his first mission has failed. Then he falls back on the desire at least to gain one year's respite and agrees to fulfil the demand of the suitors that, if he finds out for certain that Odysseus is dead, he will marry-off his mother. This was not the original intention: negotiations had been opened with a different purpose and different expectations. Only failure has forced him to think of climbing down, reaching a new agreement and asking for a respite in which to make enquiries.

On the other hand in Book 1. 271 ff., in Athena's words of exhortation which in every detail exactly anticipate Telemachus' behaviour in Book 2, i.e. his appearance before the assembled people, his plan to leave and enquire about Odysseus appears as a premeditated calculation and, according to Kirchhoff, precisely for that reason, as an absurdity. Telemachus is supposed *first* to order the suitors from his house in front of the people, *second* to go to Pylos and Sparta, and *third*, according to what he finds out, wait for a year or marry-off his mother. But the second is superfluous if the first succeeds. But if the second is supposed to apply only if the first fails, it is an unforgivable mistake on the part of the poet not to say it.

---

[1] First *Rh. Mus.* 15 (1860), 329 ff.

From this, Kirchhoff drew the famous conclusion—which had serious consequences—that the narrative of Book 2 was the original and that the narrative of Book 1 was added later in the light of Book 2, and a [17] thoughtless botch it was too. This is where he was confident that he had caught an editor at work. He considered the action of Book 2 to be logically unified and self-contained; but that of Book 1 he reckoned to be embarrassingly absurd and so much in need of Book 2 to be comprehensible at all, that the servile dependence of a different author, that is, the unfortunate editor, undoubtedly gave itself away here.

Now it is true that today people have long stopped regarding Book 2 as self-sufficient overall. We know that Athena had to advise Telemachus to make the journey beforehand, both in the assumed *Telemachy* as well as in our *Odyssey*.[2] And yet under Kirchhoff's influence critics still continue to judge the plan to depart as a mere compromise, as a retreat, as a makeshift, just in case Telemachus' attempt to make the suitors give in before the people immediately should fail. So they still regard Book 2 as so self-contained and self-sufficient that they see the unity of these two themes in it established by the course of the action itself. To them, both themes bring out the same desire in Telemachus, with the result that the travel plan can emerge as a substitute for the actually intended actions with the suitors.

If things are seen this way, the true relationship between the themes has been displaced. For it is not true that in Book 2 everything takes place logically and comprehensibly in the way suggested. If you look more closely, in his appearance before the people, Telemachus' announcement that he is going to go to Pylos and Sparta is only loosely connected with the quarrel about the right of the suitors to hospitality and about marrying-off Penelope. His speech (2. 209–23), or more precisely, that part of his speech which holds out the prospect of possibly marrying-off Penelope (218–23), is not placed firmly but only superficially in context.

The scene[3] was devised and shaped not so much as a genuine attempt to get rid of the suitors, but rather as a battle for justice in

---

[2] Differently P. Von der Mühll, *RE* 'Odyssee' 705. There 212 f. is quoted as evidence that Telemachus himself comes to the decision to reach certainty about his father's fate—hardly correctly.

[3] On this, see esp. Wilamowitz, *Die Heimkehr des Odysseus* (Berlin, 1927), 99 f.

which the suitors, the permanent parasitic guests, who claim [18] that their violent doings are justified self-help in the face of Penelope's foul play, put themselves openly in the wrong in the eyes of the people and gods, a wrong which demands the punishment at the end of the poem.[4] This clearly emerges in the strands of argument of the scene.

A long interval of time has come to an end; something new and important is beginning. The people of Ithaca are assembling for the first time since Odysseus' departure. What is going to happen? Perhaps the people who went to Troy will return home? So from the first the thought anticipates the final goal, the homecoming of Odysseus. The beginning of the description is set up in such a way that everything seems to point to a happy result—Telemachus' appearance, radiant and received with pleasure, in the first few verses (1–14), and the introductory words of old Aegyptius (25–7), which Telemachus interprets as a good omen. Telemachus now laments the ruin of his house and the injustice of the suitors, asks the assembled people for a solution, appeals to their feelings of honour and shame, and warns of the gods (40–79). Antinous' answer (85–128) makes a counter-accusation against Penelope, a counter-demand from Telemachus, and a threat. Telemachus rejects the suitors' claim by proving that what they demand is unjust; men and gods would blame *him* if he expelled his mother from the house against her will. And so he gives them a choice: either to acknowledge the injustice they are committing and leave his house in peace, or to prepare themselves for him to call on the gods for help and for Zeus to take revenge on them. If things worked out properly he would *have* to be successful. To crown it all, Zeus adds his own confirmation. Telemachus has hardly made his threat in Zeus' name when he sends him two eagles as a sign. And a warning voice appears, Halitherses, who interprets the sign as referring to Odysseus' homecoming and solemnly announces that he is near. Everything now urges people towards the right decision, when the momentum of the scene suddenly takes an evil direction. The suitors disobey the clear requirements of the situation, Eurymachus, their spokesman, disdains the divine sign and warning voice and even casts suspicion on and threatens the warner (178–207). If Antinous had previously spoken in such a way that the dispute had

---

[4] Herkenrath, *Der ethische Aufbau der Ilias und Odyssee* (Paderborn, 1928), 227 ff.

to be taken absolutely seriously as a battle for [19] justice[5]—the listener, even more the listener of the poet's own time, sees the scales of justice tremble for a moment—so now the behaviour of the suitors degenerates into pure violence and sin; and so it follows logically that Telemachus refuses to talk about it any longer because the gods and the people now know what the situation is (209–11). The matter is left to them. Then Telemachus' old friend and protector Mentor once more opposes this evil turn of events and tries to rouse the people and incite them to step in: what will things come to if they forget a king as paternal and good as Odysseus was, and calmly stand by and watch his goods and chattels being violently consumed by the suitors? If that is their reward, well, kings should be harsh and unjust (229–41)! So he appeals to the people's conscience in order to persuade them to take an interest in Telemachus' cause. In vain: a third suitor, Leocritus, talks him down unhindered (243–56), and at this point the brutality of the rabble element among the suitors manifests itself without limits or inhibitions—if one is allowed to use that description of the large crowd in this noble society in order to distinguish it from Antinous and Eurymachus, who are still of a different kind—and sweeps everything away with itself. No more attempts are made to keep up appearances of right. All they really want to do is eat and drink, and in this they will not be put off by anybody. Even Odysseus would fare badly if he were to appear suddenly. In these extravagant, sinful words, behind whose madness the near truth uncannily threatens, the injustice of the suitors is completely [20] exposed. And with this, the people allow themselves to be dismissed, after the meeting had begun under such favourable omens and they had been summoned to help in such an unambiguous matter of right and wrong. Justice has been violated: legal proceedings have begun over an issue of justice which cannot rest until the great punishment comes.

[5] For the legal side of this for the present, see Wilamowitz, *Heimkehr*, 103 n. 2. The legal conditions of the *Odyssey*, with special emphasis on clan, inheritance, and widow-law, deserve to be investigated specifically by an expert not only on early Greek but also on Indo-European law in general. Works from the last decade about marriage laws of the Indo-Europeans and Germans would help here, e.g. those by Alfred Schultze on Old Norse marriage laws and marriage laws in the older Anglo-Saxon kings' laws, *Sächsische Sitzungsberichte* 91 (1939), 1; 93 (1941), 5. Admittedly one should not make the mistake of taking the poet at his word too strictly, as if his story had to be calculated over as a law case from beginning to end.

After these comments one cannot fail to recognize the uniform movement of this scene. In dramatic opposition of forces, it comes close to the triumph of justice; there it is intensified and brought to a head; and then it goes into reverse, takes an evil direction and, bottled up once more by a counter-movement, finally plunges with all its force into mad injustice. In all this, the central point at issue, especially in the last speeches, is the fact that the suitors in Odysseus' house are dissipating his goods and chattels.

Into this uniform structure, with its clearly drawn, large-scale lines of development, where everything spreads and swings out properly, a new motif now suddenly intrudes which, if considered correctly and taken seriously, would require a second climax to the plot's movement—Telemachus' request for a manned ship for his departure to Pylos and Sparta, and the announcement that, depending on the news of his father, he will either tolerate everything for another year, or if Odysseus is dead, that he will immediately marry-off Penelope (212–23).

If Telemachus himself speaks like this, i.e. if he abandons his cause, then the dispute really is all over. At best an old friend of the house like Mentor could exhort the suitors now at least to spare the house until Telemachus returned. Or he or another speaker would, as usual, react to his step. None of this happens: but, as stated earlier, people continue to talk generally about the suitors' dissipation. Only right at the end does Leocritus say that Telemachus' old friends Mentor and Halitherses will forward the journey for him but that it probably won't happen anyway.

This topic, then, Telemachus' request for a ship and his announcement about his future actions, strangely intrudes upon an otherwise uniform and tightly knit structure, but does not develop within it.

On the other hand, immediately after the scene, Athena and Telemachus talk to each other in such a way as if the scene had dealt mainly with [21] Telemachus' journey and not with the pernicious and improper behaviour of the suitors in Odysseus' house. Telemachus pours out his sorrow to Athena, not that people have vilely deserted him or not stopped the ruin of his house, but that they are impeding his journey (2. 262–6). Athena disguised as Mentor encourages him not to worry any more about the suitors' plans; she says that he will soon effect the journey without them, but with her, the goddess's, help (270–95). Then, when the suitors for the first time after this conversation meet him again in the house, they speak to him as if all he had done was negotiate with them about the ship and the crew (303–8; cf. Telemachus' reply, especially 318–20). Next, it is indeed described how, in spite of the suitors, Telemachus gets the ship and crew and departs.

Again, even before the people's assembly, there is a passage referring to the journey and nothing else as the enterprise which lies ahead. For Telemachus, as it says in the last verse of Book 1, in the night before the assembly, does not think about his attempt to get rid of the suitors, but only about the journey which Athena has advised him to make.

So, the appearance before the people has on the one hand been devised and shaped as a dispute over the activities of the suitors in Odysseus' house. Right and injustice dramatically oppose each other. The victory of injustice demands the punishment which Odysseus will mete out; and, especially towards the end of the scene, everything points beyond the immediate context to him and his return. On the other hand, through the 'departure' motif which has been inserted—Telemachus' request for a ship and his announcement of his journey and his future action—the scene has been carelessly and superficially adapted to meet the needs of the more immediate context of the Telemachus story, which at this point requires the attempt to obtain a ship, and its failure.[6]

[22] Before the *Odyssey* took on its present shape, was there once at this place a dispute about the departure which later, when the poem as a whole tightened up towards its goal, would have been sacrificed for the sake of the higher purpose? Or was such a scene never composed? But as soon as the context of the Telemachus story had developed, was another scene (the one which, in view of the punishment, had to clear the legal side) from the beginning given the additional burden of having a request for a ship put forward and refused? These are questions for which this work is too modest. It is enough that one Homeric scene has been explained, both how it is related to the whole of the *Odyssey*, and how it is inserted into the context of Telemachus' departure.

[6] The old grammarians noticed the difficulty and queried 214–23; cf. on this Wilamowitz, *Heimkehr*, 103, who, rather helplessly, still defends the group of verses. It cannot simply be deleted because otherwise ταῦτα μέν (210) is left hanging and because 253–6 still refer to it, which in turn cannot be taken out because of λαοὶ μέν before (252) which otherwise would also be left hanging.

There is another consequence. Kirchhoff's attempt to prove that Athena's conversation with Telemachus and everything else in Book 1 connected with this was subsequently patched on to Book 1 by the editor in slavish dependence on Book 2 has had one of its two main reasons taken away from it, i.e. the assumption that in Book 2 Telemachus' request for a ship and even his intention to go on a reconnaissance mission develop with inner consistency out of the attempt to get rid of the suitors by bringing a case before the people. That the other main reason, the scathing judgement about Book 1, is not valid either, will become evident soon. Here, first of all, I discuss simply what is necessary about the relation between the two themes of lawsuit and departure in Book 1.

In Telemachus' appearance before the people, the two themes do not depend on each other, as has just been shown. The enterprise of the departure does not arise only as a compromise or in any other way either from Telemachus' attempt to get the suitors out of the house with the help of the people or from the failure of this attempt. It does not just replace the real, primary intention as a necessary makeshift either. Both themes stand there simply unconnected, or connected only externally and roughly, one related to the conflict between Odysseus and the suitors which begins indirectly in the conflict between Telemachus and the suitors, the other related to Telemachus' search for news about his missing father. *How* these [23] two matters and consequently those two topics are related to each other, how they are connected, is not stated in Book 2 but on the contrary it *is* stated in Book 1 so that, especially in this scene, the second book depends on the first and cannot stand without the Mentes-scene of Book 1 in the way it is shaped in our *Odyssey*. For there the poet makes the two topics in question emerge from the single strand of the initial situation (1. 95 ff.).

Telemachus is sitting among the parasitic suitors, helplessly thinking about his missing father (114 ff.). His misery is highlighted by the presence of the guest Mentes. In front of him Telemachus is ashamed of the embarrassing festivity in the house and because of this embarrassment he explains his hopeless situation.

> Τούτοισιν μὲν ταῦτα μέλει, κίθαρις καὶ ἀοιδή,
> ῥεῖ', ἐπεὶ ἀλλότριον βίοτον νήποινον ἔδουσιν.   160

This is the one aspect of his misery which is obvious, *the plague of the parasitical suitors*. Through the word ἀλλότριον he immediately

leads us to the other aspect: (161) ἀνέρος, οὗ δή που λεύκ’ ὀστέα
πύθεται ὄμβρῳ . . . The *head of the household* is away, missing and
probably dead. This is what Telemachus continues to lament
(161–8), and the dialogue in its first part (161–223) stays with this
one question, whether *Odysseus* is still alive and can return home.
Then a question asked by the guest (244 ff.) refers back to the
beginning, to the subject of the *offensive festivity* (cf. 159); and now
the conversation develops this aspect of his misery which at first
(159 f.) had been mentioned briefly but immediately put aside: the
ruin of the house through the *suitors* (224–51). It is from these two
members of the expository conversation (161–223 and 224–51)
which, as said above, carefully develop the two aspects of
Telemachus’ misery, that afterwards twofold advice emerges in
Athena’s speech of encouragement (253–305): to tell the *suitors* to
leave the house in front of the assembled people, and to enquire
about his missing *father* in Pylos and Sparta. It is easy to see how
the themes originate and are from the beginning separately articulated.

This is a matter of more than the external motivation and
mechanics of the action. It is a question not only of where from and
how [24] the external impulse for the two actions—dispute in front
of the people and departure to foreign lands—derives; but in particular a question of how the two themes, the two actions, spring
internally and intrinsically from the misery of Telemachus which is
developed in two aspects, and (so to speak) merely brought to the
surface by Athena.

Precisely for this reason—to come back once more to Kirchhoff’s
assumption—it is not possible to dismiss the Mentes-scene in Book
1 as a patchwork one-sidedly dependent on Book 2. That
Telemachus’ encounter with the disguised deity is also in other
respects a piece of poetry valuable in its own right is to be shown in
the next chapter of this work. But there is reason to begin initially
further back.

TELEMACHUS’ AWAKENING

The visit of the guest in whose shape Athena conceals herself to
Telemachus in Odysseus’ house—the actual opening scene of our
Odyssey—contains the beginning of the movement on the earthly
stage. The peculiarity of this section of the poem becomes obvious

when it is compared with the supposed beginning of the *Telemachy* in the way Kirchhoff's followers tend to imagine it. E. Schwartz reproduced this in his sketch of the *Telemachy*, in more detail and more intelligibly than Wilamowitz. Therefore we will keep to his version.

In the 'original' *Telemachy*—so he roughly presents it (234 ff.)— Athena visited Telemachus who poured out his heart to her and disclosed his intention to make an end of the problem of the suitors through an assembly of the people of Ithaca. At this the goddess advised him, if this plan were to fail, to depart in order to make some enquiries; after this he would be able to decide what to do next. The voyage developed from the assembly, in fact from the compromise to which the defeated Telemachus was prepared to agree (235). This in turn generated the suitors' plan to murder Telemachus, and with that the knot was tied which later was untied through the failure of their plan and through Odysseus' revenge. The real theme was the adventures of a young prince, his difficulties, travels, dangers, and finally also his deeds in battle (252), and his eventual success, the triumph of a princely family which for generations had been dependent on a son, [25] whose royal dignity was under threat (254 f.). But this free-standing work of fiction now as epic had to be connected with the heroic past. So the poet introduced his hero into a world illuminated by the gleam of epic, to his father's war comrades whom we now surprisingly see in their domestic setting, like any other people. This, according to E. Schwartz, would be the purpose of the stay in Pylos and Sparta.

In this attempt to reconstruct and interpret the context of the *Telemachy*, at the beginning the connection between the two themes of the fight for justice before the people and the departure has been—erroneously as we think we showed in the previous chapter—constructed out of the problematical verses in Telemachus' speech where he seems to fall back on a compromise (2. 218–23); and as a result of that, the narrative of our first book, Athena's visit to Telemachus, has also been rebuilt. For it is Telemachus' own initiative to decide to end the problem of the suitors before the people, but Athena foresees that he will fail in this and advises him to make the voyage as a line of retreat.[7] In this

---

[7] The thought of distributing between Telemachus himself and the goddess the impulse for Telemachus' stand against the suitors and his departure stems, as far as I see things, from H. Düntzer, *Jahrbuch für klassische Philologie* (1862), 813 ff. =

way, of course, one thing now seems to follow the other more logically. But apart from the fact that this connection in the second book is untenable, so in turn in the first something epically impossible has been countenanced and something artistically essential has been sacrificed. For if this interpretation were right, the primary impulse would come from a human, Telemachus, who in fact [26] would have made the essential decision to stir himself up and do something of his own accord, and the deity would only complement that which the man had already decided. This is not the way an epic works. The second point is even more serious. For the sake of this reconstructed beginning of the *Telemachy* the first book of our *Odyssey* is abandoned; for the sake of a beginning which may rationally motivate the external sequence of things but artistically does not bear looking at, an essential artistic conception is foregone which no one will forego once he has inwardly perceived it.

Our *Odyssey* does not begin with the violent movement of the *Iliad* or the *Aeneid*, but in a static, confused, dangerous state of misery in Odysseus' own land. The head of the household has been away for twenty years and missing for ten. The young nobles, while wooing the queen, have lodged on the estate and eaten themselves into it in such a way that they almost treat it as an abandoned property, already their booty. In the meantime the son, who is just growing up and not yet taken seriously, is sitting among these parasites but giving them in their thoughtlessness no cause for concern yet. Penelope does not know whether she must regard herself as a widow and remarry. For soon her son will take over in the house, when she will become superfluous. We see: a state precariously balanced; only little is needed, and Odysseus' home, wife, estate, and royal dignity will all be lost. What will become of the young heir, helpless as he is, when, having come of age, he becomes a danger to these parasites and they notice it? One can only ask with concern about this, and then one will also immediately recognize the real

---

Homerische Abhandlungen (Leipzig, 1872), 429 ff.; there 444: 'Athena only advised him to prepare a ship and to depart. She did not tell him that he should call an assembly of the people and call up the Ithacans against the suitors. Telemachus, encouraged by the goddess, does this of his own accord.' In Düntzer this thought stems from his analysis of Athena's speech in Book 1 (253 ff.) where the advice to call an assembly and the order to take revenge (269–78, 293–305) are seen as out of place so that only the advice to depart remains. So we understand the origin of the thought which in Wilamowitz and Schwartz, separated from the analysis of Athena's speech and not further explained or substantiated, in fact seems to originate in an arbitrary way.

danger that the old royal tribe will perish in distress, without glory. But everything is still in a static state: only inside, unnoticed, the thoughts of the son reach out towards Odysseus, grieving and worrying whether he will at some time return, scatter the suitors, and regain his status and property (I. 114 ff.). This is the situation in Odysseus' homeland.

And now one day a stranger arrives—Athena in disguise—and gives the impetus which stirs up everything that was motionless and muddled. But this happens so secretly that it is hardly noticed. Nobody in the merry and unsuspecting [27] throng has observed the arrival of the stranger[8] except for Telemachus who, because he is yearning for and worrying about his distant father, is alert enough immediately to notice the guest who (so to speak) brings something of Odysseus with him. Telemachus is also looking for and anticipating something of this sort in his guest, so that from the beginning the two of them secretly have Odysseus indirectly present as a third party in their secret collusion. Only stealthily, heads together, are host and guest able to talk to each other: for the secluded, concealed togetherness in the hall which Telemachus was intent on as soon as he received him, because he was sympathetic to the stranger and hoped to hear something about his father, is disturbed by the intrusion of the rowdy suitors from whom there is obviously no escape anywhere. But the sound of singing and playing of strings, which at the beginning and the end of the scene is set as a contrasting background to the secret conversation (152 ff., 325 ff.), and the whole din of the deluded suitors do not just press and threaten: they also shield the two of them, as the disguised deity awakens Telemachus to himself.

This concealment in the midst of superior enemies and their

---

[8] The mysterious stranger in Book 1 and the unrecognized Odysseus in the Eumaeus book belong together. The one is a kind of precursor of the other. Connected with this in both parts of the poem is the motif that deceptive news tries to deceive Telemachus and Penelope and that one does not trust it any more; that all the travellers who claim to know something of Odysseus mean on the one hand deception but on the other hand a prelude to the truth; cf. 1. 166–8 and 414–16 with 14. 122–72. In this respect one could call the Mentes scene a kind of shadow of the Eumaeus scene. Consider also the way in which Telemachus, when he addresses his guest (158 ff.), almost automatically and unintentionally always ends up talking about Odysseus. This can be compared with the style and development of Eumaeus' speeches to whom of course the same thing happens. Slightly differently but essentially agreeing U. Hölscher, *Untersuchungen zur Form der Odyssee* (Hermes-Einzelschriften 6; 1939), 75 n.

untroubled cacophony is a kind of prelude to the later concealment of the directly present Odysseus, which is itself so stealthily secret as well. Doubly secretly, light and faint like a breeze, the first movement begins here at the start of the [28] poem and then, as it progresses, maintained and controlled with consummate art,[9] will come forward and swell until the shattering reversal at the end.

Later, in the next scene (the clash with the suitors in the hall (325–424)) the stealthy secret is indirectly hinted at, in the two passages where the spokesmen of the suitors in their speeches unknowingly stumble across it and nearly touch on it—Antinous, when he replies to Telemachus' changed, forceful language with the mocking remark that the gods have probably taught him to speak like that (387 f.), and the crafty Eurymachus when he asks him: 'Who was that stranger then? He has probably brought you news from your father. He disappeared with such strange suddenness without revealing himself'; whereupon Telemachus, reservedly, protects his secret from this intrusive enquiry (405–20).[10] It is as if nothing had happened, and yet some decision has been reached, something has been set in motion which will not come to rest again until the destruction of the suitors.

There is from the beginning a tense, contrasting relationship which without doubt shapes the introductory scene. It is between the insensitive hustle and bustle of the suitors, which spreads noisily out, pushes itself to the forefront, imposes itself, pushes from behind, and thinks it has no rival, but neither feels nor even suspects what is actually happening, and the wakeful but stealthy, shy being which smoulders like a spark under the ash, which at first works and weaves only in Telemachus' thoughts and concerns, but then begins to emerge in the collusion of host and guest, the first sign of the (so to speak) indirect spiritual presence of Odysseus. But its impetus develops in such a way that—to stay with the image— the embers of the spark are nourished and fanned more and more [29] until they burst into flame—but a flame which is still concealed.

---

[9] I here use the expression of J. Burckhardt, who has certainly hit on something essential about the art of the *Iliad* and the *Odyssey*.

[10] This secretive, reserved character is certainly typical of Telemachus in Book 1. As soon as he has received the guest he intends to ask him about his father. But in the conversation with him he deliberately spurns what is secretly his burning wish, namely that someone might come and tell him that Odysseus is coming home (166–9).

The Fight for Justice and Departure of Telemachus

The mere presence of the guest arouses in Telemachus the thought that he might know something about Odysseus. So he sits with him to one side to ask him. There is another reason. He also senses in advance the aversion of the stranger to the rowdiness of the parasites—a thought, incidentally, from which the impetus is born that will soon afterwards (144–58 ff.) initiate the actual conversation.

αὐτὴν δ᾽ ἐς θρόνον εἷσεν ἄγων . . .   130
πὰρ᾽ δ᾽ αὐτὸς κλισμὸν θέτο ποικίλον, ἔκτοθεν ἄλλων   132
μνηστήρων, μὴ ξεῖνος ἀνιηθεὶς ὀρυμαγδῷ
δείπνῳ ἀδήσειεν, ὑπερφιάλοισι μετελθών,
ἠδ᾽ ἵνα μιν περὶ πατρὸς ἀποιχομένοιο ἔροιτο.

But before it comes to the intended question and the conversation about Odysseus, the suitors intrude into the hall and fill it with their feasting, dancing, singing, and lyre-playing. It is this dramatic counter-movement, which points as with a gesture, that on the other hand keeps the impetus going, and after the meal initiates the conversation between Telemachus and Athena. Telemachus senses how the guest feels in his soul—offended, reproachful or at least curious about the reason for this festival activity—and explains it to him.[11]

ξεῖνε φίλ᾽, ἦ καί μοι νεμεσήσεαι, ὅττι κεν εἴπω;
τούτοισιν μὲν ταῦτα μέλει, κίθαρις καὶ ἀοιδή,
ῥεῖ᾽, ἐπεὶ ἀλλότριον βίοτον νήποινον ἔδουσιν   160
ἀνέρος, οὗ δή που λεύκ᾽ ὀστέα πύθεται ὄμβρῳ . . .

This soon turns into a lament for Odysseus. And when Telemachus stops himself, remembers his duty as a host, and politely turns to his guest with the usual question who he is, it is with this too that, after a few words, he hits on the one thing which concerns him, and the question about the guest turns suddenly into a question about his father: 'Were you by chance a friend of his already?'

[30]   καὶ μοι ταῦτ᾽ ἀγόρευσον ἐτήτυμον, ὄφρ᾽ ἐῢ εἴδω,
ἠὲ νέον μεθέπεις, ἦ καὶ πατρώιός ἐσσι   175
ξεῖνος, ἐπεὶ πολλοὶ ἴσαν ἀνέρες ἡμέτερον δῶ
ἄλλοι, ἐπεὶ καὶ κεῖνος ἐπίστροφος ἦν ἀνθρώπων.

Thus from the start the conversation, though it seems simply to fulfil the polite formalities of hospitality, is secretly steered by that alert, lurking tension within Telemachus, to centre upon Odysseus.

---

[11] The scholia to 1. 158 are very good: προκαταλαμβάνει τὴν κατηγορίαν, ἵνα μὴ νομισθῇ παρὰ τῷ ξένῳ τῆς ἀταξίας αἴτιος εἶναι.

Yes, Odysseus is present before it starts, not only in the worry and longing of Telemachus (114 ff.) but even before that, where Athena is said to reach the forecourt of *Odysseus* (103), and then later when Telemachus takes his guest's spear and puts it in the rack together with those other spears of *Odysseus* (127 ff.)—with a significant gesture which points forward to the final battle but first reminds us of Odysseus.

If Odysseus is already indirectly present both before the start of the conversation and in the polite formalities of its beginning, so is he all the more in its more serious continuation, first in the guest's answer to Telemachus' question (179–212). Here the image of Odysseus appears to his son in ever new perspective and shape, inciting him, shaking him up, arousing hope in him, and intensifying his feelings of isolation and humiliation. The image stirs him up, for example, when by the rumour which the stranger claims to have heard, for a moment, the arrival of Odysseus is envisaged as if it had happened already; and also, by the way Athena confidently interprets Odysseus' absence and announces his return home, and all the more when she becomes aware of the fact that, in this Telemachus here, there is the Odysseus of former times, the traveller to Troy (so to speak) present again; so much does Telemachus resemble him. Both look for and see in the other something of Odysseus.

The last group of verses in this speech of Athena (205–12) mentioned just now builds a bridge of thought between the young Odysseus who once went to war and his image who is now standing in front of the guest, between the one who, in time and space, is far away, and the one who is present. Yes, in addressing Telemachus she is close to addressing an Odysseus who has grown up again and (so to speak) returned, in the course of a conversation which plays around Odysseus and so, more and more, points to Telemachus. And in this way, these verses already aim at the goal to which the whole [31] scene is directed—to awaken a new Odysseus in Telemachus. The goal is not yet reached here. After the first attempt, a counter-movement is twice led against it (214–20, 231–51). Then at last the transforming power of Athena's will emerges victorious (205–305). In this development, which begins with one end in view and is interrupted by counter-movements, there is clear evidence of a mature, long-sighted technique of extended scene-building at work.

The Fight for Justice and Departure of Telemachus

So Athena's words at first do not get as far as converting Telemachus' grief and longing into determination and energy. They only arouse new pain and bitter laments about being the son of Odysseus instead of being the son of a man favoured by fate, who would leave his son an intact, rich, and easily appropriated inheritance. As at the beginning (114 ff.), Telemachus is, as far as he is concerned, still nothing but a helpless martyr. And so, in order to achieve her purpose, Athena has to intensify his pain even more and touch his sorest point, the pain which is torturing him directly.

And here again there is the chance to observe the superb artistry of this lengthy conversation. It is the passage where the one theme, Telemachus' grief over his missing father and his own isolation, ceases to hold centre stage on its own, and where the second theme, the plague of suitors, comes to the fore after it had appeared briefly at the start of the whole conversation (159 ff.) only to be quickly dropped. This method of presenting the two themes together to start with but then developing them one after the other was referred to earlier in a different context.[12] Now we want to show how at the point of transition, where the second theme is picked up again, consistent continuity is joined with the return of the initial situation of the conversation.

Telemachus started by answering his guest's question about the reason for the feasting, even before it had been framed:

> τούτοισιν μὲν ταῦτα μέλει, κίθαρις καὶ ἀοιδή,
> ῥεῖ', ἐπεὶ ἀλλότριον βίοτον νήποινον ἔδουσιν   160
> ἀνέρος, οὗ δή που λεύκ' ὀστέα πύθεται ὄμβρῳ . . .

[32] Here now the stranger actually asks it:

> τίς δαίς, τίς δαὶ ὅμιλος ὅδ' ἔπλετο; τίπτε δέ σε χρεώ;   225
> εἰλαπίνη ἠὲ γάμος; ἐπεὶ οὐκ ἔρανος τάδε γ' ἐστίν . . .

and Telemachus explains it to him. They are the suitors of his mother, who are frittering away his goods and chattels. This answer refers us back to the beginning.

And yet the dialogue continues logically. The guest's question does not only refer back to the beginning of the conversation—it does this almost perfunctorily, as if of its own accord—but it also takes into account Telemachus' last lament which immediately precedes it.

---

[12] p. 199.

ὡς δὴ ἐγώ γ' ὄφελον,   217

he lamented,

μάκαρος νύ τοι ἔμμεναι υἱὸς
ἀνέρος, ὃν κτεάτεσσιν ἑοῖς ἔπι γῆρας ἔτετμεν.

He loses himself in the ideal of a rich master and a prosperous *house*
and estate, and laments that fate withholds this from him. It is this
which Athena goes into after she has first insisted on her theme—
bringing Telemachus to a consciousness of himself (225 f.).

τίς δαίς, τίς δαὶ ὅμιλος ὅδ' ἔπλετο; τίπτε δέ σε χρεώ;   225
εἰλαπίνη ἠὲ γάμος; ἐπεὶ οὐκ ἔρανος τάδε γ' ἐστίν.

'How does this make sense?' she asks. 'You are lamenting, yet here
there are what look like a feast and a wedding in a rich *house*. What
does this mean?' This is how speech and counter-speech would
logically interlock.

The 'wealthy *house*' is the keynote further on as well.[13] [33]
Athena's question evokes Telemachus' last and most violent lament,
in which the suitor theme now predominates: 'Yes, it did once look
as if this *house* would in the future be wealthy and of impeccable
standing. But things have turned out differently. The whole of the
young nobility is wooing my mother and using up the house; they eat
everything up and waste my house away.' This paraphrase summarizes the broadest scope of Telemachus' speech, which is shaped at
the same time in a varied and unified way. Recall the Greek:

μέλλεν μέν ποτε οἶκος ὅδ' ἀφνειὸς καὶ ἀμύμων ἔμμεναι . . .   232
νῦν δ' ἑτέρως ἐβόλοντο θεοί . . .   234
ὅσσοι . . . ἐπικρατέουσιν ἄριστοι . . . . . . ἠδ' ὅσσοι . . .   245
κοιρανέουσιν,
τόσσοι μητέρ' ἐμὴν μνῶνται, τρύχουσι δὲ οἶκον.
. . . τοὶ δὲ φθινύθουσιν ἔδοντες οἶκον ἐμόν . . .   250

---

[13] It is amazing how the mention of Penelope too is secretly prepared in
Telemachus' last lament (248 ff.) in that Telemachus' answer to the question
whether such a grown-up son of Odysseus' is really standing before him is given the
turn: 'My mother tells me that I am his son' (215) and in that in the guest's reply
Penelope is now given a place of honour: 'I am not worried about the house since
Penelope has given birth to such a son' (222 f.). In the latter passage it would have
been sufficient to say: '. . . since you are such as I see you here before me.' But obviously the listener is supposed to be prepared for Penelope without his realizing it
when he meets her as the main figure in the following lament of Telemachus': 'The
whole nobility of the islands is wooing my mother. And she cannot definitely say yes
or no' (245–50).

The Fight for Justice and Departure of Telemachus

Into the momentum of the broad structure spread over twenty verses, a link has been introduced which through μέν is related in advance to what is going to come, which travels far afield, extends over nine verses, and is itself rich in life. In this link the earlier theme, Telemachus' lament over his missing father and his own isolation, seems to have reached its climax. Here, then, all of Telemachus' concerns so far, with the new theme, the plague of suitors, definitely dominating, are accumulated together and intensified to the highest pitch—the whole misery of the son of a man utterly lost, who has been abandoned, helpless, to enemies who are fleecing him, a misery worse than that of the son of someone who has fallen in war; for he would at least inherit his father's glory and have a free hand. All this points acutely towards danger for the house and—mentioned here for the first time—danger for the heir.

> τοὶ δὲ φθινύθουσιν ἔδοντες   250
> οἶκον ἐμόν· τάχα δή με διαρραίσουσι καὶ αὐτόν.

Only after the insidious evil has come out into the open so forcefully does the conversation reach the goal at which it has been aiming for some time [34] (208 ff., 222 f.). Athena transforms suffering into energy and thus (so to speak) awakens Telemachus to himself (253–305).

And although this speech of Athena's may be difficult and controversial in details, one thing is certain: that precisely this is its purpose in the whole *Odyssey*. First (253–66) it contrasts Odysseus with the pressing need and danger which emerged from the end of Telemachus' last lament (we have drawn attention to the widely ranging structure which gathers all its force towards the end): how Odysseus is imagined as avenger in Telemachus' desire for him (115 ff., 163 ff.), how Odysseus has come alive in the guest's words (196–212) in fullness of life, strength, and intelligence, and armed with dangerous weapons (257–64), although, of course, only as an ideal:

> εἰ γὰρ νῦν ἐλθὼν δόμον ἐν πρώτῃσι θύρῃσι   255
> σταίη, ἔχων πήληκα καὶ ἀσπίδα καὶ δύο δοῦρε
> τοῖος ἐών, οἷόν μιν ἐγὼ τὰ πρῶτ' ἐνόησα
> οἴκῳ ἐν ἡμετέρῳ πίνοντά τε τερπόμενόν τε
>
>   *   *   *
>
> τοῖος ἐὼν μνηστῆρσιν ὁμιλήσειεν Ὀδυσσεύς·   265
> πάντες κ' ὠκύμοροί τε γενοίατο πικρόγαμοί τε.

Friedrich Klingner

Then she dismisses the ideal:

ἀλλ' ἦ τοι μὲν ταῦτα θεῶν ἐν γούνασι κεῖται,
ἦ κεν νοστήσας ἀποτίσεται ἠὲ καὶ οὐκί.

Its place is taken by Athena's advice. In contrast to a mere ideal, she expresses the demands of the real situation and turns Telemachus' thoughts from the father for whom he can only long to himself, the son who is present and duty bound to act: σὲ δὲ φράζεσθαι ἄνωγα (269).

This forms the second and larger section of the speech (268–302). If you examine the varied contents of this advice in detail, it seems that you move from clarity to confusion, from the indisputable to the disputed. Yet you will without doubt distinguish three themes. They all spring from the conversation as it has developed up till now and they all lead from one ordeal of Telemachus' to a determination to do something about it.

[35] Telemachus' departure stands out particularly clearly (279–92). It has emerged from the conversation before, which has gone as follows: the father is missing, the mother is being pressed by suitors and in a state of indecision, and house and son are in danger. From this now springs the resolve to make enquiries in the outside world, to clarify what the prospects are, and then to act sensibly, depending on the situation: either to wait for Odysseus for another year—he would be able to put everything right—or to put an end to the indecision, declare his father to be dead, and marry-off his mother so that he can then be master in his own house. So there will be either a sensibly limited period of waiting, or a strong-minded reconciliation of himself to the inevitable, and the dismissal of his mother. The advice is restricted to this. Of course, it does take courage to depart to make enquiries. But in this theme there is comparatively little to be felt of the theme of the father in the son, of the return of Odysseus in Telemachus, at least as regards the main problem—the situation at home and the enemies who have lodged there.

A second theme would be the fight for justice before the people (272–8). The suitors have committed injustice and behaved improperly—this has been enthusiastically referred to earlier on—and for this they deserve punishment. From this arises the advice to send them packing in front of the people, i.e. after that which is the real theme of Book 2: tying them down as criminals before people and gods, starting legal proceedings over the matter, and thus preparing their punishment. This requires much courage and prudence, and since by undertaking it, Telemachus represents the cause of his house against the suitors, he has already (so to speak) come closer to Odysseus. One senses more of the father in the son, and also that the son has been given his own part in the feud between Odysseus and the suitors.

It is this that completes itself in the third theme, the command to take revenge (293–302). This also springs from the fact that the suitors have violated justice. If Odysseus, who is the first one responsible for taking revenge, does not come, the responsibility will pass over to Telemachus, now that he has fully grown to noble stature. The example of Orestes, the avenger of his father, also acts as an admonition. The age of the young man who has just grown up is that main piece of poetic invention here on which the whole of the awakening scene, and indeed of the first books of the *Odyssey*, are based. To bring this noble rounded personality, this image of the young Odysseus, to a state of self-consciousness has already been clearly recognizable as Athena's [36] purpose (206–12, 222 f.). Finally, the example of Orestes is due to the poetic idea of seeing Odysseus and his house in the image of the house of the Atridae. This idea has been present from the beginning of the *Odyssey* (1. 35 ff.) and particularly helps to shape on a large scale the story of Telemachus' stay with Nestor and Menelaus. In fact Athena's words here have been taken for a full four lines from one of Nestor's speeches of exhortation (1. 229 (at end)–302 = 3. 197 (at end)–200). In fact this paraenetic theme here is actually related most closely to Nestor's *paraenesis* there. If you look at the whole introductory scene, the impetus which strives to awaken in Telemachus a new Odysseus is vigorously fulfilled in our third theme. In Athena's speech, Telemachus as a potential avenger corresponds at the end to the hoped-for ideal avenger Odysseus at the beginning. Finally, in the context of the whole poem, the structure of this speech points to Odysseus and Telemachus taking this vengeance together.

'If only Odysseus would come to take revenge!' Athena says. 'But since this is uncertain, you have to prepare to take revenge yourself, if the worst comes to the worst.' The two alternatives expressed by Athena will in fact occur simultaneously. Incidentally, Telemachus' feud with the suitors is prepared most vigorously in this theme, e.g. 2. 325 where it is said among the suitors: 'Telemachus is probably plotting our death.'

These three themes are bundled together very unconcernedly in Athena's advice. No attempt has been made to combine and balance them with each other in such a way that Telemachus' plan can be seen as a set of logical alternatives. One would ask in vain: 'How is the attempt to get rid of the suitors by a lawsuit before the people's assembly connected with the departure? What does the voyage mean, if the ultimate goal is revenge? Is it perhaps a means of ascertaining in advance whether the true avenger can still return, or whether Telemachus will finally have to act on his own? But in the context of the second theme, the voyage was supposed to achieve something different, i.e. ascertain whether Telemachus could wait for another year, or would have to marry-off his mother soon in order to preserve his estate. Further: Is the decision possibly to marry-off his mother compatible with the intention of taking revenge?'

[37] Have several situations been confused here? In what sense should this be understood? One thing is certain: the three themes all spring from the previous conversation and they all continue throughout the story.

People have tried to create order by deletion. So, for example, Düntzer[14] removed everything concerned with punishment from Athena's speech, i.e. everything belonging to the second and third themes (269–78, 293–305), and admitted only what belongs to the departure. Consequently, verses 279–92 would follow 253–68, so that the advice to depart and make enquiries is linked with the idealized Odysseus and the verses leading to the advice. But, how will everything which has been directed at awakening a new Odysseus in Telemachus be fulfilled by nothing but a voyage? All this does is bring clarification—a wait of one year under favourable circumstances, or liberation by marrying-off his mother. Others, among them Finsler,[15] deleted at least the command to take revenge at the end of the speech (293–305). But what then happens to the speech as a whole? See it whole, and its movement is all the more apparent. For whatever the details, as a whole it is precisely and grandly shaped. It starts powerfully and importantly, and is passionately

---

[14] *Homerische Abhandlungen*, 435 ff. (orig. *Jahrbücher für klassische Philologie* (1862), 813–23).

[15] *Homer*[2], ii. 265; similarly Ameis–Hentze to 295.

expounded, with an idealized picture of Odysseus and his revenge, and this image magnificently soars far and wide (253–66). The *paraenesis* is in clear contrast to this (267 ff.), but again, in keeping with the content and power of the speech's movement, it is intensified at the end with the command to take revenge. The result is that the realization that the duty of revenge ultimately lies with him, Telemachus, corresponds to the ideal vision portrayed at the beginning: the moving, grandly shaped ending corresponds to the strong opening. On the other hand, try to stop before the last theme (293–302) with the following words:

> σῆμά τέ οἱ χεῦαι καὶ ἐπὶ κτέρεα κτερεΐξαι   291
> πολλὰ μάλ᾽, ὅσσα ἔοικε, καὶ ἀνέρι μητέρα δοῦναι.

Then the whole movement of the speech runs like this: 'Yes, Odysseus should intervene to take revenge—but you have no [38] control over this. It is your task to try to get justice before the people, and then to ascertain whether Odysseus is still able to return. Then, at most, you can wait for another year. After that— or if the news is unfavourable, immediately—you will have to decide to marry-off your mother.' A fine way to galvanize the martyr into action! The whole burden of the suitors' outrageous injustice is not shifted at all. What opens so grandly ends with a whimper. How much worse than our traditional text!

Finally, one can try to cut out precisely the meek advice to Telemachus to marry-off his mother in the event of unfavourable news (290–3). At first, there seems to be something in this. In the event of unfavourable news, the advice, instead of being:

> νοστήσας δὴ ἔπειτα φίλην ἐς πατρίδα γαῖαν   290
> σῆμά τέ οἱ χεῦαι καὶ ἐπὶ κτέρεα κτερεΐξαι
> πολλὰ μάλ᾽, ὅσσα ἔοικε, καὶ ἀνέρι μητέρα δοῦναι . . .

would then be:

> φράζεσθαι δὴ ἔπειτα κατὰ φρένα καὶ κατὰ θυμόν,
> ὅππως κε μνηστῆρας ἐνὶ μεγάροισι τέοισι   295
> κτείνῃς ἠὲ δόλῳ ἢ ἀμφαδόν· οὐδέ τί σε χρὴ
> νηπιάας ὀχέειν, ἐπεὶ οὐκέτι τηλίκος ἐσσί.

And who knows whether sometimes it was not recited like this, the one being able to replace the other? But the group of lines in question cannot be deleted as a late addition quite so easily. Otherwise we would remove from the speech a motif which is rooted deeply in the conversation. For precisely when Telemachus' final lament reaches its climax, Penelope comes to the fore in it; her indecision endangers house and son (248 ff.). Seen from the point of view of the heir and of the estate, her status, which is ambiguous and unclear, is very dangerous. Who would then want to delete this motif from Athena's advice?

If you try to create order by deletion, you damage the poetry. If, with Kirchhoff, you condemn the disorder as a bungling patch-work and explain it as he does as genetic, you cannot account for the beauty of the movement of the whole, [39] quite apart from the fact that the well-known assumption which he made to explain the dif-ficulty is based on a faulty understanding of the corresponding place in Book 2.

So this is it: in the part of Athena's speech which looks ahead with its advice and instruction, the themes as they emerged prob-ably gradually with the genesis of the tale are put together with an astonishing lack of concern, without any harmonization of their factual contents. And yet the movement of the speech, seen in con-nection with the whole, is beautiful and plausible. Again, if one looks at the whole, the speech as a part of the 'awakening' scene brings the action to a climax and a goal which you would find it dif-ficult to improve on; whereas Athena's announcement of future developments in its details is done roughly, negligently, weakly even, and largely in verses which lack full poetic inspiration, verses which are written for those parts of the story which are announced and prepared here, but told only later.

The conversation between Telemachus and his guest which has been analysed here does not just provide the impulse for the exter-nal action, does not just relate a decision that has been made already and describe the clever advice given.[16] Within the impasse described at the beginning of the poem, at the moment of Telemachus' maturity, a power has been awakened and set in motion with great intelligence. There is more than a prince in whom the courage to perform his first deeds has been awakened. Here as well as in the people's assembly of Book 2, if you look at it closely, everything is directed towards the homecoming of Odysseus. Fatherland, house, estate, family, dignity, and people, everything he left behind is shown to be in a critical state in which

[16] As in the attempt by E. Schwartz, *Die Odyssee* (Munich, 1924) to reconstruct the genuine *Telemachy*.

the concealed contrasts step apart and begin to move. This begins with the rising grief and laments of Telemachus. But while Odysseus' cause begins to stir energetically (so to speak) in Telemachus, it also brings the opposition forces to the surface. This shows itself immediately after that 'awakening' scene, in the first encounter with the suitors after it (1. 365–425), when for the first time Telemachus [40] makes use of his rights as householder, and thus gives rise to an exchange of words about both the future kingship of Ithaca and his inherited goods and chattels. It continues in the conflict before the people in Book 2, and when the suitors do not succeed in turning Telemachus back into his previous harmless self by their jokes, it then leads to the scene where he refuses to treat with them, and insists on his departure, but they for the first time, even though still joking and mocking, turn their minds to quarrel over life and death, and his destruction (2. 305 ff., 325 ff.). Then Eurycleia anticipates with foreboding the coming attempt on his life (2. 363 ff.). Accordingly the suitors, as soon as they find out, to their surprise, that he has after all summoned the will-power to act on his own (4. 630 ff.), plan to lie in wait for him. While his impending death appears anticipated in Penelope's fears for him (4. 675 ff.), the suitors set up their ambush (4. 768 ff., 842 ff.). It seems as if Telemachus was bound to run straight into the trap. But Eurycleia's optimistic presentiment (4. 754 ff.) and a dream which Athena sends Penelope (4. 795 ff.) vaguely point to future deliverance—though behind this prospect the total uncertainty about Odysseus becomes apparent for a moment. Thus ends Book 4.

The narrative says roughly this (and it says it far better than any summary, which is only good for stimulating the attention): the situation in Odysseus' fatherland has become deadly dangerous. Then the gods decide to free him from his unwelcome sojourn with Calypso and to send him out again into the storms and anguish of the high seas. Telemachus—his breed, his heir (1. 222, 4. 753) who represents everything which he left behind at home and which belongs to him—ends up in a feud and nearly dead as soon as he starts acting independently and trying to take on the role of his father. So, just at the time when, to get back home, Odysseus exposes himself to the last and greatest dangers of his whole homecoming, also at home, his cause has never been more seriously endangered. The time has almost come when he will find nothing there that belongs to him, but only enemies. The listener now sees him with different eyes when he appears for the first time on Calypso's island in the next book (Book 5). Homecoming, life, and fatherland are at stake all together.

Everything which has been illuminated here—the 'awakening' scene and [41] the purpose of the movement which starts there and which in the departure of and danger to the heir unquestioningly relates to Odysseus—is sacrificed by those who interpret and reshape the *Telemachy* as E. Schwartz does. And he who, with Bethe or with von der Mühll, separates the feud from the *Telemachy*, assigns it to a late and inferior author, and because of that pays it no more attention, has to face the question whether the important relationships of our *Odyssey* which have been demonstrated do not make their supposedly so far superior *Telemachy* appear poor and insignificant.

Homer and the *Telemachy*, Circe and Calypso, The Phaeacians

K. REINHARDT

Who was Homer? A fiction or a human being? One poet or two? Or
a dozen? An original genius or an editor? The legendary head of a
school of rhapsodes? The hero of popular stories about a 'wandering minstrel'? Is his name—'hostage', 'guarantor', or 'guild comrade'—a proper name or a generic one? And what are the *Iliad* and
the *Odyssey*? Are they what the ancients thought they were? The
work of the same poet in his prime and his old age? Or the legacy of
a guild of rhapsodes? Of what time? Do they divide into smaller
epics or into strata? Should we divide them, as it were, by vertical
sections? Or strip them off each other, layer by layer? Mycenaean
and geometric? Or products of different hands, styles, and tem-
peraments? In order to reach the essential do we first have to free a
central core from its wrappings? Did a second master builder alter
the original work of a first? Are different plans interlocked? Did the
whole epic originate from rhapsodic competitions? So many questions, so many answers. Apart from an isolated precursor in the
seventeenth century, the Abbé d'Aubignac, the guessing, or the
'Homeric question', has been going on in uninterrupted succession
since the end of our classical period, since the time of Herder,
Christian Gottlob Heyne, Robert Wood, and especially Goethe's
friend Friedrich August Wolf and Goethe himself.

Homer was the god of our classical period. On a period which
believed in art, Wolf's famous introduction, the *Prolegomena ad
Homerum* 1795, had an effect of the voice of an ambitious atheist
founding a school. It excited, dismayed, and aroused assent and

From: K. Reinhardt, *Tradition und Geist* (Göttingen, 1960; [originally *Von Werken
und Formen* (Godesberg, 1948)]), 37–46, 77–87, 112–24. First section written to go
with an edition of Voss's translation. Every effort has been made to trace and contact the copyright holder prior to printing.

dissent. The analytical and the creative spirit, philology and the appreciation of art, clashed here for the first time in a decisive way. Hence Wolf's importance. His theory (together with the conclusions drawn from it by others), i.e. the denial of the person of Homer, the argument that writing began later, that the two epics were late records of orally transmitted common rhapsodic property, collected and put in order in Athens under Peisistratus (c.550), was not absolutely new—the latter being in a certain sense an assertion of antiquity already—but what was new was its methodical approach, its [38] historico-critical consciousness, its sharpness. It was perceived as the signal of the new era, of the historicizing epoch (which was then beginning). No philologist really liked referring to Herder and to Wood (*Essay on the Original Genius of Homer*, 1769). It was in Wolf that the intellectual conflict came to a head.

After agreeing with him initially, Goethe began to defend himself against Wolf's criticism more and more as he entered the world of the *Iliad* as an imitative poet when he was working on his own *Achilleid*. Indeed, displeasure had been his first reaction: 'The idea may be good and the effort is respectable, if only those gentlemen in order to cover their weak flanks did not occasionally have to lay waste the most fertile gardens of the aesthetic realm and turn them into disagreeable entrenchments. And at the end there is more subjective matter in all this business than one thinks' (to Schiller, 17 May 1795). But soon in the elegy 'Hermann und Dorothea' he drinks to 'the health of the man who, boldly freeing us at last from the name Homeros, calls us into a fuller orbit'. Another phase of study with Wolf's work at hand follows in April 1797: 'Here I have the most wonderful revelations.' Decisive discoveries are indeed beginning to be made, discoveries which only the most recent development in philological criticism has been able to appreciate, especially the discovery of the importance of 'preparation' and 'retardation'. 'A main characteristic of the epic poem is the fact that it is always going forwards and backwards, so all retarding motifs are epic.' In December 1797 the essay 'On epic and dramatic poetry' is sent to Schiller and at the same time work on the *Achilleid* is started. The result is: 'I am more than ever convinced of the unity and indivisibility of the poem [the *Iliad*] and that there is nobody now living, nor will there ever be, who would be capable of evaluating it. I at least find time and again that I am judging subjectively. This has happened to others before us and will happen to others after us' (to Schiller, 16 May 1798).

Schiller had always rejected Wolf and so had Voss. Goethe's later point of view is described in the 'Tag- und Jahreshefte' 1821: 'One remembers what pain began to be felt among the friends of the art of poetry and of its enjoyment, when the personality of Homer, the one-ness of the author of those world-famous poems, was disputed in such a bold and excellent way. Cultivated humanity was most profoundly upset and although it could not refute the arguments of this extremely important opponent, [39] it was nevertheless unable to extinguish completely its old instinct and inclination to imagine only *one* source for the poem. This fight had been going on for more than twenty years, and a revolution in the opinions of the whole world was necessary to restore at least some breathing space to the old view.'

But if it seemed to Goethe at that time that Wolf's view had been superseded, he was mistaken. Scholars began to split up into 'unitarians' and 'Wolfians'. The Wolfians were the more important. One Wolfian was Gottfried Hermann, who distinguished between original (Ur-) epics, an initially small original *Iliad* and original *Odyssey*, and their gradual extensions. Even more Wolfian was Hermann's follower Karl Lachmann, whose theory of individual songs was finally refuted only by Andreas Heusler's proof that epic and song are separate forms, not only in extent but also in character, and that an epic is never composed of songs. That the *Odyssey* was composed, or more precisely 'compiled', of epics instead of songs was claimed by Adolf Kirchhoff (*Die homerische Odyssee*, 1859, 1878[2]) who, with this claim, became the father of all the newer analytical approaches to this poem. According to his view, the *Odyssey* contained three poems, first, an 'old' one about Odysseus' return home, second, one of inferior quality about the killing of the suitors, and third, the one about Telemachus' journey. At a time when to be unitarian meant the equivalent of thinking unhistorically, Jacob Burckhardt's superior judgement, which had been the result of a comparison of world literature, was expressed in vain. As the most important analyst, Wilamowitz continues the work of Kirchhoff, but in his reconstruction of the poems contained in the *Iliad* as well as the *Odyssey*, his solutions become so complicated, and doubling of episodes spreads so far and wide, that the opposite, unity, can be seen more and more clearly through the thicket of hypotheses. And so, in the end, analytical criticism, the glory of the nineteenth and twentieth centuries, turned back on itself, similarly to the way Goethe did through his poetic imitation. At the end, there was no escape from the ever deepening confusion but to restore the poet to his poem. [. . .]

[41] . . . The *Odyssey* appears as testimony to a slightly younger spirit than that of the *Iliad*, and is presented against a younger background. Idyll is reflected in the fairy-tale, and in the era of heroes, the hustling merchantman and piracy of the sea-ruling Phoenicians are presented with realistic contemporary detail. The Cimmerians, on the way from southern Russia to Asia Minor in the seventh century, dwell in the far north. Family rule begins to threaten the old tribal kingship. The contrast between two generations, in the *Iliad* a rare perspective into ancient times, here broadly envelops and foregrounds an old revenge tale, to express a new interpretation and reflection. But above all, it seems that the divine has become different, and with it, consequently, that which is taught and imprinted here: the human. The avenger's trick, the disguise, develops into social perspective and the experience of all the bitterness of an old and rightless person among a supercilious young nobility. [. . .]

Of course, this is valid for the *Odyssey* as a whole, and it must not be concealed that precisely this whole has recently again been called in question. Two opinions, although more congenial to each other than before, are struggling to win approval. For the one group, the *Odyssey* is, in spite of the rather different story on which it is based, a whole, gathered up into one, which has been constructed out of days, scenes, and manifold destinies after the model of the *Iliad*. For the others, one poem, the 'Homecoming of Odysseus', which runs through it and is contained in it, has been extended by the *Telemachy*, and a few poetic insertions and imitations by the same hand. One poet, they claim, complemented the other. The older, greater poet began to tell [42] how in the council of the gods Athena intercedes for Odysseus, how Calypso, instructed by Hermes, lets him go, how he comes to the Phaeacians and to his home, how he meets his son at Eumaeus' place, how they unite for revenge, etc. They claim that another poet added the description of the situation on Ithaca, Telemachus' journey to Sparta, and the suitors' plot to kill him on his journey back home with all the minor matters connected with this. If the younger poet pursues his religious and educational goals with good fortune and skill, they say, it is only the older one who is of 'Homer's' kind, if he is not the poet of the *Iliad* himself.

These, roughly, are the thoughts of Wolfgang Schadewaldt.[1] And without doubt this theory perceives something about the *Odyssey*. What runs through it as its main theme, Odysseus' wanderings and homecoming, has been depicted far more strongly than the secondary theme, the distress his son suffers and his entry into the world of heroes, his quest and his maturing. The main action shines in all the splendour of the melody, while the weaker secondary action is courting it, as if in accompaniment. Again, the main theme has claimed nearly all the fairy-tale elements, all of the old mythical traditions, while the secondary theme makes do with invented material. And yet there are quite a few objections to this method of analysing the poem.

That older poet who is supposed to have existed brings his hero out of his wanderings via three stages: from Calypso via the Phaeacians to Eumaeus. But do Calypso and Nausicaa, the goddess and the barely matured princess, stand as counterparts to that unique woman about whom we hear only very late, only after the other two have long since disappeared from our view and are no longer in competition? Furthermore: everybody loves and entertains Odysseus—his two hosts even without knowing who he is— but Eumaeus among his swine is more royal than Alcinous in his fairy-tale splendour in that he is a king in servant's shape. Calypso and the Phaeacians are thus separated from the other fairy-tale adventures and develop into separate structures rounded in themselves in the manner of the great epic, while the other fairy-tales pass over into the first-person singular narrative. This device—it has been admired and imitated ever since, from the *Aeneid* to *Wilhelm Meister*, and yet never again mastered with such perfection—establishes an uninterrupted continuity of sequence, from the council of the gods (which provides the impulse) to the meeting of father and son. The swineherd's farmstead is the resting point, the place from which we [43] look round. But in this sequence there remains—if we leave out the second theme—an unfilled space. The miracle is: exactly that space remains which the 'second' poet needs, in order to insert that which *he* has in mind. How providentially the older poet must have composed his work in such a way

[1] *Taschenbuch für junge Menschen* (Berlin, 1946), 'Die Heimkehr des Odysseus' [repr. in W. Schadewaldt, *Von Homers Welt und Werk*[3] (Stuttgart, 1959), 375 ff.].

that the younger one only had to compose what he wanted to and the space which his predecessor had left for him would be filled! Both of them, son and father, are steered towards the same destination from two different directions; even the days interlock; at the end, there is even a simultaneous change of scene with pointed contrasts. Not to count the contrasts between the two hosts, Menelaus and Eumaeus: in the one, there are the great traditions of guest-reception with their indispensable heroic formalities, in the other, the hospitality of the swineherd, unencumbered by formalities, meal set against meal, care set against care, request for departure set against request for departure, desire to keep against desire to keep. And how at the end great tradition becomes retardation of the ever more urgently necessary haste!

But whatever its relation to the other parts, the *Telemachy* is in any case a part of the *Odyssey* which captivates less through the forcefulness of its episodes than through its development as a whole. Only in the whole does the relationship between god and man, so characteristic of its poet, emerge. As a divine action, Telemachus' journey is an *aristeia* of Athena. What do all the other helpful actions she grants her favourites mean, compared with this steering, inspiring, and putting right of the man who has lost his way? Without always being conscious of it when we think of it—how much is actually based on this part of the poem! In other instances too it is her function to stand by in combat and danger with shrewd advice, cunning and even divine malice. But what is all that compared with this multiplicity of masks of hers, this leading up the garden path of hers, this confusing and rewarding!

But, after the model of the *Iliad*, divine action has a double aspect. What amongst the gods is will against will, intention and decision, looks, when perceived with human eyes, like blind chance and arbitrariness. The divine element almost resembles what Hegel called the cunning of the idea. When, after the most solemn oaths, the Trojans and Achaeans have every reason to believe that the war is over, a disastrous, glory-seeking, stupid Pandarus intervenes for the first time and, with an arrowshot from an ambush, brings all reason to nothing again. But what is called stupidity or chance on earth is based on the quarrel and sport of the gods for the ruling of the world. Now admittedly, such sport is not there in the *Odyssey*. Not even [44] the rivals, Athena and Poseidon, clash. If we disregard the storm which Poseidon eventually stirs up once more before his part has been played out, divine action exists only as Athena's action. But how the counter-current is shifted into her own intervention now! It begins with the fact that she can no longer witness her hero's misery. But what does she do? With all her changing appearances, pedagogical advice, and careful guiding, she eventually causes the two who are supposed to meet each other to be further apart than ever before. Telemachus' journey was not only useless, but, in addition to all the danger already present, has brought a new, extreme danger to Odysseus' house. But the same thing which, when regarded with human eyes, is a deplorable trick of chance becomes in the goddess's mind a means for the two people not just to meet physically but also to find each other inwardly, for the son to mature for his encounter with his father. He can find his father in such a blissful way, only if he has set out, if he has searched—if, through the goddess, the experience has happened to him that we call 'awakening', which begins only with self-doubt: is this really me? [. . .]

The Odysseus whom Telemachus discovers is not hidden, as a divine image in Silenus' clothing, as Socrates was to Alcibiades in Plato's *Symposium*; not as soul, as something to be contemplated in the flesh; but as the one who has been transformed in an instant, whom the goddess reveals at the right hour, only once, but in such a way that the sight will be imprinted for ever. Through awe and shock one will probably fancy the man to be a god. The joy, now that it finally breaks out, becomes as violent as pain . . . In such a revelation Eumaeus can of course not participate, for his perception is of a different kind. The fact that he sometimes no longer understands his master properly is part of his lot, part of his love . . . He remains excluded, is charged with an errand and this, too, is according to the goddess's plan. [45] In her the interior, the finding of oneself, and the exterior, the being steered, are combined in one. The secret of all great composition in general, the way in which purpose becomes means and means in turn purpose, is revealed in Eumaeus, in his person and in his function within the whole, which is as the knot of the connections, more than in anything else in this work of a *concordia discors* of poetic forces in plan and conception. Eumaeus is a means for steering the plot, but at the same time what an end in itself he is as a character! How distinctive even when compared with his guest and master! He is the only one who, although a slave, is worthy to be addressed with the poetic 'you', as is Patroclus in the *Iliad*, the friend and hero, before he is killed.

Right from the beginning Eumaeus has been designated as the destination in the plan of the goddess . . . If you look carefully, the great turning point does not yet lie in Odysseus' awakening on his home soil, nor at the beginning, but only at the end of Book 13 (404 ff.). It is the swineherd there who keeps all three of them together, Telemachus, Odysseus, and Penelope . . . There, in Eumaeus' place, the goddess says, Odysseus is supposed to wait until she has brought in his son (this last point almost casually). Then follows the outburst of a man now really full of consternation, who has only now learnt where he is: 'you who knew everything, why did you not keep him back?' Whereupon the goddess: 'don't worry yourself too much: I myself led him.' I do not know of any more charming transformation of a poetic plan into poetic dialogue.

Then what a play of contrasts there is in the encounter itself! First, when the two of them find each other, Odysseus is the one who is excluded; then Eumaeus is excluded, and as a result does not understand properly any more . . . But if Telemachus has not come home after being away and escaping, how can Eumaeus, in front of the real father, first take the father's place and first kiss the returning son? And then there is Telemachus who—only son, only grandson, without family—first laments over his helpless loneliness in front of the beggar. And after the revelation, when Eumaeus informs them about the suitors' ship which he saw arriving heavily laden with weapons, what a different kind of person is he now, as with a smile, which he conceals from Eumaeus, he casts a single fleeting glance at his father, a glance which says everything!

If Telemachus' journey is removed, what happens to all this? Telemachus, the one who has been searching and is now awoken, becomes an unknown [46] quantity. And the encounter, from which that play of contrasts disappears, would instead be burdened with a description of people's different conditions, an exposition which it really cannot carry. It is true that retelling, however much it may retard the action, is not impossible, even in moments of the greatest suspense. But it is *events* which are retold, not states of mind; states of mind are depicted. And since the essential thing which Odysseus finds in his homeland is such states of mind, and what has happened as a retellable event is hardly more than Penelope's 'ruse' which (on top of everything else) would be abolished as well if one deleted the travels, then this law would have to have been broken for the sake of a poem which has not come down to us.

These are some of the considerations out of which we would like to ascribe the 'homecoming of Odysseus' and 'the journey of Telemachus' to the same poet, in spite of their indisputable difference.

[77]   CIRCE AND CALYPSO

The Circe adventure does not enjoy great favour with scholars. It is true that the legend is old and good, so they say, but according to them the poet who tells it is a later one, an editor, an imitator under obligation to the inventor of Calypso, who must be rated as so incomparably higher, right down to the wording of whole verse passages. 'Even more than the heroic', Eduard Schwartz thinks (after Wilamowitz), 'human greatness has been lost. The relationship with Calypso is of a purity which is accessible only to original poets, poets who discover depths of the heart; the Circe adventure could almost be a Milesian tale.'[2]

Of course, in the reproach of base sensuality, the rhythm of the tale is already being overlooked. The joy of passion in the love affair is minimally accentuated as the purpose of the adventure. After the passion of the love affair has been enjoyed, Odysseus, bathed and clothed miraculously by nymphs, sits opposite Circe—silent with grief! The spell is broken only by the retransformation of his companions.

To demand that the magic of Circe should be described with the same soul magic as Calypso's grotto, or with the same charming bucolic atmosphere as Polyphemus' cave, means to prescribe an aim which in this case is not being aimed at. Before it has been proved that what is aimed for here does not befit the creator of Calypso and Polyphemus, we cannot deny the poet the Circe adventure for such reasons of taste.

For there is here another component to join the ones considered so far: that of the changing relationship between the hero and his companions. That Odysseus should look after his men and as leader feel responsible for his companions is again not part of the

[2] Eduard Schwartz, *Die Odyssee* (Munich, 1924), 270. U. v. Wilamowitz-Moellendorff, *Homerische Untersuchungen* (Berlin, 1884), 115 ff. P. Von der Mühll, Article 'Odyssee' *RE*.

old fairy-tale material as such. It is in fact something so characteristic of the *Odyssey* poet that this is one of the major points of difference between him and the *Iliad* poet. In the *Iliad*, the men serve
no other purpose than to be [78] led, to create crowd moods, and in
attack or flight to construct the surge of battle, but the great heroes
care nothing for them. In the *Odyssey*, the rescue of the companions is stressed right at the beginning as Odysseus' concern. The
more adventures there are, the more obvious it becomes that they
themselves are responsible for their own destruction. So the more
Odysseus' care for his men must grow for precisely that reason.
This causes the relationship between leader and companions to
become strained, and even, in the end, a counter-leader to rise. For
the sake of this component it is not by coincidence that the Circe
adventure is to be found in the middle between the Cyclops adventure and Thrinacia. In the Cyclops adventure Odysseus is still
more daring than caring, so that adventure could never be placed at
the end. In the Thrinacia adventure, Eurylochus mutinies. What
erupts there is prepared for in the Circe adventure, where the
blockage which subsequently leads his men to disaster is only just
sorted out amicably. Thus the adventure, so to speak, looks forwards and backwards. Nowhere more than here does Odysseus put
himself in danger for the others. The fairy-tale adventure turns
into an epic this time through the fact that the magic test at the
same time turns into a test of loyalty between the leader and his
companions. And nowhere else is he rewarded with such heartfelt
thanks either. The magic fairy-tale becomes a tale of happiest
reunion; the men's heartfelt words this time are allowed to sound
all the stronger—in the critics' censure 'more sentimental'—since
soon enough, in their crime against the Sun's cattle, they turn into
their opposite and Eurylochus, here still humiliated one more time,
will triumph.

But what jumping for joy there is! Can we misjudge the irony in
it? (10. 410) 'It was like the scene at a farm when cows in a drove
come home full-fed from the pastures to the yard and are welcomed
by all their frisking calves, who burst out from the pens to gambol
round their mothers, lowing excitedly. My men were as deeply
moved as if they had reached their homeland and were standing in
their own town in rugged Ithaca, where they were born and bred.'

But this actually means: those who are jumping like this now will
never see Ithaca again! The contrast which the poet has in mind

here is the mutiny and breach of oath on Thrinacia: 'And meanwhile Eurylochus advised the others disgracefully: "Listen to me,
friends, however many sufferings you have endured . . .".'

[79] As the prelude to Thrinacia this at the same time points back
to Polyphemus. The more Eurylochus refers here in his rebellion
to the Cyclops adventure—people have wanted to delete the lines
which are really indispensable[3]—the more the Circe adventure as it
develops must become the counterpart to the Cyclops adventure.
For this very reason it starts just like the other; the fact that smoke
is seen rising is enough for the outburst of general misery . . . But
in the Cyclops adventure, after the most terrible loss, the survivors
escaped by the skin of their teeth; there Odysseus the daring at the
very last moment risks everything, and does not rest until he incurs
Poseidon's curse; with Circe, after the most terrible beginning, a
fairy-tale happy ending! And not just for Odysseus! The retrans-
formed companions become much more beautiful than they had
ever been before! The life of luxury of all of them, freshly washed
and clothed, is described with all the conventional epic detail and
how is the conventional, as a contrast to the fattening of the pigs,
now becoming unconventional again, emphasized—heroic eleva-
tion at the end of its most terrible opposite. It is only out of this
contrast that we can understand why the poet, instead of the manifold transformations into wolves, lions, etc., which the fairy-tale
offered, uses only the one into pigs. The others, often supplied on
vase paintings, are mentioned briefly, it is true, at the beginning
and in Eurylochus' speech, but in the narrative they are not

---

[3] *Od.* 10. 435–7 is usually deleted: 'Deleted by Kirchhoff; the Cyclops did not
lock up Odysseus and his companions to serve as his guards' (Schwartz, *Die Odyssee*,
318). But devouring for the ogre is really nothing different from casting a spell for
the witch. The verses are necessary if only to explain that Odysseus can be calmed
down only with difficulty. A hero reacts in this way only after an insult, e.g. *Il.* 1.
190. Someone like Odysseus does not cut off anyone's head straight away just
because he was anxious and warning him. Fr. Focke, *Die Odyssee* (Stuttgart and
Berlin, 1943), 254 follows Schwartz and he also distinguishes two series of adventures by different poets. But that referring back of the Circe adventure to the
Polyphemus tale is not based just on these lines, as has been shown. *Od.* 10. 437 in
the accusation: 'Through his (Odysseus') sin they also perished' (in the Cyclops'
cave) presupposes the opposite, 1. 7: 'Through their own sin they perished.' Thus
the proem, Circe, and Thrinacia are very closely linked. On the other hand, the justification loses its point of reference if there is not at least an appearance also of the
opposite. But from where should this appearance come if not from the Polyphemus
story? If people are serious about removing the Polyphemus story, they will realize
that as a result Circe and Thrinacia would not blend in either.

required: the pigsty becomes the counterpart of the description of the heroic banquet.

But lest we miss the landscape round Circe's house, the stag hunt corresponds to the Cyclops' goats' island as the idyll, [80] but the prelude is different from the one before the Cyclops adventure; it is a heroic idyll. The stag, going to its drinking place, falls like an Iliadic hero[4] . . . At the same time the hunt already shows Odysseus' care for his men . . .

But what is the relationship between the Circe story and the Calypso episode? Is Calypso really the original and Circe the copy? Wilamowitz once made it his task to prove line by line how the imitator failed and until very recently others followed him in this. But here it is necessary not just to compare line with line but also style with style and stage with stage.

Circe, the mistress of Aeaea, sister of the insidious Aeetes, reminds us of the magic land of the East of which Aeetes is king, the country to which the Argonauts sailed, the later Colchis on the east coast of the Black Sea. But incomparably stronger according to the poet's will than the merely shadowy geographical connection between the two magic lands is the mythic and atmospheric element which such a genealogy and neighbourhood imply. It does not mean that Aeaea (in 'Homeric' geography to be identified with Colchis) is situated in the north-east, but that Odysseus is setting foot on a soil on which magic and malice are hereditary.

Sorceresses instead of witches, women like Circe and Medea, her niece, only become possible as characters in a world which is no longer magical. The countless parallels with Jason's journey or that of Odysseus in myths and fairy-tales of earlier times show that the older they are in their stage the more magic is increased everywhere, until it becomes overwhelming. Where everybody uses magic and every step is a piece of magic, there can neither be specialist gods dedicated to this task (as amongst the Olympians Hermes or Hecate) nor sorceresses like Medea or Circe. Both these sorceresses again have differentiated roles—one turning to the dreadful and the other, Circe, to the propitious side—similarly to Hecate and Hermes among the gods. While Medea, as a demonically loving person who ruins others and herself, becomes a tragic figure, so Circe on the other hand becomes the fairy who is danger-

---

[4] *Od.* 10. 163 = *Il.* 16. 469. Wilamowitz-Moellendorff, *Homerische Untersuchungen*, 121.

ous but brings good luck to the real hero. The Circe adventure is the only one in which magic is overcome by counter-magic. According to the stage this is very old, one of those many magic tests through which the fairy-tale hero proves himself.[5]

[81] Beside Circe, Calypso illustrates the poet's psychological awareness at its height. The fairy-tale is not interested in that. And yet, if we dispute the psychological in it, this does not mean that it proceeds unpsychologically or with faulty psychology. It only means that the psychological should not be used as its yardstick. If Circe changes in a flash from fiend to friend, we are expected to accept something psychologically which, if it were told directly, would hardly be tolerated by great epic. Nevertheless, it would be easy to transcribe the motif of fairy-tale magic into a musical key of psychological developments of which no novelist should be ashamed. Why otherwise would Circe be described as so beautiful, as so enticing, so seductive, so inviting, so mockingly triumphant over all the other menfolk, if it were not her predestined fate to have to be like this until she came across the one man whom she acknowledges as her master, the lucky and courageous hero who is neither taken in by her like the stupid companions nor runs away from her like the cowardly Eurylochus? For whom it is more appropriate to seize the sword in the style of epic than to swallow a counteractive magic potion in the style of a fairy-tale? The encounter with the lucky god Hermes expresses nothing else but that Odysseus is just that hero. The favour of the gods is bestowed only upon one receptive to it. And now, finally, when this happens to her—it is the unconscious goal of all her gloating schemes—a miracle happens also to her. She is transformed, as if released from a spell, and immediately invites him to her bed and becomes his divine and most sincere lover.

The law of the psychologically possible is not violated, but certainly psychological elements are represented by other ones. But these other elements are no longer just fairy-tale ones; later elements, ones characteristic of the novella, come into play. Again, the fact that a prophecy is fulfilled, and that her conqueror is the one

---

[5] For the fairy-tale parallels cf. Grimms' fairy-tale about Jorinde and Joringel and what J. Bolte and G. Polivka, *Anmerkungen zu den Kinder- und Hausmärchen der Brüder Grimm*, say about it (Hildesheim, 1915, ii. 69). Also see E. Bethe, *Die Gedichte Homers* (Wissenschaft und Bildung 180; Leipzig, 1922), 29. Hermann Güntert, *Von der Sprache der Götter und Geister* (Halle, 1921), 95 f. Ibid. 92 ff. also about the Moly.

who was prophesied to her, so that instead of putting a spell on Odysseus she is released from one herself, and by recognizing him recognizes her fate, and is released by him who becomes the turning point for her—all this belongs here too. Tales which end with the fulfilment of a prophecy (like the ones known from Herodotus) must have been circulating: see the end of the Cyclops and Phaeacian adventures (9. 507 and 13. 172). But the fairy-tale shows itself to have come closer to the novella in this respect too, that the spell which breaks the original spell is already virtually in the process of transition towards symbolically pointing to something psychological; [82] through the magic force, a different force is recognized, a force of the spirit (10. 329): 'But you have a heart in your breast which is proof against magic.'

Is she mistaken in not recognizing the force of the Moly and attributing to his 'mind', his νόος, that which is the gift of the magic god? This conclusion will be reached only by the person who is not moved by the enigmatic, the more than fairy-tale dimension of the story. And how the poet now revels in the contrast between the two Circes, the hostile and the loving one!

But Odysseus as the unknown arrival and as the one to be recognized, the test of relationships between hosts and guests of the most manifold kind, this is not in the old fairy-tale tradition; this is the invention only of our *Odyssey*. As with Circe (which the prophecy made to her expression), a destiny fulfils itself too; at the same time the fairy-tale turns into poetry. Now that they recognize each other, they are allowed to love each other. Odysseus is allowed to stay with her for a year, and he is not allowed to fend off her magic for such a long time that we almost begin to fear that he might forget himself and Ithaca. So this adventure ends differently from the others (which are suddenly intensified at the end) with a long drawn-out pause. Odysseus, who elsewhere is always the one who admonishes the others, this time has to be reminded of himself by the others— also an adventure! The Calypso adventure on the other hand is like an inversion of this. Circe remains his companion through her directives; the Circe adventure stretches out; it in turn frames other tales, standing like a happy kind of forgetting before the sombre revelations of the underworld . . . How many, varied relations does this ordering of events create! How unconnected everything becomes if, as scholars did until very recently, one changes it!

But now Calypso compared with Circe! If Circe is the sister of the 'malicious' Aeetes, then this is what she is *qua* sorceress. But Calypso too is the daughter of a malicious character, of the 'malicious' Atlas (1. 52). But how does her paternal heritage show itself? As is shown at the end, her malice consists—only in the mistaken fears of the hero. Circe's malice fills her story. There is no tellable story about Calypso at all. What Odysseus has to watch from her is, it is true, described by the same word as that with which he is threatened by Circe: 'bewitching' (1. 57 = 10. 213, 291, 318). But the means of 'bewitching' for Circe is the magic potion and magic wand, for Calypso it is only the word and the miracle of her figure. The psychological takes the place of the magical. 'She always tries to bewitch him with soft and flattering words [83] that he might forget Ithaca but Odysseus is yearning to see even only the smoke rising from his home and wishes he were dead.' For Circe the territory she inhabits, the way she appears, how people first stand in front of the gate and then hear her voice—in short everything around her—relates to her 'magic'. She sings, lures, invites, feeds . . . It is characteristic of her story that the interest it arouses is directed only towards the sequence of events. With Calypso on the other hand, it is the inner situation, which no longer has any need for external miracles, that commands all our interest. Surprises happen in the sphere of the heart, instead of the sphere of action and miracle. And yet what similarity! With all the transition from the fairy-tale almost to the novel, what insistence on the formal! As Circe sings, so does Calypso. They both sing in a beautiful voice, walking up and down along the loom. Here, as there, the same verse. But Circe's song cannot be omitted from the story about her. It is an essential part of the adventure—and how the triple repetition is enjoyed to the full in narrative terms, first in the fate of the comrades, then in the tale of Eurylochus who escaped, and finally confirmed in Odysseus' experience. But for whom then, we ask, does Calypso sing? Does she also sing so that a surprised stranger will wish to enter, so that she is summoned and can open the door and invite him in? Odysseus sits in a remote spot by the sea. Does she sing for Hermes? But she is not in fact expecting him. Or for herself? Perhaps she *has* to sing? What with Circe is deceit and malice becomes truth with Calypso?

Circe's singing cannot be separated from her magic. True, with Circe too the old fairy-tale magic is added to with a piece of that other magic, the magic of figure, of beauty; she is no longer a witch, as in the fairy-tale parallels. But for whom does Calypso sing? Her singing is part of a different whole: the magic of a landscape, of a rock grotto, of fragrances which flow from her hearth, springs, poplars, and cypresses, birds in the branches . . . her singing becomes an accompaniment. The magic fairy-tale has been replaced by the magic of the idyll. But now it is a magic before which even a god, even Hermes stands quietly for a while. It is a picture for its own sake—and yet again not without reference. Where the god admires, Odysseus sits by the sea with his back to it and groans and weeps. One picture against the other. Thus, the immortality with which the nymph tempts him relates to his yearning for his home; thus, Calypso's love relates to that of Penelope. For it is indeed only Penelope, present as something far away, who makes the whole into a whole, who really makes two into three. An *Odyssey* starting with [84] Calypso, in which there had not been a word about Penelope before: wouldn't there be something missing from Calypso's grotto in such a telling? Would she not cease to be what she after all must be, a counterpart?

But there are still more similar features in the changed overall picture. The god who rescues Odysseus from the spell of both sorceresses is on both occasions Hermes, although in the first case he comes as a magic god who brings good luck by virtue of his own nature, while in the Calypso adventure he is epically stylized as the gods' messenger. This may be a coincidence. But what similarity underlies the fact that here, as with Circe, Odysseus, after the spell has been broken (i.e. after Calypso has promised to let him go), demands a divine oath 'that she is not planning further suffering for him himself!' And that both are equally willing to do him this favour! Again the same verses! And yet how different is the 'suffering' of which Odysseus is wary! In the one, the loss of his virility— if one shares the bed of Circe there is enough reason to fear that—in the other, something which cannot be named at all, something threatening in the dark future.[6]

---

[6] Wilamowitz-Moellendorff, *Homerische Untersuchungen*, 119 ff. tries to prove the dependence of the group of verses round 10. 300 and 10. 344 respectively (Circe) on the group of verses round 5. 179 (Calypso) by finding the context in 10 unsatisfactory. But the fault-finding succeeds only at the cost of an impossible construction: in 5. 179 ἄλλο is supposed to be in apposition to πῆμα κακόν μοι αὐτῷ. This is supposed to be the original. The tenth book is supposed distortingly to have made πῆμα the object and ἄλλο the attribute. But just try to read the verse and its emphasis in the form which according to Wilamowitz is the original! Such appositions

If, by demanding the oath, the cautious Odysseus reveals himself to Circe as a man of superior intelligence, the hero of the adventure, so in the case of Calypso he reveals himself through the same demand to be mistaken. But precisely because he *is* mistaken, because he remains the same old person, because he is so cautious, as if Calypso were a Circe, precisely for that reason Calypso loves him all the more. The unrequited love of a nymph could easily become dangerous (just think of Daphnis). But in this case the lamenting, spurned, and self-renouncing nymph, who in mythical examples is always angered by her fate (the transformation here is admittedly quieter, but for that reason almost even more surprising), turns into the one who smiles, loves, and cares.

[85] Odysseus' caution, his demand of a divine oath, is the motivation behind this new turn of events (5. 180): 'Calypso, the divine goddess, smiled and stroked him with her hand. "Odysseus," she protested, "what a rogue you are to say such a thing! It shows the crafty way your mind works."' But what is this other than a new variation of the epic situation in which Odysseus is groundlessly afraid? In particular, it is a variation of his encounter with Athena where, after failure to recognize his home country, he does not recognize his patron goddess and lies to her (13. 287): 'That was Odysseus' story. The bright-eyed goddess smiled at him and caressed him with her hand. She now wore the appearance of a woman, tall, beautiful, and accomplished. Then she spoke, and her words winged their way to him. "Anyone who met you, even a god, would have to be a consummate trickster to surpass you in subterfuge. You were always an obstinate, cunning and irrepressible intriguer."'

Which is the earlier passage here? Which the later? Odysseus as the one who (as with Calypso) fears without reason? Or as the one who (as with Athena) is cautious with good reason? No doubt is possible. Odysseus can fear *without* reason only after the gods will his return home, after the council of the gods with which the *Odyssey* begins. This, with all its irony, is a part of the poetic plan.

which are 'hanging' in the middle of the sentence may be possible in Aeschylus at best but they certainly are not in the epic. Also there are no parallels at all. ἄλλο does not mean: something different from the word which you talk about, i.e. an evil for *me*; but another, new evil. In Book 10 the first evil is that which she has done to the *comrades*. The new evil which he fears is that which she will do to him *himself*, which he will suffer in his own body if he does not protect himself. For linguistic usage compare *Il.* 24. 551; 16. 262; *Od.* 4. 698.

The other is a part of the old fairy-tale tradition. This cannot be older than the other.

Now back to the question which presented itself to us at the beginning: if, as it emerges, the Calypso poem also *qua* poem is dependent on the Circe adventure and in particular on its shape in our *Odyssey*, must it not then all the more be by a different poet? I do not want to go point by point through the argument which refutes this. In the best case, it leads to an *Odyssey* which would be like ours and yet should *not* be the same . . .

Enough. The question here is not, 'What is the original, what the imitation?', but 'How is the difference caused by the difference of stages which the epic has at its disposal in the interaction of older and more recent elements, traditional ones and ones created out of the spirit of the age?' This difference is caused by first creating epic *mises-en-scène* out of the tales, after the model of the *Iliad*, and then going back to fairy-tale traditions. One often becomes the other's echo. The Calypso poem relates to the Circe adventure as Hector's farewell to Andromache (as an epic situation) relates to Hector's death and Troy's destruction (as material from legend). Or, to stay with the *Odyssey*, as the story of Penelope's shroud ruse [86] relates to her approach to the deceived suitors in the epic situation of Book 18. If one wants to recall further instances, the Gyges tale, too, can be related to Herodotus' novella in a similar way. Poetry of such a kind is a poetry of transition. If, in the Phaeacian adventure, the fairy-tale element (regardless of its contradiction) stays hidden under an epic front, so here the fairy-tale and the epic elements occur separately in two different figures: Calypso and Circe.[7] The

---

[7] It remains to deal with an objection which also comes from Wilamowitz: the oath itself is sworn by Calypso solemnly enough in direct speech: 'Now let Earth be my witness, with the broad Sky above, and the waters of Styx that flow below—the greatest and most solemn oath the blessed gods can take—that I plot no other mischief against you' (5, 184 ff.). About Circe Odysseus says only: 'She swore as I demanded.' So, is the first not the model for the second after all? But the oath in its wording is only possible if exactly that which she is swearing with it follows it in appropriate breadth. In the Calypso adventure the oath is followed by the building of the raft and the whole farewell which has so many associations. But as a narrator you cannot make Circe swear a divine oath in four verses if after it nothing else follows but: 'And I lay down in the splendid bed of Circe.' A preparation must not surpass in weight that which it prepares. That this would be the case here is again a consequence of the assimilation and matching of the Circe adventure with the fateful total of all the adventures together which was explained at the beginning. The objection fails on grounds of epic economy. The oaths in *Iliad* 3. 276 ff. could not be sworn as solemnly either, if they were not followed by truce and the beginning of

Calypso adventure ends with the building of the raft: no Calypso without the raft. Whoever created Calypso had also done his utmost before to frustrate any hope (as far as human thought is concerned) that Odysseus would ever return to his native land. In the fairy-tale tradition, the shipwrecked sailor came straight to the hospitable Phaeacians. Now he comes to the most remote island, remote even to the gods, to a nymph who, on top of everything else, is in love with him! No situation can be considered more hopeless. It is obvious to anyone who has eyes how the poet of the *Telemachy*—we assume that he is the same one—on his part is concerned to bring about the same kind of hopelessness on Ithaca as there is in Calypso's island. Such situations are designed to produce unexpected solutions. In the fairy-tale traditions it is the helpful spirits who reveal a way out for the fairy-tale hero. [87] In the world of the epic the spirits too take on a different shape. Telemachus is helped by Athena herself, if no longer through magic, yet through what in the real world is called a miracle. Yet Odysseus too is helped by the nymph, no longer through a fairy-tale miracle (no veil, no winged shoes) but at Zeus' orders, through axe and hatchet and wood and instructions to build himself a raft. In the old form, what a new spirit! Magic aid transforms itself into an instruction: help yourself! Probably as the inventor of the wooden horse too Odysseus is a master builder. But how the inventive Odysseus is here given a sphere with which the *Odyssey* poet is especially concerned: the spirit of craftsmanship! Why in this case the nymph and not Athena should advise him, why the nymph in the cave of love should suddenly possess all the tools and bring them to her beloved with the eagerness of a helpful little spirit— this surprising element belongs to the licence without which the plan of the *Odyssey* could not be executed. But how charming that this is not hushed up, but simply related! What a marvel! How fruitless yearning transforms itself into support and help! What a variation on Circe!

Admittedly, Odysseus does not know from whom the order came to build the raft—Zeus. The surprising element in this change, surprising for the father as well as the son, is brought about by the second gods' council on Olympus, which is so often underestimated

a new battle in all their breadth. [For the relationship between the Gyges tale and Herodotus' novella see K. Reinhardt, *Vermächtnis der Antike* (Göttingen, 1960), 139 ff.]

in its facility and superiority. But why does Hermes then not mention the raft in his instructions to Calypso? Why does Calypso fore-
stall him (5. 140 ff.)? Perhaps because otherwise the invention would
lose some of its charm? If you think about the instruction, the way it
is written there really is better.

[112]   THE PHAEACIANS

The story of Odysseus and the Phaeacians takes place on a stage
which introduces two worlds: a fairy-tale wonder world, and a
present and intensified historical world. As the Phaeacian people in
the plan of the *Odyssey* finds itself settled on a border, where the
world of distant lands meets the world of home, where the narrow
track of fairy-tale adventures leads into the broad and richly figured
highway of great epic, [113] so their nature too has something
enigmatic about it, something of the most recent spirit of the
Odyssey in the old fairy-tale magic.

The Phaeacians have not escaped critical carving-up either. For
three days Odysseus was a guest of Alcinous. That was too long. In
order to be sent home the next day with presents from his hosts, he
ought to have disclosed his identity, and told what adventures he had
experienced, the *first* time he was asked his name, when he wept in
the hall in the evening over the bard's song. In this way, we would be
saved the displeasing incognito in which the hero wraps himself for
two days with the same gesture; in this way, the promise which
Alcinous gives right at the beginning would be kept: 'tomorrow I
will send you home'; and so at the same time the comic tale of Ares'
love affair would fit in all the better.[8]

This is all very well—if, with this tidying up, we did not throw
out what is precisely the ultimate purpose of this whole episode i.e.
the epic situation of the unrecognized hero as guest. This time
Odysseus is not the guest of a Eumaeus, nor behind a beggar's
mask: but the issue we come to is what is actually happening
between guest and host.

---

[8] 'Tomorrow' indicates the change which is imminent immediately, *Il.* 8. 535, 9.
357, 429, 18. 269; *Od.* 1. 272. Is it conceivable that Alcinous should say: 'I fix the
return home for the day after tomorrow?' Why not for tomorrow, everyone would
ask. Whereupon Alcinous would then have to explain: 'I foresee that you will not
give your name before then.' This verse can prove something only if you suppose
that it has been left standing unnoticed from an earlier plan. But since now it cannot
possibly be different, a carving-up which refers to it is a circular argument.

Admittedly, it is easy to see that the complete deletion of the
second day would leave something which, in its turn, would have
its own shortcomings. A Homeric day has its curve, ascent, climax,
and end. From its beginning, with the encounter with Nausicaa,
this day has one goal: the reception, the entering into a guest relationship. If it were also filled with the recognition, its preparation,
and the tales following it, it would become too full of too many different entities. It is true that different things can happen in one day,
but they must stand in contrast, happen in two places, and other
such things. But here the goal would become a different one from
that of reception: it would become the recognition. But recognition
is precisely the goal of the second day, as reception is that of the
first. The goals are reached, the first as well as the second, in the
evening. The sun is setting when Odysseus prays to the goddess, on
his way to the city at the shrine of Athena, where Nausicaa leaves
him (6. 321). Having reached the palace, he meets the king and the
elders just when they have finished their meal [114] and are pour-
ing their last libation to Hermes, according to their custom, before
they retire to bed (7. 138). Then suddenly, miraculously, the
stranger is among them. Long silence follows, then approval.
Among the men in the hall Queen Arete, the woman who decides,
whose knees Odysseus immediately clasps as he was told to do, does
not say a word. But she has an effect! As a 'suppliant' he is under
her protection from now on (cf. 11. 338). She would only need to
speak, if he were to be dragged away from her, but it does not come
to that. When Odysseus is being served later than the others, he
makes the excuse of being hungry so that he cannot say more about
himself then. In this way, he delays information about himself for
the first time. Another libation is most solemnly poured but now to
Zeus the lord of hospitality. Since the stranger appeared, the situation has been a sacro-legal one (cf. *Il.* 24. 480 ff., 570; *Od.* 14. 283
etc.). The question where his clothes came from would not be fitting here. It can wait until the king and queen are alone with their
guest. Before they go to bed, when the end of the day turns back to
its beginning, there is the charming half-truth about the clothes
and the daughter. For all that, Arete's question about his name and
homeland remains unanswered. If you tried to make room here for
the self-revelation as well, the whole thing would come apart at the
seams.

And yet there is that contradiction—the solemn promise of the return home the next day, which is not kept. But let us see what happens on the next day!

Odysseus has become the king's guest, but the king represents the collective will of the city nobility, with whom Odysseus must enter into the same legal relationship. The nobility is summoned to the assembly in the *agora*, and the newcomer is introduced to them by the king. An escort is granted, a ship and crew made available. The king invites the heads of the nobility into his house for the reception of his guest. During the meal, while the minstrel sings one of the famous songs about Troy (the quarrel between Odysseus and Achilles), the king sees his guest hiding his flowing tears. He interrupts, and invites him to watch the games. Everyone goes to the *agora* . . . Nothing should prevent Odysseus from travelling home on that same day, especially as the departure has been planned for the evening anyway. So Telemachus too departs to Pylos (2. 357) and again from Pylos to Ithaca (15. 296) at bedtime. During the games it happens that Euryalus insults the guest. Odysseus takes a discus, and in word and deed very nearly gives himself away. Alcinous ensures a cheerful sequel [115] to this serious moment: group-dancing to the bard's song of Ares and Aphrodite, then ball games and juggling. The hero of the *Iliad* marvels. Highly pleased, the king asks the people to offer presents to the guest. A committee of twelve of the ruling princes is made responsible for this. Each of them gives garments and a talent of gold, the insulter Euryalus gives his sword. The sun sets and the presents arrive (8. 417). Still nothing should prevent Odysseus from leaving that very evening. To the other presents, that of the king and the queen is added at the end; the chest which she has selected is secured, Odysseus is bathed and clothed, and Nausicaa encounters him; that short, wonderful farewell between the two takes place; the meal starts; the bard is fetched. Still nothing should prevent Odysseus from leaving that very evening. The presents, the encounter, the setting sun, the mood pervading the whole—everything points to the parting. Then it comes to that moment, inevitable and yet unexpected, which has been postponed for so long, yet upsets everything: the recognition.

The recognition is so powerful, and on the part of the person who asks as well as the person who answers so much pent-up energy is released all at once that its ripples spread further and further, right up to the very last of the adventures told—who *is* Odysseus? The answer to this question consists only of what he tells. The flow, it is true, is held up in one place, but in such a place where stopping is impossible, where trying to resist it pulls you back into it all the more strongly. When everything is focused on hearing about the heroism of the *Iliad* from voices of the underworld, Odysseus interrupts with a catalogue of illustrious prehistoric women: women, nothing but women; there seems no end to them. 'Night has fallen; it is time to sleep, whether on the ship which lies ready, or in the palace. As for my journey, I leave the arrangements in the gods' hands and in yours' (11. 330). Even now departure would still be possible, but then the queen keeps him back. He is also *her* guest and she thinks: he has still not received enough presents. Her word prevails. The guest is asked to be patient until tomorrow. And Odysseus replies: 'Certainly, at this price . . .'. What has happened? He who has been urging departure, who could hardly wait for it, has cheated himself out of it. Beginning with: 'Yes, I am Odysseus', he ends by doing himself out of the fulfilment of his yearning. For to close here, with this catalogue of women, is, as everybody feels, impossible. And, of course, it is not to his disadvantage either . . .

What has been stressed so far, however, relates only to one side of events, only to what is happening in the host–guest relationship of the real world. [116] And already impossible things have happened here. How can the king, in front of a gathered community, introduce and recommend his guest without naming or knowing him? 'The stranger at my side—I do not know who he is, nor whether he has come from eastern or from western lands—has in the course of his travels come to my palace' (8. 28 f.).

The guest does not even think of helping him out of his embarrassment. Yet here the king is shouldering a responsibility. For *this* right of hospitality is valid only among equals. Vagrant folk, in however friendly a way one may look after them, do not participate in it. It is the business of equals to recognize each other. If you consider the consequences which this can have, people often enough have misgivings when granting hospitality. On the other hand, it is the mark of a noble mind if you do not ask first and too insistently: 'Who are you? How did you get into this situation?' So—in Herodotus—the Lydian king Croesus does not hesitate to perform the expiatory rite on the unfortunate Adrastus even before asking him the necessary questions. But what is that compared with Alcinous? His sensitivity borders on that of a fairy-tale. Is this still the real world? And yet you think you can feel the psychological impulse in it, that his restraint increases the more his astonishment grows. Since the first long silence, he has not doubted for a moment. He has even thought of Odysseus as a god . . . and astonishingly soon, as a future son-in-law too. Euryalus, on the other hand, shows that doubt is possible. His insinuation, 'you do not know anything about games, you are a trader', implies 'You are not of the nobility, you have sneaked in here under false pretences.' But to his royal friend, the stranger becomes all the more mysterious. When the question, having been kept back to the absolute limit, finally breaks out of him, with what a rush of conflicting feelings, with what a mixture of shaking one's head, erroneous conjecture, and expectation does it emerge! For all his sympathy, with what misunderstanding! Odysseus' tears are not sadness at the loss of near relatives or friends but tears of emotion at the poet's song!

All the same, one can understand this Alcinous. But what is the solution to the puzzle with Odysseus? As the poet plans it, he is as persistently silent to us about his reasons for crying as he is to his friend. What are we to suppose? Is it grief which is gnawing at him? Yearning for home? The suspicion that, after all he has suffered, he is not himself any more? The feeling of being a foreigner? Would they believe him? Pride? Modesty? Or the fear: once they know who I am, they would keep me even longer? (Compare the way Telemachus avoids his host Nestor out of a similar fear, 15. 200.) Whatever the reason [117] for his crying is, he does not want to explain it. No motivation for his silence emerges in the narrative. In his home country, the denial of his own self has a purpose; it is a ruse and a mask. But here? Some have interpreted it as the embarrassment of an 'editor'. And yet, only via the ostinato of his silence does the path lead to the tune of his self-revelation! Only the moment sweeps him away. But the moment is that of the poet. That it is his own deepest wish which plays such a trick on him resembles his discovery by the nurse Eurycleia. But how much more wonderfully is he overwhelmed here, not so as to construct a new defence for himself but to reveal himself!

Unmotivated action rises, by stage, above the motivated. [. . .]

Even more than with the *Iliad* poet, the characteristic of the *Odyssey* poet seems to be the wealth of his invention in similar situations. When Odysseus, recently the unknown guest of the Phaeacians, returns to his house as the unknown beggar, both these situations tend towards a recognition which is delayed again and again. Here, as there, we find the same repetitions—two sets of tears, two sets of stool-throwing—the same means of gradation, the same problems for the critic. For again the situation carries more significance than that with which it seemed to be originally motiv-ated. Why must he here as there nearly give himself away, with the discus throw, as with the washing of his feet? But the difference is that discovery among the Phaeacians is not dangerous. It is a sim-ilar kind of game, in the opposite sense: in one case, when the mask is thrown off, finally erupting into terrible bloodshed and judge-ment, in the other erupting into revelation and wonderment at the person . . .

But above all, the situation here carries that which this poet com-poses as no other: the finding of each other: the finding of each other as confirmation of something of which one has had a premo-nition. So Odysseus and Penelope find each other, [118] as do Telemachus and Menelaus, Odysseus and Eumaeus, and also Odysseus and Alcinous. But a feature of this is that the one shows himself a match for the other, that he loves him without knowing who he is, that he has a deeper than conscious knowledge. If the path leads from the fairy-tale king to the swineherd, if the latter's realm is an intensification of the former's, it is also a necessary part of the former that Odysseus *eludes* Alcinous. In order to admire the famous hero, one does not need to be an Alcinous. That he in turn does not ask his guest's name immediately has, it is true, its justifi-cation in custom. But what tenderness, consideration, awe, and foreboding have joined custom here!

Not so the *Iliad*. It is true that there human beings touch each other, deeply and movingly, but then suddenly something will stand between them, separating them . . . If you follow this up, you soon discover a difference which goes through the whole of the work. The contrast and dramatic change (constantly reappearing in the *Iliad*) between excess and moderation, demonic and human, inward-looking compulsion and perception of the other, savage and vulnerable, harsh and tender (however you wish to express the play and counterplay of the same contrast), is alien to the whole *Odyssey*. Even in encounters which are on the surface so similar—as that of Hector and Andromache compared with Odysseus and Penelope— you will notice the same difference. The model for the miracle of Odysseus suddenly kneeling before Arete is the last book of the

Iliad, Priam suddenly kneeling in front of Achilles. But how different the contrasts which are there! In the actions and personnel in the *Odyssey*, those forces are missing which compel Iliadic heroes to act beyond their conscious purpose and capacity to understand. In this respect, Achilles, Patroclus, Hector, Agamemnon, Helen, and even Paris are like relatives. In the *Odyssey* not one of the characters, not even one of the suitors, could be compared with these. Even as an avenger, Odysseus will not be driven. Even the most terrible things he still does under the instruction of Athena. How much more self-imposed, self-driven suffering there is in Meleager, and in the young Phoenix compared with Theoclymenos, although Theoclymenos too is a fugitive because of manslaughter, and becomes the follower of a strange lord like Phoenix himself! . . . In the *Iliad*, as a rule, there is something of excess not only in the heroes but also in the events: hence our frequent impression of the cruel element in the *Iliad*. But the cruelty arises only from a background of tenderness. On the other hand, as we have said already, the *Odyssey* poet constructs the finding of each other in ever new tones. But with finding also goes the danger of missing each other, of losing each other, on an internal as well as an external level . . . [119] . . . On this scale lie the poet's richest tone sequences. This is the basic figure of his inventions, which remains the same in the most varied shape, from the dog Argus to the play with the means of recognition . . . Is the reason for this the age? Or the materials? Or, rather more, the poets?

This fertile situation yields even more beyond the original motif . . . and becomes a vehicle for new possibilities: it ultimately allows the poet to say in an indirect way what, if directly said, would go beyond the genre. (In *Hamlet* a similar thing happens in a different way.) This becomes especially evident when the events become internalized, when it is no longer just a question of deed and action but of tests, temptations, of souls proving themselves, of relationships like friendship, love, faithfulness, tenderness, doubt, foreboding . . . That Odysseus masks himself has its justification in the danger he is in. But sense does not exhaust itself in that justification. Why otherwise would the play of the unrecognized stranger in the beggar's mask be prolonged for such a long time, extended until a whole world of high and low, of nobility and of disgrace, of right and wrong has been covered in the relationship between the three strata of masters, servants, and vagrants? The unknown avenger becomes the 'tester', the 'tempter', the secret judge: his mask becomes the touchstone by which genuine and false are distinguished, true nobility in the servant figure and false nobility in the sons of the lords . . . What perspectives arise on the world looked at from below! What a reversal in the form of the old epic! What a load-bearing capacity exists in a mask! So it fits sometimes more loosely, sometimes more tightly, sometimes Odysseus *seems* the beggar, only transformed by Athena, sometimes he has to drink down to the dregs the cup of bitterness of one who has become old and homeless. And more: the mask carries the whole intensity of Odysseus' and Penelope's love. Love does not show itself directly. How could it show itself unless he disguised himself? And part of his mask is surely also the lies which he spreads about himself. What at first was merely a transformation by the goddess becomes the construction of a life. Is he lying just for the sake of his revenge? Why then would he lie 'like the poets'? So that Eumaeus will listen to him as if enchanted? Destinies which carry their own truth in themselves, as his own counter-example, of someone driven around who has to end up like this because he cannot give up adventuring? At the end he lies so that the born adventurer and his fate too, in addition to [120] that of the prophet, bard, beggar, king, herdsman, etc., will not be missing in the picture of the society of the *Odyssey*.

With the repetition of this general basic form, the Phaeacians participate in the real world of the poet. And yet, all these relationships appreciated, what would become of the story if it did not contradict itself? From where would its wings grow, so to speak, unless, as in Aladdin and his magic lamp, the real world again and again for some moments changes places with the wonder world of the fairy-tale. For what were the Phaeacians once?

Of the many magical peoples, giants, ogres, female fiends, vampires, and fairy-tale kings into whose power the hero fell, the Phaeacians are the only ones who help him towards his proper end, whose activity and magic are of the opposite kind to that of the others: as the 'little people' (as they have been called) of the far-away seas, during the night they escort home people driven off their course, asleep in their magic ships. In former times they were saviours, like Asclepius once was, son of Apollo, saviour of all the sick. But that was once upon a time. As Zeus with his lightning put an end to healing in order to safeguard his tribute to the god of death, so too the lord of the seas, in order to preserve his power, puts an end to this all-too-philanthropic escort service. On top of the kindly city and people he piles up a range of mountains with his trident. The 'mountain transformation', known as a motif, buries the old glory. Through the Phaeacians' entering the boundaries of the Odysseus legends, the hero from Ithaca becomes the last one whom they escort home.

But only the poet of this work of poetry has set this apart from the fairy-tale adventures, and lifted it beyond their level. If it were told us as the last in a series of adventures, its fairy-tale character would probably be preserved for us all the more purely the more it were lacking in 'Homeric' content. The more it has become a creation of a higher kind, the more the magical element is pushed from its centre towards the margin (so to speak), looking for a hiding place, and hiding in order suddenly to peep out again all the more surprisingly. For the contradiction of different worlds, far from causing difficulties, works in this new whole just as one more example of its many instances of magic. 'Are these still the Phaeacians?' one might ask the poet, doubtfully. 'Yes, they are', was his answer.

Ships as fast as wings and thought (7. 36), faster than hawk and falcon (13. 86), knowing of themselves where they are supposed to go and at the same time gliding along so lightly and gently that a wonderful sleep settles down on the passenger, so that when he wakes up at home he does not know what has happened to him— these must [121] be magic ships comparable with the artificial magic horse in the famous Indian story in *Arabian Nights*. One should not ask why the sea is never stormy when the Phaeacians are sailing: 'calm' (7. 319) belongs to their magic like the nocturnal secrecy of the voyage. The 'grey beings' are the invisible ones, not humans but spirits.

And yet this magic nature is mentioned only occasionally, in fact almost solely by Alcinous, as if it were repugnant to the epic spirit to talk about it directly. That the ships are even alive and omniscient, row by themselves in a fog which makes them invisible, know all coasts and reach any destination without needing a helmsman or a helm—about this we only hear once, only at that moment richest in suspense when, after so many tests of patience, Alcinous cannot control himself any longer and asks his guest what his name is. How fairy-tale magic is involved there in that moment which is expected and postponed again and again! For at this moment the suspense is directed at a very different matter! 8. 555 ff.

'You must also tell me where you come from, to what people and to what city you belong, so that my sentient ships may plan the right course to convey you there. For the Phaeacian ships have no helmsmen or rudders such as other craft possess. Our ships know by instinct what their crews are thinking and propose to do. They know every city, every fertile land; and hidden in mist and cloud they make their swift passage over the sea's immensities with no fear of damage and no thought of wreck.

'At the same time, I must tell you of a warning I had from my father Nausithous, who used to say that Poseidon grudged us our privilege of giving safe-conduct to all comers without ourselves coming to any harm. He prophesied that some day the god would wreck one of our fine vessels on the misty sea as she came home from such a journey, and would surround our city with a wall of mountains. That is what the old King used to say; and the god may do it, or may let things be. It is for him to decide as he pleases.

'And now, speak and tell us . . .'

(E. V. Rieu, rev. D. C. H. Rieu, Harmondsworth, 1991)

The core of the fairy-tale is given as an explanatory digression in this question which finally forces itself out of him with such power. The direct epic narrative actually touches this topic only once. But how it immediately makes the old miracle serviceable to a new one! What was once magic for its own sake now becomes [122] praise of the unique Odysseus, the sufferer, driven by nothing other than the desire to glorify his uniqueness, to reward his labours (13. 81 ff.):

And now, like a team of four stallions on the plain who start as one at the touch of the whip, leaping forward to make short work of the course, so the stern of the ship leaped forward, and a great dark wave of the surrounding sea surged in her wake. With unfaltering speed she forged ahead, and not even the wheeling falcon, the fastest creature that flies, could have kept her company. Thus she sped lightly on, cutting her way through the waves and carrying a man wise as the gods are wise, who in long years of war on land and wandering across the cruel seas had suffered many agonies of spirit but was now lapped in peaceful sleep, forgetting all he had endured.

(E. V. Rieu, rev. D. C. H. Rieu, Harmondsworth, 1991)

The purpose and function of these tensions is poetic transcendence. What the poet of the *Iliad*, whatever he composes, achieves again and again in a new way with the most natural inevitability, the *Odyssey* poet achieves by putting one layer on top of the other, through the tension between the old fairy-tale and the new epic spirit, by animating the fairy-tale in a new way and by giving the new spirit its support in tradition. Again, that obvious tension which lies in the fact that the Phaeacians take home any ship-wrecked person, whoever he is, yet the gift of return home is given only to Odysseus as such a high favour and distinction; that among these hospitable people nevertheless strangers are not welcome; that Odysseus almost like Priam in Achilles' tent has to ask for that which is actually granted to everyone else so willingly; all this also points to the same phenomenon, the contradiction between the fairy-tale and the epic. For it is only thanks to this contradiction that that higher consistency develops, which turns the Phaeacian adventure into the great turning point, which is how it has its place and rank in the epic. For the turning point, being at someone's mercy is necessary, the moment of anxiety, i.e. the pause while Odysseus is kneeling in front of Arete; the presentiment which dawns more and more on the Phaeacians that the stranger is greater than others, greater than they themselves; the granting and delay-ing of the voyage; the revelation which is further and further delayed. . . .

One more word about the ending. Before, it had finished with the mountain transformation. This widespread motif does not need any references. In the *Odyssey*, the narrative is replaced by an epic situation: the angry Poseidon turns to Zeus—in a divine scene after the model of the *Iliad* (*Od.* 13. 145 after *Iliad* 4. 37 etc.). Does this not [123] pick up the Polyphemus story after all? But here too it is unnecessary to make that connection for the sake of the fairy-tale. If the lord of the sea one day puts an end to the Phaeacian magic which he himself had tolerated for so long, this does not happen because Odysseus blinded his son, but because this rescue service is getting out of hand. So in the explanation of the mountain trans-formation in the gods' discussion (13. 151), as well as in Alcinous' oracle (13. 174), Odysseus is not referred to. The epic can be re-cognized by the overlapping, connecting motifs, the fairy-tale by the conflicting ones.

The model of the *Iliad* hardly ever becomes as clear as in that divine scene. And yet, if Poseidon in the part he plays in the *Iliad* complains to Zeus as an Olympian who fears for his authority, how again here has that which has been modelled on the *Iliad* been tran-scribed into the key characteristic of the poet! What a different object to the quarrel! In the *Iliad*, the gods quarrelled about the fates of kings and peoples. In the *Odyssey*, Poseidon declares that he agrees with the success of the will of the other gods. May Odysseus come to his homeland if this was promised to him by Zeus—but should he do so with such presents and such honours, with richer treasures than he would if he were coming straight from Troy, that would offend Olympian honour. What is new is that the concern of the offended god is all the greater the less he is concerned with the outcome itself, and the more he is concerned with the form of the outcome. That means that he takes offence at precisely what the poet has caused to emerge from the adventure, at the glory of the turning point—at the fact that the one who was recently naked and unknown is now suddenly so famous and richly rewarded! And how well indeed does Zeus know his Poseidon! 'OK, you just do to the Phaeacians what you want! But if you want to shatter the ship on its return, why don't you turn it into stone instead, so that all the people will be absolutely amazed at it?' Poseidon would not be Poseidon if he did not see that. He hits the ship with his flat hand and plants it firmly as a rock in the sea. Then he leaves—or rather, he has left already! The turning into stone becomes an Olympian explosion. In the sufferings of Odysseus in his homeland, as much as Polyphemus had asked him for these, Poseidon no longer participates. He becomes angry, but he does not hate. He disappears from the scene as after a storm at sea. His moods sublimely change.

And what becomes of the Phaeacians? While the people are amazed—this again after the model of the *Iliad* (*Od.* 13. 145 after *Iliad* 4. 37)—Alcinous sees his father's prophecy fulfilled, exhorts them to desist from escorting [124] people, and has twelve bulls sacrificed to Poseidon. Since the otherwise usual formula 'but he did not heed this' is avoided, the fate of the Phaeacians remains in suspense. Here, then, Odysseus who has happily returned: there, the Phaeacians who sacrifice in terror. The transition from one sphere into the other is marked by the contrast of the two situations which are held like musical pauses. Epic does not end by tapering off like a story, but broadly, in contrasting images. The *Odyssey* poet seems to owe the manner of leaving an episode in suspense to the *Iliad* poet.

The adventures of the *Odyssey*—has this topic been exhausted with what has been said? Is that which awaits the hero in his homeland not also an adventure? Being cast up again, if not in a distant land, nevertheless still in the deep? Self-denials, but of a quite different kind from those among fiends and monsters—namely among humans? The transformation into the beggar (almost as in Ovid's *Metamorphoses*), the magic, the magic wand, the hocus-pocus of this so very unhocus-pocussy Athena—is that not a reminiscence of Circe? Once more, the fairy-tale element enters the 'realism' of the great epic. This too would probably be impossible in the *Iliad*. But here, too, it represents and frames something transcendent: the miracle of finding each other. Through the magic wand, the revenge of Odysseus is connected with the adventures . . . But this leads to further questions, questions beyond the ones posed here. Here the purpose was merely, within a restricted orbit, and without building castles in the air, to lead the question about origins (which had lost its way) back to a path it could follow better. All methods, however they change, depend on what is seen in each case.

The Song of Ares and Aphrodite: On the Relationship between the *Odyssey* and the *Iliad*

WALTER BURKERT

On the issue of the 'Homeric question', since we still have one opinion against another, one hypothesis against its counterpart, without the slightest hope of reaching an agreement, it might seem pointless to want to add a new little stone to the mountain of literature. In spite of the common desire which should unite unitarians and analysts—interpretation of individual parts with a correct view of the whole—we have still got no further than missing each other's point. It is evident that in these controversies one fundamental uncertainty emerges again and again, i.e. which categories of understanding, which criteria, are appropriate for the subject matter; and the reason for this in turn is the complete isolation in which Homeric epic, at least the *Iliad*, presents itself to us. We know nothing about its poet and we ultimately know the world in which it originated only through its own testimony. Consequently, we can obtain those criteria and categories which are the basis of any interpretation only from the poem itself, or bring them in from outside without any proper legitimization. The greatest care must be taken to avoid the accusation of a circular argument or a *petitio principii*.

And yet we are faced with this basic difficulty to its full extent only as far as the *Iliad* is concerned. Perhaps people overlook at times that we are in a far better position concerning the *Odyssey*. For even though we cannot talk of an undisputed *communis opinio* about the relationship between the two epics, there is still a clear majority of research which from very different starting points came to the conclusion that the *Odyssey* as it presents itself to us originated later than the *Iliad*, and even more: that it presupposes the *Iliad* as its model and can be understood only in this kind of relationship. Even unitarians and analysts can meet at this juncture,

Originally published as W. Burkert, *Rh. Mus.* 103 (1960), 130–44, reproduced by kind permission of Sauerländer's Verlag, Frankfurt.

although one group will talk about the poet of the *Odyssey* and the others about the editor, and in many individual pieces of research this principle [131] has shown its fruitfulness.[1] Its significance, even if you want to allow it only as a working hypothesis, is obvious: for in this way we have for the *Odyssey* what we miss for the *Iliad*, i.e. certain and appropriate material for comparison; we have the opportunity to put together similar things, to separate the typical from the extraordinary, the new from the traditional [132], in short, to grasp exactly the originality of the *Odyssey*. Much has already been gained by this method but for the interpretation of

[1] The unity of authorship of both epics has been defended again and again. So, in addition to Franz Dornseiff (*Die archaische Mythenerzählung* (Berlin, 1933), esp. 44; cf. also *Gnomon* 29 (1957), 586 ff.), recently e.g. A. Severyns (*Homère* (Brussels, 1944/8), esp. iii. 159 ff.) and L. A. Post (*From Homer to Menander* (Berkeley, 1951), esp. fn. 2, p. 273). Even analysts approached this point of view: Peter von der Mühll, after separating the great original poet A from the later editor B, in his parallel analysis of the *Iliad* and the *Odyssey*, is inclined to identify these in both epics (*Kritisches Hypomnema zur Ilias* (Basle, 1952), esp. 348–90); Wolfgang Schadewaldt distinguishes two layers in the *Odyssey* and attributes the older poem to the *Iliad* poet Homer (*Taschenbuch für junge Menschen*, ed. Peter Suhrkamp (Berlin, 1946), 177 ff.). In contrast to this it was Ernst Bickel especially (*Homer. Die Lösung der Homerischen Frage* (Bonn, 1949), 97 ff.; 103 ff.) who elaborated the point of view of the *chorizontes*. All the theses mentioned here include rather than exclude the later origin of the *Odyssey* (e.g. Post, *Homer to Menander*, 12: 'The *Odyssey* is not only a sequel but a complement to the *Iliad*.'). That the *Odyssey* as a whole was composed before the *Iliad* has as far as I know been put forward recently only by Giovanni Patroni (*Commenti mediterranei all' Odissea di Omero* (Milan, 1950), esp. 146 ff.), but no one has taken up this idea. In his framework of radical analysis Benedetto Marzullo (*Il problema Omerico* (Florence, 1952), esp. 269 ff., 387 ff., cf. *Atene e Roma* NS 3 (1956), 141 ff.) tries to prove dependence of individual passages in the *Iliad* on passages in the *Odyssey*—but in complete contrast for the religious uses of the *Odyssey* he assumes influences from the *Iliad* (179 ff.). Keeping all this in mind I think that interpretations which from the point of view of the *chorizontes* contrast the originality of both epics have had convincing results. (Older material in Wilhelm Schmid, *Geschichte der griechischen Literatur I*, i (Munich, 1929), 124 ff.; Felix Jacoby, 'Die geistige Physiognomie der Odyssee', *Antike* 9 (1933), 159–94; Walter Nestle, 'Odyssee-Interpretationen', *Hermes* 77 (1942), 46–77; 113–39; for differences in the concept of the soul Bickel, *Homer*, 108 ff.; Karl Reinhardt, 'Die Abenteuer der Odyssee', *Von Werken und Formen* (Godesberg, 1948), 52 ff.; *Tradition und Geist im homerischen Epos*, Studium Generale 4 (1951), 334–9; Hermann Fränkel, *Dichtung und Philosophie des frühen Griechentums* (Lancaster, 1951), 120 ff.; Alfred Heubeck, *Der Odysseedichter und die Ilias* (Erlangen, 1954); Walter Marg, *Das erste Lied des Demodokos*, Navicula Chiloniensis (Festschrift Jacoby) (Leiden, 1956), 16–29; with analytic interpretation for the *Odyssey* Ernst Howald, *Der Dichter der Ilias* (Zurich, 1946), 166 ff.). Denys Page's opinion (*The Homeric Odyssey* (Oxford, 1955), 149 ff.), according to which the *Iliad* and the *Odyssey* originated without any connections and even in different districts, is admittedly based on commendable collations of linguistic material but to my mind untenable in its radicalism.

individual items more will need to be done. By using this method
of comparison and juxtaposition, this essay will try to come closer
to a passage of the *Odyssey* which is as well known as it is contested:
the song of Ares and Aphrodite.

Certainly this method has its problems too. The question as to
which demonstrable connections were intended and desired by the
poet, and which ones conversely have been artificially 'worked up'
and 'adjusted' by the comparison, often remains unanswered.
Nevertheless, interpretation does not require the poet's thoughts as
a psycho-biographical fact, but the objective spiritual structure of
the work; and here the right viewpoint stands the test in the very
fact that from it, individual items connect to a meaningful picture
in the most perfect way. It would certainly be self-deception if we
wanted to begin our work totally 'without any presuppositions'.
Everybody proceeds from a first view of the whole which then may
be verified or also modified in individual details. And so in this
essay too the unitarian cause will not and cannot be concealed; but
the attempt will be made as far as at all possible to leave aside the
'question of authorship' and to grasp only the demonstrable as precisely as possible.

From the outside, the song of Demodocus too is impossible to
approach in a conclusive way. Older scholarship agreed that such a
'divine-burlesque' could only be a late corruption of an originally
pious tale[2] and the analysis of Homer's work met this half-way by
actually eliminating the song as an interpolation[3] or at least
attributing it to the last editor.[4] It has since become clear that
wrong and inappropriate postulates are being applied to the epic
here [133]. Farce about the gods seems as a form to be very old;[5]

[2] Wilhelm Nestle, 'Anfänge einer Götterburleske bei Homer', *Njbb* (1905) =
Griechische Studien (Stuttgart, 1948), 1–31; likewise in principle, in spite of many
differences Karl Bielohlawek, 'Komische Motive in der homerischen Gestaltung
des griechischen Göttermythus', *ARW* 28 (1930), 106–24, 186–211.

[3] Friedrich Blass, *Die Interpolationen in der Odyssee* (Halle, 1904), 269 ff.; Georg
Finsler, *Homer II²* (Leipzig, 1918), 315; Ulrich von Wilamowitz-Moellendorff, *Die
Heimkehr des Odysseus* (Berlin, 1927), 25. Conversely according to Wolfgang
Schadewaldt (*Homer, Die Odyssee* (Hamburg, 1958), 330) the very song of
Demodocus 266–369 is by 'A' and the framework by 'B'.

[4] Eduard Schwartz, *Die Odyssee* (Munich, 1924), 25; Peter von der Mühll, 'Odyssee',
RE Suppl. VII, 717 f.; Friedrich Focke, *Die Odyssee* (Stuttgart, 1943), 147 ff.

[5] Paul Friedländer, 'Lachende Götter', *Antike* 10 (1934), 209–26; esp. Karl
Reinhardt, 'Das Parisurteil': *Von Werken und Formen* (Godesberg, 1948), 20 f. with
note; the Hittite myths already contain burlesque elements according to Margarete
Riemschneider, *Die Welt der Hethiter* (Stuttgart, 1954), 116 ff.

Walter Burkert

interpretation must try to work out individually for each case whether it is naïve-grotesque myth in the framework of matter-of-fact religious structures, or conscious poetic play taken to extremes, or subversive mockery.

Looking for earlier stages or sources of our song does not help us to reach really firm ground either. Admittedly, the connection between Ares and Aphrodite is obviously firmly rooted in cult and myth:[6] on the other hand, the connection with the marriage of Aphrodite and Hephaestus is very dubious.[7] Wilamowitz [134] reconstructed as the source of Demodocus' song a hymn about Hera being chained by Hephaestus and Hephaestus being led back to Olympus by Dionysus.[8] The priority of this divine legend,

[6] The most detailed investigation: Karl Tümpel, 'Ares und Aphrodite', *Jahrbuch für class. Philologie*, Suppl. 11 (1880), 639–754; Preller-Robert, *Griechische Mythologie I⁴* (Berlin, 1894), 176; 339 f.; Dümmler, 'Aphrodite' *RE* I, 2747 f. That the *Iliad* (5. 357 ff., 21. 416 ff.) alludes to the connection is disputed too harshly by Wilamowitz (*Der Glaube der Hellenen I* (Berlin, 1931), 323). Hesiod (*Theog.* 933 ff.) knows about their marriage. In the circle of the twelve gods the two belong together (Weinreich, 'Zwölfgötter' *RML VI*, 764 ff., esp. 830 ff.). Poets without any embarrassment call Ares Aphrodite's husband (Pindar, *Pyth.* 4. 87 f.; Aeschylus, *Hik.* 664 ff., *Sept.* 105, 140); the fine arts connect the two (François-Vase; Cypselus chest *Paus.* 5. 18. 5). Common cult at Thebes is certain. Between Argos and Mantineia stood a double temple for both deities: the images of the gods were allegedly donations by Polyneices, so apparently ancient (*Paus.* 2. 25. 1). If Harmonia wife of Cadmus appears as daughter of Ares and Aphrodite, this seems like transparent allegory (cf. Plut. *Pelopidas* 19, the affinity with Empedocles is stated by Heraclitus *qu. Hom.* 69 and Scholion *Od.* 8. 267, Eustathius *Od.* 8. 367) but myth has at all times contained a speculative element in addition to its pictorial one; already Babylonian myths know personifications of abstract conceptions (H. G. Güterbock, *Kumarbi* (Istanbul, 1946), 114 f.); cf. Deubner, 'Personification' *RML*. For the whole problem also Marie Delcourt, *Héphaistos* (Paris, 1957), 76 ff.

[7] Dümmler *RE* I, 2747 f. thought of cult connection on Lemnos; main support is *Apoll. Rh.* 1. 859 ff. w. Schol.; Demodocus' song would then be a play with the intersection of Lemnian and Theban cult legend. Evidence against this is the old Cabeiri cult on Lemnos. If Akusilaus (*FGrHist.* 2 F 20) and Pherecydes (*FGrHist.* 3 F 48) mention Kabeiro as the mother of the Lemnian Cabeiri, the sons of Hephaestus, this does indeed look like a genealogical construction (Jacoby in comm.) but this construction could only fill an empty space and could not replace Aphrodite. Cf. Bengt Hemberg, *Die Kabiren* (Uppsala, 1950), 160 ff.—*Iliad* (18. 382 f.) and Hesiod (*Theog.* 945 f.) mention as Hephaestus' wife one Charis—is she a substitute for Aphrodite or the other way round? The discrepancy, an argument of the ancient *chorizontes*, is dissolved by the A scholium to *Il.* 21. 416 into a succession (one after the other) while Lucian, *Dial. D.* 15 blesses the god with Charis on Lemnos and Aphrodite on Olympus at the same time. Cf. Malten, 'Hephaistos' *RE* VIII, 354 f.

[8] Wilamowitz, 'Hephaistos', *NGG* (1895), 217 ff. = *Kleine Schriften V*, ii (Berlin, 1937), 5–30; the pictorial material in Frank Brommer, 'Die Rückführung des Hephaistos', *Jahrbuch des Deutschen Archäologischen Instituts* 52 (1937), 198–219. Agreeing with Wilamowitz e.g. Malten *RE* VIII, 346; Bielohlawek (above n. 2) 196 ff.; opposition now in Walter Marg, *Homer über die Dichtung* (Münster, 1957), 43 n. 55.

which is well attested in archaic times, is very likely, but many
details remain doubtful, especially since a vase fragment was found
on Lemnos which seems to be nothing less than an illustration of
our Demodocus song from the seventh century.[9]

However, if we confront the Demodocus song not with hypothetical predecessors but with our extant *Iliad*, an abundance of
surprising connections emerges. The whole song culminates in the
verse [135] ἄσβεστος δ' ἄρ' ἐνῶρτο γέλως μακάρεσσι θεοῖσι
(326)—a verse which has become so well known and even prover-
bial that because of that we might almost forget that it has its

---

[9] That the *Iliad* (18. 395 ff.) presupposes and does not mention the leading back
(thus Wolfgang Kullmann, *Das Wirken der Götter in der Ilias* (Berlin, 1956), 12)
cannot be excluded but cannot be proved either. The oldest palpable evidence is
Alcaeus 9 D = 349, 381, inc. auct. 8 Lobel–Page; Bruno Snell has stated (*Festschrift
Ernst Kapp* (Hamburg, 1958), 15–17) that this is not a hymn about Hephaestus but
Dionysus. Wilamowitz's arguments for its priority are (*Kleine Schriften V*, ii. 12 f.):
(1) Only the Hymn explains the connection of Aphrodite and Hephaestus which is
presupposed in *Odyssey* 8. (2) In contrast to the Hymn the invention of *Odyssey* 8 is
totally ignored by the fine arts. Against this it can be argued that (i) we hardly have
sufficient idea of how much impromptu work a singer in Homeric times could present his audience with (the dissolution of the marriage suggested in *Od*. 8. 318 could
be understood as a retraction of the invention); above all: that Aphrodite is the price
for Hera's solution has solely been concluded from the representation of the
François-Vase; the retelling (Ps. Libanius, *Prog.* 7) does not mention Aphrodite at
all. So in this respect it cannot be decided what Book 8 owes to the Hymn. (ii) The
leading back of Hephaestus invited representation as an example of a Dionysian thi-
asus with the content of the story quite unimportant here (Brommer, 'Die
Rückführung des Hephaistos'). But this very fact of being firmly rooted in the
Dionysus cult suggests that the legend is very old, it can be regarded as a downright
αἴτιον of the Dionysian κῶμοι (reference by Professor Reinhold Merkelbach),
whereas the song of Demodocus is completely independent of the cult. In this cultic context Wilamowitz's (*Kleine Schriften V*, ii. 24) reference to the remarkable
phenomenon of the chained gods-images is attractive (cf. Martin P. Nilsson,
Geschichte der griechischen Religion I² (Munich, 1955), 82 f.); nevertheless the
Greeks themselves used to tell each other different αἴτια for this, cf. *Paus*. 3. 15. 11;
7 for the chained Aphrodite Morpho and for the chained Enyalius in Sparta; *Ath*.
15. 672c about the Hera statue of Argos which had willows wound around it. In 1939
a vase fragment from the Hephaestus sanctuary of Hephaestia on Lemnos was published (M. A. Della Seta, *Arch. Eph.* 1937 (pub. 1939), 649 ff.; thoroughly interpreted by Charles Picard, *Rev. Arch.* 20 (1942/3), 96–124), which shows a naked
goddess—Aphrodite—and opposite her a man with greaves, both in a squatting
position and obviously chained. Since the finding place establishes the connection
with Hephaestus there is hardly any doubt that this is an illustration of Demodocus'
song, dedicated to the god whose τέχνη won; therefore sculpture has not ignored the
song completely after all. Conjectures about cultic background in Picard 103 ff.,
Delcourt 81 ff. Whereas Della Seta dated the vase as early as the 8th cent. Picard
suggested the last third of the 7th without excluding the early 6th. The fact that the
truly sensational find hardly seems to have caused a stir may be due to the War.

unique, fixed, and unrepeatable place in the *Iliad* (1. 599). In fact there is no other scene in the *Iliad* in which all the gods come together for such untroubled laughter. The linguistic formulation too is not quite usual; the metaphor ἄσβεστος γέλως seems to need to be explained by the *Odyssey* scholia.[10] So this is not a formulaic verse which could be used as often as desired.

Conclusions could not be drawn from one single borrowing of a verse; but the connections continue straight away: the verse following the gods' laughter ὡς ἴδον Ἥφαιστον διὰ δώματα ποιπνύοντα (1. 600) reappears in *Od.* 8.285 f.

> οὐδ' ἀλαὸς σκοπιὴν εἶχε χρυσήνιος Ἄρης,
> ὡς ἴδεν Ἥφαιστον κλυτοτέχνην νόσφι κιόντα.

When looked at closely the two verses do not quite fit together in the *Odyssey*, because literally it says 'Ares was not blind' 'when he saw . . .'. Certainly 8. 285 is a formulaic verse which occurs several times;[11] ἀλαοσκοπιή, as the manuscripts usually write,[12] has practically fused into one word with the meaning of 'careless' or 'fruitless' watch, but it is remarkable that the catachrestic conjunction with ὡς ἴδε is found again only in the Dolon episode (*Il.* 10. 515 f.) [136] in contrast to the other examples in the *Iliad* and in Hesiod.

Further: here as there Hephaestus is at the centre of the laughter which arises half at his initiative and half at his cost; and although the island of Lemnos is mentioned in many other places[13] the Σίντιες are mentioned only in these two.[14] All this seems to be more than mere coincidence.

Coincidence is excluded completely as soon as the two scenes from *Iliad* and *Odyssey* are juxtaposed in their context: in their whole structure they appear related and connected with each other. In the divine scene of *Iliad* 1, Zeus has first answered Hera's jealously insistent questions evasively, then with coarse threats. The consequence is the offended silence of his wife (569) and the discontent of all the other gods. Then Hephaestus begins to speak, in a mediating and appeasing tone. He reminds the gods of their

---

[10] It only occurs in *Od.* 20. 346 apart from here.

[11] *Il.* 10. 515, 13. 10, 14. 135; Hes. *Theog.* 466.

[12] The scholia seem to presuppose word-separation. ΑΛΑΟΣΣΚΟΠΙΗΝ is written by several papyri and Venetus A, but Allen keeps in his *Iliad* edition the Vulgate ἀλαοσκοπιήν.

[13] *Il.* 2. 722, 7. 467, 8. 230, 14. 230, 21. 40, 46, 58, 79, 24. 753.

[14] *Il.* 1. 594, *Od.* 8. 294. A Thracian tribe according to Hellanicus *FGrHist.* 4 F 71.

superiority and gets the feast going again; all the tensions dissolve in 'Homeric' laughter, the shadows which had fallen on the gods' existence because of human fate disappear. Serene and cloudless the gods' day ends. A similar arc of tension stretches through Odyssey 8: Euryalus has offended Odysseus, he has replied angrily, and embarrassing silence (234) ends the *agon*. Then Alcinous finds the right word, he gives his guest his due honour and at the same time demonstrates the true superiority of the Phaeacians. Odysseus admires the dance and singing (265); the song of Demodocus in which the gods laugh so vigorously delights him too (367 f.); and when at the end he praises Demodocus in well-chosen words (382 ff.) there is joy again in the whole company.[15]

The fundamental difference between the two scenes—there the serene action of the gods juxtaposed with the other pole of the one comprehensive reality, tragic human affairs, here a [137] poem within a poem for the mere exhilaration of the fictitious (and real) listeners—will have to be discussed later. But the similarity is impossible to overlook: in both cases laughter conquers ill-feeling, in both cases it is caused by Hephaestus, the skilful cripple; and if in addition to this there are individual linguistic and factual correspondences, the finding is confirmed: the 'Homeric' laughter has not been taken over thoughtlessly, *Iliad* 1 is present in the *Odyssey* scene.

But this by no means exhausts the connections with the *Iliad*. In terms of riskiness of topic, of offensiveness to ancient and modern critics,[16] there is only one scene of the *Iliad* comparable: the Διὸς

---

[15] Already the meaningful gradation θαύμαζε—τέρπετο 'praise' is evidence against the assumption of a subsequent, disturbing insertion of the song. The main argument of the analysis is the assertion that the song interrupts the dance performances without a motive (above nn. 3–4, esp. Blass, Focke, furthermore Margarete Riemschneider, *Homer* (Leipzig, 1950), 47). This is contradicted by the following consideration: after the detailed announcement 250 ff. the round dance cannot be dealt with in the few verses 262/4, but how can music and dance be described in detail in epic language if not by reporting the dancing song? Cf. Wilhelm Mattes, *Odysseus bei den Phäaken* (Würzburg, 1958), 97, 2; cf. also Dornseiff, *Die archaische Mythenerzählung*, 44 ff.; how far we need to presuppose mimetic dance remains doubtful, Delcourt 80 mentions the Cordax.—By the way, is purely instrumental music, which would come in if we deleted the song, not much more striking and 'offensive' for Homeric time?—We cannot argue with the unique form ἥλιος 271 when we consider the character of Homeric artistic language; an equally unique contraction, e.g. *Il.* 18. 475 τιμῆντα, instead of τιμήεντα, cf. Pierre Chantraine, *Grammaire Homérique*, i² (Paris, 1948), 47.

[16] Already Xenophanes, VS 21 B 11, 3 = 12, 2: μοιχεύειν καὶ ἀλλήλους ἀπατεύειν; Plato, *Rep.* 390b–c, *Ath.* 3. 122c censures both scenes together. The song

Walter Burkert

ἀπάτη. And again detailed connections can be found. Certainly the fact that the verse δεῦρο, φίλη, λέκτρονδε, τραπείομεν εὐνηθέντε occurs here as well as there (*Il.* 14. 314 = *Od.* 8. 292, but also *Il.* 3. 441) is caused by the content. Another verse repetition is more remarkable: οὐκ ἔστ᾽ οὐδὲ ἔοικε τεὸν ἔπος ἀρνήσασθαι. With these words Hephaestus finally complies with Poseidon's request (*Od.* 8. 358). The same words are spoken by Aphrodite to Hera (*Il.* 14. 212), only there they mean immediate concession, as is 'becoming' for the wife of Zeus (213), whereas in the [138] *Odyssey* the verse somewhat abruptly and surprisingly concludes longer negotiations.[17]

The following is even more important: Hera, having achieved the object of her plan, prudishly delays with the words (*Il.* 14. 333 ff.):

πῶς κ᾽ ἔοι, εἴ τις νῶϊ θεῶν αἰειγενετάων
εὕδοντ᾽ ἀθρήσειε, θεοῖσι δὲ πᾶσι μετελθὼν
πεφράδοι

and Zeus calms her (342 ff.)

. . . μήτε θεῶν τό γε δείδιθι μήτε τιν᾽ ἀνδρῶν
ὄψεσθαι· τοῖόν τοι ἐγὼ νέφος ἀμφικαλύψω
χρύσεον· οὐδ᾽ ἂν νῶϊ διαδράκοι Ἥλιός περ . . .

In *Od.* 8 Helios sees the two first (270) and then Hephaestus in a loud voice calls πᾶσι θεοῖσι (305). This is more than similarity simply conditioned by the situation: the whole embarrassing and comical situation of Demodocus' song is contained potentially in the Διὸς ἀπάτη; what is only suggested here is there elaborated in detail.

Again connections of language and content come together: this *Iliad* scene too is behind the song of Ares and Aphrodite.

And a third episode is reflected there: the battle of the gods. The fact that in *Iliad* 20/21 and in *Od.* 8 the same gods appear, Poseidon, Hermes, and Apollo, may not be considered remarkable since they are the most important Olympians. But already the verses describing their appearance are almost identical:

of Demodocus was deleted (scholium to Aristoph. *Pax* 778) or purified by removing the most offensive bit (scholium to *Od.* 8. 333) or interpreted allegorically (Heraclitus *qu. Hom.* 39; 69 = scholium to *Od.* 8. 346; *Ath.* 12. 511 b–c).

[17] Walter Diehl, *Die wörtlichen Beziehungen zwischen Ilias und Odyssee* (diss. Greifswald, 1938), 72. Attempt at a legal interpretation of the passage in *Od.* 8: Adalbert Erler, 'Die Bürgschaft Poseidons im 8. Gesang der Odyssee', *ZSRG romanische Abteilung* 65 (1947), 312–19.

The Song of Ares and Aphrodite

Od. 8. 322 f.: ἦλθε Ποσειδάων γαιήοχος, ἦλθ' ἐριούνης
             'Ερμείας
Il. 20. 34 f.: ἠδὲ Ποσειδάων γαιήοχος ἠδ' ἐριούνης
             'Ερμείας

—the strange epithet ἐριούνης occurs only in these two places in epic—and the anaphora compared with the simple conjunction of the *Iliad* should probably be understood as a conscious further development. Even more clearly than in *Iliad* 5 (355 ff.), Ares and Aphrodite in Book 21 are close friends. The goddess wants to lead him, injured, out of battle and at the end they both lie on the ground next to each other (*Il.* 21. 416 ff.). The whole [139] presumably reflects the (to be presupposed) myths about the connection of Ares and Aphrodite (above n. 6). But it is the unmistakable similarity in the whole way the gods behave, in their characterization, which is most important: Poseidon, of a deliberate and slow nature, is felt to belong to the older generation; he knows what is becoming for his age (*Il.* 21. 439 f.); and so he is the only one who cannot laugh with the others in *Od.* 8 but feels obliged to end the matter with a light touch. Because of his αἰδώς Apollo cannot start any scuffles with Poseidon in *Il.* 21 (468 f.); Hephaestus does not want to accept Poseidon's bail because he cannot seriously make his superior liable (*Od.* 8. 350 ff.). On the other hand, Hephaestus knows that it is 'not becoming' (358) to reject his words. But especially Hermes: in his answer to Apollo (*Od.* 8. 339 ff.) he rejects convention and custom with the same unembarrassed and flippant gesture with which he breaks the rules of the gods' battle in refusing to fight Leto (*Il.* 21. 498 ff.)—'boast anyway of having defeated me'. The happy, cunning god of shepherds and thieves, as the *Hymn* describes him, appears here sublimated in a very subtle way—typical of Homer—from κερδαλεόφρων to εἴρων, who by resigning his own dignity in smiling self-detraction unmasks appearances and in this very way proves his independence. Precisely this subtlety is common to both *Iliad* and *Odyssey*. Again the comparison has led from the linguistic to the factual: the gods' individuality in Demodocus' song has been formed under *Iliadic* influence.

To sum up: clear connections with three gods' scenes from the *Iliad* emerged: inextinguishable laughter around Hephaestus as in Book 1; risky situations as in Book 14; gods' conversations and gods' characterization as in Book 21. The parallels became evident each time in individual formulation, in borrowed verses and formulas as well as quite particularly in the contents as a whole, in the disposition and function of persons and scenes. Not all these cases can be coincidental and nobody will postulate for all of them—though for individual cases this would be conceivable—a hypothetical common source to explain the correspondence. Demodocus' song does presuppose the *Iliad*.

But then Demodocus' song does not remind us of any randomly chosen scenes from the *Iliad* but of those three divine scenes which by their extent and content decisively coin the image of the *Iliadic* gods as ῥεῖα ζώοντες; from this [140] results the decisive perspective for the understanding of Demodocus' song.

For the world of the *Iliad* the contrast between the serene life of the gods and deadly serious human fate is constitutive;[18] it was possible to call this coexistence virtually 'the inner necessary form of the *Iliad*'.[19] the 'sublime unseriousness' (Reinhardt) of the gods is the counter-world to that of human suffering, the ironic mirroring[20] of human tragedy. The three gods' scenes mentioned must be seen in the context of the poetical work. Among humans, harmless events entangle themselves into an inextricable knot of guilt and fate. From Olympus, after a short disagreement, the inextinguishable laughter of the easy-living gods answers back. On earth, battle rages, demanding victim after victim. At that precise moment, the world-ruler Zeus, whose decree is to be fulfilled, succumbs to his wife's cunning. Achilles rages terribly, and the final battle with Hector looms. The battle of the gods with each other becomes a game, which results in tears at the most, and Zeus is amused by it. Later theology regarded the gods' laughter as diminishing their dignity; in reality it is rather an expression of a dreadful, uncanny superiority, of a truly divine freedom and security, far removed from all calculating human reason.

The divine scenes of the *Iliad* in which this takes shape are united in sharply concentrated focus in Demodocus' song; and yet something completely different has emerged. It is true that one could

---

[18] Cf. esp. Karl Reinhardt, 'Das Parisurteil' (above n. 5), 22 f.

[19] U. Hölscher, *Untersuchungen zur Form der Odyssee* (Berlin, 1939), 48 ff.

[20] 'Irony' not in a Socratic sense but in the more general sense of having a 'double bottom', of the two elements cancelling each other, as has been shown especially by Karl Reinhardt, 'Das Parisurteil', 22 f.

The Song of Ares and Aphrodite

find here, too, some ironic reflection. Ancient commentators (Ath. 5. 192 d/e) already draw a parallel between the content of Demodocus' song and the theme of the *Odyssey* as a whole. In both there is the question of marital faithfulness, and again what causes only laughter on Olympus becomes deadly serious on earth. But whereas in the *Iliad* image is set against image in an unforgettable way, in the *Odyssey* at best only analysis can discover a connection.

[141] For indeed that serene world of the gods as a contrast to human reality has in general been abandoned in the *Odyssey*. The nature of the gods has changed.[21] Right at the beginning Zeus programmatically says

ὦ πόποι, οἷον δή νυ θεοὺς βροτοὶ αἰτιόωνται (*Od.* 1. 32).

He feels that he has been forced onto the defensive. But in the *Iliad* no one answers when, for instance, Menelaus calls

Ζεῦ πάτερ, οὔ τις σεῖο θεῶν ὀλοώτερος ἄλλος (*Il.* 3. 365).

At the end of the *Odyssey* we find the confirmation

Ζεῦ πάτερ, ἦ ῥα ἔτ᾽ ἐστὲ θεοὶ κατὰ μακρὸν Ὄλυμπον (*Od.* 24. 351)

—the fact that there are 'still' any gods left at all has to become clear to man through his experience of life, through the victory of justice in the world. Zeus, as far as he is there at all, has the task of watching over morals and justice. And so his involvement with earthly matters is quite different from that in the *Iliad*. The many-coloured life of the gods in the *Iliad*, an expression of that infinite freedom, must atrophy under the burden of ethical responsibilities. Divine assemblies are rare and they have as their topic only human circumstances, the restoration of justice. Compared with Zeus and Athena, who are connected by the same desire, the other gods stand well in the background. It is only in Demodocus' song that they are given individual life. When faced with this view of the world the gods' laughter must grow silent—with the one exception of Demodocus' song.

From this perspective Demodocus' song could be regarded as an

---

[21] More recent literature about the religious differences of *Iliad* and *Odyssey* in Alfred Heubeck, *Gymnasium* 62 (1955), 130 n. 42. Most outstanding but already a little overrefined is Werner Jaeger's formulation that the Zeus of the *Odyssey* is the 'philosophically purified world conscience' (*Paideia* I³ (Berlin, 1954), 85 f.).

alien element in the *Odyssey* after all, and yet it is linked through a variety of relationships with the whole scene and indeed with the entire poem. It has become clear already (above n. 15) that it cannot simply be removed from the context of *Odyssey* 8. Ancient and modern commentators[22] have often emphasized how, with its light nature, it has been fitted into the playfully serene world of the Phaeacians. But more important still is the special emphasis which dominates the story and incorporates it completely into that [142] framework which, with Jacoby, could be called the 'spiritual physiognomy of the *Odyssey*'.

At the centre there is no frivolity but the victory of τέχνη, of cleverness over nature. So we can observe everywhere in the *Odyssey* how deliberation and even calculation take the place of spontaneous feeling and action. It is not only Odysseus who is completely moulded by this. When after twenty years' waiting his return home is announced, he by no means seizes the opportunity immediately (*Od.* 5. 171 ff.): when he finally knows that he is at home he quickly contrives a story full of lies (13. 253 ff.). But when Telemachus rejects inappropriate presents (4. 601 ff.), and Penelope remains suspicious right up to the end (23. 166 ff.), this is the result of a basic attitude similar to that of Hephaestus who, instead of resisting openly, lures the wrongdoers into a trap, in indirect revenge. The victory of deliberation over simple spontaneous acting or living is the discovery of the *Odyssey* as compared with the *Iliad*. The values of the world of the nobility diverge in this way: as Odysseus knows how to distinguish outward appearance from spiritual qualities (*Od.* 8. 167 ff.), so Aphrodite is καλή, but also οὐκ ἐχέθυμος.[23] The taste for material goods corresponds to the advance of calculation: the fine seems to be the most important thing for Hephaestus.[24] So Demodocus' song, in spite of its special status, turns out on a spiritual level to belong fully to the *Odyssey*.

Yet even if the most moralistic sentiment of the *Odyssey* is found just here—οὐκ ἀρετᾷ κακὰ ἔργα (329)—there is still enough danger. It has been emphasized, no doubt correctly, to what extent

---

[22] *Ath.* 12. 511b–c; Heraclitus, *qu. Hom.* 69; scholium to *Od.* 8. 267, 272; Eustathius to *Od.* 8. 267, 335.

[23] ἐχέθυμος *Od.* 8. 320 is ἅπαξ λεγόμενον—a new word for a new view. Comparable formations are ἐχεπευκής or ἐχέφρων, but with a different meaning of the first element.

[24] Cf. Jacoby, *op. cit.* 180 ff. on the role of 'possession' in the *Odyssey*.

offensive elements have been repressed,[25] in contrast for instance to Lucian (*Dial. D.* 17): Ares and Aphrodite do not seem to be taken completely seriously in the *Iliad* either; besides, Ares has reached his goal anyway and Aphrodite is as it were in her element. But at least in the dialogue between Poseidon and Hephaestus no remnant of divinity can be discovered;[26] anthropomorphization cannot go further [143] than this. Even if we are extremely conservative in judging what original religious feelings could and could not tolerate, Demodocus' song makes an unbridgeable contrast with the conception of the gods in *Odyssey* Book 1 as well as with the sublimity of the gods of the *Iliad*.

And yet everything fits together: for the tale of Ares and Aphrodite is not as the world of the gods is in the *Iliad*, the other side of the one reality. Nor is the poet speaking in his own name. It is significant that it is Demodocus of all people who recites the song among the easy-living Phaeacians. It is not 'Homer' who is the speaker here, but Δημόδοκος τῇ ἰδίᾳ μυθοποιίᾳ as the scholium (to *Od.* 8. 267) rightly says. As the fairy-tale-like adventures of Odysseus have receded into the distance through the artifice of the first-person singular narrative,[27] so also the song of Ares and Aphrodite has been put in quotation marks, so to speak, and thus rendered harmless. One little detail is striking, especially in comparison with the *Iliad*. In the *Iliad* it is a matter of course that while Zeus, e.g. during the fight of the gods, watches and enjoys it (*Il.* 21. 388 ff.), in our song his name is mentioned only in Hephaestus' exclamation (306), and in what follows he seems to have been forgotten. In reality, I suppose that he has been consciously excluded.[28] And thus *Odyssey* Books 1 and 8 correspond: in Book 1 the poet wrestles with the question of divine justice, whose representative is called Zeus, in Book 8, in a non-committal, even precarious, game, this name is missing. Zeus in the *Odyssey* has been

[25] Esp. Walter F. Otto, *Die Götter Griechenlands* (Frankfurt, 1956⁴), 239 ff.; Friedländer (above n. 5).

[26] It is significant that Otto (above, n. 25) passes over this conversation. Aristarchus' reading εὐθύνοιμι instead of δέοιμι v. 352 mitigates the most outrageous part, the god's detention for debt.

[27] Jacoby, *op. cit.* 166 f., Heubeck, *Der Odysseedichter und die Ilias*, 97 f.

[28] Apollodorus wonders why Zeus or Phobos and Deimos do not plead for Ares instead of Poseidon who is not as close to him: scholium *Od.* 8. 344 Ἀπολλόδωρος ζητεῖ, διά τί τῶν ἄλλων θεῶν οὐδεὶς ἦν . . . Dindorf conjectures ἀπῆν without reason.

raised so far above the other gods that he cannot be drawn into such a situation.

The whole problem of *Odyssey* 'analysis' has so far been intentionally omitted, because it is impossible to make a decisive statement from such a narrow base. As a result, it can be said in summary that Demodocus' song on the one hand is firmly rooted in the total structure of our *Odyssey*, and on the other that it condenses the most important divine scenes of the *Iliad* at the same time as it transforms them.

If we dare to end by interpreting this finding further, we can come up only with a conjecture, but one which may seem plausible: the *Odyssey* poet, who created his work according to [144] whatever models after the pattern of the *Iliad* but with a new ethico-religious attitude, saw that in his model there remained a vacuum in his own far-too-serious image of the world and its gods. So he undertook the task of uniting the whole Olympic serenity of the *Iliad* in one image. That thus—if you come this far you might as well go all the way—the most precarious of all divine scenes resulted is characteristic rather than astonishing. The *Odyssey* poet has already reached the point at which uninhibitedness about the myths of the gods has been lost; under the influence of ethical reflection, there occurs a split into a 'purer' conception of god on the one hand, and into a religiously irrelevant or even risky fiction on the other. The poet of the *Odyssey* took over the laughing gods from the *Iliad*, but with much cushioning and distancing he separates the 'divine burlesque' from his actual religious concern, which crystallizes around the figure of Zeus.

The Ending of the *Odyssey*: Linguistic Problems

HARTMUT ERBSE

In this chapter those linguistic peculiarities will be discussed with which people tried to justify the deletion of the ending of the *Odyssey* (arguments compiled in Page, *The Homeric Odyssey* (Oxford, 1955), 102–11). It is advisable to make a few general remarks before individual passages are examined.

1. People like to use *hapax legomena*, or other rare forms of a Homeric word not otherwise found, as evidence against the authenticity of a text.[1] In the case of the ending of the *Odyssey* Spohn has already done this, considering the number of *hapax legomena* unusually high here (157): 'At vero in hac extrema Odysseae parte numerum deprehendimus ἅπαξ εἰρημένων non solum pro ambitu ingentem, sed etiam multas formas continentem, quae et linguam et ingenium processisse docent, ita ut iis vis et momentum in indicanda origine concedi possit.' I regard this conclusion, at least as regards the number of words found only once in the epics, as methodologically unsound in every case where it can be shown that the unique word is called for by situation, metre, and sentence structure. As the Aristonicus scholia teach us, Aristarchus already used to mark *hapax legomenon* with a *diple*, but he used such a *hapax legomenon* to recommend deletion only in exceptional cases (cf. e.g. Ariston. to *Iliad* 7. 475: ἀθετεῖται, ὅτι νεωτερικὴ ⟨ἡ⟩ [addidi] ὀνομασία τοῦ ἀνδράποδον). Incidentally, he knew very well that the Homeric epics contain many *hapax legomena* (cf. Ariston. on *Il.* 3. 54a). A rough glance at the *Iliad* scholia still extant today which deal with these

From: H. Erbse, *Beiträge zum Verständnis der Odyssee* (Untersuchungen zur antiken Literatur und Geschichte 13; Berlin, 1972), 177–229, reproduced by kind permission of Walter de Gruyter & Co., Berlin.

[1] By *hapax legomena* I understand in the following such words as appear only once in both epics. Post-Homeric references do not affect this definition.

words[2] shows quite clearly that lexically unique words are distrib-
uted over the whole poem. They bulk excessively large only where
the subject matter is unconventional (e.g. in *Od.* 23). Consequently,
anyone who wants to justify deletion by reference to *hapax legomena*
would have to demonstrate in each case that [178] the thought
intended at the place concerned could have been expressed just as
clearly by more common synonyms. Something similar is valid for
rare forms in as far as they are formed in accordance with the laws of
epic language or have fitting analogies. We must never forget that,
among the forms we frequently meet, we accept quite a few strange
formations, for the obvious reason that we have become used to their
existence. We become suspicious only when faced with rarity. But
before we condemn a rare form, we should ask whether the poet ever
had any opportunity to repeat the peculiarity.

2. It is no different with the word combinations which people usually describe in the broadest sense of the word as formulae. A formulaic expression which cannot be found elsewhere does not
necessarily indicate a later (e.g. post-Homeric) origin, if it becomes
clear that the usual formula needed to be changed in order to
describe a particular situation more precisely. The problem can be
explained with an example: e.g. the unique combination at *Il.* 20.
79: λαοσσόος ὦρσεν Ἀπόλλων is contrasted with numerous verse
endings of the form Φοῖβος Ἀπόλλων, ἑκάεργος Ἀπόλλων,
ἀργυρότοξος Ἀπόλλων. But the choice of the unique expression in
Il. 20. 79 can be explained by the special purpose of the description.
While Achilles is trying to find Hector in the turmoil of battle in
order to avenge the death of his friend Patroclus, Apollo in the
shape of Lycaon, son of Priam, incites Aeneas to go into action
against Achilles: Αἰνείαν δ' ἰθὺς λαοσσόος ὦρσεν Ἀπόλλων | ἀντία
Πηλεΐωνος. Only here, where he provokes a level-headed man to an
unusually rash step, does he receive the epithet 'stirring up to battle', which elsewhere the battle-deities Athena (13. 128), Ares (17.
398), or Eris (20. 48) have. The formation of the new word combination was easy since adjective and proper name were able to take
the verb (ὦρσεν) between them. For this reason, it takes up a place
in the verse at which it is found in other places too.[3]

---

[2] Cf. the compilation in Martinazzoli, *Hapax legomenon* (Rome, 1953), i. 26. The
meagre Aristonicus scholia to the *Odyssey* do not allow any certain conclusions.

[3] Cf. *Il.* 2. 451, 13. 83, 794, 15. 694, 17. 273, 18. 218, 23. 108, 153, 24. 507, always
in the fifth trochee.

The Ending of the Odyssey: Linguistic Problems

But, so people object (cf. Dihle 73), is it not a violation of the practice of oral poetry to break up stock phrases and put them together in a new way? Is not the oral poet obliged to speak in traditional word combinations because it is only in these that he thinks? Would not his audience refuse to approve of unknown combinations?

3. These questions lead us into a wide field. It will be impossible to avoid entering it, since otherwise the accusation could be made against the ensuing examination of details about the language of the ending of the *Odyssey* that it does not take into account the different principles on which [179] oral and written epic poetry are composed. So we could be in danger of old-fashioned practices. I freely admit that I offer an opinion on these matters only hesitantly, although I have been pursuing the problem of oral poetry and its application to Homer for years. But I regard it as a great disadvantage that I have been able to get to know the work of Serbo-Croat singers and other poets composing orally only in translation. This is all the more regrettable since I have not succeeded in finding evidence of high epic art in the songs of the guslars.[4] Nevertheless, I cannot do anything other than present my arguments.

Following M. Parry, Lord (152)[5] claims that Homer was a poet who composed through oral performance. The *Iliad* and *Odyssey* originated in this way. Both epics, Lord assumes, were written down at Homer's dictation. Other scholars (e.g. recently Dihle) assume that the writing down happened only centuries later; so they assume that

[4] Cf. M. Parry and A. B. Lord, *Serbocroatian Heroic Songs*, i. *Novi Pazar* (Cambridge, Mass. and Belgrade, 1954). This volume contains the compositions of the singers Salih Uglianin, Sulejman Fortić, Demail Zogić, Suleyman Makić, and Alija Fjuljanin (the latter probably the most gifted narrator). These are heroicized, partly fairy-tale-like, partly gruesome, robber and war stories. With the Homeric epics there are hardly any points of contact in terms of content, let alone of composition. Everyone who ascribes the *Iliad* and *Odyssey* to oral poetry should feel duty bound to read this volume first. (The valuable treatise by F. Dirlmeier should be mentioned with special emphasis, *Das serbokroatische Heldenlied und Homer* (*Sitzungsberichte der Heidelberger Akademie der Wissenschaften, philologisch–historische Klasse*, 1971, 1; Heidelberg, 1971). Dirlmeier's judgement on Homer and the problem of writing (p. 19), and on the quality of Serbian folk art (p. 29, 'But we do not have high art') are in both cases congruent with the conclusions presented above.)

[5] *Passim.* On oral poetry and its relationship to Homer cf. the level-headed presentation by Lesky, *RE* Suppl. 11 (1968), 693, 59, esp. 703, 27. The thought that the epics were written down with Homer dictating them has, as is well known, been represented by Raphael on his famous fresco, cf. H. von Einem, *Das Programm der Stanza della Segnatura im Vatikan* (Opladen, 1971), 33.

there was an oral tradition over longer periods of time. But these details are of minor importance. Only the question whether both Homeric epics can be products of genuine oral poetry is important to us. Some suppose that they originated in the same way as the songs of the guslars collected by Parry and Lord, because their language has numerous fixed formulae at its disposal which, if used economically (i.e. if varied as economically as possible), could have been very useful for a poet composing orally. Scholars think that a literate poet must actually have been hindered by them.

On this, I would like to make the following observations. Today it is undisputed that pre-Homeric oral poetry developed a great wealth [180] of formulaic phrases. But this general observation must not tempt us to the conclusion that a Homeric formula (for example ἀργυρότοξος Ἀπόλλων) must be inherited just because it is found frequently in our epics. Even a combination as common as κορυθαίολος Ἕκτωρ which Page tried to prove to be Mycenaean cannot be regarded as pre-Homeric without conclusive argument.[6] Because of this, it cannot be decided whether the *Iliad* poet composed the famous farewell scene of Book 6 in the shape we have it because the most important Trojan hero had an inherited epithet which suggested to him the conception of Astyanax's fear, or whether it was the planning of the scene that determined the choice, perhaps even the invention, of the epithet. I confess that I regard the latter as more probable, but cannot present definitive arguments. But, *vice versa*, proof that formulae are inherited succeeds only where their linguistic form (e.g. εὐρύοπα Ζεύς, Διὸς νεφεληγερέταο, μελαινάων ἀπὸ νηῶν)[7] or perhaps content (e.g. *Il.* 2. 319: Κρόνου πάϊς ἀγκυλομήτεω) make it possible. Hoekstra[8] proved in an important investigation that many Homeric words and word combinations can have originated only under the influence of Ionic dialect: metathesis of quantities and loss of the digamma are clear indications of lateness, whereas the free use of

---

[6] Cf. D. L. Page, *History and the Homeric Iliad* (Berkeley, 1959), 249. J. B. Hainsworth, 'The Homeric Formula and the Problem of its Transmission', *Institute of Classical Studies London, Bulletin* 9 (1962), 57–68 has already shown that Mycenaean remains in Homeric formulaic language can only be small. Attempts at a distinction between individual and traditional epithets only in Whitman 113.

[7] These examples after Parry 316. But Parry himself admits the possibility 'that the later poets may have used one of the old words in a new formula'.

[8] A. Hoekstra, *Homeric Modifications of Formulaic Prototypes* (Verhandelingen der Koninklijke Nederlandse Akademie, N. R. 71:1, 1965), 1–172. Cf. with this L. E. Rossi, *Göttingische Gelehrte Anzeiger* 223 (1971), 161 ff.

v-ephelkustikon may have become normal earlier. So the special mixture of Homeric dialect and the formulae coined for it cannot have been in existence for centuries. These results expose the one-sidedness of Parry's system, according to which nearly every word which in the concordances is shown to occur at least twice in the same place in the line has to be regarded as part of an inherited formula.

Parry (301) and Lord (143) identify e.g. οὐλομένην at the beginning of a verse as part of a formula given to the singer because it does not occur just in *Il.* 1. 2 (referring to μῆνιν) but also in *Il.* 5. 876 (referring to κούρην), in *Od.* 17. 287 (referring to γαστέρα) and similarly in *Od.* 17. 474. The meaning of the word is identical only in the last two places, but these are presumably imitations of the *Iliad* references. On what grounds then does it follow that οὐλομένην found twice at the beginning of a verse [181] is a traditional formula, or even part of one? On the same grounds one could claim that the artificially lengthened participle was created only for *Il.* 1. 2 and then picked up again in Book 5. In the place mentioned first, it summarizes the basic theme of the whole poem; in the other it is given an unquestionably original function (Ares describing Aphrodite).[9] One could at the most think of regarding the so-called unperiodic enjambement which is frequent in Homer as it occurs in *Il.* 1. 2 and 5. 876 as an inheritance from oral poetry.[10]

It is even stranger when Lord (143) counts *Iliad* 1. 13–15 as formulaic just because they appear again in lines 372–4 (in Achilles' report). Where is the justification for this procedure? Parry (302) in this case was more restrained, since he also considers *Il.* 1. 16 = 375, and does not call all the word combinations of the four verses formulae at all.[11]

---

[9] This result would not change either if one included the other cases of the participle at the beginning of the verse in the investigation: οὐλομένη (*Il.* 19. 92), οὐλομένης (*Od.* 20. 273), οὐλόμεν᾽ (*Il.* 14. 84; *Od.* 17. 484), οὐλομένων (*Od.* 11. 555). Parry probably left them aside because they are not followed by a relative clause, in *Od.* 18. 273 only after a pronoun (οὐλομένης ἐμέθεν, τῆς τε Ζεὺς ὄλβον ἀπηύρα).

[10] Terminology after Parry 262. We call an enjambement (i.e. when a sentence runs on over the end of the period after the 6th catalectic dactyl and thus over the metrical pause into the next verse) 'unperiodic' if the first verse contains an already syntactically completed sentence. On the other hand an enjambement is called 'necessary' if the construction of the sentence in the first verse cannot dispense with the word which runs on. This enjambement is missing in oral poetry (cf. Lord 54) and is twice as rare in Homer as in later Greek epic poets. Cf. further Hainsworth 105.

[11] Lord (144), it is true, adds this disarming remark to his analysis of *Il.* 1. 1–15: 'The divisions of the lines do not always agree with those of Parry, and it is very

Hartmut Erbse

Only Hainsworth (cf. especially 110) exercises more appropriate caution in dealing with these problems. He acknowledges that in the *Iliad* there are parts which contain relatively few formulaic phrases, and tries to bring this fact into line with his observations about the flexibility of the Homeric formula.[12] He has successfully refuted the erroneous view that the language of the two Homeric epics was mechanically put together solely from formulae (cf. 122). If one follows his suggestions and assumes that the authors of the two epics preserved for us were also able to coin new formulaic phrases, one can support the claim with reference to the many combinations which occur only in the *Odyssey*. Three examples of this: the combination Διὸς μεγάλου (μεγαλοι᾽) ὀαριστής (*Od.* 19. 179, of Minos) can hardly be derived from an old lost song; for obviously the poet had *Il.* 13. 450–1 in mind. One can hardly call the comparison of an especially fine shirt with an onion skin (*Od.* 19. 233 οἷόν τε κρομύοιο λοπὸν κατὰ ἰσχαλέοιο) traditional. Something similar is true of the phrase which occurs three times in the *Odyssey* Κακοΐλιον οὐκ ὀνομαστήν (*Od.* 19. 260 = 597 = 23. 19), a bitter indictment of her fate created specifically for Penelope. But if the poet of the *Odyssey* could create such formulaic [182] combinations, we must grant the same ability to his predecessor as well.[13]

Even the so-called unpermitted hiatuses and the short syllables which take the place of one *longum* (*breves in longo*) do not prove cogently that they could have come into being only through the use of traditional formulaic stock. Parry has shown in a particularly impressive discussion (191–239) that such irregularities originated through the modification (e.g. declension) or combination of formulaic phrases. He says (227): 'There is nothing in the *Iliad* and *Odyssey* to indicate that the poet ever refrained from this interchange of formulae, nothing to indicate that he ever replaced them by words of his own finding, as long as he was able to use the old

---

likely that someone else would divide them in still another way.' But what kind of proof is that which must dispense with clarity from the start? Cf. besides the important remarks by R. Cantarella, 'Omero tra formula e poesia', in *La poesia epica e la sua formazione* (Rome, 1970), 68.

[12] I would just like to note by the way that the sentence (40): 'Despite their generous bulk (27,800 verses) the two Homeric epics cannot be more than a sample of the production of Greek heroic verse in its heyday' (similarly 70) constitutes in this formulation an unproven *petitio principii*.

[13] Cf. for this the happy formulations of U. Hölscher in the review of Kirk (*Gnomon* 39 (1967), 441).

words to express his thought.' But everything depends on this last condition. For only relatively small parts of our texts, and certainly not the most interesting and valuable ones, can have originated from this game of modifying formulae and parts of formulae, interchanging them, and combining them in new ways. It is impossible for all of those metrical anomalies to be explained in this way.[14] Thus one is forced into the assumption that a brilliant poet had further developed the procedure of the bards and, according to the models learned, formed new combinations, some also with metrical irregularities (cf. Parry 229 and 238 bottom). This is a possibility which would have to be rigorously excluded by anyone who regards the *Iliad* and *Odyssey* as combinations of inherited formulae. As long as this cannot be done, there is room for the more natural view that the author of the older poem (Homer) treated the inherited stock of word combinations in a free and original manner.

The idea that the poet fills gaps in the line with formulae is not binding either.[15] For he could consider in advance which of the available formulae and parts of formulae were appropriate for the present context and then construct the verse in such a way that it formed a suitable frame for the best formula. One would imagine that this would be the normal procedure for a poet who is consciously creating. If this were the case, it would be the duty of the interpreter to examine the relation of the formula to its context.

But people raise the objection to this that this is precisely the way the oral poet does not proceed. Only a poet using writing would have felt the stilted formulaic language of epic to be an unnecessary obstacle which he must have jettisoned immediately. This point of view, however, must be put briefly aside until we have considered some further consequences of the thesis of the oral origin of the Homeric poems.

It is particularly instructive to discover from the Serbo-Croatian songs recorded by M. Parry and Lord what opportunities of expressing themselves were at the disposal of those illiterate [183] bards. The length of their songs alone, i.e. the size of their feat of memory, cannot fail to impress the observer. And yet we cannot fail to observe how far removed these products of genuine oral poetry

---

[14] Whitman's observation is especially important (82): 'The lapses and inconsistencies which dot all oral poetry are remarkably few in Homer, especially considering the size of the poems.'

[15] Cf. for this Hainsworth 57.

are from the Homeric epics. Adam Parry rightly stressed this with great emphasis in an important essay[16] (p. 190): 'The greatness of the *Iliad* cannot be that of any poem composed in the formulary style examined and described by M. Parry.' The oral poet—this is roughly how we may express it—simply follows the traditional sequence of events, orienting himself by the structural models of the songs known to him (Lord's 'themes'). Actual problems of composition do not exist for him, or do so only in the simplest form. Questions of transition, of change of scene, of parallel developments, of shaping character evenly, of the material being penetrated from a general formulation of a question—all this is not decisive for his kind of account. Even if he were aware of such problems of form, he would hardly be able to pay attention to them in the act of improvisation. But they are fundamental to Homeric epic. The art of exposing, of leading up to, of preparing, of interrupting, of surprising, of tying and untying, is so perfect in both Homeric poems that the assumption has to be ruled out that these complicated and artful connections could have been added by coincidence, so to speak, to the 'formulae' and 'themes' during oral performance. Lord (168) proceeds quite logically when he disputes the significance of an artistic (geometrical or symmetrical) model of composition for an orally created text.[17] But in Homeric epic the symmetrical patterns of structure (ring composition and others) are unmistakable: indeed, they leap to the eye, if only one wants to see them.[18] They cannot be products of improvisation; for while the oral poet proceeds mostly by making associations, it is evident [184] that Homer only rarely does so. Who also would want to believe that Homer's creativity can be compared with the routine of

[16] A. Parry, 'Have we Homer's Iliad?', *YClS* 20 (1966), 177–216. In his reply ('Homer as Oral Poet', *Harv. Stud.* 72 (1967), 1–46) A. B. Lord to my mind did not do justice to A. Parry's exposition. Cf. also Whitman 13 and the points presented by J. B. Hainsworth in the essay 'The Criticism of an Oral Homer' (*JHS* 90 (1970), 90–8), esp. the final words of his exposition.

[17] 'It does not seem likely that the force of the artistic pattern, *qua* artistic pattern, in a traditional oral song would be great enough in itself to cause either the placing or displacing of incidents' (in the polemic against Whitman).

[18] Cf. e.g. D. Lohmann, *Die Komposition der Reden in der Ilias* (Berlin, 1970) and the literature mentioned there pp. 289 ff., also Clarke 65, and esp. Whitman's 11th chapter (249) where it is explained correctly that ring composition and *hysteron proteron* are already 'building shapes' of oral poetry (one should even say: of natural speech). If Homer handles them in a masterly way, this however does not mean that he composed the *Iliad* during an oral performance.

a card player, an analogy which A. van Gennep[19] offers to help us understand the technique of the guslars? Again, Radloff's comparison (quoted in Parry 334 n. 1) of the improvising bard with the improviser on the piano cannot explain the origin of the Homeric epics either, since it does not take into account the perfection of their composition. Our *Iliad* could hardly have materialized at all if Homer had proceeded in the way Lord (148) imagines it: 'An oral poet spins out a tale; he likes to ornament, if he has the ability to do so, as Homer, of course, did . . . The story is there and Homer tells it to the end. He tells it fully and with a leisurely tempo . . .'. This judgement[20] sounds like something from the Romantic period. At any rate, it does not apply to the authors of *Iliad* and *Odyssey*, because it does not acknowledge their brilliance.

Its limitations become obvious as soon as it is applied to the objects of our examination. Lord (159) thinks that the reference to the legend of the Atridae at the beginning of the *Odyssey* is strange: 'Such a reference to another tale is highly sophisticated and unusual for oral epic.' Lord can understand it only as a reference to a great homecoming epic involving all Greek heroes. But, quite apart from the dubious existence of such a pre-Homeric epic, this does nothing to help us determine the function of such a reference. On the other hand, we know that the references to the return of Agamemnon in our *Odyssey* are firmly linked to the fate of Odysseus. Indeed, the comparison Odysseus–Agamemnon belongs to the basic theme of the whole poem. Of course this is not a 'theme' in the sense of Serbo-Croat oral poetry. Thus Lord draws conclusions from the text before he has interpreted it exhaustively.[21]

Hainsworth's careful investigation moves on quite a different level. Here a clear picture is drawn of the formulaic nature of epic language. We learn that many words could be used only within the framework of fixed formulae, and in this combination were tied to certain places in the verse; that the same formula became mobile through modification, expansion, or separation and distribution of

---

[19] *La Question d'Homère* (Paris, 1909), quoted in Parry 329. Cf. also Hainsworth 15, 1 who rightly rejects the comparison from his refined method.

[20] It is based on the views of Parry (324): 'At no time is he (sc. the singer) seeking words for an idea which has never before found expression, so that the question of originality in style means nothing to him.'

[21] Cf. incidentally the succinct sentences of K. Reinhardt, *Die Ilias und ihr Dichter* (Göttingen, 1961), 15 f.

its single words to certain other places of the verse[22]—indeed, even to two verses (the so-called 'runover technique'). Hainsworth also [185] stresses the importance of the associations possibly triggered off by formulae. Thus we get to know the tricks (so to speak) which Homer practised as a budding oral poet and which he later developed further for his own particular purposes. But this way of looking at things also has its limitations. Since it cannot be ascertained with sufficient certainty what formulaic material Homer inherited, we cannot establish to what extent he modified and enriched that inherited language. We can only observe that his utterances in the epics handed down to us are subordinated to certain principles of composition. I regard this as decisive: for this criterion cannot be reconciled with the theory of an origin of the Homeric poems from pure improvisation—unless, in order to save Parry's thesis after all, one introduces with Hainsworth (128) an irrational (and thus uncontrollable) unknown quantity: 'The role of free creation cannot be ignored, but the talent for free creation is, of course, God-given and is not part of technical craftsmanship.' We do not want to deny the miracle of Homer's creativity but feel obliged not to put excessive weight on this unknown quantity. We would be better off if we admitted that the structural connections anchored in the text can be understood only as products of conscious artistic creation.[23] Otherwise it would be impossible to understand why in other parts of the world where oral poetry was cultivated over long periods of time, nothing was produced remotely comparable to the Homeric epics. You look there quite in vain.

People who count the authors of the Homeric epics among the oral composers should also realize that there is another consequence which they can avoid only if they adhere to Lord's thesis. For if the poems were not written down when they originated, but handed down from bard to bard, they were exposed to far-reaching changes. A. Parry[24] demonstrated the probability of a text the size of the *Iliad* being completely transformed after six generations. Nor can we imagine the survival of an oral text in the early period

[22] The latter ('separation') is the most important instance; for now such expressions too are covered by the concept of formula which do not occur under the same metrical conditions (cf. E. Heitsch, *Gnomon* 42 (1970), 438).

[23] A. Parry's golden words should be quoted here (*YClS* 20 (1966), 200 n. 45): 'No one could seriously argue that the self-revelation of Helen as we have it in Book III (sc. of the *Iliad*) is an automatic creation of the formulaic system.'

[24] *YClS* 20 (1966), 189.

of a tradition in the way U. Hölscher (*Gnomon* 39 (1967), 444) describes it as the handing on of a rehearsed, not improvised, text which the rhapsodes (successors of the *aoidoi*) would have to have taken over from their master (the creator of the large epic), and passed on until it was finally written down; for they could not have done without the control [186] imposed by a standard text, fixed in writing. Thus those who begin the history of the transmission of the Homeric epics with a longer period of oral tradition (as Dihle recently) would have to give reasons for the fact that nearly the whole text still shows meaningful relationships but not the modifications and disorganization which are the consequence of uncontrolled transmission.

These considerations forbid us to conclude that it is proven that Homer must have been an oral poet. But if we ask why, if he really used writing, he did not compose without formulae, why e.g. he did not say Ἕκτωρ instead of more elaborately κορυθαίολος Ἕκτωρ, then we can only answer: because he did not know any other poetry than genuine oral poetry. He grew up with it, and without its rules he could not have done justice to such a demanding verse form. But in the epic which was handed down to us—we restrict ourselves to the *Iliad* in the present discussion—he already stands on a higher plane than the average bard of his time. In a new medium of representation, in the great epic which was fixed in writing (and performed orally afterwards), he gave the impression, by this artificial technique of imitation, that he was still an ἀοιδός of the old time. In the way he archaizes the content, describes heroes, weapons, activities, and divine miracles which supposedly could be encountered in a heroic past, he assimilates his description of an idealized form to that way of singing which in his lifetime was still in vogue but perhaps already beginning to decline.

Nowhere has this peculiar position of the poet of the *Iliad*, poised in the middle between genuine oral poetry and rhapsodic poetry, been described better than in Sir M. Bowra's great work about heroic poetry.[25] His words should stand here:

When we look at Homer's use of language, a paradox emerges. On the one hand his use of formulae is more extensive, more homogeneous and more governed by rules than any other poetry.[26] On the other hand the range of

[25] *Heroic Poetry* (London, 1952; 2nd edn. 1961), 240–1, trans. H. G. Schürmann (Stuttgart, 1964). Cf. also Whitman 78.

[26] He means the representatives of oral poetry of many nations.

his effects is greater, and his purely poetical achievement is far richer and more subtle than any other heroic poet's. The explanation of this is probably that he stands in the middle of an important change produced by the introduction of writing. That it came in the eighth century we can hardly doubt, and it is quite possible that its special character was determined by a desire to use it to record poetry. In this case we can understand Homer's ambiguous position. Behind him lie centuries of oral performance, largely improvised, with all its wealth of formulae adapted to an exacting metre; these he knows and uses fully. But if he also knows writing and is able [187] to commit his poems to it, he is enabled to give a far greater precision and care to what he says than any improvising poet ever can. Since it is almost impossible to believe that the *Iliad* and *Odyssey* were ever improvised, and the richness of their poetry suggests some reliance on writing, we may see in them examples of what happens when writing comes to help the oral bard. He continues to compose in the same manner as before, but with a far greater care and effectiveness. He can omit and correct and rearrange and take his time as the improvising poet cannot, and the result is a great enrichment of his texture. Indeed the dazzling use which Homer makes of his traditional formulae is perhaps an indication that he has passed beyond their purely functional use in composition to something that is almost purely poetical. Perhaps he learned his craft in the old tradition, but in his lifetime the alphabet appeared, and he had the insight to see what great advantages it brought in turning the old technique to a nobler and richer purpose.[27]

The *Iliad*, the older of the epics handed down under Homer's name, is therefore a work artificially stylized in terms of content and language, whose author gives the impression of an 'as if'.[28] He only affects the singing of the bards and the historicity of the heroic world. People are the victims of a brilliant deception, if they understand his poetic formulae as evidence of genuine oral poetry without appreciating his conscious artistic purpose.

If these thoughts are correct, one probably cannot claim that a high percentage of Homeric language consists of traditional formulae. It is true that there are groups of words which are regularly used under the same metrical conditions in order to express a cer-

[27] Cf. M. Parry's idea of Homer's method of creation (261): 'But Homer put all his trust in a technique of formulas which he accepted without thought of change: it was the traditional style and by it he could put together rapidly and easily his spoken verses.' Cf. also ibid. 375.

[28] Cf. also U. Hölscher, *Gnomon* 39 (1967), 441: Homer takes over from oral poetry 'only quite generally the possibility of repetition as an epic stylistic device but creates something completely different from it'.

tain thought (formulated after Parry), or there are groups of words which have been modified in the way described by Hainsworth, but these are not necessarily inherited formulae, and they are certainly not combinations which were coined only during performance, but rather magnificent, often original imitations of several basic models provided by improvising predecessors.[29] Expressed in Lord's terminology, [188] Homer was thus not an oral poet but an imitator—though an imitator of the highest perfection. His apparently unique ability to develop formulaic phrases into images and coherent sequences of images, an art which continues to be cultivated by the *Odyssey* poet as well (Whitman 121 compares e.g. *Il.* 20. 95 with *Od.* 19. 33–4), also belongs to this sphere of imitation. But Homer does not just draw new word combinations out of the diction of the *aoidoi* but also some entirely novel ideas, conceptions which leave nothing to be desired in terms of originality, especially since their existence is justified only in the context of the particular description. He who admits this will understand that in the development of Greek poetry a truly new beginning was made when Homer's creation began to spread and assert itself, while the old sank into the darkness of the past. One may assume with some justification that the better creations of Homer's predecessors, namely the songs imitated by him, were not bad, at least in comparison with the songs of the guslars. But it is impossible for us to know this. Yet we can understand why eighth-century Greeks did not want to hear the more primitive songs any more when they had fallen under the spell of the master.

On these conditions we may claim that what Dihle (127) says about Hesiod is in fact valid for Homer:

The quota of untraditional expressions which have been formed after the pattern of oral formulae, and the frequency of the metrical displacement of traditional or slightly modified formulae, are so great that one can best explain the breadth of variation by reference to the written composition of the poems. In oral poetry this procedure would be too uneconomical.

Here the following too should be considered: if Hesiod had set himself the task of creating an extensive epic work but did not have any

---

[29] Certainly Homer took over the principle of economy from the practice of oral poetry, i.e. the principle of using the same word combinations under the same conditions in terms of content and metrics. The principle is probably just as natural for a poet who is familiar with writing and relying on new formations as for a bard who composes orally. Cf. L. E. Rossi, *Göttingische Gelehrte Anzeiger* 223 (1971), 167.

ambition to express new observations and modern thoughts in original phrases, we would find more Homeric 'formulae' in his work. In Hesiod's case too it is the special situation, articulated more simply, the new kind of purpose, which has forced a modification of older modes of expression.

Now as far as word-forms and word-usage are concerned, the *Odyssey* stands between the *Iliad* and Hesiod. Its poet was still able to describe many things in the same phrases as his predecessor, but quite a few things demanded new modes of description—not just new words and new formulae but also different dispositions of the facts. This is sufficiently understood and need not be explained here.[30] Our concern is with the simple conclusion which goes as follows: [189] an epic poet who is always striving to set old word combinations in different relations to their surroundings, or even to coin new ones, cannot be denied the right to go his own way if he regards this as necessary. The peculiarity of the language of the ending of the *Odyssey* is not denied by what follows—nothing would be more wrong than that. Rather it will be shown that the unique expressions that occur in this ending can be reconciled with modes of expression common to epic as long as one bears in mind the special circumstances of so complicated an action.[31] Those who are not prepared to do this, but consider only individual passages, should (to be fair) admit that they can make similarly one-sided examinations of all parts of the epic, as long as they do not concern themselves with typical scenes.

It would be methodologically justifiable to put the following passages in order according to subject groups: for Page's list of alleged offences against epic diction indeed combines important and justified reservations with quite trivial things, even obvious mistakes. However, clarity would suffer in a grouping according to degrees of importance; some repetitions could not be avoided. I therefore choose the simpler option and will discuss the passages dealt with by Page in the order in which they occur in the poem. The discussion of some questions of content has been included in this list only because Page also put them in his list. The actual problems of composition are to be discussed in the next chapter.

---

[30] Cf. esp. Whitman 286, 293, above all 295.
[31] So the concern can only be to prove that what has been rebuked as 'anti-traditional' is merely 'untraditional'.

The Ending of the Odyssey: Linguistic Problems

Od. 23. 321: Page (103) subjects the abstract word πολυμηχανίη to censorship as follows: 'a singularly unsuccessful novelty, not to be found again before Plutarch'. The following needs to be said about this. The *Odyssey* is rich in novel abstracts. In this case, the origin of the new formation is particularly transparent; for ἀμήχανος (*Il.* 13. 726 *et al.*) is in the same relationship to ἀμηχανίη (*Od.* 9. 295) as πολυμήχανος[32] to πολυμηχανίη. Also ἀμηχανίη is found only in the place quoted. The one new formation is as successful as the other (cf. already Spohn 157). But the fact that the noun πολυμηχανία does not occur again until Plutarch does not argue against Homeric origin. It could be a consequence of our incomplete knowledge of Greek literature. But even if we disregard this, it makes no difference; for quite a few Homeric words are not used subsequently. Or did Page want to characterize Plutarch as a lover of unfortunate word formations?

23. 326: ἠδ' ὡς Σειρήνων ἀδινάων φθόγγον ἄκουσεν. On this, Page (102): 'Σ· ἀδινάων is an almost, if not quite, meaningless expression; the author has [190] misunderstood the Epic usages of this adjective.' This judgement follows statements by Spohn (183). In the article ἀδινός in *LfgrE*. (as in Ebeling's *Lexicon Homericum*) a meaning 'singing loudly' is given. But this can hardly be proven. The author's (V. Pisani) categories of meaning are: (1) 'thronging'; (2) 'repeatedly', 'continuous . . .'; then also 'loud', finally 'singing loudly' (the sirens); (3) 'violently' (beating, of the heart).[33] It is true that the translation 'loud, singing loudly' is able to refer to Buttman's learned article in his *Lexilogus* (4th edn., Berlin, 1865, i. 193), but it can be brought into line with the transparent etymology of the word only with difficulty.[34] On the other hand, all the passages in which 'loudness' could be meant are in line with the sense which corresponds to the etymology 'thronging densely, plentiful, repeated, intensive'. Compare ἀδινοῦ ἐξῆρχε γόοιο (*Il.* 18. 316, 22. 430, 23. 17, 24. 747); ἀδινὸν στοναχῆσαι (*Il.* 18. 124; similarly *Od.* 4. 721, 10. 413); ἀδινὰ στεναχίζων (*Il.* 23. 225, similarly 24. 123; *Od.* 7. 274, 24. 317); κλαῖ' ἀδινά (*Il.* 24. 510); ἀδινῶς ἀνενείκατο (*Il.* 19. 314). The possibility that great loudness is indicated is not

---

[32] In the vocative (πολυμήχαν') it is a standing epithet of Odysseus' in both epics.
[33] The third claim only refers to *Il.* 16. 481 and *Od.* 19. 516. The translation assumed by Pisani is controversial. But the question is not important for our purposes.
[34] Cf. Frisk, *GEW* i. 21 s.v. ἅδην.

mentioned in the scholia either. Several times these even suggest the opposite, cf. the scholion to *Il.* 18. 316a (ex., with testimonies) while Aristarchus (cf. the exegetic scholion to *Il.* 22. 430) explains the gloss with ἀθρόος.

The genitive used in *Od.* 23. 326 has its formal model in *Il.* 2. 87 (ἔθνεα εἶσι μελισσάων ἀδινάων) or in 2. 469 (μυιάων ἀδινάων ἔθνεα πολλά). Here already the ancient school commentaries understood correctly, cf. schol. D to *Il.* 2. 87: τῶν ἄδην καὶ ἀθρόως πετομένων. παρὰ τὸ ἄδην. διὸ καὶ δασύνεται, namely 'flying in a dense throng'. When in *Od.* 23. 326 φθόγγος Σειρήνων ἀδινάων is mentioned, this probably must have meant the voice of 'the sirens who are singing continually';[35] for singing is the characteristic occupation of these creatures. This view is not only logical but also appropriate to the subject matter; for the sirens are dangerous precisely in that they do not stop singing when a victim has come within range of their tempting voices. According to the imagination of our poet, they make a high-pitched, penetrating song (cf. *Od.* 12. 183 λιγυρὴν δ᾿ ἔντυνον ἀοιδήν) sound continually with a sweet tone (cf. *Od.* 12. 187 μελίγηρυν . . . ὄπα).[36] Perhaps the use of the [191] adjective ἀδινός in the meaning intended here was promoted by *Od.* 16. 216, where the sharpness and duration of the plaintive cry are connected with each other (father and son are the subject in hand): κλαῖον δὲ λιγέως, ἀδινώτερον ἤ τ᾿ οἰωνοί etc.[37] Ameis–Hentze–Cauer (on *Od.* 23. 326), whose explanation Page quotes to confirm his judgement, are right in starting from the basic meaning 'densely thronged' to understand our passage. But they should not have claimed, without evidence, that the adjective had here possibly become the epithet of the song of the sirens 'by a misunderstanding of the late poet'.[38] They obviously refer to a misunderstanding only because this is common in discussions about the language of *Odyssey* 23 and 24. But the survey of meanings presented above does not contain any unusual leaps. It gives us the right to reject Page's reservations.

[35] Apollonius Soph. 9. 6 also understands it this way (συνεχῶς ᾀδουσῶν); cf. also the schol. to *Il.* 23. 17.

[36] Cf. also Stanford ad loc.: 'It is not entirely impossible that something of the kind is meant by H. there (i.e. in *Il.* 2. 87 and 469) and here—"the eversinging Seirens".'

[37] Cf. Ameis–Hentze–Cauer: ἀδινώτερον 'in a denser sequence', 'more continuous'. Stanford: 'more intensely'.

[38] 'Here it has become (perhaps through a misunderstanding of the later poet?) the epithet of the singing ones. We must take the expression with φθόγγον: the uninterrupted voice.'

23. 330: ψολόεντι κεραυνῷ and 24. 539: ψολόεντα κεραυνόν. The noun κεραυνός in other places is linked with the adjective χαλεπός (only *Il.* 14. 417) or ἀργῆς. At the end of a verse only the formulae ἀργῆτα κεραυνόν (*Il.* 8. 133), ἀργῆτι κεραυνῷ (*Od.* 5. 128, 131; 7. 249; 12. 387), and the two combinations mentioned above appear. There the combination ἀργῆτα κεραυνόν or ἀργῆτι κεραυνῷ respectively is used for the sequence – – ∪ ∪ – –, the combination ψολόεντα κεραυνόν or ψολόεντι κεραυνῷ respectively for the verse end ∪ ∪ – ∪ ∪ – –. It is probably not too bold a conclusion to say that the poet did not have any use for the formula ψολόεντι (-α) κεραυνῷ (-όν) in Books 1–22, quite apart from the fact that lightning is not often mentioned. Page's objection (102) that ψολόεις is alien to Homeric language is thus unfounded. The verse in Hesiod, *Th.* 515 (εἰς Ἔρεβος κατέπεμψε βαλὼν ψολόεντι κεραυνῷ) is obviously an imitation of *Odyssey* 23. 330; for the epithet is an original modification of the phrase known from 5. 128, a luxury so to speak: ἀργῆτι κεραυνῷ could really have stood just as well while this was impossible in 23. 330 (or 24. 539 respectively). Obviously it was the meaning ('sooty') which mattered to Hesiod.

23. 347: αὐτίκ' ἀπ' Ὠκεανοῦ χρυσόθρονον ἠριγένειαν | ὦρσεν. Page (102) objects that ἠριγένεια is treated as a noun whereas it usually stands next to ἠώς as an adjective. He has to admit, however, that the same usage can be quoted in 22. 197 (οὐδέ σέ γ' ἠριγένεια παρ' Ὠκεανοῖο ῥοάων | λήσει ἀνερχομένη χρυσόθρονος) (thus already Stanford ad loc.). So this is not a peculiarity of the author of verses 23. 297 ff. Besides we know ἠριγένεια as an adjective especially from the formulaic verse ἦμος δ' ἠριγένεια φάνη [192] ῥοδοδάκτυλος Ἠώς (the verse occurs twice in the *Iliad*, 20 times in the *Odyssey*). Besides, the adjective is found in *Il.* 8. 508, *Od.* 12. 3 and 13. 94 (Ἠοῦς ἠριγενείης), and further in *Od.* 4. 195, where it is separated from the noun to which it belongs by the end of the verse ἀλλὰ καὶ Ἠὼς | ἔσσεται ἠριγένεια). So the two passages castigated by Page are to be set against five formulations in which ἠριγένεια is a pure adjective. As a result, the unusualness of the usage in *Od.* 22. 197 and 23. 347 is considerably reduced. One should also ask, particularly in this case, whether we have an overview of all the material. Presumably the bards had other formulae at their disposal for expressing sunrise, among which there may have been phrases with ἠριγένεια used as a noun.

Hartmut Erbse

23. 361: The lengthening ἐπῑτέλλω (σοὶ δέ, γύναι, τόδ' ἐπιτέλλω πινυτῇ περ ἐούσῃ), as Page (102) and Kirk (249) state correctly after Spohn (244) and Monro, contradicts the rules of Homeric prosody; for metrical lengthening is permitted only where the form in question cannot be avoided in the hexameter. The attempt of a Ryland papyrus from the third century AD and of the *editio princeps* to write ἐπιστέλλω instead condemns itself, since this verb is not poetic. Besides, the poet introduces Odysseus' speech with the words (*Od.* 23. 349): . . . ἀλόχῳ δ' ἐπὶ μῦθον ἔτελλεν, to which he refers back in 23. 361. But the conjecture that such an exceptional form suggests—that there was a later poet—is not plausible: Homer's successors in particular would have kept to the well-known rules, if necessary by sacrificing subtleties of content, especially since familiar formulations for expressing the intended thought offered themselves, for instance σοὶ δ' αὐτῇ τόδ' ἐγὼν ἐπιτέλλομαι ἠδὲ κελεύω (after *Il.* 19. 192).[39] Since an explanation cannot be found within the scope of the rules of metrical lengthening known to us, this is probably an author's error. Two possibilities offer themselves by way of explanation:

1. A poet who knew nothing about the digamma and handed down its effects only in traditional or imitated formulae could have inferred from the beginning of a verse μῆνιν ἀποειπών (*Il.* 19. 35) that it was permitted to scan as a *longum* the short final syllable of the prefix to a verb. This suggested itself all the more since the *Odyssey* is familiar with a lengthened final syllable of the preposition ἐπί (12. 209: οὐ μὲν δὴ τότε μεῖζον ἔπι κακόν, lengthening according to rule). So the combination τόδ' ἐπιτέλλω (∪∪ – – –), which could not be avoided because of the beginning and the ending of the verse (σοὶ δέ, γύναι and πινυτῇ περ ἐούσῃ) [193] could be regarded as permissible.[40] One could well imagine that a poet who has allowed himself prosodic peculiarities like Διονύσου (∪∪ – –, *Od.* 11. 325)[41] and οὐδόν (instead of ὁδόν, – ∪, 17. 196) (cf. also 6.

---

[39] σοὶ δέ, γύναι, τόδε νῦν ἐπιτέλλομαι ἠδὲ κελεύω would also be conceivable (in order to keep the beginning of the verse). However, one gets into difficulties straight away if one wants to keep the traditional end of the verse, πινυτῇ περ ἐούσῃ, i.e. the reference to Penelope's cleverness.

[40] The frequent normal lengthenings of the final syllable of the prefix ἐπῑ may have had an effect, cf. e.g. from: *Od.* 7: ἐπιτρέψειεν 149; ἐπικρῆσαι 164; ἐπιπλόμενον 261; ἐπισκύσσαιτο 306.

[41] Cf. G. A. Privitera, *Dioniso in Omero* (Rome, 1970), 77. The author tries to my mind in vain to perceive in the prosody of Book 11 of the *Odyssey* the effect of a pre-Homeric formula.

45 ἀννέφελος and 9. 490 καταννεύων) might make this or a similar association. But I consider the second possibility as more likely.

2. Stanford has referred to *Od.* 16. 297 (ἐπῑθύσαντες, ∪ – – – ∪). Admittedly, this is no genuine analogy to ἐπιτέλλω; for in 16. 297 we have a compound of ἰθύω. But it is uncertain whether the poet recognized it as such. He read the same compound in *Il.* 18. 175 (Τρῶες ἐπ-ιθύουσιν), but in addition knew phrases like περὶ πρὸ γὰρ ἔγχεϊ θῦεν (*Il.* 11. 180, 16. 699), οἴδματι θύων (21. 234), ὑψόσε θύων (21. 324, of Scamander), and above all οὓς ἔκτανες ἔγχεϊ θύων (22. 272). How could he save himself from the temptation of using ἐπ-ιθύω like ἐπι-θύω? He would have had to have been aware that the simplex ἰθύω with a similar meaning appears nine times in the *Iliad*. This at any rate did not exactly suggest itself, especially since the language of the *Odyssey* contains the verb only twice, each time linked with an infinitive and only with the meaning 'to be about to'.[42] So the opportunity to interpret the available compound ἐπ-ιθύω as ἐπι-θύω was there—in fact it practically begged to be used. If this is correct, then what we have found in *Od.* 16. 297 is a model which, in a metrical dilemma, made the unusual lengthening ἐπῑτέλλω possible for the poet. We need have no recourse to a later poet who knew less about versification.

Od. 24. 40: In the underworld, Agamemnon's soul praises that of Achilles as lucky because Achilles fell before Troy, and a hard battle flared up about his corpse: σὺ δ' ἐν στροφάλιγγι κονίης | κεῖσο μέγας μεγαλωστί, λελασμένος ἱπποσυνάων. The poet of the *Iliad* ends the tale of the battle for the corpse of Cebriones with the same words (*Od.* 24. 40 = *Il.* 16. 776, here κεῖτο, not κεῖσο). Page (103) regards the repetition of the verse in *Od.* 24 as inappropriate: '. . . to apply such an expression to Achilles would be unthinkable in the older Epic.' He says that only Tryphiodorus (629) had repeated the error.

It is true that the genitive ἱπποσυνάων in *Il.* 16. 776 refers to Hector's charioteer. So the art of steering a chariot must be meant, just as in *Il.* 23. 289 (of Eumelus) and in 23. 307 (of [194] Antilochus). Here in Book 23 of the *Iliad*, by the way, the skill is praised in two heroes who otherwise appear as hoplites.[43] So every

---

[42] *Od.* 11. 591: τῶν ὁπότ' ἰθύσει ὁ γέρων (scil. Tantalus) ἐπὶ χερσὶ μάσασθαι and 22. 408: ἴθυσέν ῥ' ὀλολύξαι (sc. Eurycleia).

[43] Eumelus may also be counted among the *promachoi* since he is the leader of a contingent, cf. *Il.* 2. 713–14.

nobleman had to be able to function as a charioteer simply because he wanted to participate in the races. The noun ἱπποσύνη however does not describe this art alone but nearly as frequently the skill of fighting from a chariot. This is clearly obvious from *Il*. 11. 503: Ἕκτωρ μὲν μετὰ τοῖσιν ὁμίλει, μέρμερα ῥέζων | ἔγχεΐ θ' ἱπποσύνῃ τε (the charioteer is Cebriones). Similarly *Il*. 4. 303 (Nestor to those fighting from chariots): μηδέ τις ἱπποσύνῃ τε καὶ ἠνορέηφι πεποιθὼς | οἶος πρόσθ' ἄλλων μεμάτω Τρώεσσι μάχεσθαι. We also have to understand *Il*. 16. 809 like this where it is said of Euphorbus: ὃς ἡλικίην ἐκέκαστο | ἔγχεΐ θ' ἱπποσύνῃ τε πόδεσσί τε καρπαλίμοισι, i.e. 'with the spear, in fighting from chariots and in running' (Rupé).[44]

Our conclusion may now be: the poet of *Odyssey* 24 probably took over verse 16. 776 of the *Iliad*, but he linked the genitive ἱπποσυνάων with the idea of a chariot fighter, which was quite appropriate for Achilles.[45] Such procedures can be observed everywhere in the *Odyssey*. One may call it a principle of living mimesis. It is certainly wrong to want to force the unchanged meaning of the model onto the imitation too. Naturally one must try to do this if one wants to see a bad poet in an imitator. But in doing this one abandons the path of unprejudiced interpretation.

24. 60: 'All the nine Muses' lament in antiphonal singing the greatest hero of the Greeks (Μοῦσαι δ' ἐννέα πᾶσαι ἀμειβόμεναι ὀπὶ καλῇ | θρήνεον). The *Odyssey* otherwise knows only one single ('the') Muse, the *Iliad* several, in an indefinite number. The canon of the nine Muses (and their names) is not mentioned before Hesiod (*Th*. 57. 76). From these facts, Page (103) concludes that in *Od*. 24. 60 there is 'a numeration alien to the Homeric tradition'. The reader is tempted to assume that verse 60 of Book 24 is composed under Hesiodic influence.

But we should ask ourselves: Why did Hesiod invent names for precisely nine Muses? That this is his invention is hardly doubted by anyone today.[46] But however magnificent his [195] creation of

[44] Cf. also the explaining verses *Il*. 16. 810–11!

[45] That neither *Il*. 16. 775–6 nor *Od*. 24. 39–40 have anything to do with the allegedly pre-Homeric *Aithiopis* has been shown by Hölscher, *Gnomon* 27 (1955), 395 and Dihle 23.

[46] Cf. P. Friedländer, 'Das Prooimion der Theogonie', in *Studien zur antiken Literatur und Kunst* (Berlin, 1969), 75; Wilamowitz, *Die Ilias und Homer* (Berlin, 1916), 468 and 474; Solmsen, *Hesiod and Aeschylus* (New York, 1949), 39; M. L. West on Hesiod *Th*. 76.

names may be,[47] the number nine is not demanded by the subject-matter (the function of the Muses). One must therefore assume that it was given to the poet; for other numbers would have suggested themselves much more readily. Three Muses were worshipped at Helicon, in Delphi, and also in Sicyon (cf. Plut. *Mor.* 744c and 746e). The epic poet Eumelus also (fr. 17, *EGF* 195) knew three Muses, Epicharmus (fr. 41 K.) seven, and the numbers four and five also have supporters.[48] If Hesiod disregarded all these possibilities, especially the numbers three and seven consecrated by cult,[49] one must believe that he felt committed to a respected model in which precisely nine Muses were mentioned. In order not to have to regard the Second Nekyia as older than the *Theogony*, one could talk about an epic tradition unknown to us. But this would be methodologically contestable; for it is not permitted to prefer a hypothetical tradition to an extant text, as long as it has not been proved that the extant text's statement belongs to a later time.

The modern objection against *Od.* 24. 60, that the Homeric epic is not familiar with the number nine for the Muses, goes back to Aristarchus, cf. schol. *Od.* 24. 1 (p. 725, 10 Ddf.): ἀλλὰ καὶ τὸ ἀριθμεῖν τὰς Μούσας οὐχ Ὁμηρικόν, similarly T to *Il.* 24. 720: ἀθετητέος δὲ ὁ Μουσῶν ἐπ᾽ Ἀχιλλεῖ θρῆνος. But this argument is bad: for its author does not consider that only in this passage particular emphasis is supposed to be placed on the fact that, on this most solemn occasion, a large but surveyable number of divine female singers is appearing (Μοῦσαι δ᾽ ἐννέα πᾶσαι). For such purposes the epic has the number nine at its disposal. Its individual members can under certain circumstances be enumerated by name (cf. *Il.* 2. 591–4, 7. 161–8, 8. 261–6, 24. 249–52), a procedure which e.g. in the catalogue of Nereids in Book 18 of the *Iliad* can no longer be carried out. Nine, then, is a typical number in Homer.[50]

[47] But cf. B. Snell, *Die Entdeckung des Geistes* (Hamburg, 3rd edn. 1955), 67, where Hesiod's authorship is disputed.

[48] Cf. in detail M. Mayer, *RE* 16, 1 (1933), 687, 50 s.v. Musai C.

[49] That the number seven for the Muses is older than nine is assumed with reason by W. H. Roscher, *Die Sieben- und Neunzahl im Kultus und Mythus der Griechen* (Abhandlungen der Königlichen Sächsischen Gesellschaft der Wissenschaften 24; Leipzig, 1904), 19, 35, 71. Anyhow groups of nine are not frequent in cult and myth.

[50] Cf. J. W. S. Blom, *De typische getallen bij Homeros en Herodotos I* (Nijmegen, 1936), 259; G. Germain, *Homère et la mystique des nombres* (Paris, 1954), 13 ('le nombre 9 sert essentiellement à exprimer un temps'), 17 ('c'est par 9 que l'on présente *groupes* des *êtres vivants*, en particulier . . . des hommes'), 27, 29, 32, 34, 44, 78; further D. Fehling, *Die Quellenangaben bei Herodot* (Berlin, 1971), 155.

Aristarchus had already recognized Homer's special liking for the number nine, cf. Aristonicus on *Il.* 6. 174: ὅτι ἐπίφορός ἐστι πρὸς τὸν ἐννέα ἀριθμόν, similarly T on *Il.* 12. 25. In both epics, periods of time and persons in particular are understood in groups of nine, but less frequently animals, measures, countries, places, and [196] other objects. I here give the references, but do not consider the so-called hidden enneads[51] which can be found in Blom.

1. *Iliad. Periods of Time*: For nine days the plague rages in the army (1. 53); nine (scil. long) years have passed since the beginning of the war (2. 134); for nine days Iobates is host to Bellerophontes before he asks him about his wishes (6. 174); for nine nights Phoenix is guarded by his relatives (9. 470); the rivers need nine days in order to destroy the Greeks' wall at Poseidon's and Apollo's instructions (12. 25); for nine years Hephaestus forges precious jewellery for the sea goddessses Thetis and Eurynome (18. 400); for nine days the gods quarrel over Hector's corpse (24. 107); for nine days the daughters of Niobe lie in their blood (24. 610); for nine days Hector is supposed to be mourned (24. 664); and for nine days wood is gathered for the funeral pyre (24. 784). *Persons*: Nine heralds keep the assembled warriors in check (2. 96–7); three times nine men are killed by Patroclus in the last onslaught (16. 785); cf. besides the references already given above 7. 161, 8. 261, 24. 249. *Animals*: Nine sparrows are devoured by the snake in Aulis (2. 313, cf. 327); nine dogs follow the four shepherds on the shield made by Hephaestus (18. 578); nine dogs are owned by Achilles (23. 173), and the armour of Glaucus is as valuable as nine head of cattle (6. 236). Further, nine ships (2. 654) and once nine cubits (24. 270) are mentioned. Cf. also 2. 591 (already mentioned above).

2. *Odyssey*. For nine days Odysseus travels with his ships in order to get from Cape Malea to the land of the lotus eaters (9. 82); nine days and nine nights is the time the voyage takes from Aeolus' island to the mountains of Ithaca (10. 28); for nine days after his shipwreck Odysseus drifts to the island of Calypso (12. 447, cf. 7. 253); and nine days the beggar claims to have spent on the ocean sitting astride a plank (14. 314). Apart from this, the nine years' duration of the Trojan War is mentioned four times (3. 118, 5. 107, 14. 240, 22. 228). Nine judges supervise the games of the Phaeacians (8. 258); each ship's crew kills nine goats (9. 160); in nine rows of seats

---

[51] i.e. series of nines of different kinds, groups of nine verses and similar things.

the people is assembled on the shore of Pylos and in each row nine bulls (i.e. 81 altogether) are sacrificed (3. 7–8, cf. above *Il.* 2. 591–4 where the nine cities subject to Nestor are enumerated); the size and breadth of the nine-year-old giant children Otos and Ephialtes are measured in nines (11. 311–12; cf. Germain, *Homère et la mystique des nombres*, 23); the body of Tityus stretches over nine plethra (11. 577); the beggar claims to have owned nine warships before the expedition to Troy (14. 230) and he claims to have fitted out nine ships many years previously for the voyage to Egypt (14. 248).

[197] For our purposes *Il.* 7. 161 is especially important: οἱ δ' ἐννέα πάντες ἀνέσταν 'but they got up, nine altogether'. Aristarchus remarks, not badly, that πάντες is redundant in terms of content. The exegetic scholium to the passage (ad *Il.* 7. 161b) mentions another opinion: πλεονάζει τὸ "πάντες"· οὐ γάρ, ὥς τινες, οἱ ἅπαντες ἐννέα. So these interpreters understood 'all nine' as if there had been no other *promachoi* apart from the ones mentioned in the text.[52] There are no ancient explanations of our passage, *Od.* 24. 60. But one can state with some certainty that the poet wanted to say that a large number of goddesses appeared for Achilles' funeral rites, so 'nine altogether' (Stanford 'nine in all'). But for a later poet who wanted to fix the number of the Muses and announce their names (as the symbol of their essence), there was nothing which prevented him from interpreting the phrases of the verse in the same way as the ancient interpreters just mentioned understood the similar expression in *Il.* 7. 161, i.e. as 'all the nine Muses'. Hesiod could have interpreted in such a way.

If our analysis is conclusive, the consequences are as follows:

1. The poet of the Nekyia uses a typical number.
2. He wants to indicate a quantity appropriate for the situation, but does not want to fix the number of the Muses. His formulation does not involve him in a contradiction with other statements in the epic.
3. The predicatively used πᾶσαι could be understood attributively. Thus 24. 60 fulfils all the requirements which one would expect from a model of Hesiod's verses *Th.* 57 and 76.

---

[52] The scholiast refutes their opinion with the reference to the phrase δέκα πάντα τάλαντα (*Il.* 19. 247, 24. 232) where indeed 'ten talents altogether' must also be understood.

The use of nine as a typical number in epic is a hard fact. Page should have taken note of this and not pushed it aside with a disparaging remark.[53]

24. 88–9: ὅτε κέν ποτ᾽ ἀποφθιμένου βασιλῆος | ζώννυταί τε νέοι καὶ ἐπεντύνωνται[54] ἄεθλα. Page (103) calls the first verb mentioned (ζώννυται) 'an unlikely subjunctive form' because the two comparable subjunctives are δαινύῃ (*Od*. 8. 243 and 19. 328). W. Schulze[55] wanted to write δαίνῡαι in the place mentioned first and δαίνῡ᾽ (αι) in the second.[56] He thus regarded the type δαινύῃ with the long vowel as later [198] than the subjunctive represented by ζώννυνται. This belongs to a group of athematic subjunctives 'whose distinguishing vowel shows the vowel length of the indicative form' (Schwyzer i. 792 with references of epichoric origin). Certainty cannot be achieved in the judgement of the subjunctive appearing in *Od*. 24. 89 because there is no more evidence than the references mentioned. In line with the thematic inflection of athematic verbs one expects the subjunctive ζωννύωνται with a metrically lengthened υ but it is very doubtful whether such a formation would deserve precedence over the traditional ζώννυνται (cf. the forms quoted by Schwyzer from Arcadian and Lesbian). So there is possibly an archaism here. In any case, the reference does not permit any conclusions about the time of its origin.[57]

24. 111–13: Agamemnon's soul asks that of Amphimedon who is entering Hades with the shades of the other suitors: 'Did Poseidon destroy you at sea?'

ἦ που ἀνάρσιοι ἄνδρες ἐδηλήσαντ᾽ ἐπὶ χέρσου   111
βοῦς περιταμνομένους ἠδ᾽ οἰῶν πώεα καλά,
ἠὲ περὶ πτόλιος μαχεούμενοι ἠδὲ γυναικῶν;   113

Verses 109–13 are derived from *Od*. 11. 399–403. There Odysseus wants to know from Agamemnon's soul: 'Did Poseidon destroy you at sea?'

---

[53] Page 103: 'Some have alleged that our poet need not be charged with believing that the number of the Muses was nine: out of an unspecified total number (they suggest), nine are mentioned here merely because nine is a convenient and favorite number in Epic verse. It is difficult to imagine how special pleading could go further.'

[54] ἐπεντύνωνται Thiersch, ἐπεντύνονται codd. (thus also Stanford).

[55] *Quaest. ep.* 331.   [56] Cf. Chantraine, *Gr. Hom.* i. 458.

[57] In literature a corresponding subjunctive cannot be found before Hipponax (fr. 25, 4 D. = 34, 4 M.) (ῥηγνῦται; the form, conjectured instead of the traditional ῥίγνυται, is probably secure in spite of weak manuscript testimony).

ἠέ σ' ἀνάρσιοι ἄνδρες ἐδηλήσαντ' ἐπὶ χέρσου   401
βοῦς περιταμνόμενον ἠδ' οἰῶν πώεα καλά,
ἠὲ περὶ πτόλιος μαχεούμενον ἠδὲ γυναικῶν;   113

i.e. '. . . or did hostile men do you harm on the mainland while you
were trying to cut off cattle and beautiful flocks of sheep or were
perhaps fighting for a city and for women?' (after Schadewaldt).

The changes in Book 24[58] concern only three words: ἦ που (111)
instead of ἠέ σε, περιταμνομένους (112) instead of περιταμνόμενον,
and [199] μαχεούμενοι (113) instead of μαχεούμενον. Thus in the
last case, evidently for metrical reasons, the participle is made to
agree not with the object but with the subject. Page (103) sees a
grave shortcoming in this formulation: 'Hence μαχεούμενοι here,
agreeing with the *subject* of the main verb, to the great confusion of
the whole sentence.' Is this reproach justified?

Odysseus enumerates several possibilities—a storm at sea, stealing of flocks, or an attack on a hostile city. That the participle
μαχεούμενον (*Od.* 11. 403) could be understood as describing the
defender is perhaps linguistically possible, but it is virtually
excluded in Agamemnon's case.[59] Book 24 contains the same number of possibilities, but the question how μαχεούμενοι should be
understood is immediately answered through the new agreement:
'Did enemies destroy you when you wanted to steal their flocks or
when they were fighting with you (scil. in a defensive fight) for their
city and their women?' In the modified form, too, the text leaves no
doubt that the suitors are meant as the aggressors in the fight for the
city. Thus the poet made a virtue out of the problem posed by the
verse even though the sentence did not turn out very elegantly.
There is no reason to talk about a 'great confusion'.

Page calls μαχεούμενον (or μαχεούμενοι respectively) a linguistic
monster ('a unique monster'). This is also unjustified. It is true that
there is not a linguistically accepted explanation of the form

[58] The verses *Od.* 11. 399–403 were deleted by Aristophanes Byz. (and perhaps
also by Aristarchus, cf. Ludwich, *AHT* i. 590. 22; Page 103 imprecisely). If one
accepts this deletion then Odysseus' question consists of a meagre two lines (11.
397–8). But these do not correspond to the passionate answer of the murdered man
(cf. also Besslich 30). Odysseus must mention several possibilities without being
able to hit the right one. So the deletion is certainly wrong. But it justifies the
assumption that the Alexandrians saw the better formulation in the verses of Book
24 (Aristophanes Byz. does not seem to have deleted the second Nekyia).

[59] For μάχομαι περί τινος describing the attacker cf. *Il.* 18. 265 (of Achilles):
ἀλλὰ περὶ πτόλιός τε μαχήσεται ἠδὲ γυναικῶν (Ameis–Hentze–Cauer).

μαχεούμενος.[60] But Witte's conjecture should recommend itself, that the phrase of verse 11. 403 περὶ πτόλιος μαχεούμενον ἠδὲ γυναικῶν, cf. 24. 113) was formed on the model of passages like *Il.* 18. 265 (περὶ πτόλιός τε μαχήσεται ἠδὲ γυναικῶν), similar to μαχειόμενος κτεάτεσσι (*Od.* 17. 471) being formed after μαχησόμενος Δαναοῖσιν (*Il.* 17. 146).[61]

As in *Od.* 24. 40, the imitation of a known model offers no ground for conjecturing that it must have been made by a later or even a bad poet.

24. 208: No conclusions can be drawn about the noun κλίσιον ('outhouse, columned hall', Lat. *vinea*), since there was no opportunity to use it anywhere earlier in the epic. Dorotheus [200] of Ascalon dedicated a whole book of his Λεξέων συναγωγή to this word (cf. Porph. 2. 132. 1; further testimonies in Spohn 145–53). Cf. incidentally Frisk, *GEW* i. 874.

24. 231: αἰγείην κυνέην κεφαλῇ ἔχε, πένθος ἀέξων. Page (109) translates: 'He had a goatskin cap on his head, *thus* (or, *because he was*) *cherishing his grief.*' One is at first tempted to assume that the words after the bucolic diaeresis are corrupt. But the violently differing conjectures should already make us suspicious. Compare: πνῖγος ἀλέξων, Schulze; ψῦχος ἀλέξων, Bérard; αἶθος ἀλέξων, Schadewaldt. Besides J. Dingel[62] has proved that Euripides took the received text into account in his *Electra* (55–8), thus understanding the wearing of a goatskin cap to be a demonstration [of grief]. This changed interpretation is admittedly only meant for the theatre, but it contains a correct core; for it is evident that the old man, in his despair, is intensifying his pain, cf. 11. 195–6 (Anticleia is speaking): ἔνθ' ὅ γε κεῖτ' ἀχέων, μέγα δὲ φρέσι πένθος ἀέξει, | σὸν νόστον ποθέων. Not inappropriately has Stanford (with reference to Hayman) compared Laertes with a Heautontimorumenos. Page was badly advised when he exclaimed: 'Such desperate remedies are certainly called for.'

---

[60] Cf. W. F. Wyatt Jr., *Metrical Lengthening in Homer* (Rome, 1969), 135.

[61] Cf. K. Witte, *RE* 8. 2 (1913), 2224, 64 s.v. Homeros Nr. 1. The participle *μαχεόμενος presupposed in both lengthened forms can also be justified through reference to μαχέοιτο (*Il.* 1. 272). Both lengthenings obey the rule, cf. Schulze, *Quaest. ep.* 363, Meister, *HK* 37. Incidentally the scholiast to *Od.* 11. 403 (Hrd. 2. 152. 5) noted the peculiarity of the form μαχεούμενον without being able to explain it satisfactorily with his means: παράλογος ἡ διαίρεσις. θέλει γὰρ εἰπεῖν μαχόμενον. ἐπέκτασις οὖν γέγονε διὰ τὸ μέτρον. Cf. also the testimonies to *Il.* 12. 216.

[62] J. Dingel, *Rh. Mus.* 112 (1969), 105 f.

24. 237: Page (104) writes: ' εἰπεῖν ὡς ἔλθοι: this use of the optative in *oratio obliqua* is the idiom of a much later era; it never occurs in the Homeric poems.' This is a statement of a well-known fact about which discussion is pointless. But Page's claim that the phenomenon belongs to a *much* later time is exaggerated; the Hymn to Aphrodite (214) is already familiar with the optative in an *oratio obliqua* statement. But the main difficulty in our passage does not lie with the optatives at all. The sentence runs (24. 235–8):

> μερμήριξε δ' ἔπειτα κατὰ φρένα καὶ κατὰ θυμὸν 235
> κύσσαι καὶ περιφῦναι ἑὸν πατέρ' ἠδὲ ἕκαστα
> εἰπεῖν, ὡς ἔλθοι καὶ ἵκοιτ' ἐς πατρίδα γαῖαν,
> ἦ πρῶτ' ἐξερέοιτο ἕκαστά τε πειρήσαιτο.

The subordinate clause introduced with ὡς need not be a statement. Ebeling (*Lexicon Homericum* ii. 498 s.v. ὡς) sees in it an indirect question ('ubi non est: se venisse . . ., sed quomodo venisset'), Gildersleeve[63] supports the same view and Schwyzer–Debrunner (ii. 332 a) describe ὡς as a modal relative adverb ('as' or 'that'). So the construction of the hymn could have originated from our place: εἶπεν δὲ ἕκαστα . . . Ἀργεϊφόντης ὡς ἔοι ἀθάνατος, [201] sc. Ganymede.[64] Indeed the view put forward by the interpreters describes Odysseus' indecision perfectly: if the son really wanted to reveal himself to his father, he could do this only by connecting it with a description of the special nature of his return—which does indeed happen later (cf. *Od.* 24. 321–6). Schadewaldt translates:[65] '. . . whether he should kiss and embrace his father or tell him all the details *how* he had come and reached his native land or whether he should ask him first and test him in details.' Stanford stays closer to the wording of the original: 'Then he deliberated in his heart and mind to kiss and embrace his father and tell him everything, *how* he had made his way back to his native land—or should he first question and test him in every way.'

This correct translation shows that the structure of the sentence is much more striking than the use of mood; for the poet has in a unique way combined two Homeric constructions: μερμηρίζω can either be connected with an infinitive ('to consider doing something') or with an indirect question ('to be undecided whether to . . .

---

[63] *AJPhil.* 27 (1906), 205.
[64] Thus F. Urtel, *Über den homerischen Gebrauch des Optativs der abhängigen Rede* (Progr. Wilhelm-Ernstisches Gymnasium; Weimar, 1884), 5.
[65] Similarly already Voss.

or'). One should compare (*a*) *Od*. 10. 151–2: μερμήριξα δ᾽ ἔπειτα κατὰ φρένα καὶ κατὰ θυμὸν | ἐλθεῖν ἠδὲ πυθέσθαι[66] and (*b*) *Od*. 4. 117–19: μερμήριξε δ᾽ ἔπειτα κατὰ φρένα καὶ κατὰ θυμόν, | ἠέ μιν αὐτὸν πατρὸς ἐάσειε μνησθῆναι, | ἦ πρῶτ᾽ ἐξερέοιτο ἕκαστά τε πειρήσαιτο.[67] To lose the mixture of constructions in our passage, Nauck deleted *Od*. 24. 238 (= *Od*. 4. 119).[68] The context now goes: 'He considered kissing him and saying . . . But it seemed to him to be appropriate this way . . .'. But the price of this smooth, quite ordinary construction is the unacceptable destruction of the point. For it is precisely in the unexpected transition from one form of expression to the other (24. 237–8) that the embarrassment of our wily hero is reflected, as he stands under the pear tree, crying and weighing up the two possibilities against each other. So deeply is he affected by the sight of his long-suffering father. In Nauck's text, the possibility which is rejected at the end would be no more than a passing idea. So the peculiarity of the formulation is justified: From considering the simple self-introduction (μερμήριξε . . . κύσσαι καὶ περιφῦναι . . . ἠδὲ ἕκαστα εἰπεῖν), the thought turns to the question whether one should not [202] first investigate and examine (ἦ πρῶτ᾽ ἐξερέοιτο ἕκαστά τε πειρήσαιτο). Thus the moods of the possibilities override the more determined statement of the first clause, and lead up to what Odysseus will eventually do (cf. *Od*. 24. 239–40). So one cannot stress with enough emphasis the peculiarity of the construction of our passage; at the same time, one has to add (to be fair) that it is quite appropriate to what is a unique situation (cf. also Stanford *ad loc.*). An imitator would have done without such subtleties, and applied inferior medicines.

24. 240: πρῶτον κερτομίοισ᾽ ἐπέεσσιν πειρηθῆναι. The lengthening of the fourth biceps by position offends against Wernicke's Law (cf. P. Maas, *Greek Metre* §125). Page (104) regards the alleged metrical mistake as especially grave because ' νῦ ἐφελκυστικόν cannot be added to assist the lengthening of a naturally short vowel before the fifth dactyl of the line'.[69] But such a tightening of

[66] Similarly *Il*. 8. 167 and *Od*. 10. 438.

[67] Cf. also *Il*. 1. 189, 5. 671; *Od*. 6. 141, 10. 50, 17. 235, 18. 90, 20. 10, 22. 333. Further instances in which a simple question is dependent on the verb are not considered here. Cf. for the rest Spohn 197.

[68] Agreeing Wilamowitz, *Die Heimkehr des Odysseus* (Berlin, 1927), 81, 3.

[69] See also Stanford *ad loc.*: '. . . the only instance in *Od*. of a lengthening by means of νῦ ἐφελκυστικόν in the 4th foot'. The treatise quoted by Page without author's name *CR* 11 (1897) (Tyrrell, Agar, Platt?) is not available to me [R. Tyrrell,

Wernicke's Law is not justified. The ν ἐφελκυστικόν often served Ionic epic language to bridge a hiatus or make position.[70] So if Wernicke's Law allows any exceptions at all, making position of the kind cited should be permitted.

Since the discovery of Ryland papyrus P 28 in Allen (third–fourth century AD, published 1911), people have often thought that the difficulty had disappeared; for there we find the variant ἔπεσιν διαπειρηθῆναι. Wilamowitz (*Die Heimkehr des Odysseus* (Berlin, 1927), 81 A. 3) called it a remedy and Von der Mühll adopted it in his text. Page on the other hand regards it as an unsuccessful conjecture—probably rightly; for διαπειρηθῆναι is a word alien to epic language and at home almost exclusively in prose. Again, why should the metrically smooth formulation of the papyrus have been changed to a sequence of quantities unfamiliar to Homer's readers (ἐπέεσσιν πειρηθῆναι)? This is without doubt the *lectio difficilior*. Do we have the right to criticize it? Probably not, because every reader of Homer knows verses which make position with a consonant at the end of a word in the fourth biceps, cf. *Iliad* 18. 400: τῇσι παρ᾽ εἰνάετες χάλκευον δαίδαλα πολλά, 5. 734 (= 8. 385): πέπλον μὲν κατέχευεν ἑανὸν πατρὸς ἐπ᾽ οὔδει and other examples enumerated in Leaf (*Iliad* ii. 637 f.).[71] Leaf sees the reason [203] for the dislike of verses formed like this in the effort not to make the fourth foot sound like the end of a verse ('that the fourth foot should not sound like the end of a line'). Meister expressed himself similarly (K. Meister, *Die homerische Kunstsprache* (Leipzig, 1921), 55): '. . . lest through a spondaic word ending and a predominantly dactylic third foot the verse end would be (as it were) anticipated.'

With such considerations in mind, one approaches the problem of trying to explain Hermann's bridge. But this whole discussion has in fact been unnecessary for decades, since Th. Stifler[72] showed convincingly that in the Homeric hexameter there can be no question of conscious avoidance of a long syllable originating through

'Can a Short Vowel Resist Position?' (28) and P. L. Agar, 'The Lengthening of Final Syllables by Position before the Fifth Foot in the Homeric Hexameter' (29–31), in response to A. Platt, 'Note on Hom. *Hymn. Dem.* 268', in *CQ* 10 (1896), 431–2. *Ed.*]. But cf. W. Leaf, *The Iliad*, ii. 634 (App. N. para. 9).

[70] Cf. *Il.* 1. 211 and Chantraine, *Gr. Hom.* i. 92.

[71] A 4th trochee ending in a vowel is never lengthened by a double consonant beginning the following word.

[72] Th. Stifler, 'Das Wernickesche Gesetz und die bukolische Dihaerese', *Philologus* 79 (1924), 323–54. Cf. B. Snell, *Lexikon der Alten Welt* (Zurich, 1965), 3271.

making position at the end of a word in the fourth biceps. So the law referred to by Page, which Wernicke had found when he was commenting on Tryphiodorus and established for 'poetae docti',[73] is not valid in Homer. The rarity of such position-making at the end of a word after the fourth biceps can be explained (1) through the use of spondaic forms in the hexameter and (2) through the restrictions which lie in the nature of position at the end of a word.

On (1): All words of the type (∪) ∪ − − are restricted to the second half of the verse and are normally at the verse end.[74] Only if more than one bacchaic or ionic word has to appear in the verse, i.e. if the metre demands this, do they appear before the bucolic diaeresis. On the other hand, this metrical demand is not binding for words of the type (∪) ∪ − ∪ (our ἐπέεσσι); for they can find a place in the first half of the verse. So there must be exceptional conditions if such words appear immediately before the bucolic diaeresis.

On (2): Here is meant the proportion of final syllables long by nature to those long by position (i.e. the ones which need a consonant or double consonant at the beginning of the following word). According to Stifler's calculations this proportion is 3 : 1. This reduces the possibility of final syllable position-making before the bucolic diaeresis.

That these conclusions are correct is shown by a simple observation (cf. Stifler *loc. cit.* 330). In our passage, the poet could have written πειρηθῆναι ἐπέεσσι just as well, in order to avoid the offensive position. He did this just as little as the author of the *Iliad* in 2. 522 (Κηφισὸν δῖον ἔναιον: *δῖον Κηφισὸν ἔναιον), 2. 813 (Βατίειαν κικλήσκουσιν: *κικλήσκουσιν Βατίειαν), 5. 734 (ἑανὸν πατρὸς ἐπ᾽ οὔδει: *πατρὸς ἐπ᾽ οὔδει ἑανόν), 7. 436 (ποτὶ δ᾽ αὐτὸν τεῖχος ἔδειμαν: *τεῖχος ποτὶ δ᾽ αὐτὸν ἔδειμαν), 22. 494 (κοτύλην τις τυτθὸν ἐπέσχε: *τυτθὸν κοτύλην τις ἐπέσχε).[75] The poets preferred to follow the natural word order.

---

[73] Where we have to observe that this rules itself out from the start for the hexameter of the Alexandrians since there no word may end after a monosyllabic 4th biceps.

[74] Cf. E. G. O'Neill, 'Word-Types in the Greek Hexameter', *YClS* 8 (1942), 142, 145, 153; H. N. Porter, *YClS* 12 (1951), 53 and 63.

[75] All the examples in Stifler, *Philologus* 79 (1924), 330. The metrical peculiarity in *Od.* 24. 364 (ταμνομένους κρέα πολλὰ κερῶντάς τ᾽ αἴθοπα οἶνον) arose because here the poet modified 15. 500 faithfully to the sense (δεῖπνόν τ᾽ ἐντύνοντο κερῶντό τε αἴθοπα οἶνον).

The author of our verse (*Od.* 24. 240) was presumably restricted particularly by the peculiarity of the statement intended: the infinitive πειρηθῆναι appears in other instances only at the end of a verse (*Il.* 5. 220, 20. 349, 21. 225, 23. 804) but is never linked with ἔπεσσι (or similar).[76] But the dative ἐπέεσσι(ν) is mostly found in the second and third or in the fifth and sixth dactyl. Now as soon as the attribute κερτομίοισ(ιν), which is indispensable for the context, is put in, difficulties arise which one can see in the verse as preserved. The poet was unable to use any of the established formulae, but had to accept a prosodic peculiarity if he wanted to keep the usual word order but not (like the writer of the Ryland papyrus) remedy things with a new compound. The prevalence of the poet's concern for content here is quite clear. Something else becomes evident in this example. Homeric epic represents a stage of development of epic style at which the succinctness of the individual statement counts for more than the consistent use of the usual formulae, even if the new coinage this entails is laborious (and so, in the sense of oral poetry, uneconomical).

24. 242: ἦ τοι ὁ μὲν κατέχων κεφαλὴν φυτὸν ἀμφελάχαινε, 'holding his head down'. This usage—Page (104)—contradicts the normal use of the verb. He says that the *GEL* does not mention it (Passow incidentally does not either) and that it occurs again only in Euripides (fr. 410, 3): καὶ κατ' ὀφθαλμοὺς ἔχει. Page does not ask whether anyone else in Homer ever had reason to hold down a limb of his body when digging like Laertes. The absence of any other reference can probably be explained through the lack of such occasions. But for the poet who wanted to express the content of 24. 242 it was easy to take the primary meaning which κατα- has as prefix from related compounds. One should compare places like *Il.* 13. 17 (ἐξ ὄρεος κατεβήσατο), 4. 149 (= 5. 870: αἷμα καταρρέον ἐξ ὠτειλῆς, also 1. 527 (ὅ τί κεν κεφαλῇ κατανεύσω) and others. Faesi rightly says of our passage that κατέχων is used here in its actual meaning ('demittens').[77]

[205] *Od.* 24. 244: The abstract noun ἀδαημονίη is criticized by Spohn (177), Page (109), and Kirk (250), rightly, as an irregular, quite unique formation. But they withhold the fact that an ancient version ἀδαημοσύνη has also been handed down (Schol. *Il.* 7:

---

[76] An exception is the combination ἔπεσιν πειρήσομαι (only *Il.* 2. 73, ⏑⏑–––⏑⏑).

[77] But presumably it is not etymologically the oldest, cf. Schwyzer–Debrunner 474.

γράφεται "*ἀδαημοσύνη*" and Ap. p. 8, 25), and this should be preferred to the Vulgate. One should compare Buttmann, *Lexilogus* (2nd edn. Berlin, 1860), ii. 121 and Cobet, *Miscellanea critica* (Leiden, 1876), 376. But the noun ἀδαημοσύνη is formed regularly; for as εὔφρων (*Od.* 17. 531) is related to εὐφροσύνη (*Od.* 9. 6 and others), so ἀδαήμων (cf. *Od.* 12. 208) to ἀδαημοσύνη. That word is not unique either; for Apollonius Rhodius formed a corresponding noun δαημοσύνη after it (cf. 2. 175, 4. 1273).

24. 245: (ὦ γέρον, οὐκ ἀδαημοσύνη σ' ἔχει ἀμφιπολεύειν | ὄρχατον), ἀλλ' εὖ τοι κομιδὴ ἔχει . . . This is the oldest reference for the combination εὖ ἔχειν, so common later. It appears neither in Pindar nor Bacchylides nor in Aeschylus, as Page (104) observes. One is tempted to see in it a phrase alien to epic language. However, nothing can be determined about its age, and before one can use it against the genuineness of Book 24 one has to ask how presumably it originated. Odysseus says: '. . . your garden stands to you well looked after . . . you yourself do not stand well looked after' (Schadewaldt). So the incriminated phrase is in opposition to 24. 249: αὐτόν σ' οὐκ ἀγαθὴ κομιδὴ ἔχει. This expression is formed like other combinations frequent in the *Odyssey* ἄγη μ' ἔχει (3. 227), σέβας μ' ἔχει εἰσορόωντα (3. 123, 4. 75 and more frequently), θαῦμά μ' ἔχει (10. 326) and others. In 24. 245 one expects a corresponding formulation. Presumably it would have been possible metrically.[78] But apparently the combination abstract noun + ἔχει could not take an impersonal object. Thus the poet made do with the intransitive ἔχω. Such usage has models in both Homeric poems; (*a*) of persons: *Il.* 24. 27 ἀλλ' ἔχον (sc. Hera, Athena, and Poseidon), ὥς σφιν πρῶτον ἀπήχθετο Ἴλιος ἱρή (= they held out, persevered, continued to behave). *Od.* 19. 494 ἔξω δ' ὡς ὅτε τις στερεὴ λίθος (= I will hold out, will behave); (*b*) of things: *Il.* 13. 520 (= *Il.* 14. 452) δι' ὤμου δ' ὄβριμον ἔγχος | ἔσχεν (= penetrated), *Od.* 12. 435 ῥίζαι γὰρ ἑκὰς εἶχον (= they were situated, cf. Erbse: Schol. V: *Od.* 13: ἀντὶ τοῦ ὑπῆρχον). So it can be said here too: 'The tending of the garden is found in an excellent state.' So Odysseus does not give a general description of the situation ('bene res se habet' Page paraphrases), but praises the whole activity of his unhappy father. The difference between the two views becomes obvious immediately, if one compares the *Odyssey* verse with the

---

[78] e.g. ἀλλ' ἀγαθὴ κομιδὴ ἔχει ὄρχατον or something similar.

formula usual in Attic [206], cf. Soph. *Ai.* 684: ἀλλ᾽ ἀμφὶ μὲν τούτοισιν εὖ σχήσει. Also, in the present case, the construction of 24. 245 could have become the model for the later impersonal expression (which of course cannot be proved), but the expression itself still belongs fully to the Homeric language with which we are familiar.

24. 247: The *synizesis* (*synaloephe*) οὐκ ὄγχνη, οὐ πρασιή τοι ἄνευ κομιδῆς κατὰ κῆπον has been called 'incredible' by Wilamowitz (*Die Heimkehr des Odysseus*, p. 81, n. 3) and he tried to remove it by deleting οὐ before πρασιή. But the suppression of the negative, common in lyric poetry, is not found in Homer. Following Spohn, who defends the traditional version, Page (104) mentioned three verses of the *Iliad* and one of the *Odyssey* which fully justify the use of synizesis in 24. 247. But by preferring to recognize conjectures and bad variants, he wanted to eliminate two of the parallels, which would diminish the basis of confirmation for the expression handed down in 24. 247. We will examine only this part of the question here:

1. *Il.* 17. 89: φλογὶ εἴκελος Ἡφαίστοιο | ἀσβέστῳ· οὐδ᾽ υἱὸν λάθεν Ἀτρέος ὀξὺ βοήσας (ἀσπέτῳ Bentley; ἀσβέστῳ· οὐδ᾽ υἷα λάθ᾽ Barnes and Bothe. Both suggestions are arbitrary).

2. *Od.* 1. 226: εἰλαπίνη ἦε γάμος.

3. *Il.* 18. 458: υἱεῖ ἐμῷ ὠκυμόρῳ δόμεν ἀσπίδα καὶ τρυφάλειαν.

Chantraine (*Gr. Hom.* i. 84) recommends υἷ᾽ ἐμῷ ὠκυμόρῳ (as does Page). But the manuscript basis for this is too slender. The Vulgate ἐμ᾽ ὠκυμόρῳ was already commented on by Herodianus: ἔξω τοῦ ῑ τὸ ἐμωκυμόρῳ· συνεκτέθλιπται γὰρ τῷ ω τὸ ῑ AAint. Herodianus was accustomed to interpreting Aristarchus' text. His lemma makes us assume that he erroneously regarded a *synaloephe* recorded in writing (crasis, ΕΜΩΚΥΜΟΡΩΙ) as an elision. So here too, the text approved by the Alexandrians expected elision.

4. *Il.* 2. 651: Μηριόνης τ᾽ ἀτάλαντος Ἐνυαλίῳ ἀνδρειφόντῃ.

Chantraine (*Gr. Hom.* i. 84) rightly rejects the attempt to read Ἐνυαλίῳ as four syllables (∪–∪∪ with consonantic υ and long α). But his own suggestion (110) to accept the weakly attested (ancient) variant ἀνδριφόντῃ and scan it after the pattern of ἀνδροτῆτα (∪∪– –)[79] is not convincing; for in compound nouns containing

ἀνδρ(ο)- that peculiarity, which is only found twice (sc. *Il.* 16, 857
[= *Il.* 22. 363] and *Il.* 24. 6), cannot be attested.[80] So one would
have to [207] take up ἀδριφόντῃ in the parallel verse *Il.* 8. 264,
which is only preserved in Codex P17, and regard it as original. But
the origin of today's vulgate version (*Il.* 2. 651, 7. 166, 8. 264, 17.
259) would then become extremely complicated.[81]

To my mind, the four cases of rare *synizesis* (i.e. of the combination of two long vowels or one long vowel with a diphthong not
shown in writing) support each other. Those who support this
judgement must also accept the traditional version of *Od.* 24. 247 as
Homeric.

24. 250–3:   αὐχμεῖς τε κακῶς καὶ ἀεικέα ἕσσαι.
οὐ μὲν ἀεργίης γε ἄναξ ἕνεκ' οὐ σε κομίζει,
οὐδέ τί τοι δούλειον ἐπιπρέπει εἰσοράασθαι
εἶδος καὶ μέγεθος.

In this series of verses Page's sensitive feeling for language (105) is
offended by the words αὐχμεῖς, ἀεργίη, δούλειον . . . εἶδος καὶ
μέγεθος, ἐπιπρέπει, as well as by ἀρτίφρων (ἀνήρ . . . | οὔ τι μάλ'
ἀρτίφρων) used slightly later (sc. 24. 261). The poet allowed these
words into our passage, or formed them newly for it, because he
wanted to register some very specific ideas. Is this procedure legitimate, or is the author now leaving the typical framework of the
Odyssey?

1. That the unkempt body of the poor man is 'dry', i.e. surrounded by encrusted dirt and shaggy, is also said by Penelope (*Od.*
19. 327–8): εἴ κεν ἀϋσταλέος . . . | δαινύῃ. This adjective is also a
hapax legomenon like the verb αὐχμεῖν, and since the speaker in both
scenes is thinking of the contrast (i.e. with the bathed, well-tended
body), he hits the nail on the head each time. Those who criticize
the expression must identify a situation in the *Iliad* or *Odyssey*
where the poets were forced to say something similar, but did so

---

[79] For the prosody of ἀνδροτῆτα (for ἀδροτῆτα = being man, vigour of life) cf.
J. Latacz, *Glotta* 43 (1965), 62–76.

[80] Page seems to refer to this when he remarks of *Il.* 2. 651: 'ἐνναλίωι
ανδρειφόντηι is capable of other treatments than ἐνναλίωι ἀν' (104).

[81] Cf. Latacz, *Glotta* 43 (1965), 66, 4. Latacz himself regards ἀνδριφόντῃ (∪∪--)
as original.

with more usual words. The verb αὐχμεῖν also shows that the poets had more words at their disposal than they usually reveal.

2. Page himself probably justified the new formation ἀρτίφρων ('sensible, pleasant') by enumerating the other compounds formed with ἀρτι- found in the epic. Common to both poems (*Il.* 9. 505; *Od.* 8. 310) is ἀρτίπος 'swift'; the formation ἀρτιεπής ('rash with his word', 'mere blatherer') belongs only to the *Iliad* (22. 281). For the native who would be able to give information to the stranger quickly and readily ἀρτίφρων is a particularly suitable description, especially since here, equipped with a negative, it is supposed to describe [208] a rather dense, even stubborn man. It is difficult not to admire the magnificent realism of Odysseus' false story. The creation *de novo* of such apt expressions is hardly the business of bad poets.

3. The noun ἀεργίη, as Page has correctly observed, is no more remarkable than κακοεργίη (*Od.* 22. 374).[82] But he should have added that κακοεργός (*Od.* 18. 54) relates to κακοεργίη just as ἀεργός (cf. *Od.* 19. 27) does to ἀεργίη. So this form has been correctly developed from the acknowledged word-stock of the *Odyssey*. It is not valid to suspect its originality.

4. δούλειον (– – ∪) according to Page is unhomeric since the epics otherwise have δούλιος. But there we are dealing with a single combination (δούλιον ἦμαρ), apparently a very strong one, which is at the end of the verse in the *Iliad* (6. 463); in the second and third (14. 340), or in the fourth and fifth (17. 323) dactyl in the *Odyssey*. In our passage it has been separated, developed, and so placed that the adjective closes with the third trochee. So the poet needed to lengthen it. It can only be an analogical formation. For the ending -ειος originated either from *-εσ-ιος or from *-ηϝ-ιος. The former belongs to the s-stems, the latter to nouns in -ευς. Where -εῖος is derived from nouns of the o-declension the adjective developed by analogy with the genuine derivation.[83] Such words can be found in Homer, cf. e.g. χρύσειος (from χρυσός), χάλκειος (from χαλκός), ἵππειος (from ἵππος). So the poet of Book 24 did nothing unusual when he rejected the adjective of the formula δούλιον ἦμαρ, which was useless for his purposes, and created δούλειος, an analogy to

---

[82] For the lengthening of the -ῑ- cf. Meister, *HK* 36 (metrical lengthening or transformation?). The writing -είη suggests itself in both cases, cf. also Herodianus to *Il.* 9. 73a, incidentally Spohn 177.

[83] Cf. Debrunner 144 (para. 285); e.g. ἄνθρωπος—ἀνθρώπειος.

δοῦλος. The phenomenon has been judged on principle correctly by Debrunner.[84]

5. ἐπιπρέπει has a model in *Od.* 8. 172: μετὰ δὲ πρέπει ἀγρομένοισιν. But the poet who has a *hapax legomenon* μεταπρέπει at his disposal can also form a new compound for himself, especially since a splendid picture thereby emerges. However, one has to construe the words according to sense and rules. One could understand: οὐδέ τι δούλειον εἶδος καὶ μέγεθος ἐπιπρέπει. This could be justified if need be (καὶ must then stand for οὐδέ).[85] But it is really better to separate τι δούλειον from the nouns and regard these as accusatives of respect: 'And there is nothing slavish either [209] which comes to the fore in you when one looks at you, neither in appearance nor in size' (Schadewaldt).[86]

24. 267–8: Page (105) sets the following verses against each other:

19. 350–1: οὐ γάρ πώ τις ἀνὴρ πεπνυμένος ὧδε
ξείνων τηλεδαπῶν φιλίων ἐμὸν ἵκετο δῶμα and

24. 267–8: καὶ οὐ πώ τις βροτὸς ἄλλος
ξείνων τηλεδαπῶν φιλίων ἐμὸν ἵκετο δῶμα.

His interpretation claims (as does Kirk 250), that φιλίων in 19. 351 is a genitive and in 24. 268, through misunderstanding, a comparative. His judgement is: 'φίλος φιλίων, like κακὸς κακίων; no Greek ever repeated this blunder.'[87]

The following arguments contradict this view:

1. φίλιος does not exist in epic language.
2. What is one supposed to imagine the ξεῖνοι τηλεδαποὶ φίλιοι to be? Only tragedy speaks about a φιλία γυνή or δμωΐδες φίλιαι and the like. The scholiast (B) to *Od.* 19. 351 says: φιλίων. ὡς ἡδίων, συγκριτικὸν ἀντὶ τοῦ φίλτερος. One needs only to survey the complete sentence in order to recognize that he is right (19. 350–2):

---

[84] Debrunner 149, 3: 'The form -ειος which also occurs in the epic (χρύσειος etc.) probably originated under the influence of the form -ειος from para. 285, perhaps simply under the pressure of metre.' Unfortunately Page did not take note of Debrunner's observations.

[85] Cf. Kühner–Gerth ii. 291 m, where *Il.* 1. 603–4 are quoted.

[86] Ameis–Hentze–Cauer punctuate before εἰσοράασθαι so that εἶδος καὶ μέγεθος depend on this infinitive: '. . . when one contemplates your appearance and your size'. I have not been able to find a parallel for this combination (εἰσοράασθαι εἶδος καὶ μέγεθος in the sense of 'when one . . . contemplates').

[87] Page refers to a translation of the pair of verses *Od.* 19. 350–1 by Monro: 'Monro said "no man so wise has ever come to my house".'

ξεῖνε φίλ᾽· οὐ γάρ πώ τις ἀνὴρ πεπνυμένος ὧδε
ξείνων τηλεδαπῶν φιλίων ἐμὸν ἵκετο δῶμα,
ὡς σὺ μάλ᾽ εὐφραδέως πεπνυμένα πάντ᾽ ἀγορεύεις.

Three things should be noted here: (*a*) φιλίων takes up φίλε again, intensifying it; (*b*) it is used predicatively; indeed, next to the negated main verb, almost in the sense of a consecutive clause ('so that he would have been dearer to me'); (*c*) ὧδε is picked up by ὡς (352). Schadewaldt's translation is highly commendable: 'For never yet has such a sensible man among the strangers from far away come to my house who would have been dearer to me, the way you say everything sensibly and in a well-thought-out way.'

24. 273: καί οἱ δῶρα πόρον ξεινήϊα, οἷα ἐῴκει. Our poet, so Page (105) more or less explains, regarded ξεινήϊον as an adjective. But, he says, in epic language it is used as a noun. He rejects the possibility of understanding ξεινήϊα as being in apposition to δῶρα—presumably rightly; for the juxtaposition of genus and species is admittedly Homeric (cf. the examples in Chantraine, *Gr. Hom.* ii. 13 and 14, [210] para. 18). But the usage is restricted to certain groups of meaning into which our example does not quite fit. The following fact is decisive: The phrase δῶρα δίδωμι τινί τι is standard; it means 'to give someone something as a present'; the accusative δῶρα is in apposition, not the object. One should compare *Iliad* 16. 867: (ἵπποι|) ἄμβροτοι, οὓς Πηλῆϊ θεοὶ δόσαν ἀγλαὰ δῶρα (similarly 24. 278), 14. 238: δῶρα δέ τοι δώσω καλὸν θρόνον ἄφθιτον αἰεί, but also 11. 124: (ὅς ῥα μάλιστα|) χρυσὸν Ἀλεξάνδροιο δεδεγμένος (expecting) ἀγλαὰ δῶρα, | οὐκ εἴασχ᾽ | Ἑλένην | δόμεναι ξανθῷ Μενελάῳ.[88] So, apparently, the poet does not do what the common commentaries affirm, but is imitating the outlined phrase of the *Iliad*; and in his newly created construction δῶρα is in apposition, not the object: 'As a present I brought him a friend's gifts as they are proper.' Again, it is not the author's fault in this case that his sound, epic mode of expression was misinterpreted.

24. 278–9: χωρὶς δ᾽ αὖτε γυναῖκας ἀμύμονα ἔργα ἰδυίας | τέσσαρας εἰδαλίμας, ἃς ἤθελεν αὐτὸς ἑλέσθαι. Εἰδάλιμος, a rare word, at which Page expresses surprise (106: 'this unpromising neologism'), is not a unique (i.e. unexplained) word formation. Leumann (*HW* 248 with n. 1) gave the explanation: Εἰδάλιμος is modelled on the

---

[88] Ameis–Hentze too, like Leaf, understand ἀγλαὰ δῶρα in apposition to χρυσόν and punctuate accordingly.

Hartmut Erbse

frequent κυδάλιμος. So from the single occurrence of this unexceptional form no conclusion can be drawn about its relative time of origin—as little, in fact, as one may conclude that the tale about the lotus-eaters was inserted later[89] from the regularly formed ἄνθινον εἶδαρ (9. 84), which is also found only once in epic. That the new adjective εἰδάλιμος is found again only in Mnasalcas (cf. Page 106) is a result of the taste of the post-Homeric poets or of our limited knowledge of their works. The author of 24. 279 could not know anything about the future success of his new formation.

More important, but also more difficult, is the question why the poet was not content with a usual word for 'beautiful' in 24. 279 (cf. Page: 'It is not as if there were any lack of Homeric epithets meaning "beautiful" '). Perhaps we may assume that the speaker who, as we know, lays it on thick in his false tale, wants to improve on the pale epithet καλαί with which the physical assets of female slaves are normally emphasized (cf. Il. 9. 130): Odysseus, so he reports, had chosen the women not just because they [211] were good at their work but also because they were a feast for the eyes. But certainty cannot be achieved on this point.

24. 285–6: τῷ κέν σ' εὖ δώροισιν ἀμειψάμενος ἀπέπεμψε | καὶ ξενίῃ ἀγαθῇ. ἡ γὰρ θέμις, ὅς τις ὑπάρξῃ, i.e. 'then he would have rewarded you well for it with presents and also would have sent you away after feeding you well; for this is the custom, if someone has done this first' (Schadewaldt). Page (106) criticizes the prosody ξεν- instead of ξειν-, the noun ξενίη because it appears again only in the fifth century, and the compound ὑπάρξῃ.

1. With ξενίη there exist six references in the Odyssey for ξένιος (14. 158, 389; 15. 514, 546; 17. 155; 20. 230 [here v. 1]). In all places ξειν- could be written and bisyllabic pronunciation (with slurring of the final syllables) could be possible, as also in our verse and in Od. 24. 314 (μείξεσθαι ξενίῃ). W. Schulze already realized this.[90]

2. The noun ξενίη (or ξεινίη respectively) is derived according to rule from ξένιος (ξείνιος) which in turn originated from ξένος

---

[89] These considerations could be supported with numerous examples. I only want to mention ἐπιβώτωρ (only Od. 13. 222); it relates to the simplex βώτωρ (cf. Il. 12. 302 and others) as ἐπιβουκόλος does to βουκόλος. Also the abstract nouns δουλοσύνη (Od. 22. 423, from δοῦλος), ἀλαωτύς (Od. 9. 503, from ἀλαός and ἀλαοῦν), γραπτύς (Od. 24. 229, from γράφειν) are formed regularly, cf. Debrunner 188 (paras. 374–5).

[90] Quaest. ep. 85 f. (quoted in Wackernagel, Spr. Unters. zu Homer (Göttingen, 1916) [SU] 120, 2 in the place quoted by Page).

(ξεῖνος).⁹¹ It is found in Herodotus in the form ξεινίη (1, 69, 3; 2, 182, 2 and others), so seems to have existed in Ionic.⁹²

3. The compound ὑπάρξῃ stands with the simplex (cf. apart from the *Iliad* references also *Od.* 22. 437: ἄρχετε νῦν νέκυας φορέειν) without an essential difference in meaning being visible (in our verse of Book 24 probably 'once someone has started with it'). Similarly ὑπάλυξε (*Od.* 5. 430) relates to ἀλύξαι, ὑπέμεινα (10. 258) to μεῖναι, ὑποδάμνασαι (3. 214; 16. 95) to δάμνασθαι. See further 16. 70 (πῶς γὰρ δὴ τὸν ξεῖνον ἐγὼν ὑποδέξομαι οἴκῳ;) with 17. 110: δεξάμενος δέ με κεῖνος ἐν ὑψηλοῖσι δόμοισι. Why should one deny the poet of Book 24 this liberty? Incidentally, ὑπάρχω also occurs in Herodotus (cf. Stanford *ad loc.*), so it does not appear in Attic for the first time.

24. 288: Laertes asks: πόστον δὴ ἔτος ἐστίν, ὅτε ξείνισσας ἐκεῖνον; Page (106) follows Wackernagel who (*SU* 157) explains as follows: 'πόστος, "the how manyeth?".' As Brugmann⁹³ has seen, this is derived from ποσ(σ)οστός by haplology and so is connected with the formations ἑκατοστός . . . derived from -κοστός. This formation does not look as if it is very old, and one would find it quite normal if there were no older references than the one in [212] Aristophanes . . . (Fr. 163 Kock). Only 24. 288 is older πόστον δὴ ἔτος ἐστίν; . . . Is this supposed to come from Ionia? For Ionic πόστος is attested as little as for any other dialect, apart from Attic.' Looked at in the cold light of day, this is only a Non liquet.⁹⁴ We are satisfied with the observation that 24. 288 offers no evidence in relation to our question. At any rate, one should not forget that in the rest of Homer no situation is described in which the question 'the how manyeth year is it?' is necessary. It is at any rate conceivable that a poetic language which had ordinals like ἐεικοστός at its disposal also had a corresponding question word, or could form one if necessary.

24. 289–90 and 301: Page (109) quotes 24. 289–90 (σὸν ξεῖνον δύστηνον, ἐμὸν παῖδ᾽, εἴ ποτ᾽ ἔην γε; | δύσμορον, ὅν που κτλ.) and

---

⁹¹ Cf. Debrunner 145 (para. 287).

⁹² Page's remark is a bit enigmatic: 'Though there is wide scope for its use, if it had existed, in the Homeric poems and elsewhere . . .'. One would surely have to ask first whether there was opportunity to use the word.

⁹³ Cf. Schwyzer i. 596.

⁹⁴ Schwyzer i. 612 leaves the question open ('πόστος since Homer'); Frisk, *GEW* ii. 585 says without comment '*Od.* 24. 288, Att.'.

301: (οἱ δ᾽ ἐκβήσαντες ἔβησαν). On this he remarks: 'Our poet has hardly done himself justice, or at least credit, in writing . . .'. Nothing is less justified than this verdict. One should compare Bekker's collection (*Homerische Blätter* (Bonn, 1863), i. 185) who begins his well-known chapter with the words: 'Homer loves repetition in almost every shape, so much so that there are few verses in which he does not somehow remind us of certain other verses. He certainly also understands how the repetition of the same sound has a charming and powerful effect on the ear and appreciation.' As references for the epanalepsis of the first of the examples mentioned above, *Od.* 3. 472 (οἶνον οἰνοχοεῦντες) or 20. 280 (δασσάμενοι δαίνυντ᾽ ἐρικυδέα δαῖτα) should be mentioned, for the parechesis of the second *Il.* 20. 61–2 (ἔδεισεν . . . δείσας) or 12. 295–6 (ἐξήλατον . . . ἤλασεν).

24. 299: ποῦ δαὶ νηῦς ἔστηκε θοή; Page (106) claims that the manuscript tradition attests the particle here; in *Od.* 1. 225 (τίς δὲ ὅμιλος) he says it was introduced by Aristarchus against the majority of the manuscripts in order to avoid hiatus; as for the third reference (sc. *Il.* 10. 408: πῶς δαὶ τῶν ἄλλων Τρώων φυλακαί τε καὶ εὐναί), he says it is one of several well-attested variants. If one puts this accurately, one gets the following results:

In *Il.* 10. 408 the Vulgate has δ᾽ αἱ, a small number of manuscripts (among them A) δαί.

In *Od.* 1. 225 the Vulgate reads δέ, only one manuscript δαί.

In 24. 299 the Vulgate offers δέ, Allen's classes d and f, manuscript P 1 and the Ryland Papyrus (third and fourth century AD) have δαί.

Apollonius Dyscolus' report (*synt.* 106. 1) shows clearly that Aristarchus wanted to ensure that δαί was read in all three places, cf. 107. 8: ἀλλὰ φαίνεται ὅτι τὸν Ἀρίσταρχον ἐκίνει τὸ ἔθιμον τοῦ ποιητοῦ, ὡς [213] συνήθως μὲν ἐλλείπει τοῖς ἄρθροις, συνάπτει δὲ μετὰ τὰ πύσματα τὸν δαί σύνδεσμον, "τίς δαί ἐστιν ὅδε ὅμιλος;" (cf. *Od.* 1. 225), "ποῦ δαὶ νηῦς ἔστηκεν;" (24. 299). If one follows Apollonius, Aristarchus was faced with the question whether in *Il.* 10. 408 he should interpret the letter sequence ΔΑΙ as δ᾽ αἱ or δαί. In considering the question, he referred to the fact that Homeric language lacks the definite article. His second argument consisted of reference to the two verses from the *Odyssey*. It would be significant evidence if he really had found δαί there. But the testimony of the Vulgate speaks against this, quite apart from the observation that δέ is of course a *lectio difficilior* and could hardly have been inserted later. So presumably Aristarchus changed the text of the *Odyssey* in both places in order to be able to prove his case. He did not have to take exception to the fact that he was attributing a typically Attic particle to the text of the poet; for he regarded Homer as an Athenian.[95] If these thoughts are correct, all disparaging statements about 24. 299 take care of themselves since presumably in pre-Alexandrian times it did not contain the offending particle. At the same time, one should realize that Atticisms can have come into the Homeric text only relatively late (this is not the only case).[96]

24. 307: Odysseus says to his father (ἀλλά με δαίμων |) πλάγξ' ἀπὸ Σῐκανίης. Page (109) claims: ' "Sicania" is not known to Homeric geography.' This is a relic of a thesis by Kirchhoff (528):[97] 'Sicels and Sicania on the other hand are geographical terms which occur only in the additions of the editor.' But it is arbitrary to delete the mention of Sicily in *Od.* 20. 383 (ἐς Σικελοὺς πέμψωμεν)—not to mention the three passages in Book 24 (211, 366, 389: γυνὴ Σικελή and similar). But if the *Odyssey* poet knew of the existence of Sicily, he could also have known the old name of the island (Σικανίη, cf. Hdt. 7. 170. 1) which for metrical reasons offered itself on a plate. On the other hand, it is improbable that a later poet, who allegedly was the first to introduce the term 'Sicily' into the *Odyssey*, should have caused confusion in our passage through preferring an antiquated name of the country. Probably in post-Homeric times this described only a part of the island.[98]

24. 314: 'διδώσειν: this *monstrum rhapsodicum* has a parallel in *Od.* 13. 358' (Page 109, cf. also Kirk 250). The recurrence of the [214] form in a second passage should have warned us against thoughtless categorization. Indeed, formations of the future from characterized present stems are not rare. They can be attested already in Homer, cf. κιχήσομαι (*Il.* 2. 258 and more often), χαιρήσειν (*Il.* 20.

[95] It is enough to suppose that he suggested the conjectures for both places in the *Odyssey* in his commentary where Apollonius seems to have found them. But Aristarchus' explanation is a circular one.

[96] Our passage has on principle already been dealt with correctly by M. van de Valk, *Textual Criticism of the Odyssey* (Leiden, 1949), 172.

[97] Cf. also Spohn 81 with hardly convincing arguments.

[98] Cf. Schulten, *RE* 2 A 2 (1923), 2459, 39 s.v. Sikaner.

Hartmut Erbse

363), ἀλύξειν (*Il*. 10. 371, 17. 547, 19. 558).[99] Are all these supposed to be *monstra*?

24. 318–20: ἀνὰ ῥῖνας δέ οἱ ἤδη | δριμὺ μένος προὔτυψε φίλον πατέρ' εἰσορόωντι. | κύσσε δέ μιν περιφὺς ἐπιάλμενος.[100] Page's complaints (106) concern the verbal forms προὔτυψε and ἐπιάλμενος. The word mentioned first, he thinks, is familiar to the epic only in the phrase Τρῶες δὲ προὔτυψαν ἀολλέες (*Il*. 13. 136, 15. 306, 17. 262); but he says the meaning required there does not fit the context of the passage in Book 24. To this you can object: The poet means the onset of the stinging tickle which precedes the outbreak of tears ('and already the sharp urge advanced to the front of his nose' Schadewaldt translates). This urge overwhelms man like the advancing enemy. The second criticism too is hardly appropriate. It is true that ἐπιάλμενος (*Il*. 7. 15) refers to mounting the war chariot (ἵππων ἐπιάλμενον ὠκειάων). But this meaning does not help us here. On the other hand, in *Od*. 14. 220 and 22. 305 the participle ἐπάλμενος is used of pouncing on the enemy, so of a movement which lunges violently forward (in 22. 305 in the simile vultures are mentioned). This idea exactly describes the situation which we previously tried to argue was the climax of the *anagnorisis*: Odysseus jumps up towards his father, embraces him, kisses him, and tells him who he is.

One will have to concede to Page that the judgement in both cases is a matter of discretion. But who would want to put their signature to this opinion: 'More unsuitable words for the present context would be hard to find'? One senses Page's purpose, and very unsatisfying it is.

24. 341–4: With these verses Odysseus concludes the series of signs which he gives his father in order to prove his identity. They are his personal memories of childhood in the orchard, when his father made him presents of valuable trees. The content already makes us suspect that we will find here unique expressions. The verses go:

> ... ὄρχους δέ μοι ὧδ' ὀνόμηνας
> δώσειν πεντήκοντα, διατρύγιος δὲ ἕκαστος

---

[99] Further material in Schwyzer i. 783 a 7. From post-Homeric language especially διδάξω should be mentioned. The above mentioned ἀλύξω is incidentally not a definite testimony since the stem ἀλυκ- cannot be excluded, cf. Frisk, *GEW* i. 80.

[100] Cf. with this also Casaubon in Spohn 205.

The Ending of the Odyssey: Linguistic Problems

[215]   ἤην (ἔνθα δ᾽ ἀνὰ σταφυλαὶ παντοῖαι ἔασιν),
         ὁππότε δὴ Διὸς ὧραι ἐπιβρίσειαν ὕπερθεν.

Page (107) is offended that the form ὀνόμηνας is constructed like a verb of promising; for the forms of this word (only the aorist is attested) are construed either with an accusative object (*Iliad*: 2. 488; 9. 121; 10. 522; 14. 278; 16. 491; 23. 178; 24. 591; with double accusative 23. 90) or with accusative and indirect question (*Od.* 4. 240; 11. 328, 517). Once (*Od.* 11. 251) the verb is used absolutely. Nevertheless, Page's objection is not justified. Ameis–Hentze–Cauer already realized that the related word ὀνομάζω is used twice (*Il.* 9. 515 and 18. 449) with the meaning 'to promise, namely that'.[101] By analogy with ὑπισχνεῖσθαι the infinitive could easily appear after ὀνομαίνω ('in this way you promised me, enumerating them, to give (me) 50 vine rows as a present').[102] For the *hapax legomenon* διατρύγιος Page (rightly) accepts Ebeling's translation (*diversis temporibus fructus ferens*). The word expresses the idea that each row can be picked at any time of year, because the grapes ripen in turn. Although the formation is transparent, the poet confirms what he means with an explanation in the parenthesis of the next verse: 'For there are indeed grapes of manifold kind (i.e. in different states of ripeness) on the vines.' With this enlightening reference to reality, Odysseus shows that he knows all about the vineyard. So the parenthesis is not unsatisfactory (thus, for example, Monro and Stanford) but logical. Only in it does the present ἔασιν make full sense, and given the sequence the temporal clause follows the finite verb ἤην pleasingly. The form ἤην itself is attested four times (*Il.* 11. 808; *Od.* 19. 283; 23. 316; 24. 343). In *Od.* 23. 316 there are no variants, in the other places only weakly attested ones. Schulze's change to ἦεν is today no longer regarded as probable or even necessary: ἤην is morphologically the latest form in the series *ἔεν, ἦεν, ἦν, ἔην, ἤην.*[103] The Ionian singers, Homer already among them, could have known and used it (by which I imply nothing about the orthography of the oldest text of Homer).

---

[101] *Il.* 9. 515: εἰ μὲν γὰρ μὴ δῶρα φέροι, τὰ δ᾽ ὄπισθ᾽ ὀνομάζοι (sc. Agamemnon) and 18. 449: καὶ πολλὰ περικλυτὰ δῶρ᾽ ὀνόμαζον.

[102] If instead of ὀνόμηνας one read the participle ὀνομήνας so that a verb of saying (from ἔειπες *Od.* 24. 339) would have to be added, then a familiar construction would result. But the ellipsis would be extraordinarily harsh.

[103] Cf. Meister, *HK* 109; Chantraine, *Gr. Hom.* i. 289.

Even this passage, which seems so strange, does not contain any unhomeric expressions, and if one considers it calmly, one can observe that it contributes well to the rounding-off of the Laertes scene. [216] 24. 347–9:

> ἀμφὶ δὲ παιδὶ φίλῳ βάλε πήχεε· τὸν δὲ ποτὶ οἷ
> εἷλεν ἀποψύχοντα πολύτλας δῖος Ὀδυσσεύς.
> αὐτὰρ ἐπεί ῥ᾿ ἄμπνυτο καὶ ἐς φρένα θυμὸς ἀγέρθη . . .

The phrase τὸν δὲ π(ρ)οτὶ οἷ | εἷλεν is a formation modelled on *Il.* 21. 507–8 (τὴν [sc. Artemis] δὲ π(ρ)οτὶ οἷ εἷλε πατὴρ Κρονίδης), but the participle ἀποψύχοντα with the meaning 'fainting' has no epic model (cf. Spohn 184). The verb ἀποψύχω = *efflare* occurs again only in the fifth century (mostly connected with an accusative object). In epic, the compound is otherwise only used with the meaning 'to blow off, to refresh', *Il.* 11. 621 (= 22. 2): ἱδρῶ ἀπεψύχοντο and 21. 561: ἱδρῶ ἀποψυχθείς. The same is true of ἀναψύχω, see 5. 795: ἕλκος ἀναψύχοντα, 13. 84: ἀνέψυχον φίλον ἦτορ, 10. 575: ἀνέψυχθεν φίλον ἦτορ and *Od.* 4. 568: ἀναψύχειν ἀνθρώπους (of winds). But does this finding lead to the conclusion that the expression of *Od.* 24. 348 is close to the language of the fifth century, or at any rate, no longer epic (Page 108: 'contrary to Epic usage')?

Our decision on the expression must start from two comparable places in which fainting is described, *Il.* 5. 696–7 (τὸν δ᾿ ἔλιπε ψυχή . . . | αὖτις δ᾿ ἀμπνύνθη) and 22. 467–75 (ἀπὸ δὲ ψυχὴν ἐκάπυσσε . . . | ἡ δ᾿ ἐπεὶ οὖν ἄμπνυτο). Both passages show that people imagined fainting as a temporary departure of the soul. But soul is the breath of life; the Greeks were always conscious that ψυχή belongs to ψύχω. From this consideration alone, it follows that ἀποψύχω in Book 24 of the *Odyssey* was used in a more original sense than in the other places. Of course, both meanings are very close to each other: 'The shift which must be assumed—"blow > cool down (in the wind)" (also "make dry [in the wind]")—has nothing strange about it, especially for a seafaring people' (Frisk, *GEW* ii. 1142). One may even assume that the *Odyssey* poet could have inferred the basic meaning *efflare* from the *Iliad* references, if the compound in its actual sense had not been known to him. But it is not very probable that it should have remained completely alien to the older epic, especially in its early oral stage. We just do not have any testimony, since the poet of the *Iliad* described fainting and sudden feelings of weakness in different ways (Hector's fainting too, cf. *Il.* 14. 418–39), but in the *Odyssey* this is the single case (Irus does not faint, cf. *Od.* 18.

96–9). Finally one could refer to the structure of the sentence: the phrase taken from *Il.* 21 (τὸν δὲ ποτὶ οἷ | εἷλεν) which should have closed with the subject described in a formula (πολύτλας δῖος ’Οδυσσεύς) left only little room for the description of the fainting. Evidently the participle ἀποψύχοντα was effectively unavoidable. [217]

24. 360: (ἔνθα δὲ Τηλέμαχον καὶ βουκόλον ἠδὲ συβώτην |) προὔπεμψ’, ὡς ἂν δεῖπνον ἐφοπλίσσωσι τάχιστα. Page (108) quotes Monro: 'The only Homeric instance of a compound of προ- in which we cannot write the uncontracted form προε-.' He could also have referred to van Leeuwen.[104] The diphthong which originates from the crasis does indeed stand in a *longum* position (the *arsis*) only in our passage. In the other instances in the *Iliad* and the *Odyssey*, the vowel contraction could be dissolved. But it has been very doubtful for a long time whether by doing this one would find the original word sound. Rightly, Chantraine (*Gr. Hom.* i. 85) expresses himself much more cautiously than Page: 'Enfin dans le cas un peu différent de προὔφαινε, προὔχουσας, προὔχοντα etc., on peut penser que la forme contracte s'est substituée à la forme non contracte.' Since Meister's research, we have known that contraction is not in the least alien to the language of our epics. We are e.g. not justified in doubting the tradition of *Od.* 22. 385 (κοῖλον ἐς αἰγιαλὸν πολιῆς ἔκτοσθε θαλάσσης) with Nauck because the stem syllable of the adjective κοῖλος in all other places in Homer can be dissolved into two short ones.[105] The assumption can be confidently made that the poet of Book 24 had already met the diphthong which had originated through crasis in the compounds with προ-. For he himself in 24. 82 (προὔχούσῃ) and 24. 319 (προὔτυψε) put the diphthong in the *thesis*.[106] To my mind, Monro's observation only implies the following: In compounds with προ-, the augment did not originally blend with the prefix, so the prefixes (προ-ε-) had to stand in a biceps (i.e. in the *thesis*). This position was also usually kept in the Homeric poems at a time when crasis had already occurred. The existence of the false diphthong was regarded as so unexceptional that the author of our verse could dare to begin it with the form προὔπεμψ’.[107]

[104] *Enchiridium Dictionis Epicae* (2nd edn. Leiden, 1918), 70.
[105] Cf. Meister, *HK* 50.
[106] One is hardly allowed to presuppose that in these two cases the text was modernized but in *Od.* 24. 360 conceived of in the contracted form.
[107] Page thinks that he can support his judgement with reference to *Od.* 24. 240 (supposed violation of Wernicke's Law). We regard this attempt as unsuccessful. Cf. above pp. 290 ff.

24. 386: ἔνθ' οἱ μὲν δείπνῳ ἐπεχείρεον. On this Page (108):[108] 'This poet is far from the main stream of Epic tradition: the common formulas are forgotten or despised—not οἱ δ' ἐπ' ὀνείαθ' ἑτοῖμα προκείμενα χεῖρας ἴαλλον or the like, but δείπνῳ ἐπεχείρεον: the verb, and this construction with the dative case, are common in the prose and poetry of the fifth century (esp. Attic).' Page seems to regard the poet as a self-willed ignoramus: instead of using the formulae ready to hand, [218] he is supposed to have patched together Attic constructions! But one should have a closer look at what he is saying! Here something unexampled is happening: One has hardly started 'to fall to the food' when along comes old Dolius with his sons (ἀγχίμολον δέ | ἦλθ' ὁ γέρων Δολίος). The meal is temporarily stopped for people to greet each other. Odysseus himself says quite clearly that the food is standing there hardly touched (394–6): 'Old man, sit down for your meal, and you, stop being amazed! For we have been waiting in the halls for a long time, eager to stretch out the hand for the bread (δηρὸν γὰρ σίτῳ ἐπιχειρήσειν μεμαῶτες | μίμνομεν ἐν μεγάροισ'), and we have been waiting for you all the time' (Schadewaldt).

We should be reminded that the formulaic verse quoted by Page introduces a typical dining scene in which the meal goes by in a way familiar to the audience of epic poetry. Apart from two exceptions the formulaic verse: αὐτὰρ ἐπεὶ πόσιος καὶ ἐδητύος ἐξ ἔρον ἔντο . . . always follows.[109] The *Odyssey* is rich in surprises. Our scene also corresponds to its mode of representation: here the stream of the narrative is interrupted just at that moment at which the listener expects to hear the most usual words.

24. 387–8: ἦλθ' ὁ γέρων Δολίος, σὺν δ' υἱεῖς τοῖο γέροντος, | ἐξ ἔργων μογέοντες, '. . . then old Dolius came along and with him the sons of the old man, tired out from working on the fields' (Schadewaldt). Page (108) rightly emphasized the meaning of the participle, which is unique in the epic. Μογεῖν means 'to suffer' (~ *perpeti*) but that is not the meaning here. The model for our passage is likely to be one of the two *Iliad* verses in which μογέων is used intransitively, in place of an adverb, *Il.* 11. 636: ἄλλος μὲν

---

[108] Cf. also Spohn 205; Schwartz 135 n. 2.

[109] The two exceptions are *Od.* 4. 218 where something special which is closely connected with the meal follows (ἔνθ' αὖτ' ἄλλ' ἐνόησ' Ἑλένη Διὸς ἐκγεγαυῖα) and 20. 256 (Telemachus seats Odysseus who is now a guest of the house at a special table near the threshold).

The Ending of the Odyssey: *Linguistic Problems*

μογέων ἀποκινήσασκε τραπέζης ('with effort') or 12. 29: τὰ θέσαν μογέοντες Ἀχαιοί ('with trouble'). So one would have to translate the reference in the *Odyssey* in the following way: 'Dolius and his sons came home from work on the fields with trouble.' But this surely does not correspond to the poet's intention; the word order alone makes it clear that μογέοντες belongs to the prepositional phrase (meaning 'to be in a bad state').[110]

So the peculiarity of the use of the word consists in the fact that the participle μογέοντες, instead of being taken with the main verb, is taken with the prepositional phrase. By this means the slight shift of meaning from *perpetiens* to *laborans* automatically results. It is probably not too bold to claim that such a use of the participle could be derived at any time from the two references in the *Iliad*. [219] This assumption should also be maintainable if the participle were attested elsewhere in the *Odyssey*, possibly even with the same function as in the older poem.

Page compares three places from tragedy with *Od.* 24. 388 (Aesch. *Ag.* 1624 and *Prom.* 275 as well as Eur. *Alc.* 849) and expects his reader to conclude that the *Odyssey* verse was composed under the influence of Attic phrases. Such a suggestion is not justified.

24. 394: ὦ γέρον, ἷζ' ἐπὶ δεῖπνον, ἀπεκλελάθεσθε δὲ θάμβευς. The verse contains two peculiarities: the form ἀπεκλελάθεσθε and the genitive θάμβευς in the sixth dactyl.

1. That multiple compounds are more numerous in the *Odyssey* than in the *Iliad* is well known. One should for instance compare the following forms: ἀποπροέηκε (14. 26, 22. 327; see 22. 82); ἐκπρολιπόντες (8. 515); ἐπεντανύσας (22. 467) and others. The prefixes ἀποπρο-, ἐκπρο- and ἐπεν- are alien to the *Iliad*, ἐπεν- also occurs in the *Odyssey* only in the passage just mentioned. So this could be as suspect as the form ἀπεκλελάθεσθε. Since forms of ἐκλαθέσθαι ('to forget') are known to both epics (cf. ἐκλελαθέσθαι (*Il.* 6. 285) and ἐκλελάθοιτο (*Od.* 3. 224)), in our passage the meaning must be 'complete forgetting'. One is probably not allowed to discredit this *ad hoc* formation by pointing out that the combinations with ἐξαπο- predominate overall over ἀπεκ-. In all of these cases, the prefix ἀπο- immediately preceding the verb means

---

[110] Cf. Schol. D to *Il.* 1. 162: ἐμόγησα· ἐκοπίασα, ἐκακοπάθησα, similarly Schol. *Od.* 24. 207.

'firmly', or even 'darkly'.[111] Also, in our case, an intensifying second prefix has come before the firm combination ἐκλελάθεσθε. So a transposition of the prefixes was not permitted. But we must exclude the obvious possibility of writing ὑπεκλελάθεσθε instead of ἀπεκλελάθεσθε (cf. ὑπεξαλέασθαι *Il.* 15. 180, ὑπεξαναδύς *Il.* 13. 352, ὑπεξέφυγον *Od.* 11. 383) because the meaning would be distorted.

2. Page emphasizes that a contracted genitive singular of the neuters in -ος is otherwise never 'in the unemphasized half of the dactyl' (so in the biceps). I regard the deviation from this practice in our verse as less astonishing than the fact that the contracted ending -ευς coincides several times with a *longum* (thus filling the *arsis*).[112] These diphthongs which originated through contraction cannot be removed. But once the ending -ευς was accepted, the opportunity arose [220] of occasionally putting a contracted genitive at the verse end. As the poet used τέο next to τεῦ, σέο next to ἐμεῦ, ἔρχεο next to ἔρχευ, so he will have regarded θάμβευς next to ὄρεος as permitted and at his permanent disposal. The opportunity of locating it at the same position as in 24. 394 was not often given anyhow; for most of the epic neuters in -ος have a short stem vowel.[113]

24. 398: (ὡς ἄρ' ἔφη, Δολίος δ' ἰθὺς κίε χεῖρε πετάσσας |) ἀμφοτέρας, 'Οδυσεῦς δὲ λαβὼν κύσε χεῖρ' ἐπὶ καρπῷ. The genitive 'Οδυσεῦς is a rarity; for according to our knowledge the group ε(F)ο- is not contracted (cf. Chantraine, *Gr. Hom.* i. 34). Page (108) calls the construction 'absolutely contrary to Homeric law'. But it depends on how one defines the scope of validity of this law. It should only be noted in passing that it is not difficult to mould this verse into a more pleasing shape, e.g. ἄμφω, 'Οδυσῆος δὲ λαβών (Nauck). So there could also be a mistake in the tradition here.

Nevertheless, it is advisable to keep the tradition even without having to ascribe it to an inferior poet. There are three forms of the

---

[111] Schwyzer–Debrunner 428. There the impressive example ἐξαπατήσειν *Il.* 22. 299, 'next to which only ἀπάτησε and similar, not simple ἀτάω'.

[112] Cf. the cases compiled in Chantraine, *Gr. Hom.* i. 58: *Il.* 8. 368 (ἐξ 'Ερέβευς, $\overset{\perp}{\smile}\smile-$), *Il.* 3. 10 (ἠύτ' ὄρευς, $\overset{\perp}{\smile}\smile-$, v. l. ant.), *Od.* 11. 37 (ὑπὲξ 'Ερέβευς, $\smile\overset{2}{\smile}\smile-$), *Il.* 16. 743 (εὐεργέος, $\overset{2}{\smile}--$), *Il.* 17. 573 (θάρσευς, $-\overset{3}{\smile}$), *Od.* 7. 118 (θέρευς, $\smile\overset{3}{\smile}$), *Od.* 15. 533 (γένευς, $\smile\overset{4}{\smile}$).

[113] So it is unnecessary to think of a mistake in tradition and consider θάμβεος which would have had to be measured in analogy to ᾦκεον (*Od.* 9. 400), ἠρίθμεον (10. 204), ἐφόρεον (22. 456).

The Ending of the Odyssey: Linguistic Problems

genitive, Ὀδυσσῆος, Ὀδυσῆος, and Ὀδυσσέος. But the last one occurs only once in both epics, namely *Il.* 4. 491: τοῦ μὲν ἅμαρθ᾽, ὁ δὲ Λεῦκον Ὀδυσσέος ἐσθλὸν ἑταῖρον. Now if a genitive scanning ∪∪– was really needed, could one not believe oneself to be justified in creating it through contraction after the model of the neuter genitives of the s-stems (cf. the form θάμβευς, *Od.* 24. 394 which has just been dealt with)? Such genitives of nouns in -ευς were known to the old interpreters of Homer anyhow, cf. Schol. T to *Il.* 13. 424 (Ἰδομενεὺς δ᾽ οὐ λῆγε μένος μέγα): τινὲς περισπῶσιν. One should compare the references in the grammarians collected for this scholium, especially Choiroboscus (Th. 1. 172. 21): ἰστέον δὲ ὅτι τὸ ε καὶ τὸ ο τριχῶς συναιροῦνται ἤγουν κίρνανται ... (24) οἷον Ἰδομενέος Ἰδομενεῦς, "Ἰδομενεὺς δ᾽ οὐ λῆγε μένος μέγα" ἀντὶ τοῦ Ἰδομενέως οὐκ ἔληγεν ἡ δύναμις (next *Od.* 24. 398 and *Il.* 8. 368 are quoted). Bekker even wanted to extend the contraction to *Il.* 2. 566 (= *Il.* 23. 678) (Μηκιστεὺς υἱός instead of the traditional Μηκιστέος υἱός) and on top of everything write Πηλεῦς instead of Πηλέος.[114] Although we are not allowed [221] to go that far, we will nevertheless leave untouched the contracted form in *Od.* 24. 398, which is unanimously attested. For Page's conclusion would not be cogent even if the poet of the *Odyssey* had taken over the uncontracted form of *Il.* 4. 491 (Ὀδυσσέος) in another place.

Finally, if Ἀτρέος, Τυδέος, Πηλέος were formed only from the patronymics as Meister (*HK* 150) assumes, we would not be allowed (with the editors) to put in Πηλῆος for traditional Πηλέος, so we would have to read διογενὴς Πηλέος υἱός in *Il.* 1. 489. If this thesis were correct (it is convincingly disputed) the poet at *Od.* 24. 398, supported by such a position of the proper name, could have written: ἀμφοτέρας, Ὀδυσέος (to be read with synaloephe).[115] But this is not probable.

24. 402: οὐλέ τε καὶ μέγα χαῖρε, θεοὶ δέ τοι ὄλβια δοῖεν. The solemn form οὐλε[116] occurs again only in the Hymn to Apollo 466,

---

[114] I. Bekker, *Homerische Blätter* (Bonn, 1863), i. 40 f. In any case it cannot be denied that in *Il.* 2. 566 (= 23. 678) either Μηκιστέος (Μηκιστεὺς Bekker) υἱός or Μηκιστῆος υἱός (thus Bekker in the edition Bonn 1858) must be read. Allen had Μηκιστέος printed in the first, Μηκιστῆος in the second place although the majority of the MSS offers Μηκιστέως there and here (sc. *Il.* 23. 678) Μηκιστέος. Cf. also Herodianus on *Il.* 9. 106.

[115] So we would have only a slight mistake in the traditional version.

[116] Originally vocative (cf. Schwyzer i. 723 n. 5), but used like an imperative by the poet ('salve'). Uncontrollable associations in G. E. Dimcock Jr. in *Essays* 70.

where our verse is repeated. Conclusions concerning the time of origin of this verse of the *Odyssey*, our oldest evidence for this interesting word, are not possible.

24. 416: μυχμῷ τε στοναχῇ τε. Μυχμός (groaning) is an Ionic formation like πρῆχμα (later μυγμός); it belongs to μύζω.[117] Page (110) notes: 'A novelty, not elsewhere in poetry.' But the principle is valid here too that words which have been formed regularly, even if they are attested only once, do not allow any conclusions about their age.

24. 432: . . . ἢ καὶ ἔπειτα κατηφέες ἐσσόμεθ᾽ αἰεί. This new formation is in addition to epic κατηφείη (*Il.* 3. 51 and more often) which belongs to κατηφεῖν (cf. κατηφήσας *Il.* 22. 293, similarly *Od.* 16. 342). Page (110; cf. also Spohn 180) has the references mentioned to hand, and also notes that the *Iliad* knows the noun κατηφόνες (*Il.* 24. 253) besides. Under these circumstances, however, he should not have been surprised about the existence of the adjective κατηφής; for this relates to κατηφείη as ἀληθής (*Il.* 12. 433) to ἀληθείη (cf. *Il.* 23. 361) or as ἀναιδής (cf. *Il.* 1. 158) to ἀναιδείη (cf. 1. 149). So the formation is regular; it could be coined at any time by an expert user of epic language.

24. 437: Eupeithes challenges the Ithacans to take revenge before Odysseus escapes to the mainland with his people: ἀλλ᾽ ἴομεν, μὴ φθέωσι περαιωθέντες ἐκεῖνοι. This verb meaning 'to cross (over)' is not otherwise attested in epic. περᾶν is used once to mean 'to cross the sea', [222] cf. *Od.* 5. 174: ἤ με κέλεαι σχεδίῃ περάαν μέγα λαῖτμα θαλάσσης. But this finding does not give us a reason for surprise (cf. Page 109); for at 24. 437 a crossing from coast to coast is evidently meant, and this fact alone explains why the verb later occurs so often in Greek historical literature. In classical poetry, it is found only in Aristophanes (*Ran.* 138, Dionysus in conversation with Heracles): εἶτα πῶς γε περαιωθήσομαι 'How shall I get across there (sc. across the lake of the underworld)?' It goes without saying that there was no opportunity for such usage in the *Odyssey* apart from here; for even in the formulation of *Od.* 5. 174, the full emphasis is on the perilous length of the voyage, not on the possibility of getting across. So the *Odyssey* offers the oldest evidence for περαιοῦσθαι. It is no coincidence that this epic word gained new life only in the fifth century.

[117] Cf. Frisk, *GEW* ii. 264 (with lit.).

24. 465: οὐ γάρ σφιν ἅδε μῦθος ἐνὶ φρεσίν, ἀλλ' Εὐπείθει |
πείθοντ(ο). Page (109) on this: 'Εὐπειθεῖ: the contracted dative in
-ει in the unstressed half of the dactyl is absolutely contrary to
Homeric law.' The statement is not accurately formulated, unless
Page means the second half of the sixth dactyl. The dative of the s-
stems is found in the *thesis*, but always with hiatus shortening (so it
forms the second *breve* of the *biceps*), e.g. *Il.* 11. 109: Ἄντιφον αὖ
παρὰ οὖς ἔλασε ξίφει, ἐκ δ' ἔβαλ' ἵππων, or *Il.* 20. 172: γλαυκιόων
ἰθὺς φέρεται μένει, ἥν τινα πέφνῃ, or 23. 189: ἐν λέχει ἀσκητῷ.
Meister (*HK* 128) has proved that this position was chosen because
the contraction was not acceptable to the poets. Such forms therefore take the place of the *longum* only rarely. e.g. *Il.* 16. 792 (= *Od.*
13. 164): χειρὶ καταπρηνεῖ, *Il.* 17. 647: ἐν δὲ φάει (beginnings of
verse), *Il.* 23. 515: οὔ τι τάχει γε (²∪∪–∪), *Od.* 3. 91: εἴτε καὶ ἐν
πελάγει, *Il.* 21. 262 χώρῳ ἐνί προαλεῖ (beginnings of verse). The
places mentioned last show anyhow that contraction was acceptable
although it was used only rarely.

So the irregularity of *Od.* 24. 465 consists in the fact that the
dative with a contracted final syllable forms the end of the hexameter. For this we do not have any other evidence. There is a
second peculiarity too: 422 and 469 in Book 24 show that the poet
wanted the proper name, which in the preceding books appears
only in the formula προσέφη Εὐπείθεος υἱός (∪∪⁴––∪∪–×), to
be read as three syllables. But as a Molossian word, the dative
Εὐπείθει would have had to be placed in such a way that its middle
syllable took the place of a *biceps* (was in the *thesis*).[118]

[223] So in this case one can only take note of the irregularity.
Presumably the poet felt that he was allowed to put the contracted
dative of the rare proper name at the end of the verse. We do not
want to excuse him. Certainly a more pleasing expression could
have been found. On the other hand this violation of the rule—it is
the only place where Page's criticism is really justified—is not sufficient to condemn the whole ending of the epic.[119]

[118] On the exceptions cf. Ludwich, *Aristarchs Homerische Textkritik* i, ii
(Leipzig, 1884–5) ii. 247: 'Only in two places within the verse did Homer at times
allow himself to deviate from the regular stress of the Molossus: before the bucolic
dihaeresis and at the end of the verse (in the hexameter *spondiacus*); there only
extremely rarely, here a little more frequently.'

[119] Whether one should think about an influence of the genitive θάμβευς (⁶-, *Od.*
24. 394) discussed above is debatable. But quite possibly the poet could have been
looking for the parechesis Εὐπείθει | πείθοντο. But this certainly is not sufficient to
justify the position of the *nomen proprium*.

24. 485: (ἡμεῖς δ' αὖ παίδων τε κασιγνήτων τε φόνοιο |) ἔκλησιν
θέωμεν. Page (110) emphasizes with disapproval that the noun has
a parallel only in Pindaric ἐπίλασις (*P*. 1. 46). He says besides that
the phraseology is just as unhomeric as the phrase σκέδασιν θείη
(*Od*. 1. 116, 20. 225) (quoted by the commentators).[120] Both accusations are inappropriate: The formation ἔκλησις is faultless (cf.
ἔκβασις *Od*. 5. 410).[121] But one can effortlessly detect this supposedly unhomeric phraseology in both epics. As in *Od*. 24. 485, the
verbal abstract is used as a paraphrase in other places as well, when
a special intensity of the action is supposed to be expressed, cf. *Il*.
15. 69–70 (ἐκ τοῦ δ' ἄν τοι ἔπειτα παλίωξιν παρὰ νηῶν | αἰεὶ ἐγὼ
τεύχοιμι), *Od*. 4. 544 (οὐκ ἄνυσίν τινα δήομεν), *Od*. 9. 421 (εἴ τιν'
ἑταίροισιν θανάτου λύσιν ἠδ' ἐμοὶ αὐτῷ | εὑροίμην).[122] In this
case, Page's misgivings are totally groundless.

24. 486: Zeus finishes his speech with the words: πλοῦτος δὲ καὶ
εἰρήνη ἅλις ἔστω. Page (111) regards this as strange too because
πλοῦτος appears elsewhere in the *Odyssey* only at 14. 206, and on
top of that in a formula which stems from the *Iliad*, and because
εἰρήνη on the other hand belongs to the older poem only (in the
combination ὥς ποτ' or τὸ πρὶν ἐπ' εἰρήνης respectively, cf. *Il*. 2.
797, 9. 403, 22. 156). We add that πλοῦτος is used six times in the
Iliad and ask how the poem about war could have fitted in the word
'peace' in any other way than in phrases of the kind 'as once in
peacetime'. But in *Od*. 24. 486 both [224] nouns, and especially
εἰρήνη, have their full sense: they hint at the fulfilment of the
action.

24. 491: ἐξελθών τις ἴδοι, μὴ δὴ σχεδὸν ὦσι (σχ. ἔωσι Schwartz,
σχεδόν εἰσι Kirchhoff) κιόντες. Page (110) seems to regard such
Attic forms as evidence of later origin (sc. under the influence of the
Attic dialect). In this case even Wackernagel (*SU* 110) does not go
this far. But should one suppose that the author of *Il*. 14. 274

---

[120] The construction of the sentence (ὅρκια ... ταμόντες ὁ μὲν ... ἡμεῖς δ'. ...)
follows a typically Homeric scheme, cf. *Od*. 12. 73 ff.; Stanford on *Od*. 24. 485. Cf.
also Aristonicus on *Il*. 5. 27–8 (with test.). The irregularity consists only in that in
the imagination of the speaker the thought that the gods are responsible for what will
happen pushes itself to the front; so instead of 'the Ithacans are supposed to forget'
it is said 'we (the celestial ones) will make them forget'. This is a psychologically
understandable anacoluthon. Good description in Eust. 1968, 11. Spohn's objections (198) are not justified.

[121] Cf. the literature mentioned in Frisk, *GEW* ii. 81!

[122] Cf. Schwyzer–Debrunner 357.

The Ending of the Odyssey: Linguistic Problems

(μάρτυροι ὦσ' οἱ ἔνερθε θεοὶ Κρόνον ἀμφὶς ἐόντες) was able to form
an epic participle, but on the other hand fell back upon the Attic
form for the subjunctive? This is improbable. Either he also had
the subjunctive ὦσι at his disposal as an epic form or the passage is
corrupt (μαρτυρέωσ' οἱ van Leeuwen, μάρτυροι ὅσσοι Voss). Only
the second possibility can be reconciled with our knowledge of
Homeric dialect. The few Attic forms which can be found in both
epics (cf. Chantraine, *Gr. Hom.* i. 286 ff.) were corrected by conjectures a long time ago:[123] κεν ἧσιν (κ' ἔησιν quoted by Zonaras)
Od. 8. 147; ἧσιν (ἔησιν) 8. 163; ἵνα ἧσι (ἵν' ἔησι) 8. 580; ἧσιν (ἔησιν)
Il. 19. 202; ὄντας (ἐόντας) *Od.* 7. 94; οὔσης (ἐούσης) *Od.* 19. 489;
ὄντες (v. l. ἐόντες) *Od.* 19. 230. So we can recommend assuming
that *Od.* 24. 491 is also corrupt.

24. 497: τέσσαρες ἀμφ' 'Οδυσῆ', ἐξ δ' υἱεῖς οἱ Δολίοιο. Page (110)
accepts only *Il.* 20. 181 (τιμῆς τῆς Πριάμου) as an exact parallel;
but this verse appears in a part athetized by Aristarchus.
Nevertheless, it is sufficient to justify the formulation in *Od.* 24.
497; for Aristarchus' deletion of *Il.* 20. 180–6 is unsound, cf.
Aristonicus: . . . ὅτι εὐτελεῖς εἰσι τῇ κατασκευῇ καὶ τοῖς νοήμασι.
Chantraine (*Gr. Hom.* ii. 163) classifies the verses mentioned under
a use of the article which is only beginning to develop in epic language. Page rejects his further examples (*Il.* 9. 342, 23. 348, and
probably also *Od.* 22. 221) with a certain amount of justification;
for in them the noun which belongs to the article has been left out;
so they cannot definitely be compared with our verse.[124] But one
can very well bring in the cases in which the article stands after the
noun with an explanatory or a qualifying adjective. For τιμῆς τῆς
Πριάμου is nothing other than τιμῆς τῆς Πριαμηΐης (to insert a
later adjective for the sake of clarification). So one should compare:
Il. 16. 358 (Αἴας δ' ὁ μέγας), [225] 14. 279 (θεοὺς δ' ὀνόμηνεν
ἅπαντας | τοὺς ὑποταρταρίους), *Od.* 12. 252 (ἰχθύσι τοῖς ὀλίγοισι
δόλον κατὰ εἴδατα βάλλων, i.e. 'and in fact to the small ones which
are not caught with harpoons'). So one should leave the formulation of 24. 497 unchallenged, especially since the use of the article

---

[123] In most cases it is enough to put in the corresponding Ionic form and to read
with synizesis. Cf. Wackernagel, *SU* 110; Schwyzer i. 677; Chantraine, *Gr. Hom.*
i. 41, 64; Thumb–Scherer, *Handbuch der griechischen Dialekte* (Heidelberg, 1959),
ii. 257. Cf. also Meister, *Die homerische Kunstsprache* (Leipzig, 1921) 195 (who
seems to admit οὔσης next to regular ἐούσης).

[124] *Il.* 23. 376: αἱ Φηρητιάδαο ποδώκεες ἔκφερον ἵπποι mentioned as an example by Monro (cf. Stanford *ad loc.*) must probably be discarded as well.

in the *Odyssey* is more modern than in the *Iliad* (cf. Chantraine, *Gr. Hom.* ii. 165).

24. 499: καὶ πολιοί περ ἐόντες, ἀναγκαῖοι πολεμισταί. 'A fine Homeric line' (Stanford). Page (111) on the other hand notes: 'πολιός: grey, meaning grey-haired, aged, is characteristic of fifth-century Attic, especially Drama; the usage is unknown to the Epic.' But how about the references in which a grey i.e. grey-haired head is mentioned? Cf. *Il.* 22. 74 (similarly *Il.* 24. 516): πολιόν τε κάρη πολιόν τε γένειον and *Od.* 24. 317: χεύατο κὰκ κεφαλῆς πολιῆς. It would probably be nit-picking to treat this problem by distinguishing between head and person, cf. e.g. *Il.* 8. 281 (Τεῦκρε, φίλη κεφαλή), further *Il.* 11. 55, 23. 94; *Od.* 11. 549, 557. The expression which is permissible for the head must therefore also be valid for the person.

24. 511: ὄψεαι, αἴ κ' ἐθέλῃσθα . . . τῷδ' ἐνὶ θυμῷ (| οὔ τι καταισχύνοντα τεὸν γένος). Page (111) need not have included this passage in his catalogue of linguistic offences; for the mistake is corrected by Wolf's conjecture (τῷδ' ἐπὶ θυμῷ), cf. *Il.* 13. 485 and *Od.* 16. 99 (in both places Aristarchus read ἐπί instead of ἐνί. A large part of the manuscript tradition agrees with him). This kind of corruption is not rare, cf. M. L. West on *Od.* 16. 282 (*Philol.* 110 (1967), 147).[125]

24. 514–15: τίς νύ μοι ἡμέρη ἥδε, θεοὶ φίλοι; ἦ μάλα χαίρω | υἱός θ' υἱωνός τ' ἀρετῆς πέρι δῆριν ἔχουσι. Page (110) thinks: 'The Epic was very sparing of interjections (ὤμοι, ὦ πόποι): neither this expletive, θεοὶ φίλοι, nor anything else of the kind occurs elsewhere in the Homeric poems.' Then he quotes Spohn (206), who reports that the young Gottfried Hermann read this verse with displeasure. If Page had also known Faesi's remark about these verses, he would probably have enjoyed quoting them: 'An immensely feeble expression which makes Laertes appear to us as an almost childishly weak and vain old man.' This is certainly one method of interpretation which will quickly get rid of the difficulties. Wackernagel (*SU* 230) remarks quite correctly that Laertes' words are less a question than an 'expression of a feeling of happiness'. They combine suitably enough with the exclamation 'merciful gods', and

---

[125] Stanford defends tradition since he regards the meaning 'in my present spirit' as more suitable than the interpretation 'with, in possession of . . .'. The reference to *Il.* 13. 485 and *Od.* 16. 99 to my mind militates against this opinion.

describe a climax of mood in a similar way to [226] the one in which the words of Philoetius (*Od.* 20. 209: ὢ μοι ἔπειτ' Ὀδυσῆος ἀμύμονος) form an exclamation of horror. Wackernagel also referred to *Od.* 24. 351–2 by way of comparison: Ζεῦ πάτερ, ἦ ῥ' ἔτι ἐστέ, θεοί, κατὰ μακρὸν Ὄλυμπον, | εἰ ἐτεὸν μνηστῆρες ἀτάσθαλον ὕβριν ἔτεισαν. They describe a similar feeling of happiness as 24. 514 f., but Zeus and the gods are actually addressed in them. On the other hand the exclamation θεοὶ φίλοι, taken as a mere assertion, does indeed lack a proper analogy in Homer.[126] But the special peculiarity of Book 24 must in this case also be emphasized: in a relatively short compass, the poet is describing unique situations which, as we have been able to state several times already, brought unique expressions to life. One would have to find in the *Iliad* the occasion when Laertes' exclamation would have been appropriate. To reverse the argument: Which more usual Homeric phrase should the old man have used, in order to describe the unexpected happiness which he is now allowed to enjoy at the end of his life? He who ponders these questions will soon realize that not only were Faesi and Page wrong, but also the young Gottfried Hermann.

24. 519 Athena goes up to Laertes and urges him to pray to Zeus and his daughter (sc. Athena) and then to hurl his spear at the enemy: αἶψα μάλ' ἀμπεπαλὼν προΐει δολιχόσκιον ἔγχος. The last words (προΐει δολιχόσκιον ἔγχος) are formulaic. They occur in the *Iliad* another ten times (3. 355 = 5. 280 = 7. 244 = 11. 349 = 17. 516 = 22. 273 = 22. 289, cf. further 5. 15, 7. 249, 20. 273), but there προΐει is in each case imperfect indicative. Page (111) therefore speaks of an artificial adaptation of the formula in *Od.* 24. 519 since προΐει is here to be understood as an imperative. But the point of the *Odyssey* reference consists in the fact that Laertes obeys Athena's advice and launches the spear successfully: the narrative of the poet (24. 521–2) now takes up the verses of the goddess (24. 518–19) almost literally (24. 519 = 522), but in verse 522 προΐει is now an imperfect, as in the descriptions of the *Iliad*. Again, from a hackneyed phrase new splendour has been won (cf. above to *Od.* 24. 40).

24. 528: καὶ νύ κε δὴ πάντας (τ') ὄλεσαν καὶ θῆκαν ἀνόστους. This adjective, which is a combination of an α-privative and a verbal

---

[126] Cf. Bekker, *Homerische Blätter*, i. 201.

noun, is found only here in the Homeric epics. Like Spohn (181)
and the commentaries, Page too (111) refers to the related and isolated formation in *Od.* 4. 182: (θεός,) ὃς κεῖνον δύστηνον ἀνόστιμον
οἶον ἔθηκεν. Furthermore he thinks that he needs to state that
ἄνοστος would be 'a useful word, if the Epic had known it'. I regard
this assumption as incorrect, since there were [227] paraphrases
with νόστος and νόστιμον ἦμαρ as well as personal constructions
with νόστιμος at the poet's disposal for representing the thought
that someone did not or could not return home. Cf. *Il.* 9. 413
(ὤλετο μέν μοι νόστος), 16. 82 (φίλον δ' ἀπὸ νόστον ἕλωνται); *Od.*
12. 419 (= 14. 309: θεὸς δ' ἀποαίνυτο νόστον), 1. 9 (ὁ τοῖσιν
ἀφείλετο νόστιμον ἦμαρ), 4. 806 (ἐπεί ῥ' ἔτι νόστιμός ἐστιν), 20.
333 (νῦν δ' ἤδη τόδε δῆλον ὅ τ' οὐκέτι νόστιμός ἐστιν). In all these
cases, a return home from war is referred to; he who grants or
denies it is a god. But in *Od.* 24. 528 only a return from Laertes'
estate is meant. The object of the sentence is Eupeithes' followers,
the agents Odysseus and his comrades. Perhaps the poet felt
obliged to choose a word which had not been used before in order
to describe these peculiarities, either a word which was known to
him already or one which he created for the present purpose.[127]

24. 534: τῶν δ' ἄρα δεισάντων ἐκ χειρῶν ἔπτατο τεύχεα (| πάντα
δ' ἐπὶ χθονὶ πῖπτε . . .). Page (111 and 113) is scandalized by the
misuse of the word τεύχεα. No poet to whom epic language was
familiar could have talked about the whole armour, the harness, if
he meant only 'weapons'. Page says that the author of our verse had
imitated *Od.* 12. 203 (τῶν δ' ἄρα δεισάντων ἐκ χειρῶν ἔπτατ'
ἐρετμά) but that this imitation miscarried, proving multiple
authorship. But the second part of this judgement is false. Let us
recall the verses in which the recovery of weapons is mentioned:
ἀρήϊα τεύχεα (*Od.* 16. 284, 19. 4) describes clearly all the parts of a
warrior's equipment, namely protective and offensive weapons but
especially sword, spears, and shield (cf. *Od.* 16. 295–6; cf. further
Od. 22. 109, 139, 180; 24. 165, 219). What is the *Iliad* poet thinking of when he describes the last flight of the Achaeans in the following way (*Il.* 17. 760): πολλὰ δὲ τεύχεα καλὰ πέσον περί τ' ἀμφί
τε τάφρον | φευγόντων Δαναῶν, or when in describing the river
battle he says (21. 301): πολλὰ δὲ τεύχεα καλὰ δαϊκταμένων αἰζηῶν

---

[127] The formation ἄνοστος could not cause any difficulties, cf. Debrunner 28
(para. 54), cf. ἄ-νοστος with ἄ-νουσος, ἄ-γονος (*Il.* 3. 40), ἀ-θάνατος, ἀ-κάματος,
ἄ-υπνος and others.

| πλῶον καὶ νέκυες? Both references are crystal clear. The fleeing Greeks are obviously throwing away their cumbersome shields in particular. But there are not just spears floating on the floods of Scamander but corpses and probably shields covered with ox hide (βοάγρια, cf. *Il.* 12. 22), or rather the light shields of barbarian auxiliaries (λαισήϊα . . . πτερόεντα, cf. *Il.* 5. 453 = 12. 426).[128] It is a logical assumption that in our passage in Book 24 too, shields in particular are described by τεύχεα. The [228] Ithacans throw them away, in order to be able to run for the city at speed. The question whether they are taking their spears along at the same time is irrelevant.

24. 535: πάντα (sc. τεύχεα) δ᾽ ἐπὶ χθονὶ πῖπτε, θεᾶς ὄπα φωνησάσης, i.e. 'when the goddess let her voice sound'. The half of the verse after the middle caesura is a phrase from the *Iliad* (*Il.* 2. 182 = 10. 512, similarly 20. 380); here the accusative ὄπα depends on the finite verb (ξυνέηκε or ἄκουσε respectively), but in the construction in Book 24 it depends on the participle. Page sees in this combination of words a reprehensible deviation from epic tradition (110: 'our poet is so far from the tradition . . .'). On the other hand, syntactical regroupings of given phrases are important characteristics of epic verse formation and no evidence at all that the poet had mastered his art inadequately. As Leumann (*Homerische Wörter* (Basle, 1950) *passim*, esp. 183 ff.) showed with notable examples, the *Iliad* poet already proceeds like this with the formulaic material given to him, and a similar relationship can be traced between quite a few of his word combinations and those of the *Odyssey*. So its poet reshaped the phrase γούνων ἁψάμενοι λιτανεύσομεν (*Il.* 24. 357) into the construction γούνων ἐλλιτάνευσα (*Od.* 10. 481), presumably not without the influence of *Il.* 9. 451 (ἐμὲ λισσέσκετο γούνων).[129] The verb στεῦμαι is combined with the infinitive in the *Iliad*, cf. *Il.* 2. 597: στεῦτο γὰρ εὐχόμενος νικήσεμεν ('he boastingly presumed to win') and 5. 832–3: στεῦτ᾽ ἀγορεύων | Τρῶσι μαχήσεσθαι ('talking, he asserted that he would fight against the

---

[128] For their description in the commentaries of the ancients cf. H. L. Lorimer, *Homer and the Monuments* (London, 1950), 195.

[129] Cf. Leumann, *Homerische Wörter*, 189. For the dependence of *Od.* 10 on Book 24 of the *Iliad* cf. G. Beck, *Philologus* 109 (1965), 1–29. Beck also noticed singularities in language usage in *Od.* 10 which can have originated only under the influence of *Il.* 24, e.g. ἱμερόεις . . . γόος *Od.* 10. 398, θαλερὸν γόον 10. 457. On the other hand in *Il.* 24. 760 it says γόον δ᾽ ἀλίαστον ὄρινε which could not be used in the new context and was recoined into the phrases mentioned which were alien to the *Iliad*.

Trojans'). But the *Odyssey* (sc. *Od.* 11. 584) gives the impression that its author had taken the opportunity from the references mentioned to combine στεῦτο with the participle: στεῦτο δὲ διψάων, πιέειν δ᾽ οὐκ εἶχεν ἑλέσθαι ('he behaved like a thirsting man', of Tantalus).[130] So after the pattern ἐπίουρος (*Il.* 13. 450: Κρήτῃ ἐπίουρον, originally Κρήτῃ ἔπι οὖρον),[131] originating from misjudging or neglecting postposition, the *Odyssey* poet formed from βουκόλοι ἄνδρες (*Il.* 13. 571 and sim.) the compound ἐπιβουκόλος ἀνήρ (*Od.* 3. 422) and from βώτορας ἄνδρας (*Il.* 12. 302) a new *nomen agentis* ἐπιβώτορι μήλων (*Od.* 13. 222) etc.[132]

[229] 24. 535 also belongs to this group of obviously intentional changes of construction and shifts of meaning. It should not be permissible to assume an error on the poet's part, that he could not have constructed the simple verse *Il.* 2. 182 (ὣς φάθ᾽, ὁ δὲ ξυνέηκε θεᾶς ὄπα φωνησάσης). Rather, since a transitive use of a verb employed in the *Iliad* only absolutely suggested itself by analogy with λέγειν or εἰπεῖν respectively (cf. e.g. *Od.* 4. 389 = 10. 539), he seems to have seen a possibility here of giving a new and more effective sense to a known formulaic combination. We had observed similar phenomena several times already (cf. *Od.* 24. 40 and 519).

All the expressions which Page, following Spohn's investigation, regards as unepic have now been mentioned. The new examination has shown that only four places present difficulties: the gloss word ἀδινάων (*Od.* 23. 326) whose intended meaning cannot really be known, the unique form πόστον (24. 288) which cannot be given in Ionic, the genitive 'Οδυσεῦς (24. 398), and the metric peculiarity of verse 24. 465 (contracted Εὐπείθει at the end of the verse). All the other objections are not justified, since sufficient analogies can be found in the acknowledged stock of epic diction. But the deletion of the final part of our epic cannot be justified merely on the strength of these four peculiarities. That the language of the last two books is rich in rare expressions and unique word combinations is presumably, as we have emphasized several times already, the result of the multiplicity of themes which come together here in a relatively confined space.

[130] Cf. Leumann, *Homerische Wörter*, 211 who on the other hand also considers the possibility of construing πιέειν with στεῦτο. However, if Agar's conjecture is correct (στεῦτο δὲ διψάων πιέειν, οὐδ᾽ εἶχεν ἑλέσθαι), this example would anyway be unsuitable for our purposes.

[131] Thus already some unknown sources of Herodianus, cf. Schol. A *ad loc.*

[132] Cf. Leumann, *Homerische Wörter*, 92.

Index Locorum

Index Locorum

THUCYDIDES
   1. 9   54
   1. 13. 1   4

VIRGIL
  Aeneid
    10. 515   167 n. 55
    11. 45   167 n. 56

XENOPHANES
  VS 21 B 11,3 = 12,2   255 n. 16

General Index

abstract, verbal 314
abstract nouns 277, 294
abstraction 76, 102, 120
Achilles:
  and Agamemnon 3, 69, 94, 166
  armour 60, 122 n. 35, 157–8, 163
  connections to Hector 141–2, 165
  and death 166–7, 169, 184–5
    foreknowledge of 142, 158, 159,
      161, 163–5
  decision to fight 16–18, 143–69
    context 146–50, 166–7
    fate and freedom 16–18, 169
    Hector and Achilles' fates 161–9
    speech 158–60
    structure 151–60
    text 143–6
  horses 148, 162–3
  and Myrmidons 81
  and Odysseus 37–8, 65–6
  and Paris 185, 187, 189
  and Patroclus' death 152–4, 167–8,
    184–5
  and Priam 72–3, 141, 164
  rustic utilitarianism 63, 66
  similes 68
  speeches 72–3, 80 n. 18, 82, 89–90,
    141, 158–60, 164
  and Thetis 80 n. 18, 156–60
action 132
  Achilles' speech as 160
  audience attention to plot 9–10
  events outside sequence of epic
    action 173–5
  states of mind expessed through
    129–30, 153–4, 157, 224
adjectives formed from a-privative and
    verbal noun 317–18
Adrastus 239
Aeneas 167
Aeolus 33
Aeschylus:
  Myrmidons 168
  Prometheus 156
  see also Index Locorum

Aethiopis 36, 156
Agamemnon:
  and Achilles 3, 69, 94, 166
  aristeia 2–3
  armour 110 n. 16
  homecoming 271
  leadership 3–4, 54, 97 n. 51
  and Odysseus 95–7, 271
  report of Hector's threat 79–80
Agenor 100–1
age of material 5, 120, 173, 187–90,
    194, 266
  contemporary culture reflected 54–5
  see also Odyssey, ending; relics
agora 51, 84
agriculture 49, 55
Ajax 67, 80–1, 140
akropolis 51
Alcinous 236, 238, 239–40, 241, 255
allusions, spotting of 34–5
American Indian folklore 33–4 n. 7
analogy, creation of forms by 297–8
Andromache 153
  female archetype 13, 131–2, 132–4,
    136, 137–8, 138–9
  see also Hector and Andromache
    episode
anger 140
animals:
  groups of nine 284–5
  Odyssey's attitude to 110
  personal names referring to 62
  transformation into 227–8
  see also individual animals and under
    similes
anticipation:
  of future events not included in
    poem *per se* 167
  of heroes' deaths 130, 138, 141–2,
    152, 156
  of Odysseus' homecoming 203,
    204–5, 205–6, 211–12, 215–16
  see also expectations
Antilochus 74–8, 83–4
  see also chariots